SELECTED LETTERS of SERGEI PROKOFIEV

SELECTED LETTERS of

SERGEI PROKOFIEU

Translated, edited, and
with an introduction by

HARLOW ROBINSON

NORTHEASTERN UNIVERSITY PRESS • BOSTON

Northeastern University Press

Copyright 1998 by Harlow Robinson

Library of Congress Cataloging-in-Publication Data
Prokofiev, Sergey, 1891–1953.
[Correspondence. English. Selections]
Selected letters of Sergei Prokofiev / translated, edited,
and with an introduction by Harlow Robinson.
p.   cm.
Includes index.
ISBN 1-55553-347-7 (cloth : alk. paper)
1. Prokofiev, Sergey, 1891–1953—Correspondence.
2. Composers—Soviet Union—Correspondence.
I. Harlow Robinson.
ML410.P865A4 1998
780'.92—dc21
[B]   98-9604
MN

Designed and composed by Scott-Martin Kosofsky
at The Philidor Company, Boston.
Set in Fairfield, Berthold City, and Modula types.
Printed and bound by Maple Press, York, Pennsylvania.
The paper is Perfection Antique Recycled, an acid-free sheet.

MANUFACTURED IN THE UNITED STATES OF AMERICA
02 01 00 99 98   5 4 3 2 1

to the memory of

ALEKSEI MIKHALEV
1944–1994

Translator and friend *extraordinaire*

On revient toujours à ses premiers amours.

—FRENCH PROVERB

CONTENTS

ACKNOWLEDGMENTS

MANY PEOPLE and institutions have contributed time, talent, and money to this project. I am particularly grateful for the fellowships and grants I received from the State University of New York Research Foundation, the Faculty Research Awards Program at the University at Albany, the Kennan Institute for Advanced Russian Studies at the Woodrow Wilson International Center for Scholars in Washington, D.C., the Fulbright-Hays Faculty Research Abroad Program, and the International Research and Exchanges Board Program for the USSR. Completion of this volume would have been impossible without their generous financial and moral support.

No less essential was the assistance provided by my colleagues and graduate students in the Department of Slavic Languages and Literatures at the University at Albany, SUNY, where I taught from 1980 to 1996. Over a period of several years, they collaborated with me in translating and editing hundreds of letters and in preparing them for publication, taking to the task with enthusiasm and commitment. Thanks, then, to Marjorie McShane, Liza Rudneva, Geoffrey Carlson, Eileen Fisher, Tatiana Poliakova, David Smith, Lynn Parsons, Jim Williams, Rebecca Severnyak, and Stephanie Clader. I am grateful to Prof. Sophia Lubensky for training these students so well in the difficult art of translation, and for her invaluable advice. Kay L. Shaffer of the library staff at the University at Albany also provided expert, good-humored, and deeply appreciated assistance.

During my several research trips to Moscow, I received warm hospitality, encouragement, and guidance from the members of the staff of the archives at the Glinka Museum. I am particularly indebted to Irina Andreevna Medvedeva, Deputy Director for Scholarly Work, for welcoming me into the archives and for granting permission for previously unpublished materials to be used in this collection.

The members of the staff of the Music Division of the Library of Congress in Washington, D.C., also gave me invaluable assistance during my work on the Prokofiev letters stored in their archival collection.

To Oleg Prokofiev I am grateful for nearly twenty years of support, advice, and insight. His devotion to his father's memory and legacy has been an inspiration to me while working on this project.

William A. Frohlich, Director of Northeastern University Press, a visionary editor and publisher, embraced and shaped this project from the very beginning. His energy, patience and tact sustained and prodded me through to its conclusion.

Last, but far from least, I thank Robert Holley, my companion of sixteen years, not only for believing in the importance of this collection, not only for his editorial assistance and computer skills, but for his enduring love and creativity.

BOSTON
SEPTEMBER 1997

INTRODUCTION

M ORE THAN A DECADE has passed since the publication of my biography of Russian / Soviet composer Sergei Prokofiev. Much has changed since then, both in the world and in our understanding of Prokofiev (1891–1953) as a man and as a musician. When *Sergei Prokofiev: A Biography* (the first in English to draw on Soviet archival sources) appeared in early 1987, the USSR was still very much intact. Mikhail Gorbachev had only recently become leader of the country and of the Communist Party. The process of reevaluating Soviet history, including music and the other arts, from the new viewpoint of *glasnost* was just beginning. The fortress of Soviet official culture—with its artistic unions, lavish subsidies, and oppressive censorship—was still vast, powerful, and seemingly impregnable. Soviet composers and musicologists still lived in an insulated and isolated environment, their access to global information and travel severely limited.

But by 1991, the year of the hundredth anniversary of Prokofiev's birth, the political and cultural climate in Russia had changed more quickly and profoundly than anyone could possibly have imagined or predicted just a few years before. This much was clear at a symposium on Prokofiev sponsored by the Leningrad Composers Union and the Leningrad Spring Festival, to which I was invited in early April 1991. Just as Prokofiev's death had been grotesquely overshadowed by Stalin's death on the very same day (March 5, 1953), political events also conspired to overshadow the planned celebration of the composer's centenary. With the USSR in financial chaos and government subsidies to culture rapidly decreasing, the Soviet Composers Union had few resources to spend on what in earlier years would have been a large-scale event. During the symposium, the Soviet ruble was devalued to one-sixth of its former value against the dollar, creating widespread confusion and anxiety. Although attentive and large audiences turned out for the symposium and related concerts, both participants and spectators were obviously distracted by the fast-moving and unpredictable changes taking place all over what we would soon be calling the former Soviet Union.

Once again, as had happened so often in his life, what should have been Prokofiev's moment in the limelight was being upstaged by momentous events on the street.

Glasnost and *perestroika* actually turned out to be something of a mixed blessing for Prokofiev's reputation, especially in the short run. Like all prominent creative artists who lived and worked under the Soviet regime, Prokofiev came under new scrutiny for the extent to which he had collaborated with and supported what was now regarded as an evil and corrupt system. As is the case with all revolutions (and this was surely a revolution, both cultural and political), all those associated with the old regime were now perceived as somehow tainted.

Both in Russia and in the West, the initial blind rush to denounce everything and anything "Soviet" led critics and writers to extreme and rigid judgment. On what should have been the joyous occasion of his centenary, Prokofiev—who lived in the USSR only for the last seventeen of his nearly sixty-two years, never joined the Communist Party, and ended his life in near-poverty after having been attacked as an anti-Soviet "formalist" in 1948—was instead slandered in the *New York Times* as a lackey of Stalin, ready to write anything in order to defend or improve his position in the Soviet musical establishment. This trendy, "politically correct" analysis reduced the complexities of Prokofiev's difficult and contradictory career to the level of a sound bite, severely misrepresenting the nature of his relationship to the Soviet government and his role in Soviet music.

In the introduction to my 1987 biography, I observed that Prokofiev's life was full of irony: "Indifferent to ideology and politically unsophisticated, he had chosen to spend his last seventeen years in one of the most relentlessly ideological societies ever created."[1] Perhaps it is only fitting that this sense of irony has pursued Prokofiev beyond the grave, beyond even the collapse of the USSR into a new post–Cold War era. For to condemn the hopelessly apolitical Prokofiev as a scheming apologist for Stalinism is no less absurd than describing Mozart as a cynical lackey of the Hapsburg emperors.

The letters assembled and translated in this volume provide ample evidence of Prokofiev's political views—or rather, of his lack of any. Music was his god, dictator, and raison d'être. Wherever he was—in prerevolutionary St. Petersburg, in New York, Paris, and other world capitals between the wars, or in

---

1.   Harlow Robinson, *Sergei Prokofiev: A Biography* (New York: Viking, 1987), 3.

Stalin's Moscow—Prokofiev pledged allegiance to music first and foremost. Nor is there any evidence that he ever acted to improve his own position in the Soviet cultural establishment at the expense either of other people or of his personal integrity. If Prokofiev had a tragic flaw, it was his inability to see beyond his own closed world of music, a certain tunnel vision. Driven, egotistical, and applying the highest artistic standards to himself and others, he was really guilty of only one crime: a single-minded and, yes, perhaps even blind devotion to his craft. That devotion created music now beloved by millions of people all over the world, people who live in many different countries and under the most diverse political and ideological systems. As time passes, Prokofiev's popularity only continues to grow, with audiences, musicians, and even musicologists.

IF PROKOFIEV had not decided to become a composer, he would probably have become a writer. Literature always appealed to him much more than painting, architecture, or any other of the arts. As a child growing up in the remote Ukrainian village of Sontsovka, where his father managed an aristocrat's estate, Prokofiev loved to write little dramas and libretti. Some of these plays and operas (with his own music) were performed with his doting parents' approval. Prokofiev also began to keep a very detailed diary at the age of twelve, a habit he maintained sporadically throughout his life. The early diaries were later an important source for his massive *Autobiography*, written in two parts between 1937 and 1950 and devoted solely to the composer's first eighteen years. Here, in an offhand, tongue-in-cheek style, he examines his early education, adventures, and music in rich and microscopic detail.

Prokofiev's literary activity intensifed after he moved from Sontsovka to St. Petersburg, where he enrolled in the conservatory in 1904. He became acquainted with numerous poets, writers, and critics in what was then the center of Russian cultural and literary life. The Futurist poet Vladimir Mayakovsky impressed him deeply. Occasionally Prokofiev would write reviews of new music for magazines and even joked that he could have made a good—and nasty—critic if he had chosen to pursue that path. Just before and after the Russian Revolution Prokofiev also tried his hand at fiction, producing several short stories, mainly fantastic ones.

But most of his literary energy went to writing libretti for his own operas. Beginning with *Maddalena* in 1911, Prokofiev would eventually write (either solely or in collaboration) the libretti for all eight of his major operas, adapting sources as diverse as Dostoyevsky, Tolstoy, and Sheridan for the stage. The composer also wrote scores for several theatrical productions staged in Russia in the 1930s, including *Hamlet*.

Given his gregarious nature and verbal skills, it is hardly surprising that Prokofiev also showed unusual talent as a correspondent very early in his life. During the summer vacations he spent in Sontsovka, writing letters to his new classmates from St. Petersburg Conservatory was a means both of passing the time and of staying in touch with civilization. From the very beginning, Prokofiev's letters display wit, a strong sense of verbal play, and an abrupt, almost telegraphic syntax. He was always fond of dropping vowels in words, writing in a kind of consonant-clogged shorthand.

In the years just before the Russian Revolution, Prokofiev began to travel abroad, and would send long, vivid letters back home to his friends from London, Paris, Scandinavia, and elsewhere. Here, he describes concerts, performances (including those of Sergei Diaghilev's Ballets Russes), and his meetings with other musicians and composers, as well as his own often quirky perceptions of European life and customs. During the 1917 Bolshevik Revolution, Prokofiev found himself far from the action, in the Caucasus resort of Kislovodsk. In an attempt to stay in touch with his friends and colleagues in Petrograd, he wrote frequent notes, cards, and letters.

Perhaps the most valuable portion of Prokofiev's voluminous correspondence, however, belongs to the eighteen-year period (from 1918 to 1936) when he was living outside the USSR. By the early 1920s, Prokofiev had initiated regular correspondence with several of his former conservatory colleagues—the composer Nikolai Miaskovsky, the composer-critic Boris Asafiev, the harpist Eleonora Damskaya—as well as with the distinguished stage director Vsevolod Meyerhold, with whom he was hoping to collaborate. His letters to them became a vital lifeline to what was happening in the Soviet musical and theatrical world, since Prokofiev clearly intended even then to return to Russia someday. In return, Prokofiev gave them a window onto what was happening in Western music and culture. This information became increasingly important to the composer's correspondents as the years passed, since Stalin's policies were leading to growing isolation and highly restricted travel abroad.

Prokofiev also wrote letters in the opposite direction—toward the United States. Throughout the 1920s and 1930s, mainly from Paris, he maintained a lively correspondence with some of the many Russian musicians who had settled in America: the conductor Serge Koussevitsky, the composer Vernon Duke (aka Vladimir Dukelsky), the singer Nina Koshetz.

After Prokofiev returned to the USSR permanently in 1936, he wrote relatively few letters. He was now able to communicate in person with most of his former correspondents, since they lived nearby in Moscow or St. Petersburg. One of the exceptions was the great Soviet film director Sergei Eisenstein, a new friend with whom the composer began to collaborate in 1938. Their letters deal primarily with work on the films *Aleksandr Nevsky* and *Ivan the Terrible*. Strict Soviet censorship of all mail sent abroad disrupted Prokofiev's correspondence with American and European correspondents except in the most official form, usually telegrams of a congratulatory nature.

Writing letters seems to have been a form of relaxation for Prokofiev. He often composed them while traveling by train or ship, and often in longhand without the help of a secretary or typist. In Paris in the 1930s he would most often dictate them to his personal assistant, Mikhail Astrov. The great majority of Prokofiev's correspondence was written in his native Russian, but he was also sufficiently well-versed in other languages to write highly literate letters in French and English. Prokofiev also knew German well (he lived in Bavaria with his wife and first son for nearly two years in the early 1920s), and would frequently use phrases in various languages (including Italian and Swedish), most often for humorous effect.

Consistent with his unemotional, unreflective, and highly private personality, Prokofiev's letters very rarely touch upon personal or romantic matters. Like his music, they are laconic, brisk and tart, full of energy, musical gossip, and an odd—at times even brutal and voyeuristic—sense of humor. Do not look here for the soul-baring confessions typical of the self-doubting, subjective, and guilt-ridden letters penned by Tchaikovsky and Shostakovich. If anything, Prokofiev's personal and epistolary style contradicts the popular stereotype of the tortured, undisciplined Russian artist. Not much of a drinker or carouser, Prokofiev was noted for his punctuality, sarcasm, objectivity, and avoidance of sentiment. He preferred practical jokes and mechanical gadgets to fevered, vodka-driven conversations about the meaning of life.

Most often, Prokofiev's letters deal with the music he was writing and hearing, people he was meeting, and sights he was seeing on his extensive travels around the world. Because Prokofiev voyaged so widely, living and performing in so many world capitals at crucial moments in twentieth-century history, his letters provide a cultural and musical history unequalled in the correspondence of any other modern composer. Another major theme is the business of being published and performed. Since Prokofiev was in essence his own manager, impresario and promoter, he writes frequently about administrative and financial matters. He was never one of those artists who disdained involvement in the business of music—if anything, he seemed to enjoy it thoroughly.

What also emerges from the thousands of letters Prokofiev composed during his lifetime is a previously unappreciated generosity toward colleagues, especially those who remained in the USSR. During the entire long period that Prokofiev spent away from Russia, he devoted many hours to promoting the music of Soviet composers, especially Miaskovsky, arranging for publication and performances in Europe and the United States. He also did a great deal to promote the music of Vernon Duke in Europe and the USSR. To his credit, Prokofiev always strove to appreciate the music being written by his contemporaries (whether Russian, European, or American), to rise above feelings of envy and competition. This is evident even in his mostly positive assessment of the music of Igor Stravinsky, who at times seemed to be always just one step ahead of Prokofiev—wherever he might find himself.

This volume is the first collection in any language—including Russian—devoted solely to Prokofiev's letters to various correspondents. That it has taken so long lies in several factors. One is Prokofiev's nomadic existence. At the time of his death, his correspondence was spread all over the world.

Another was, of course, the terrible realities of Soviet censorship. Even though the composer's second wife, Mira Mendelson, herself a writer, devoted herself almost exclusively to bringing order to the composer's archives in the years following his death, the political situation surrounding Prokofiev remained extremely sensitive. That he had spent so many years abroad was held against him for many years after Stalin's death. Several of his important correspondents—Meyerhold, Diaghilev, Koussevitsky, Duke—had become "nonpeople" in the USSR for various reasons. This made it impossible for Prokofiev's letters to them to be published. Furthermore, Western scholars were not allowed to see many materials in Soviet archives—especially letters—until relatively recently. Some parts of his correspondence, especially letters written during the period of the Bolshevik Revolution, were long withheld even from Soviet musicologists and scholars.

The letters assembled in this volume have come from various sources, as indicated in the footnotes. Some have been published in Russian in separate editions. Others have never been published before, even in Russian. The selection is by no means exhaustive; a publication of the complete letters of Prokofiev would run to several large volumes. What I have done is to choose those which I find most accessible, representative, and enlightening. I have edited many of the letters, cutting out extensive and repetitive discussions of financial matters and excessively technical musical analysis. In most cases I have indicated with ellipsis where these cuts have been made.

The texts of Prokofiev's letters reproduced in Soviet editions used here (to Diaghilev, Meyerhold, Asafiev, Eisenstein, and Miaskovsky) were edited for publication in the USSR. I used them after consulting with Oleg Prokofiev, who has assured me that the cuts are minor and do not alter the content of the originals. I have chosen to structure the volume by individual correspondents, rather than chronologically, for two reasons: to make it easier to use, and to focus on the central relationships in Prokofiev's life.

In translating the letters, I have attempted as much as possible to retain a sense of Prokofiev's quirky, breathless prose style while providing a version that makes sense in English. As mentioned above, Prokofiev was very fond of abbreviations; in most cases I have restored the missing letters, except where the meaning would still be clear without them. In beginning and ending his letters, Prokofiev showed an ingenious creativity in the use of various nicknames, and I have attempted as much as possible to retain that ingenuity and variety. Similarly, I have retained his characteristic use of foreign salutations and phrases in their original.

With letters written in Russia before the adoption of the Western calendar in 1918, one always faces the problem of dating. Until the reform, the Russian calendar (Old Style) lagged behind the Western calendar (New Style) by thirteen days. In some cases, but not always, Prokofiev himself provided double dates (both Old and New) on letters written in Europe and sent back to Russia before 1918. When double dates were not provided, I have reproduced Prokofiev's dating. Generally speaking, he used Old Style in letters to his Russian correspondents until the calendar reform.

In transliterating Russian names, I have followed what I judge to be standard usage, so as to provide names in their most familiar forms. This practice has led to inconsistencies which I recognize and for which I accept responsibility. But each name is spelled consistently thoughout the text—except for Prokofiev's. When he used roman script, Prokofiev signed his name "Prokofieff." And yet "Prokofiev" has become the standard bibliographic form, so I follow that convention here, except where Prokofiev signs his name in the letters themselves. In the notes, most Russian-language titles are transliterated according to the Library of Congress system.

Brackets with ellipsis [. . .] indicate editorial cuts; other ellipses are Prokofiev's own. Other brackets provide information (dates, etc.) not provided in the letters.

My hope is that this volume will lead to greater understanding of Prokofiev's frequently misunderstood life, provide an insight into his creative processes and aesthetic principles, and introduce a new character to those who love his music: Prokofiev the man of letters.

CHAPTER ONE
Letters to Vera Alpers

Prokofiev's childhood letters to Vera Alpers represent only a small portion of their extensive correspondence, which spans—with an interruption during Prokofiev's absence from Russia in the 1920s—the composer's entire life. Born in 1892, just one year after Prokofiev, Alpers was a fellow student at the St. Petersburg Conservatory, where they quickly became friends and confidants. A pianist, Alpers shows up frequently in Prokofiev's childhood autobiography. There, he recalls how girls outnumbered the boys seventeen to three in the courses in academic subjects. Sheltered during his early life from contact with his female peers, Prokofiev viewed his female fellow students as exotic creatures he was discovering for the first time.

Alpers was "quiet and did not draw attention to herself," he wrote; another student described her as "pale as the day she was born."[1] Prokofiev, on the other hand, was a rosy-cheeked, mischievous prankster who loved to tease both his peers and his teachers. Perhaps it was precisely this difference in their temperaments that drew them together. In any case, Prokofiev behaved toward Alpers like an affectionate brother, giving her advice about matters both musical and romantic. It seems that the brilliant and clumsy teenager from Sontsovka, Ukraine, also knew that Vera was suffering from a crush on him—like several other girls studying at the conservatory.

Prokofiev figured prominently in the diary Alpers kept during her conservatory years, where she remembered how agitated he would become after giving piano performances: "I was even afraid for him, thinking he might have some sort of nervous attack. He rushed off the stage and suddenly sat down on the stairs. He couldn't seem to get his breath, then he jumped up like he was crazy, slammed the door and left."[2] After they became reacquainted in the 1930s, Alpers gave Prokofiev her diary to read. It was "like reading an interesting adolescent novel about a nice but clumsy girl," he told her.[3] Prokofiev included

1. Sergei Prokof'ev, *Avtobiografiia* (Moscow: Sovetskii kompozitor, 1973), 431.
2. Ibid., 551.
3. Sergei Prokof'ev and V. V. Alpers, "Perepiska." *Muzyakal'noe nasledstvo*, Vol. I, L. M. Kutateladze, ed. (Moscow: Gosudarstvennoe muzykal'noe izdatel'stvo, 1962), 425.

many excerpts (like the one quoted above) from Alpers's diary in his vivid and charming autobiography.

Unlike Prokofiev, Alpers did not leave the USSR after the Bolshevik Revolution of 1917. She stayed in Leningrad, where she worked as a piano teacher. Despite the obvious differences in their lives when Prokofiev, now world-famous, began traveling with increasing frequency to the USSR in the early 1930s, they reestablished their adolescent bond. Prokofiev would visit her whenever he came to Leningrad, and they resumed their correspondence.

Five of the six letters translated here date from the summer of 1909. Prokofiev, eighteen years old, was spending his vacation in Sontsovka, the remote Ukrainian village where his father, an agronomist, ran a large estate. Having just completed his undergraduate studies, Prokofiev was already a professional composer and pianist. In the autumn of 1909, he began graduate studies at the conservatory. The last letter dates from the summer of 1910 and relates the death of Prokofiev's father.

With War World I and the Russian Revolution still several years away, the mood of these letters is carefree and playful, full of youthful optimism and bravado. They also show Prokofiev's marvelous gift for wordplay, his fondness for playing the *enfant terrible*, and his weird sense of humor.

(These letters were published in Russian as "Pis'ma k V. V. Alpers" in *Sergei Prokof'ev 1953–1963: Stat'i i materialy [Sergei Prokofiev 1953–1963: Articles and Materials]* [Moscow: Sovetskii kompozitor, 1962], 269–74. Translated into English by Marge McShane and Harlow Robinson.)

June 1, 1909
SONTSOVKA

Most Respected Vera Vladimirovna,

I've been here a week and already want to leave this bear's lair. I'm taking a weeklong jaunt to the Dnepr to see a great friend of mine who's a musician and chess player. I'm stuck here in our awful boondocks. So far I haven't laid eyes on a single person I know—in fact there's practically no one to see. I haven't even run into the village priest. All day I keep busy with the piano, writing, and chess.

Esipova[4] would hardly have approved of what I'm doing at the piano, but it's just for fun, something to start with. I'm playing a whole lot, but to no particular purpose. I start with exercises for about half an hour, then play around with all kinds of different things, from the *Golden Cock*[5] to the sonatas of Scriabin and Glazunov, to *Islamey*[6] and *The Divine Poem*,[7] which I play solo from a four-hand arrangement.

I've written the full score for one of the five movements of a sinfonietta and have already sent it off to Miaskovsky. Let him play with it and pick it apart. As far as chess goes, this week I've sent out 17 chess letters and received 12, which means our quiet post office has experienced a surge of activity. When, towards evening, my head begins to ache from chess and my fingers from Scriabin, I drink in our May nights, which really are breathtaking, with the bright white moon and the dark garden, and the only things that irritate me are the nightingales yelling at the top of their lungs, accompanied by a whole chorus of frogs from a nearby stream.

And I recall another *May Night*,[8] and the great hall of the conservatory, and you in it, and some awkward, sleepless mermaids under horrid green lighting, and Idelson, with huge glasses, reading in a halting voice: "Second lieutentant Kozma Derkach-Drip-shpan-tovsky . . ."

Where are you living now—in Pavlovsk, Pskov, Saratov, or, maybe, somewhere in Yaroslavl again? Are you sticking to your piano diet? Are you taking

4. Anna Nikolaevna Esipova (1851–1914) was a pianist and teacher at the conservatory; among her students was Prokofiev.
5. *The Golden Cockerel* is an opera by Rimsky-Korsakov.
6. *Islamey* is a piano piece by Mily Balakirev.
7. *The Divine Poem* is a symphonic work by Aleksandr Scriabin. At the time, Prokofiev was very taken with Scriabin's harmonic experiments, even though the two composers were later considered to be polar opposites.
8. Prokofiev is referring to a performance of Rimsky-Korsakov's opera *May Night*.

two-hour naps during the day? Are they giving you, as in the past, two soft-boiled eggs in the morning when you wake up in a most nasty mood?

Please write, and don't be angry that I didn't write back immediately: your heart is amazingly kind, and therefore you aren't likely to get angry.

With great respect,
Prokofiev

What is Max's address?[9]

June 14, 1909
SONTSOVKA

Most respected Verochka,

The last time the mail came I received a ton of letters, one nastier than the next. My *mamenka*, who is still fussing around in Peter with the apartment, is a nervous wreck: she landed on me for not writing her more often. Miaskovsky is in such a foul mood that for two weeks he hasn't touched the piano, and his vicious criticism of the movement of the sinfonietta I sent him reduced it to ashes. Lesenka just can't go to Italy and is wasting away in Petersburg. Your sweetheart wanted to read Dostoyevsky and is wasting away in Pavlovsk. Finally, Kankarovich wrote me a desperate letter saying that the police are planning to throw his whole orchestra out of Voronezh because they don't have resident permits. It never rains but it pours, and all straight down on me. However, I haven't lost heart, and am really in quite a good mood.

And here's yet another storm cloud looming over my head: I had to withstand a whole week of solitary confinement—well, not totally solitary, but almost totally. You see Morolev, whom I was planning to visit on the Dnepr, sent me a telegram saying he was called away to some kind of a conference, Dad had to go to Kharkov on business, and mama was in St. Petersburg—and I stayed all by my lonesome in this backwoods with no one but the servants and the dogs. I christened two of the dogs with the names of great chess players—Lasker and Tarash. It would be great if this Lasker played chess but, naturally, he only barks, and even that not particularly well. But I didn't lose heart even from all this, and kept terribly busy the whole time. I gobbled up Dostoyevsky's *The Devils* in two evenings. Don't worry, I digested it successfully, but the next day I had

---

9.   Prokofiev is referring to Max Shmitgoff, their fellow conservatory student, who would commit suicide in 1913.

a really bad kink in my neck from having read while not sitting up straight. *The Devils*, it seems, is more palatable than a lot of Dostoyevsky's works, which, in general, I don't always particularly like. Then I traveled 25 versts to spend a week with our doctor, who has three daughters—cheerful provincial young ladies.

Max sent me a letter written when he was in better spirits. He wasn't only in a better mood, he was even pretentious enough to really let me have it. He lives in Pushkin and little by little is putting on weight. I told him that I forgive him a lot, as I would a sick man, and hope that he's back to his old self soon.

I feel very sorry for your delicate, white fingers which have become all stiff. For some reason Miss Abramycheva's little fist comes to mind.[10]

When the happy day finally comes when you sit down to the piano again, take out some Brahms exercises. They're amazing.

I wish you all the best. Write a little more, with your characteristic neatness, and have no doubt that I would ever for a minute forget my dear "pal."

> Your faithfully devoted Prokofiev.

Do you ever see anybody from our gang at the conservatory?

[July 4, 1909]

SONTSOVKA

You're right, Vera Vladimirovna, that I had a good laugh over those nasty letters, and not a good cry like you would have, and I acted quite appropriately. Because just look how all of those sour moods of my beloved correspondents worked themselves out: Kankarosh reached an agreement with the angry Voronezh police, and my sinfonietta, it seems, will be all right. Miaskovsky, to whom I replied with dead silence, sent me a charming letter that filled eight big pages; he softened towards the sinfonietta he had so besmirched, and called me his priceless angel. Charming Lesechka spent some time in Germany and Switzerland and then went to France. She has sent me a whole bunch of postcards so I've been following her travels on a map.

So you see, everything has calmed down . . . Do you have a lot of photos? For heaven's sake, send me more shots with you in them—I so want to see you! I haven't been doing much with photography. One of the doctor's daughters, by

---

10. According to Vera Alpers, Olga Nikolaevna Abramycheva, a pianist, was their fellow student at the conservatory, where her father, N. I. Abramychev, was the inspector.

the way your namesake and an avid photographer, made me clean the dust off my camera and even take a few shots. But that was enough to make us get into an argument, such a heated argument that she swore never, ever to photograph me again. Too bad. All Veras are distinguished by their stubbornness, and every time she had been taking not fewer than half a dozen shots of me. However, all three sisters are now probably gnashing their teeth at me, and here's why. They were planning to go to Svyatye Gory—a large monastery, a little resort, and an incredibly beautiful spot. A large group was supposed to go together, all their cousins and friends, on the train and in carriages, 125 versts in all. They invited me insistently to come along and even delayed their departure because of me. And then, just at the decisive moment, I got a letter from Morolev, forgot about all those plans, and instead of Svyatye Gory, I ended up in Nikopol. I spent a week there and returned home only the day before yesterday. What's happened to the sisters I really can't say.

In Nikopol it turned out that almost half the town was waiting for me—all the chess players and musicians. I played chess and music until I was in a stupor, swam in the Dnepr, took bicycle rides and went on picnics, went to the circus—in a word, I gained three pounds. Now I've returned home and am taking hematogen.

Happy seventeenth birthday! Once I was that age, too. Up until now you were two years younger than I, but now you're only one year younger, so that means little by little you're catching up to me. In any case, I'll note your most blessed birth in golden letters underlined with bright red pencil. So I send you my warmest wishes. I'm starting to really miss you and wish you all the best.

> Devotedly
> Prokofiev

[July 26, 1909]

SONTSOVKA

You haven't written me for so long, dear Vera Vladimirovna, that I'm beside myself with despair. But in fact you should be acting nicely towards me, and here's why. Honored Avraam Isakovich Kankarovich, after arguing with his impresario, proceeded perpendicularly[11] and left Voronezh, and I, with my

---

11.   According to Alpers, this is a word that one of their classmates once used inappropriately, after which it became something of a private joke between them.

charming sinfonietta, ended up like a beached whale stranded on the shore. So this damn Kankaroshka, whom I had always considered a wimpy milksop, suddenly took it into his head to behave decisively, just when it wasn't appropriate. Isn't that a joke, or what? When autumn comes I'll have to get down to serious work and get it played in Petersburg. True, they'll perform it better than they would have in Voronezh, but there will also be a lot of arranging to do. In short, every autumn I feel like an anxious *mamashenka* with a grown-up daughter who has to be groomed and introduced to society.

Kankaroshka's news got me terribly upset, but that didn't spoil my mood. Lately, I've had to go through so much with the creation of my sinfonietta that I was really happy to be liberated from the obligation to push it any further. Now I'm composing a little at a time, gradually, and in the meantime I'm writing etudes for Winkler[12] and a mazurka in which both hands play around in parallel fourths.

"Oh, you dear daughter! How did they end up letting you go to your deep blue sea!"[13] (Actually, it's probably more like gray.) I, too, am planning to exhibit some filial tenderness and visit my *mamenka*, who has been in Essentuki for two weeks already in treatment for her rheumatism. Only I'm not going to the sea but the mountains, the tall, snow-covered mountains! The three pounds I lost with God's good graces I have put back on, but now I'll probably lose them again. What can you do. . . . After all, you don't waste away living in the country!

Along with your letter I received one from your namesake (who has already managed to make up with me and even to expend a lot of film taking pictures of me). I'm sending you a shot she took following my instructions, setting up two cameras at the same time—one from the front and one from the back. Then they were pasted together. What resulted was a sort of doll. It doesn't look at all like me, but at first glance the shots and I do have something inexplicable in common.

Not long ago civilization sprang up in our backwoods in the form of a gramophone bought by one of the peasant men. And now towards evening, this damned invention stands outdoors in front of his hut and starts to wheeze its horrible songs. The crowd that gathers makes a racket, expressing its joy, and pretends to sing along. Dogs bark and howl, the cows coming in from the fields

---

12. Aleksandr Winkler was Prokofiev's piano teacher at the St. Petersburg Conservatory.
13. Alpers used to spend her summer vacations with relatives on the Baltic Sea coast near Riga. The original source of this literary quotation is unclear.

moo and run in all directions, and, to top off all this torture, someone from a neighboring hut starts to play along on the accordion, off-key. At first I try closing all the windows, then I sit down at the piano, but finally I lose my patience and go off riding on my bicycle in the fields so as to spare myself this frightful cacophony.

> Write, Verochka, adio—
> Prokofiev

August 19, 1909
[SONTSOVKA]

Welcome home, Verochka! It's been three days now since I made my way back home, with God's grace, having returned from distant travels. When I set off for the Caucasus, I decided ahead of time to do nothing, and didn't take with me any music, books, not even a chess set. I liked Essentuki very much, and I made a series of raids from there on my neighbors—on Zheleznovodsk, Kislovodsk, Beshtau (I think I even wrote you from there), Piatigorsk, and so on. For ten whole days, instead of being at home, I wound up in Kislovodsk, one of the most lively resorts in Russia. I found myself in splendid surroundings: a Shreder concert grand, an intoxicating view from the balcony, ceilings seven *arshins*[14] tall, Narzan mineral baths, a female companion with whom to play piano four-hands (one of Rubinstein's pupils), and more.

As it turned out, the whole musical world was gathered in Kislovodsk: Glazunov, Safonov, Esipova, Kalantarov, Zbrueva, Smirnov, Tartakov; and then on a somewhat lower level: Tarnovsky, the Mestechkins (M. and Mme.), even Vandsheidt,[15] and, finally, the French teacher from our academic classes.

But to tell the truth, I didn't really spend as much time as I should have with anyone.

Towards the end I started to get bored from the inactivity, and I felt like get-

---

14. An *arshin* is a measurement used in Russia; it equals .71 meters, or about 28 inches. The ceilings are thus about sixteen feet high.

15. Alpers notes that Olga Kalantorovna Kalantrova was a pianist, a pupil, and a friend of A. N. Esipova, and a professor at the St. Petersburg Conservatory through the Soviet period; Evgenia Ivanovna Zbrueva was a singer and soloist at the Mariinsky Theater; Smirnov was a tenor and a soloist at the Mariinsky Theater; Tarnovsky was a pianist and pupil of Esipova; the Mestechkins were a violinist and and former student of the conservatory and his wife; Vansheidt was a French horn player and a fellow student in academic subjects.

ting home to my work. But at home there were already guests to be taken care of—my cousin and several varieties of aunts (you probably laid eyes on them at the exam), so that it's unlikely that my work will progress as fast as it would if I were alone, but the good thing is that it's not so desolate around here now. We sometimes go horseback riding or play croquet at night by the moon.

I tore up your disgusting photograph. Be sure to thank the person who took such a pleasant shot of you.

I'm still not thinking about going to Petersburg yet. In any case I won't go any earlier than September 20. But I'm very sorry for you. What sort of desire possessed you to set off for the city ahead of time? By the way, it's clear that you are bored. In any case, your last letter carried such a strong fragrance of unrelieved boredom that I hid it as soon as possible in the farthest drawer of my desk.

Miaskovsky is also down at the mouth in PBG, Zakharov has fallen completely silent, Lesyushka and I have reached the point of exchanging very caustic letters, and Max has vanished.

And yet when I returned from the Caucasus I found waiting for me on my desk no more and no fewer than 22 letters.

Good-bye, Verochka, be well.

Yours completely S. Prokofiev

July 31, 1910
[St. Petersburg]

Dear Verochka, I send you my final greetings from PBG.

As a result of my father's death, I am abandoning the north and tomorrow morning will leave for Ekaterinoslavskaya Province. Write me more frequently and at greater length: I would be very grateful to you for that.

Greetings to you and yours.

Yours devotedly Prokofiev

CHAPTER TWO

Letters to Eleonora Damskaya

LIKE VERA ALPERS, ELEONORA DAMSKAYA was a fellow student of Prokofiev at the St. Petersburg Conservatory. Her instrument was the harp. In the words of the Russian editors of Damskaya's previously unpublished correspondence, which is preserved at the Glinka Museum in Moscow, Damskaya was an "intelligent and interesting conversationalist who involuntarily inspired Prokofiev to produce vivid, substantial, and slightly flirtatious letters."[1] So infatuated with Damskaya was Prokofiev that he even immortalized their friendship in music: the Prelude for Piano and Harp, one of the "Ten Pieces for Piano," op. 12 (composed 1906–13) is dedicated to Damskaya.

Prokofiev's correspondence with Damskaya began in 1912 and continued very regularly until May 1918, when Prokofiev left the war-torn USSR for the United States. Whenever he was away from Petersburg on one of his many trips to the Caucasus, Moscow, or Europe, Prokofiev would send postcards and letters to Damskaya. He even sent her several humorous poems. The correspondence resumed in 1920, and became very frequent once again until 1927, when Prokofiev made his first trip back to Russia. At this point it broke off for many years, however, only to be resumed in 1948, long after Prokofiev's final return to the USSR. Interestingly, one of the last letters Prokofiev wrote was to Damskaya, on February 11, 1953, just three weeks before his death.

What seems to have led to the break in the Prokofiev-Damskaya correspondence between 1927 and 1948 was a dispute that arose between them over a piano that Prokofiev had won as a graduation prize in 1914. When Prokofiev left the USSR in 1918, he left the piano and many papers (including the only score of his Piano Concerto No. 2) behind in the St. Petersburg apartment in which he and his mother had been living. During the Civil War, however, the apartment was occupied by people unknown to Prokofiev, who destroyed the documents and disposed of the piano. Writing to Damskaya from Germany and

---

1. S. S. *Prokof'ev: Pis'ma*, Gosudarstvennyi tsentral'nyi muzei muzykal'noi kul'tury im. M. I. Glinki, M. K. Starodubtseva, and M. G. Rytsareva, eds., introduction by M. G. Rytsareva (Moscow, 1980), ms, 8.

France in the 1920s, Prokofiev urged her to find out what happened to his piano, and to save it for him. Whether Damskaya's efforts caused her problems with the Soviet authorities, or whether she was simply annoyed with Prokofiev for his insistent and repeated requests for assistance is unclear. In any case, their friendship and correspondence obviously cooled after 1927. Although Prokofiev continued to correspond regularly with other friends and colleagues in the USSR in the late 1920s and throughout the 1930s, when he was still living abroad, he no longer wrote to Damskaya. Nor does he mention her in his long autobiography.

But the more than one hundred letters that Prokofiev did write to Damskaya are extremely valuable and revealing. Here, Prokofiev adopts a joking, casual tone strikingly different from that of the more formal letters he wrote to Koussevitsky, Diaghilev, and even to Miaskovsky. His observations sent from his early trips to Europe are full of energy and a strange voyeurism. Verbally complex, the letters are also full of references to common friends and acquaintances. Many of these were of only passing and topical interest, and not all can be identified. But the spirit in which Prokofiev describes their social and romantic adventures is irresistible and entirely consistent with the ironic, tongue-in-cheek aesthetic of such early works as the "Classical" Symphony and the Violin Concerto No. 1, where lyricism and naughtiness dwell comfortably side-by-side.

Prokofiev's letters to Damskaya are also very revealing of Prokofiev's political sentiments—or rather, his lack thereof—during the revolutionary months of 1917. When the Bolsheviks seized the Winter Palace in Petrograd on October 25, 1917, Prokofiev was far away in the Caucasus resort of Kislovodsk, one of his favorite places. Damskaya was in the center of action back home. His notes and letters to her from autumn 1917 to the spring of 1918, when he left Russia for what turned out to be a nine-year absence, demonstrate an anxiety over what was happening in Petrograd, but also a complete failure to grasp the immensity of the change that was occurring in all areas of Russian life. "I will come only after the civil strife ends," Prokofiev wrote naively to Damskaya on December 30, 1917. Little did he realize that the "civil strife" would last for several more bloody years, and that the outcome would eventually have an enormous influence on his own creative and personal life.

This disengaged, even frivolous attitude towards the Russian Revolution helps to explain why Prokofiev's letters to Damskaya have gone unpublished until now. In 1980, two members of the staff of the Glinka Museum prepared an edition of Prokofiev's letters, including his correspondence with Damskaya. The report prepared by the publishing house *Sovetskii kompozitor* on the proposed publication noted that the letters dating from 1917 and 1918 "would have to be cut," and further: "It's possible to publish Prokofiev's letters to Damskaya, but not necessary." Not necessary because the portrait the letters paint of the composer was inappropriate for one of the leading figures of Soviet music, and would lead to awkward questions about his acceptance of Lenin, communism, and Soviet power.

I have omitted some letters because they discuss at length unknown friends of Prokofiev and Damskaya (often referred to only by initials) and have edited those included so as to make them more accessible in English translation.

(These letters are preserved in the archives of the Glinka Museum of Musical Culture in Moscow. They were prepared for publication in 1980 by M. K. Starodubtseva and M. G. Rytsareva, as part of a larger volume of Prokofiev's correspondence, with editing, introduction, and notes by M. G. Rytsareva, but the planned volume never appeared. With the permission of the museum's administration, I have used some of the material in the notes and introduction of that planned volume in preparing these translations and notes. Translated by Harlow Robinson, with assistance from Liza Rudneva.)

June 19, 1913
PARIS

Here's the hello I promised you from the top of the Eiffel Tower.
Prokofiev

February 15, 1914
MOSCOW

Signora Leonora,

I squeezed out ten minutes of free time to scribble a few words to you and send a hello from muddy and damp Moscow, where I'm dying without galoshes and don't want to buy another pair.

I've started to rehearse the concerto only today.[2]

I haven't run across M–lle *Proika* yet.

Say hello to Vera Aleksandrovna.
S.P.

April 8, 1914
ST. PETERSBURG
[written on a postcard with a photo of Capablanca][3]

Capablanca,
Bought at the international chess tournament in St. Petersburg on April 8, 1914—at the very moment when he was winning the match with Nimtsovich.

June 2, 1914
STOCKHOLM

Mamselle Eleonora,

Having arrived successfully in the city that you see on the other side,[4] I'm looking it over in the accidental company of three happy Russian stallions.

---

2. By this time Prokofiev had composed two piano concertos: Concerto No. 1 in D-flat Major, op. 10, received its premiere in Moscow on July 15, 1912; and Concerto No. 2 in G Minor, op. 16, in Pavlovsk on August 23, 1913.

3. José Raul Capablanca (1888–1942) was a great Cuban chess player and the world champion at the time. Prokofiev competed against him in St. Petersburg on May 11, 13, and 15, 1914, and managed to win the last of these display matches.

4. He writes on a postcard with a picture of Stockholm.

I just lost them and now I'm bored again. Tomorrow I'll continue my trip along the canals.

Bye for now.

S. Prokofiev

June 6, 1914
CHRISTIANIA [OSLO]

Froken Eleonora,

I'm happy to let you know that I have safely arrived in Christiania. Tomorrow I'll walk around the city and after that will go on to Bergen. The cabin is already reserved, we'll see what happens. So far the trip was nice, and the companionship of a young German suffragette most pleasant. My best wishes.

P.

Your ink pen leaked into my pocket twice and doesn't write any more; and God knows how to feed it ink.

June 12, 1914
NEWCASTLE

Miss Eleonora,

Without absolutely any maritime embarrassments, and in fact, quite pleasantly, I crossed from Norway to England. Now I'm getting on a train to London. I'm traveling third class because my funds are already running low. Good thing I had enough for third class, or else I would have had to check myself as baggage.

A propos, did you get a chance to see Capablanchik[5] in the issue of Novyi Svet of 04/01? Isn't he sweet?

June 25, 1914
LONDON

Your Excellency Mr. Minister,[6]

I was very happy to receive your letter. True, I had to go get a magnifying glass, but that doesn't matter. Though, in all honesty, you have miserable hand-

5.   Capablanchik is an endearing Russian diminutive for Capablanca. Prokofiev uses it to show his warm feelings for the famous chess player.
6.   This was one of Prokofiev's joking nicknames for Damskaya; he often used this as a salutation to her in his letters.

writing. Nevertheless, the contents were so interesting that they made up for ruining my eyesight.

This is my "pastan"[7] in London: I sleep at night; they wake up my neighbor at 7:00 A.M., he is deeply asleep and they are knocking on his door for a couple minutes while I'm cursing at them; then I doze off till about 8:30 and at 8:30 I hear a gong banging—it's breakfast time; after breakfast, I usually go to Breit-kopf and Härtel's shop where I have an office for my studies (the same one where Nikolai Nikolaevich had written his *Red Mask*).[8] At one in the afternoon I go home for lunch; in the afternoon, I meet different people associated with music, conduct negotiations on musical business, play bridge with Nikolai Andreyev,[9] or go shopping for colored stockings. At night, I put on tails and a cloak and go to the Ballets Russes or the opera. You can hardly get a ticket, but like some kind of a governor, I have a reserved seat because Diaghilev is propos-ing that I write a ballet for next season and wants me to get to know the busi-ness. Backstage, I meet heavily made-up celebrities and half-naked ballerinas. On my way back I usually stop at a little restaurant for a big lobster and then go home to sleep. I went to see a boxing match and with delight watched them beat each other into unconsciousness and spit their teeth out in a bucket of water, which turned a soft pink color.

I'm waiting for your second letter. Your ink pen is still intact; I use it and often curse it. I sent Struve[10] a card hoping that she would be insulted, but instead received an answer that makes no sense. And so, away I go.

Yours S. Prokofiev.

My best regards to Vera Aleksandrovna.

July 5, 1914
LONDON

My dear Minister,

It seems that you graduated from the lycée or law school a very long time ago, because a high percentage of spelling mistakes have crept into your letters. Oh, of course, the contents are so interesting that they make up for these little sins, and yet you know, for a minister it's kind of embarrassing . . .

---

7.   Pastime.
8.   Prokofiev refers to Nicolai Tcherepnin, his professor of conducting. The correct title of the ballet is *The Red Death Mask*.
9.   Nikolai Andreyev was a singer of the Mariinsky Theater who went on tours with the operas staged by Diaghilev.
10. Struve was Prokofiev's fellow student in the conservatory.

Ask Vera Aleksandrovna to read dictations to you once in a while. Sorry for intruding into your private life. Now I'll turn to current events. My stay in London is coming to an end; in a few days I am going off on a long journey—to Berlin and Moscow. On July 15, I'll show up for the concert at Pavlovsk. It's a pity that you're not here to stroll in the evenings in Hyde Park. There is plenty to admire there. Hundreds of couples settle down on the soft grass in the park, kiss, lounge around embracing each other, and pay absolutely no attention to the passersby. You can stand near, watch them, learn pleasant positions, and recall your own youth. Since there was so much fun at 9:00 P.M., I decided that at 11:00, when darkness falls upon the earth, it would be even more interesting, and so I went for a walk at 11:00 P.M. Alas, the evening turned out to be wet and cold, so I didn't get a chance to see what I was hoping to spy on . . .

Somewhere in Norway, I sent a skinny postcard to that little liar Vegman, but didn't indicate the return address. Inquire of her which address she is using to carry on this lively correspondence with me. Give my best regards to Vera Aleksandrovna and to . . . God help me . . . Daniella Stanislavovna. The Petersburg paper had it all wrong about umbrellas. The weather is excellent.

Bye for now, Mr. Minister. I wish you all the best.

Yours,

S. Prokofiev.

[July 6–7] 1914
WINDSOR

You don't have any postcards of Windsor, do you? So here's one for your collection, my dear merry wife of Windsor. So far I haven't gotten a single letter from you. For this I have to reprimand you.

P.

July 25, 1914
LISKI STATION

Eleonora, forgive me for not writing to you from Moscow, but things have become tolerable only now. From Petersburg to Kozlov I was traveling not in a regular car, but in some kind of overcrowded pigsty. By the way, you probably don't have a postcard like this of charming Liski in your collection.

My best regards to that quiet sister of yours, and I'll be looking forward to a letter from you in Kislovodsk.

There were 16 cars in the train; and the locomotive overexerted itself and died. We are stuck in the middle of a field awaiting another one.

August 5, 1914
KISLOVODSK

My dear Sazosha,[11]

At present, Kislovodsk looks something like this: there're quite a few people; none are very chic, but many are chic enough. Everybody—including me—is wearing white. Lots of sun and local mineral water; trees and grass are green and fresh. Trains go to Petersburg every day, but you have to change trains; they're promising to begin a direct connection soon, so your precious Mr. Shish Kebab is talking nonsense. I'm playing chess a lot and not flirting with anybody; I stroll, sleep, work on the sinfonietta[12] a little and play bridge; I'm also following the events of the war, studying English, and failing to respond to letters; in a word, I'm relaxing. I hope that when you recall how many letters I sent you in June, you won't be expecting an answer to each line and you'll more often send me news of the capital, in which I'm extremely interested. If Struve, Vegman, Lipinskaya, and the others[13] haven't been yet taken hostage by the enemy, send them my best regards. I read the review from the *Russian Musical Gazette* earlier. It was mentioned there that a detailed report on the ceremony would appear in the next issue; that's the report I have been hoping to get from you.[14]

So, Mr. Minister, wartime obligates you to double the frequency of your dispatches. In anticipation of that let me pump your honest hand.

My best regards to Vera Aleksandrovna.

Your S. Prokofiev.

The ballet will have two or even more harps.

August 20, 1914
KISLOVODSK

My dear Minister,

I share your grief over the misfortunes that have befallen you in your private life, but allow me to question that diplomatic astuteness of yours. Military operations always follow a break in diplomatic relations, so you should've fore-

---

11. This is another of Prokofiev's nicknames for Damskaya.

12. In the summer of 1914 Sergei Prokofiev worked on the new version of the Sinfonietta, op. 5.

13. These are Damskaya's girlfriends at the conservatory.

14. Prokofiev is talking about the graduation ceremony at the St. Petersburg Conservatory, which he missed because of his trip to England.

seen that after rancorous negotiations your precious Sergusenka would want to start fighting. And stop whining; kiss your darling new cadet and forget the one you threw over, or else I won't respect you anymore.

In vain do you wish that there should be no war with Turkey; it's nothing to worry about and even interesting. Kislovodsk is beyond reach of the Turks because of the Caucasus, but all those who live in the Caucasian region will come here and it will be fun to be among these dark-eyed southerners.

Send my greetings to Struve. She says that she is related to every Struve; well you know, one of them—from the cavalry division—has been awarded a St. George's Medal. I'm still satisfied with Kislovodsk, but probably won't be sitting around here till October, so could you do me a favor: call the musical studio and in case that tavern still exists, find out—as if you're thinking of applying—when classes start there, what are the requirements, and what their teachers are like. It goes without saying that you shouldn't give me away. In case that tavern has collapsed, maybe I'll really get out of Kislovodsk and visit somebody. As for my current regime, since my last letter the following changes have occurred: I'm not playing chess, I'm answering letters and flirting; I'm learning 60 new words for each English lesson; I'm hiking in the mountains but mostly in the foothills; and I'm parting my hair.

I'm very unhappy with you for sending your dispatches so rarely. You're not earning your salary as minister.

My best regards to Verosanit.[15]

Your S. Prokofiev.

September 3, 1914
KISLOVODSK

My dear Minister,

You're terrific. Your graciousness, as well as your gift for diplomacy, exceeded my expectations three times over. I only regret that in your dispatch there was no space left for other affairs of state or for information on your private life. As for me, without your enlightening guidance I've landed in a bitter war. I'm fighting like a madman. The war, by the way, is successful, although part of a lousy town in my territory has been occupied. The name of that little town is My Heart.

---

15.   This is a jocular abbreviation of Vera Aleksandrovna's name.

Let me change the subject to Kislovodsk. The resort is deserted. As far as the weather, it has generally been very fine: sunny one day and rainy another. On the 11th I'll arrive in Petrograd, or rather "Petroalekseyevsk," as they want to name it. So then I'll see you soon. I stroll around in the rain and under the sun without a *chapeau* and have such a tan that I look like a copper basin. You won't be able to recognize me. Say hello to Vera Aleksandrovna.

Take care.

Your S. Prokofiev

February 1, 1915
EN ROUTE[16]

Oh, this awful pen! An inkblot after the first two words, and it doesn't write at all after the third. Otherwise everything else is just fine. I had breakfast, took a nap, now I'm studying Italian, and I'm in a wonderful mood. Another inkblot! God, this is too much!

4:00 A.M. February 3, 1915
KIEV

We arrived in Kiev at 3:30 A.M. instead of 7 in the evening. Sorry for this lousy postcard, but at this early hour in the morning I couldn't buy anything better. My spirits, except for the runny nose, are terrific. My traveling companion got married at 20 and got a divorce at 27, and advises me not to do such a stupid thing. I object to his point of view, observing that it would have been even better if he had divorced her at 23!

February 3, 1915
KAZATIN STATION

The weather is sunny and my nose is runny. Our new traveling companion is a singer named Bavastro who cannot stop swearing, but who is nice and cheerful and reminds me a little of Capablanca. In general the weather here is superb, the only thing is I wish my cold would go away as soon as possible. Bavastro is going to put me on a couch and pour drops of menthol and spirits in my nose.

They say letters reach Rome quickly. So write me there.

---

16. In early February 1915 Prokofiev went to Italy to meet Sergei Diaghilev. He traveled through Romania, Bulgaria, and Greece.

8:00 P.M., February 4, 1915
YASSY [ROMANIA]

There's cholera around somewhere, which is why we had to cross the border in third-class cars that looked like some sort of wagons. But now we have finally landed in a sleeping car[17] and sighed with relief. My spirits are proportionally opposite to the weather—and it's slushy outside. They are ringing the departure bell, I'd better go.

February 5, 1915
BUCHAREST

They say Bucharest is a small Paris. Maybe here and there it is, but it really is very small. On the whole it's not a bad little city. I'm swallowing foreign newspapers whole. It's provocative to see official denunciations of Petrograd and Berlin side by side. . . .

S.P.

[February 6] 1915
BULGARIA

Even though mines are floating in the Danube, none of them exploded while we were crossing the river on the steamship. Now we are traveling through Bulgaria[. . . .] I'm reading Bulgarian newspapers and understand almost everything; the only thing that surprises me is the Bulgarian letter ъ which they stick here and there for no good reason.[18]

7:00 A.M., February 9, 1915
USKYUT [SERBIA]

We finally managed to sleep in a sleeping car, but in the corridor. Today we'll end our railroad journey and will arrive in Salonika. I almost missed the train because I was writing this note. The Serbs are nice, but you can't find any postcards, stamps, or mailboxes here.

---

17. Prokofiev wrote these two words in English.
18. The letter ъ is part of both the Russian and Bulgarian alphabets, but is used differently, thus Prokofiev's surprise.

February 10, 1915
SALONIKA

Eleonora, we are by the sea, but it is gray and rough. If we are not detained by quarantines for this stupid typhoid fever, we will sail today for Athens. Our group now consists of eight people of all ages, but is very cheerful and makes quite a loud hubbub.

Greetings.

February 12, 1915
ATHENS

We sailed and sailed—some got seasick, but not me—and yesterday finally sailed into Athens. It's hot, bright, warm, green and white—and really very fine. I don't have enough money, of course. The first thing I did was to get my hair cut, but I am in a very cheerful mood.

S.P.

February 17, 1915
BARI [ITALY]

At first the sea was "like a swamp," to use Bavastro's expression, but then it got very rough; the whole boat was throwing up (excuse me for that description), but not your faithful servant, who was strolling about the deck of the dancing ship, stumbling on benches, hooks and so on. Yesterday we docked at Brindisi, spent the night nearby at Bari, which is shown on the postcard. In the evening—to Rome.

February 18[?], 1915
FOGGIA

A regrettable incident has occurred: while Bavastro and I were having lunch at some obscure station our train and all of our baggage went on to Rome. Fortunately, our train was designated *diretto*, and in four hours the *direttissimo* will come by. It arrives in Rome at almost the same time. On the one hand it's funny, but on the other a bit confusing.

February 21, 1915
ROME

I was very happy to get your postcards and reviews. It's a shame you don't feel like writing more; letters come reliably in about 15–17 days, and I am not planning a quick return to Russia. For the moment they are advertising me like the devil, and have been wearing me out with breakfasts, rehearsals, reviewers, marquises—but they have been praising me to the skies, so that I feel like some sort of Beethoven. The orchestra and conductor are excellent. The posters are handsome and about three yards tall.[19] The Italian girls are all short.

March 1, 1915
POMPEII

We just arrived in this dead kingdom from Naples, where I settled instead of Palermo. Naples is fun-loving, sunny, and noisy. Not a single one of you devils is writing me. The concert went very well.

16 [3] March, 1915
CAPRI

I am in Capri. The sea, the mountains, the light—wherever you turn, all is splendid. Maybe that is even a drawback. The Italian reviews were in part good, in part bad, and one pen-pusher called me an animal.

There are two Englishmen in the hotel here who dress for dinner in smoking jackets, which makes me very uncomfortable, because my things are in Naples. Here I have only my Swiss suit. Forgive me for relating this detail, but as it happens I am just about to go to have dinner and am feeling embarrassed.

March 20, 1915
ROME

It seems that you will soon be celebrating Easter; so allow me to extend my respectful best wishes. It's a pity that I cannot exchange the traditional Easter kiss with you in person, and push into the crowd at the conservatory for the matins service. I am starting to feel like coming home, but instead I am setting off in the opposite direction—to Switzerland, probably not for long.[20] Greetings!

---

19. Prokofiev was preparing for a concert at which he played his Second Concerto and several piano pieces from the op. 2 and op. 12. The conductor was Bernardino Molinari. The concert took place in the Augusteum on March 7, 1915 (New Style). This letter was written the day before the concert (Prokofiev dated it Old Style).

20. Prokofiev does not mention this trip to Switzerland in his *Autobiography*. It is entirely possible that it did not take place. This seems even more likely since Prokofiev returned to Petrograd from Italy, through Brindisi, Salonika, and Sofia.

25 (12) March, 1915
ROME

These idiot insurance men cannot find any way of insuring Diaghilev for half a million (and that is essential for his contract with America). As a result there is no way we can slip over to Switzerland, where I really wanted to go.

I am tired of Rome, and the weather is snivelly. I would not even be opposed to setting out for Petrograd, but I cannot think about that for the moment: there is a lot of business to be done with the ballet.

April 2, 1915
SOFIA

Our traveling company has deigned to become fatigued, so we are staying for 1½ days in Sofia.[21] It is a city something like our Simferopol; on the streets there are masses of dark-haired people who are a bit crude but occasionally colorful because of their national costumes. Ugly Bulgarian mugs. I had a quarrel with Bavastro.

July 19, 1915
[No place given; probably PETROGRAD]

Eleonora, don't be angry with me for sending so little news and for writing on such atrocious paper. I am going to Terioki for a vacation.[22] If you are in Pavlovsk on the 21st, then we can see each other.[23] In Terioki I'll be rehearsing the sonata, for I have completely forgotten it.

I was in the city for two minutes on Friday. I received your letter, and called 637 on the phone, but instead of you I got your mama. Greetings
S.

August 6, 1915
PETROGRAD[24]

Respected Eleonor Aleksandrovich,[25]

I am deeply guilty that I did not keep my promise on time, but after I fool-

---

21.   Prokofiev stopped in Sofia on the way from Italy to Russia.
22.   Terioki is a resort on the Karelian Isthmus, later renamed as Zelenogorsk.
23.   On July 21 in Pavlovsk there was a concert at which Prokofiev was scheduled to perform his Second Piano Sonata.
24.   The name of St. Petersburg was changed to Petrograd soon after the start of World War I, because St. Petersburg sounded too German.
25.   Prokofiev uses the masculine form of her name, as a joke.

ishly dug up my *Autumnal*[26] I sat with such pleasure fixing it up all evening that I did not even notice that it was after midnight. Now it's raining hard, but I am on my way: what do I have to lose? Either the sun or some eyes—someone will light the way.

All the best and—get better.

SP

Saturday
March 26, 1916
[No place given; seems to be PETROGRAD]

O, my dear child, accept my 1000 expressions of sympathy, and then the news of what I was doing yesterday. In the evening at the Andreyevs, A.G.[27] put on a white blouse and was rather unbearable to look at, but since she sat modestly in the other room, she was pleasant enough. N.V.[28] was in uniform and very nice. After winning three rubles, I went to a gathering of The Bronze Horseman,[29] or, as N.V. called it, The Bronze Forehead. There Gorodetsky and Kuzmin read their poems quite nicely;[30] Erdeli played with verve, although she got mixed up in my prelude. Overall, she conducted herself modestly and decorously. Demchinsky was there with his wife and the three of us went home together.[31] In the afternoon I played until teatime, when my darling Marinochka came to see me and stayed for 3½ whole hours. Ah—she is such a treasure! This evening I won't go to the Tcherepnins (I have an invitation to go to the Demchinskys). Mama is in a panic over today's afternoon visitor (whom I did not exhibit to her), but is going with me to the Demchinskys. Please

26. *Autumnal*, a symphonic sketch for small orchestra, op. 8, was originally composed in 1910, and revised in 1915 and again in 1934.

27. Anna Grigorevna Zherebtsova-Andreyeva.

28. Nikolai Vasilevich Andreyev.

29. This was a Petrograd literary-artistic circle of the time, named after the poem "The Bronze Horseman" by Aleksandr Pushkin, which was itself inspired by the statue of Peter the Great that stands by the River Neva behind St. Isaac's Cathedral.

30. Sergei Gorodetsky (1884–1967) was a prominent poet and a cofounder of the Acmeist movement. He wrote the scenario for Prokofiev's *Ala and Lolly* (later revised and renamed *The Scythian Suite*), Prokofiev's first ballet project for Diaghilev. Mikhail Kuzmin (1875–1936) was also a well-known Acmeist poet and a composer of considerable talent.

31. Boris Nikolaevich Demchinsky (1877–1942) was a writer and close friend of Prokofiev's. He later helped Prokofiev write the libretti for *The Gambler* and *The Fiery Angel*.

forgive the paper, ink, and penmanship. You don't have anything to do anyway, so spend your time deciphering it.

Greetings S

June 17, 1916

KUOKKALA[32]

The very first day here there were sharks and a bloody battle at cards that lasted until 6:00 A.M. I did not participate, limiting myself to ten minutes of lotto which resulted in a win of 2 rubles.

My primary occupations are the old ones: tennis and "pages" (68%).[33] V. N. and I quarreled right away, but then she went off to inquire of the neighbors what there was to see in Kuokkala and they told her that Prokofiev had settled here somewhere. After that she became completely pleasant. Boris Verin[34] is not writing you because he is trying to revive someone who drowned, a boy of about 10. A crowd gathered, the mother is wailing, the summer residents are aghast and anxious, they are running off to get the doctor—but I think they are really enjoying themselves.

July 1, 1916

RYBINSK

In the end the poet[35] and I left Petrograd on Thursday and made it without any trouble to Rybinsk. Rybinsk is bad. There are cows on the sidewalks, but the steamboat has turned out to be most elegant. The Volga is a marvel, and so is the weather. We are about to cast off, farewell!

July 2, 1916

PLES

Everything is superb: the Volga, the cities (especially Yaroslavl), the weather, even Boris Verin is bearable. We have not managed to get by without running into some people we know: Rusinov, Gorodinsky. Even Telyakovsky[36] himself

---

32. Kuokkala was another popular summer resort on the Finnish Gulf near Petrograd.
33. In the summer of 1916, Prokofiev was working on the orchestration of *The Gambler* and had by this point completed 68 percent of the full score.
34. Boris Verin was the nom de plume of Prokofiev's friend Boris Bashkirov. Verin wrote one of the poems Prokofiev set in his op. 23 song cycle ("Trust Me") and later spent time with Prokofiev in Europe in the early 1920s.
35. Boris Verin.
36. Vladimir Arkadevich Telyakovsky (1861–1924) was a Russian theater critic and director of the Imperial Theaters.

flashed by—he was accompanying from the church to our ship his daughter (age 19) and her freshly married husband (age 42, and a senator to boot). Our observation of this couple at 12 midnight yesterday provided us with some amusement and a few suggestions. Fok, friend to you and Anna Grigorevna, gave a concert in Rybinsk(!) and it was a flop(!!!).

July 7, 1916
SAMARA [now KUIBYSHEV]

We have been stuck in Samara for three days already—or, more precisely, 15 versts from it—in the large but ungainly dacha of the poet's brother. It is awfully messy here, but tolerable for a little break during our long journey.

As for the Volga, it is much bigger, and the trip much more interesting, than I had expected.
Greetings.

July 10, 1916
SAMARA

To E. A. Damskaya

Samara, skinny Samara!
You may be full to bursting with grain,
But besides that one commodity
The sky has made you bare and plain.

So pitiful you are, boring Samarka
(Although full to bursting with grain),
That I wander sadly in the lanes of the park
Searching for a place to hang myself . . .

July 16, 1916
ASTRAKHAN

We have made a stop in Astrakhan. We are eating caviar, riding in a motor boat, lying on the roof of our ship, and walking around the colorful bazaar. Tomorrow we leave for Persia. By the way, I'll be back in the north sooner than you might think from reading this. Essentuki is nearby.

Greetings

July 19, 1916
TIFLIS [now TBILISI]

It was a blow to be told here that Persia was not interesting, so I went to the Caucasus. Boris Verin overslept the ship's departure and therefore remained in Astrakhan. Today I arrived in Tiflis. I went to the Oriental baths—a sea of lather. Just now I came to have supper in the park here and suddenly—how convenient—a symphonic orchestra is playing Liszt's *Tasso*. I want desperately to sleep, but tomorrow morning I leave for Borzhomi.

July 20, 1916
BORZHOMI

Borzhomi spreads out attractively among high mountains overgrown with thick green forest. As for the water, it's better in bottles.[37] In character the resort is like a quiet Kislovodsk, in miniature. . . . On the street it's raining, and in my head there's neuralgia. Tomorrow I'm climbing some mountain or other, and the day after tomorrow I'm traveling along the Georgian Military Highway and will probably overtake this letter.

August 14, 1916
KUOKKALA

The famous international tennis star Prokofiev has arrived in Kuokkala and has taken part in a huge tennis competition. *The Gambler* suffered most of all.

Greetings. Drop a line if you are still in Mustamyaki.

November 17, 1916
KIEV[38]

Still persevering in my journey,
I have stepped on the soil of Kii.
How bright it is! What sunbeams!
And even a few clouds.

S.P.

---

37. Like Kislovodsk, Borzhomi was famous for its healing mineral waters.
38. Prokofiev made his first appearance in Kiev in the fall of 1916, playing the First Piano Concerto under the direction of his childhood tutor Reinhold Glière, who had been appointed head of the Kiev Conservatory.

May 21, 1917
MALAYA VISHERA[39]

The thermos is marvelous. Our trip is also going well. Nobody is slaughtering anybody yet. I hear that from now on chocolate will be given only to those who are sick. Please buy me five pounds, Kraft if you can get it.[40]

Greetings.

May 28, 1917
[no return address — EN ROUTE]

In Kazan I decided to betray the Volga and to take a peek at the Kama—so I set off on the Kama. I made my way splendidly to Perm and am now traveling along farther.

I send you greetings. S.P.

July 23, 1917
TULA

For the moment everything is just splendid—I am alone in my compartment, I slept well and am reading your *Derelicts*. The only problem is I did something silly: I was standing until Lyuban by an open window, enjoying the warm summer night, and as a result I caught a chill in my teeth. I am treating them with warm tea. I'm planning out a second short story.[41] Owing to my teeth, it will be an angry one. I am waiting for the letter you promised to write me "after dinner."

July 24, 1917
ROSTOV-ON-DON

The journey is continuing just as well as it began. The problem with my teeth is spoiling things just a little—which is reflected in a certain irritability in my second short story, which by the way I have now almost completely thought out.

---

39. In the spring of 1917 Prokofiev took a steamboat trip along the Volga and Kama rivers, traveling close to the Ural Mountains. On that trip he orchestrated his Violin Concerto No. 1 and finished his Symphony No. 1, the "Classical."

40. The Russian army continued to fight in World War I after the February Revolution of 1917, which led to the formation of the Provisional Government. But Russian losses at the front were huge, and civil unrest was common throughout Russia in this period. Luxuries such as chocolate were thus difficult to come by.

41. Prokofiev wrote several short stories in 1917–18; see *Sergei Prokofiev: Soviet Diary 1927 and Other Writings*, translated and edited by Oleg Prokofiev (Boston: Northeastern University Press, 1991).

Just as I feared, a lady has crept into my compartment, followed by an ailing colonel, filling up all the space. When the lady placed her dirty suitcase on top of a pillow that I had just taken out of my briefcase, I made a scene. The indignant lady—followed by the ailing colonel—ran out into the two neighboring compartments, and I can hear through the closed doors how they are now cursing me. This gives me a little idea for a third short story which I will now start working on, taking advantage of my solitude. Heartfelt greetings.

S.

August 1, 1917
Essentuki

Today I received your interesting and very fresh (it took only five days to get here) letter. I am continuing to bask in the sun and am not yet working very hard (orchestra., symphon.,[42] Kant,[43] and two short stories). A few days ago there was a roundup here of deserters and I was seized along with them, since I didn't have any identification papers in my pocket. But I was so insolent at the commissar's office that they quickly released me, requesting that I bring my documents the following day, which I was happy to do. There are few people I know here, which makes me happy. Nina Koshetz is crazy about Verin's daughter (and she really is something special) and about me, and prayed with her head on my shoulder that heaven would send me even a single drop of love for her. She must be a great sinner because heaven has so far turned a deaf ear to her prayers, and she is leaving tomorrow.

S.

August 9, 1917
Essentuki

> In verse and rhythm cloaked
> To Essentuki traveled Verin,
> Where, as is his custom,
> From dawn to dusk he sleeps.
>
> S.P.

---

42. Refers to the "Classical" Symphony.
43. Prokofiev noted in his autobiography that he devoted some of the summer of 1917 to reading the work of the German philosopher Immanuel Kant.

We spend our time here nicely,
Forgetting ills and sorrow,
In the deep quiet behind the lines
Serzh and I peer into the distance.*

Boris Verin

* telescope and newspapers

September 21, 1917
[no return address — EN ROUTE]

After the train pulled out of the station, the engineer in our compartment made a terrible scene because there was too much baggage, but the matter was settled most unexpectedly and effectively. It turned out that there were three of us and 22 pieces of luggage—and that the engineer had the wrong ticket. So at Lyuban they sent him packing to another car. I send you greetings. Bow down for me to Boris Borisovich. Why are you keeping silent?

S.P.

September 24, 1917
KISLOVODSK

Today I came to Kislovodsk to find out if I couldn't manage to get myself into the Grand Hotel, because it is after all better than the Kiselev, although Maria Grigorevna did take the trouble to arrange an excellent room for me there. As of now, I have encountered Sharoev and General Ruzsky.[44] Greetings.

S.P.

September 27, 1917
ESSENTUKI

For the moment I am spending my time in Essentuki in the company of Kant, my seven devils[45] and handsome Mt. Beshtau, which is spread out right in from of my balcony. At the Kislovodsk Grand Hotel the rooms are fully booked until the beginning of October. At that time we and Maria Grigorevna will move there. . . . .V.N. has expressed the desire to get together with me, but I replied that when presented with a choice between Kant and fools I take the former.

Greetings.

---

44. Nikolai Pavlovich Ruzsky was an amateur cellist and a family friend of the Prokofievs.
45. At the time Prokofiev was working on his cantata *Seven, They Are Seven*, set to a text by Balmont.

October 1, 1917
ESSENTUKI

I am leaving today on the Georgian Military Highway for the kingdom of air and mountains. I will return in a week, and meanwhile M.G.[46] is preparing for our move to Kislovodsk. I was there only two times, and then went to see Kirena,[47] but she was sleeping. General Ruzsky is a charmer; he and I have been discussing strategic affairs.

I send you greetings. S.

October 4, 1917
TEBERDA

Teberda is a superb little place, but has no *carte-postals* [*sic*]. An Englishman, two gentlemen from among the Russians, and I are now traveling higher, although the roads barely deserve to be called by that name. At the same time, its beauty is worth writing about it.

Greetings.

S.

October 10, 1917
KISLOVODSK

Having reached a height of 9,000 feet and traveling nearly to Sukhumi, I have now settled into the Grand Hotel in a charming room with two balconies facing two suns: the southern and the western. Today Maria Grigorevna is moving over to the Grand—for her winter stay. I am starting to think about returning to Petrograd, although he is behaving himself very badly.[48] My concert here is on the 14th. In Moscow the concert will be on November 9. I have so far from you two letters[. . . .]

Accept my greetings.

S.P.

Please be so kind as to send Maria Grigorevna the little book by Schopenhauer, the one with the aphorisms [. . . .]

---

46. M.G. are the initials of Prokofiev's mother, Maria Grigorevna.
47. Kirena Aleksandrovna Ziloti, daughter of Aleksander Ziloti (see note 50, below).
48. Prokofiev is referring to the civil unrest preceding the Bolshevik Revolution of late October 1917.

November 3, 1917
KISLOVODSK

My dear friend, you have sent me only two miserable little letters, but that's not why I have been silent. I was planning to leave here to return north four times—on the 20th, the 25th, the 31st, and the 3rd—and made all my farewell visits four times, but today, the third, I see once again that Moscow has other things to worry about besides me, so I am proposing to leave here on the 9th and go directly to Petrograd.

So things in your Petrograd are quite merry![49] But here we have quiet and monotony: the same old sun, summer suits, dinners on the veranda, sweet pastries, and so on.

Accept my warmest greeting.

S.

November 14, 1917
Grand Hotel, KISLOVODSK

My dear friend, having received a telegram from Petrograd that there will be no concerts, I decided to stay put and not to rush off anywhere—considering that no one is biting off anyone's head here, the sun is shining, and work is being worked on. But my news is uninteresting, everything here is going along as usual; we are living like normal people. It would be better for you to tell about the terrible city of Petrograd. I will remain here in any case until the end of the month and would probably receive your reply (preferably you should send it with someone coming here).

For now, I send you my warmest greetings.

Yours   S.P.

November 20, 1917
KISLOVODSK

For the moment everything is going along as it has been, that is, just fine, or rather—extremely well. The next incitement to leave for Petrograd are Ziloti's[50] concerts: a symphonic concert on the 9th, and a chamber one on the 10th. I

---

49. The Bolsheviks seized the Winter Palace on October 25 and the Provisional Government collapsed, leaving the way open for Vladimir Lenin to establish a Bolshevik regime in Russia.

50. Aleksander Ilych Ziloti (1863–1945) was a pianist, conductor, and organizer of concert series in Moscow and St. Petersburg. Prokofiev often appeared as a conductor in Ziloti's concerts. Ziloti emigrated from Russia in 1919 and taught at Juilliard 1924–42.

have sent an inquiry to him and am awaiting a telegram in reply. I was overjoyed today to get, finally, a letter from dear Glebushka.[51] There's a friend for you! My other friends seem to be illiterate.

Greetings. S.

December 5, 1917
KISLOVODSK

Only my nobility can explain why I am writing to individuals who seem to be completely illiterate. Could I ever have dreamed when we parted at Nikolaevsky Station that I would greet the month of December in Kislovodsk? Actually, this is one of the few remote places where it is possible to live decently. People feel this and more and more of them keep arriving.

I send you my greetings. Aren't you planning to come here to Sour Waters?[52]

December 30, 1917
KISLOVODSK

My dear friend, your letters have started to arrive rather regularly: the ones from December 1, 14, and 18 have shown up. The famous letter that you entrusted to the train conductor has vanished. The telegram took 14 days to get here. I sent you an answering telegram soon after receiving it. Thanks for your efforts, but what would the rats in the military command want with me? To fight against Kaledin? In fact as a resident of the Southeast Republic, I should in all fairness show up at the local military command, that is, in Novocher-kassk—but in that case they would send me to fight against Petrograd, so it would be better if your friends don't drop any hints about me, considering that I forgot about it myself. [53] Why would they want to create an extra soldier, and especially one who would fight against them? And it would be better if those two soldiers of the Red Guard did not come here to fetch me—I say this out of tender love for them: the local Chechens would slaughter them in a moment on the stairs of the Grand Hotel, if they did not manage to do so right at the train station.

---

51. Boris Asafiev was Prokofiev's conservatory classmate and a composer and critic. He used the pseudonym Igor Glebov.
52. Prokofiev writes *Kislye vody* here, which means literally "sour waters," from the mineral springs that gave the resort its name and fame.
53. The region in which Prokofiev was living was under the control of the Whites, who opposed the establishment of Bolshevik rule.

This is what I am working on: I finished the Fourth Sonata and *Seven, They Are Seven* (it's stunning).[54] I have also begun a Third Concerto, in C Major, in three movements. [. . .]

The number of my acquaintances here has grown by leaps and bounds, although among the masculine personnel one does not find any of particular significance. That is not even a bad thing, for it does not distract me from my usual life. I used my talent to find a place for Maria Grigorevna in another hotel. We have lunch and dinner together. I am very much enjoying the local scenery and air and take long walks in the mountains. I don't feel like going to Petrograd: first of all, who the hell knows what is going on there where you are; secondly, who the hell knows how I would get there. I will come only after the civil strife ends. [. . .]

So I wish you a Happy New Year—may it be no less interesting than this one has been! I hope that you have disposed of your safes wisely and have not suffered. Take a vacation from your duties and pay us a visit for a few days: you'll see what kind of weather we have—it's not for nothing that I keep writing you about it. Miller's gymnastics are flourishing, with the same cold water and in front of the open balcony.[55]

I wish you Miller-like health.

Yours

S.P.

January 11, 1918

KISLOVODSK

My dear friend, your letters at one time came quite frequently, but have now stopped: probably they are sitting somewhere in Chertkov or Yasinovataya. I am thinking a bit about coming to Petrograd, but only after the reestablishment of order at these above-mentioned stations, on Petrograd's streets, and in Petrograd's stomachs. Here the weather—but really, I can't keep writing about the weather. I have gotten mired in writing out a clean copy of *Seven*, and only tomorrow, at last, will I finish it. I send you a respectful bow. I wrote you at length at the end of December.

---

54. *Seven, They Are Seven*, op. 30, a cantata for dramatic tenor, chorus, and large symphonic orchestra, set to the verses of the Symbolist Konstantin Balmont (see note 70, below).

55. This seems to refer to Vera Miller, an acquaintance of Damskaya's at the St. Petersburg Conservatory.

May 8, 1918

VOLOGDA

We are traveling quickly and in all respects quite well.[56] I am reading, smoking, and looking out the window. The only problem is that it is very cold and snow is lying all around. I spent my time in Moscow extremely pleasantly, but deflected all attempts to keep me there longer. *Merci* for the marzipan, although I never did receive it after all.

Greetings. S.

May 13, 1918

KRASNOYARSK

My dear friend, we are approaching Krasnoyarsk. After being caught in a terrible white blizzard in Omsk, we have now emerged into sun and green—at least something relatively green. The route to Kharbin has been cut by the Cossack captain who has occupied Olovyannaya Station. We will hurry to break through to Vladivostok by way of Blagoveshchensk-Khabarovsk. My mood is ideal; I'm getting fat from lots of eating and the absence of exercise; I'm studying Spanish; I'm writing "The Tower."[57] The express train is comfortable and goes fast.

Greetings S.

May 16, 1918

10:00 P.M. our time 4:00 P.M. your time

CHITA

My dear friend, what I'm seeing through the window has become more animated, and Baikal—it's just remarkably beautiful. My mood is excellent, and my Spanish even better. I'm traveling with a Danish mission. We are circling

---

56. On May 7, 1918, Prokofiev left Petrograd, having decided to travel to America to stay for a while. In fact, he would not return to the USSR until nine years later, in early 1927. Traveling across Siberia to the Pacific was very dangerous at the time, since civil war between the Bolsheviks and Whites was raging nearly everywhere. Originally the train was to have traveled via Kharbin, in China, but had to change its route through the Russian city of Khabarovsk instead because of the fighting.

57. One of the short stories Prokofiev was writing at the time was called "The Wandering Tower," a fantastic science fiction tale.

around Khabarovsk on the new route to Vladivostok. Kharbin is impassable, so it's impossible to get into China.

I send you my greetings.

Yours
S.P.

There are no local postcards here.

May 22, 1918
KHABAROVSK

My dear friend, Khabarovsk, where we have ended up thanks to our forced detour and the impassability of Kharbin, has turned out to be a charming little patriarchal place on the shore of the wide Amur. The passage to Japan via Vladivostok is simple and without obstacles and the price—2 rubles 68 kopecks! I am rejoicing—and laughing at those who foretold that I would encounter difficulties and horrors. Everything has been so simple and pleasant. Greetings.

S.

May 28, 1918
VLADIVOSTOK

Farewell, Russia! Tomorrow the *Khosan-Maru* is taking me to Japan. I have a ticket, a visa—the only thing I don't have is any yen. Two weeks ago this wretched coinlet was worth two rubles 80 kopecks, but now it has risen to five rubles 20 kopecks. I am trying out all sorts of combinations, and maybe I can get it at a rate of 3½ to 4. The rest I'll have to make up on my concerts in Japan.[58] Greetings. Drop a line to M.G.

S.

September 1, 1920
[no return address; somewhere in FRANCE]

Dear Eleonora, I know from your Uncle Boris that you are alive in Petrograd. Boris Borisovich is in Constantinople, I'm trying to write to him. Where is Boris Verin? Is it true that the manuscripts, letters, and notes that I left in my apartment have perished?

---

58. Prokofiev arrived in Yokohama by steamer from Vladivostok on June 1. He gave piano recitals in Tokyo and Yokohama before boarding a steamer bound for San Francisco.

Write me in detail about yourself and address it C/o Mlle Jung, Conservatory, Riga.[59] I am in France and in two weeks will return to America to stay there for 3–4 months. Your prelude[60] enjoyed success in England and America—more than all the other compositions, and was reprinted in New York.

Warmest greetings and best wishes.

Mama is with me.

Yours, S. Prokofiev

July 15, 1921
Rochlé

Dear Eleonora,

Your letter of March 1, the one in which you wished me a happy upcoming birthday, took four months to reach me. I only received it a few days ago. So here's a lesson for you: if in the future you wish to be courteous, then wish me a happy birthday in December, and a happy name day in May. I approve of your intention to write me each month, but I have yet to receive your letters of April, May, or June. Nor have I received a letter from Zakharov,[61] and only today I read in *Poslednie novosti*, the Russian newspaper that is published in Paris, that Cecilia[62] is playing the Tchaikovsky Concerto with Cooper[63] for the opening of the Petrograd summer season. By the way, tell her that my violin concerto is being printed and will soon see the light of day.[64] Tell Zakharov first of all that I will be happy to receive the letter he promised to write, and second, that by chance I celebrated this New Year with two flirts—Ariadna Nikolskaya and Dagmar Godowska[65]—and that we were even planning to send him a postcard from underneath the palms of blooming Los Angeles, but our drunken state and the sad condition of the mails prevented us.

---

59. A. A. Jung was a musician and acquaintance of Eleonora Damskaya.
60. The Prelude for Piano and Harp is one of the "Ten Pieces for Piano," op. 12, and is dedicated to Damskaya.
61. Boris Stepanovich Zakharov (1887–?), a pianist and student of A. N. Esipova and Prokofiev's fellow student from the St. Petersburg Conservatory.
62. Cecilia Hansen (1897–1989), a Swedish violinist, was the wife of Boris Zakharov and a friend of Prokofiev's from the conservatory.
63. Emil Albertovich Cooper (1877–1960), a Russian conductor.
64. The Concerto No. 1 for Violin and Orchestra in D Major, op. 19, composed 1916–17, received its premiere in Paris on October 18, 1923.
65. Dagmar Godowska was the daughter of Leopold Godowsky.

Thank you for the torture you endured in rescuing my piano.[66] Mama wants to know what is left of the furniture, except for the living room. As far as I am concerned, now that I know that they used my papers for kindling, I don't even want to think about furniture. By the way, I didn't know that you still had my notes on Beethoven. I thought that they were in the desk, and had also been grilled. Rumors have reached me that the State Publishing House has printed *Seven, They Are Seven*[67] and the Fourth Sonata. One copy of the Fourth Sonata did in fact wind up in Berlin and will be in my hands in a few days, but I would ask you to make inquiries about *Seven, They Are Seven* and let me know if it has in fact been published. They should send me a copy, for the sake of decorum. I cannot figure it out. If you see Asafiev, then mention me and tell him that he should write me. A year has passed since I sent him a letter, but I never received a reply.

Since I wrote you from San Francisco, my biography has been the following: A very successful tour of California, with a New Year's celebration in sunny Los Angeles and a little excursion to Mexico. Then Chicago, New York, and a new contract for a production of *Love for Three Oranges*, which I will conduct next January in both cities (don't fail to tell Meyerhold about this, and give him my regards).[68] In February a short visit to London and Paris, and since March, a spacious house among pines and cypresses right on the Atlantic coast, at the spot where the Loire meets the sea (consult your map). I am planning to stay here until October, until my departure for America, but I have already managed to travel a bit: to Monte Carlo in April, to Paris in May, and to London in June. No, I didn't go to Monte Carlo to play roulette, but to rehearse my ballet *The Buffoon*, that famous ballet that was first outlined in 1915. I have now revised and orchestrated it and Diaghilev presented it with extreme pomp in Paris and London, with me conducting. It had an extraordinary success; the French modernists went especially crazy over it. In London 114 reviews have appeared, but 113 of them are abusive. Boris Nikolaevich[69] arrived in Paris just in time for the premiere, and then stayed a whole month with me. At the moment he is in

---

66. This was the Shreder piano Prokofiev had won as the Anton Rubinstein Prize in a competition in 1914 at the St. Petersburg Conservatory. It was left behind in the apartment in which he and his mother had lived in Petrograd when Prokofiev left Russia in 1918, along with other papers and belongings. Prokofiev had asked Damskaya to help him rescue the piano and whatever else she could.
67. *Seven, They Are Seven* was first published in 1922 by the State Music Publishers.
68. *Love for Three Oranges* received its premiere in Chicago on December 30, 1921.
69. Boris Verin (Bashkirov).

Paris, and since he lost all of his decisiveness when he left Petrograd, he simply cannot figure out whether he will leave Paris and go to his brother in New York, or whether he'll return here to see me in October. In his place Balmont[70] has appeared, and he is teaching me to swim in the waters of the Atlantic. Boris Borisovich was also at the premiere; owing to his impracticality he is having a hard time in Paris. He is writing erotic verses out of grief. As soon as I receive assurance from A. A. Jung that she is able to send the strings to you, I will buy them for you in Paris and send you the fattest chord there is. I am happy to hear that everything is all right with you and that your mother and Vera Aleksandrovna are in good health. Mama and I send you our warmest greetings. Ekaterina Grigorevna[71] has been found in Penza. Koshetz is in America, and is gradually getting used to life there; she will sing the leading witch in my opera.[72]

Take care of yourself and don't forget. *Orevuar.*

Yours,
S. Prokofiev

Mama begs you to find out about Tatiana Pavlovna Serebryakova, at 176 Zverinskaya.

September 28, 1921
ROCHLÉ

Dear Eleonora,

Your letter of September 6 created something of a sensation, first of all because of its thousands of stamps; second because it was so fresh; and finally, because of the address: to write "France-Rochlé" is about as exact as writing "Russia-Ivanovka," since Rochlé is a tiny beach with ten summer houses. How your letter got here is a mystery. You are right, the other letter sent through Jung is still wandering around somewhere, and I am not even sure if I will receive it before I sail for America on October 15. I already have a berth reserved on the *Aquitania,* a vessel of 47,000 tons. In America I will be immediately dragged into the thick of rehearsals of my opera, which I am assigned to lead, and then I will

---

70. Konstantin Balmont (1867–1942) was a Russian Symbolist poet who emigrated to France and became Prokofiev's friend there in the early 1920s. Later, Balmont was ostracized by the Soviet cultural establishment for his political views.

71. Ekaterina Grigorevna was Prokofiev's aunt, his mother's sister.

72. Nina Pavlovna Koshetz (1894–1965) was a Russian singer who emigrated in 1921 and settled in the United States. She sang the role of Fata Morgana in the Chicago production of *Love for Three Oranges.* (See also chapter 7.)

conduct eight performances. The first is in Chicago around December 1. I am sending you a photo of my ugly mug that was taken in New York about 18 months ago. Since then I haven't changed too much, except I have lost a few hairs, one tooth (when I fell off a bicycle), and have become more nasty. Boris Nikolaevich is in America, which he does not like, and he writes me well-phrased letters. Tcherepnin arrived in Paris not long ago, but I haven't seen him yet. Send me Miaskovsky's address, and whatever you know about him. I spent a very tranquil summer in Rochlé, composed a great deal, and completed the Third Concerto; recently some friends and I took an auto trip around the whole northwestern corner of France. I will soon be in Paris and will take up the matter of your strings (the fat ones). The card of little Seryozha that you sent gave the greatest pleasure to mama. She sends her kindest regards to you and yours. She will spend the winter in Paris. I have not been able to determine here in the countryside if it is possible to send packages of food to Russia. If it turns out to be possible, then I'll send you some chocolate.

So for now be a good girl, and write more often if that isn't too ruinously expensive.

Yours,
S. Prokofiev

May 5, 1922
ETTAL [Bavaria]

Dear Eleonora,

So what's going on? Why haven't I heard from you for so long? I saw Boris Borisovich not long ago in Paris, and he is also worried because he hasn't had any news from you.

After another winter trip to America; a successful production of *Love for Three Oranges* in Chicago and New York; a performance of the Third Concerto in New York, Chicago, and London; trips to Munich and Berlin (where I saw Zakharov, Souvchinsky, and Glazunov), I have firmly settled in Ettal, in the Bavarian Alps, in a very quiet and well-appointed dacha, and am now determined to get down to some serious work: the publication of *Three Oranges* and the completion of a new opera.[73]

Write me here: letters (if not every single one) sent to Germany from Russia sometimes manage to gallop over here quickly.

---

73. Prokofiev was working on *The Fiery Angel*.

Did you receive my American package that I sent to you three months ago from New York?

Heartfelt greetings from me and from Boris Nikolaevich, who is now living with me here. We hope everything is going well with you.

Yours, S. Prokofiev

June 18, 1922
ETTAL

Dear Eleonora,

From rags to riches: first I heard nothing from you since last September, and then suddenly come two certified letters: one sent to America and one sent to Ettal dated May 23. I also received Asafiev's letter, but his book has not arrived yet.

It's very irritating that we keep having such bad luck with the strings. In October I had two orders to fulfill: one from Jung's father for viola strings, and one from you for harp strings. I sent the strings to Jung, but at that time packages were not going from Paris to Petrograd—in fact they even returned to me (as you know) the certified letter I tried to send. That's why when I was leaving for America, I instructed Boris Borisovich—who was on his way to Berlin—to take care of this. But this erotic (and in consequence frivolous) poet not only did not manage to make it to Berlin the whole winter, but didn't even bother to tell me. Therefore, the checks sent to Berlin for me to pick up just rotted there. In the spring I found myself in Munich, and Boris Nikolaevich and I decided to equip two packages: I prepared one with the strings for you, and he some technically advanced fishing rods for his adored Igor Severyanin, who was in Toilu.[74] But it turned out that new rules had just been issued that prohibited the sending of any such items from Germany. So the fishing rods are still lying packed up (to the joy of the fish of Finland?), and likewise your strings—although they are still unpurchased—find themselves in a similarly desperate situation. As soon as the rules change (and they change here monthly), I will send them right along. Or perhaps you can give me some intelligent advice, if you can figure this out better from Petrograd.

Tell me also if there is a large customs fee in Russia on chocolate. I'll send you some. I have been told that the fee is so high that to send chocolate amounts to robbing the recipient.

---

74. Igor Severyanin (1887–1941), a prominent St. Petersburg poet, was in Toilu, Finland, at the time.

I have sent through Mrs. Katzman[75] the notebooks with my new compositions. Share them equally with Asafiev. Show them also to Karatygin.[76] Please tell me his address and Demchinsky's, and, if possible, Miaskovsky's. I have asked for Miaskovsky's address 45 thousand times now.

Are you in contact with Meyerhold? If you are, then I will send you the piano score of *Love for Three Oranges*, which will come out in June, to give to him.

Our life here is proceeding quietly and happily. I am working a lot, fooling around less, and playing chess with Boris Nikolaevich[77] in the evenings. He and I have invented a contest: who can better translate some classical sonnets—of course also in sonnet form. The devil himself would break his leg in trying to figure out these sonnets. Balmont and Severyanin have been selected as the jury. So far we have finished five of them. Balmont and Severyanin gave us grades and made very risqué observations. So you can see that I have gone from prose to Parnassian poetry. But in any case, since you have now learned how to bang on a typewriter, then be so kind as to copy over my notes on Beethoven and Wolf and send them here.[78]

Mama is with us and feels very well here in Ettal. She remembers you with pleasure and is planning to write you, or rather, to print to you (she also has now conquered the typewriter). She begs you to find out about her cousin Tatiana Pavlovna Serebryakova, who lives at 17-B Zverinskaya.

Boris Borisovich is still in Paris, living in poverty and hanging around with young poets and artists. Boris Stepanovich[79] has gone off to Terioki for the summer. His wife had a great success in Berlin.

I can't send the photographs with Boris Nikolaevich right now because he lost his camera en route from America, and I never had one. I promise to take appropriate measures, however, and to send some in one of my next letters. In New York in February one Austrian artist painted my portrait in oils, and it is a good likeness. As soon as I receive a photo from him, I'll send it to you.

Miller and Jung are in Germany. So don't be surprised if your letters sent via Riga didn't reach me (if the letters were sent with them). Miller has managed

75. Mrs. Katzman was a mutual acquaintance of Prokofiev and Damskaya; she lived in Riga.
76. Viacheslav Gavrilovich Karatygin (1875–1925), a Russian/Soviet music critic, composer, and teacher, had enthusiastically promoted Prokofiev's music from the start of his career.
77. Verin.
78. Prokofiev had written some literary observations on these composers.
79. Zakharov.

to translate into German my new songs and the Akhmatova songs, which will soon appear in four languages. Overall, my compositions are beginning to sell abroad, and the first edition of *Tales of an Old Grandmother* sold out in a few months.[80]

Send me programs and clippings when my things are performed in Russia. You know that every time I read your cheerful letters, I rejoice at your cheerful manner and your way of keeping your chin up. I send heartfelt greetings to you, and also to your mama and to Vera Aleksandrovna. Convey my regards to Benois,[81] Asafiev, and Dranishnikov.[82] I am writing Asafiev.

Be well.

Yours, S. Prokofiev

September 25, 1922
FREIBURG

It's somehow odd to be sending postcards to Russia while traveling around in an automobile. I'm driving with friends around the Black Forest and Alsace. In a few days I'll be back in Ettal and will write you in more detail, and also send some new opuses.

Greetings, S. Prokofiev

November 8, 1922
ETTAL

Dear Eleonora,

I received your very impressive telegram. I have been awaiting the letters you promised, but they have not yet arrived—neither have the notes on Beethoven. *Three Oranges*, the Overture,[83] and *Tales of an Old Grandmother* were sent to your acquaintance in Riga several weeks ago already. Share the Overture and the *Tales* with Asafiev; after you show *Three Oranges* to Asafiev and Karatygin, hand it over to Meyerhold (if he hasn't yet received them from

---

80. *Tales of an Old Grandmother*, four pieces for piano, op. 31.
81. Aleksandre Benois (1870–1960), a Russian artist, art historian, cultural and music critic, and stage director, best known for his set designs and costumes for Diaghilev's ballets.
82. Vladimir Aleksandrovich Dranishnikov (1893–1939) was a Soviet conductor who worked at the Mariinsky Theater 1914–36.
83. Overture on Hebrew Themes, for clarinet, two violins, viola, cello, and piano, op. 34, composed 1919.

some other source). To you, Karatygin, and Demchinsky I sent insured, precisely weighed packages with chocolate, soap, and so on. Did you receive them?

I returned a few days ago from giving concerts in Paris and Berlin. I saw Boris Borisovich in Paris, and found him, as the French would say, *"dans la purée."*[84] He has grown a beard and has no money, but I don't believe he really intends to go to Germany, where life is ten times cheaper. I told him that, if he is seriously intending to come to Germany and gets the necessary visas, I would immediately get him a ticket as far as Berlin.

[. . .]I have now settled down in Ettal, with its snow-covered mountains, sun, honeyed air, and a devilish stack of scores to be proofed—I won't make my way through them in a month.

I would be happy to get a letter from you. It's nice that you are eating chocolate, sailing around the islands,[85] and sending telegrams—but you could write me in more detail about yourself.

Greetings to you and yours from mama, Boris Nikolaevich, and me. Mama has recently been having problems with her heart. Her cousin, the one I asked you to inquire about, has turned up in the "Russia" apartment house on Kamennoostrovsky Prospect.

Be well and write.

Yours, S. Prokofiev

I'll send a photo in the next letter.

December 14, 1922
ETTAL

Dear Eleonora,

I send you greetings and best wishes for the upcoming holidays, as well as regrets and a reprimand because you haven't written in a long while. I readily believe, though, that you are not to blame, but rather the Petrograd postal service, which is very unreliable, unlike the Moscow one.

I wrote to you last time on November 8 and around the same time to Asafiev, but received nothing in reply. Actually, the most recent news I had from Petrograd was your telegram on my name day.

I carry on regular correspondence with Moscow, and yesterday at last received the orchestral score of *Seven, They Are Seven,* which was published there quite respectably.

---

84. A French expression meaning "to be very hard up."
85. The Elagin (later Kirov) islands were a resort spot near Petrograd.

Did you, Karatygin, and Demchinsky receive the small parcels I sent you containing all sorts of stuff: chocolate, soap, and so on? If not, let me know—I did insure them after all, and if they didn't reach you, then I'll create a scandal in the appropriate place.

I continue to reside peacefully in Ettal, where mounds of snow have accumulated in the mountains. Boris Nikolaevich and I are planning to go skiing, but he keeps running off to Berlin and our excursion keeps getting postponed. I am completing an orchestral suite from *The Buffoon* and writing the fifth act of my opera.[86] I'm drowning in proofs but then by now that's the same old refrain.

Don't be annoyed by the laconic nature of this letter, but I haven't heard anything from you. Write and tell me what's happening in Petrograd among our friends and acquaintances. Did you receive the second installment of my opuses?

So be well. Mama sends her heartfelt greetings to you and yours. So do I.

Yours   S. Prokofiev

January 7, 1923
ETTAL

Dear Eleonora,

Your letter of December 5 made me both happy and sad. I was happy to hear that the manuscript of *The Gambler* is still in one piece, and sad to have you confirm that my manuscripts left at Pervaya Rota were in fact destroyed.

As far as the manuscript of *The Gambler* is concerned, I was certain that it had perished in the hands of Tyulin,[87] so are you really sure that the complete manuscript of the full score of *The Gambler*—in its entirety—is really in the theater library? It's entirely possible that what's there is not the complete score, but only a small part of it—to be exact, the fragment of Act IV which Tyulin did not manage to take. It's also possible that what you think is the full score is in fact only a pencil manuscript of the piano score, which nobody needs. Please find out and write me.

I wrote to Coates[88] concerning the two acts which he took, but it seems he's

---

86. *Fiery Angel.*
87. Yuri Nikolaevich Tyulin (1893–1978) was a Soviet musicologist and composer.
88. Albert Coates (1882–1953) was an English conductor and composer; he was the conductor at the Mariinsky Theater in St. Petersburg 1910–19.

now in America, and therefore I'll have an answer only two months from now—and considering his distaste for letter writing, probably even later than that. But during the course of our numerous meetings, he didn't say anything to me about those two acts. On the contrary, he complained that his collection of scores perished when he left Russia, so one can say with confidence ahead of time that these two acts are nowhere to be found abroad. And yet if I am not mistaken, Coates told me that a certain person loyal to him had remained in Russia and protected a part of Coates's library that had survived. It seems that this is the same person who was taking care of Stravinsky's mother. I don't know his name, but it should be easier for you to make inquiries on the spot. Perhaps this person has the two acts we are looking for.

In any case, it's impossible to send the manuscript if there is no copy to be found anywhere. It would also be unthinkable to make a copy for you at my own expense, although I would ask you in any case to calculate how much it would cost in French francs to copy over the two acts, if I should decide to have you undertake that task.

However, if it turns out that this copy you refer to really is in fact a complete one, then the manuscript could be sent to Berlin, not by mail of course (that would be insane), but with a diplomatic courier; there are many of them circulating between the Russian capitals and Berlin. Neither Ekskuzovich[89] nor anyone else has the right to retain my manuscripts, since it is my private property, and was given to the theater so that a copy could be made.

And so, while awaiting information from you on these points, I now pass to the more unpleasant part of your letter—that is, the devastation of my apartment. Of course there are many to blame for the destruction of my manuscripts: the Bolshevik decree allowing irresponsible individuals to be settled in apartments; and Souvchinsky[90] with his thief of a business manager; and that scoundrel Lourié;[91] and most of all, me, for having placed too much faith in my friends. And you know I cannot help faulting Asafiev—only a ditherer like him would be satisfied to accept Lourié's refusal. If Lourié behaved like a bastard,

---

89. Ivan Vasilevich Ekskusovich (1883–1942) was a Russian/Soviet theatrical impresario. In 1917 he became the director of the Petrograd State Theaters, and from 1924 to 1928 he was the director of the state academic theaters of Moscow and Leningrad.

90. Pierre Souvchinsky (1892–1985), a musicologist and close friend of Prokofiev, emigrated to Paris in 1920.

91. Arthur Vincent Lourié (1892–1966), a composer who studied at the St. Petersburg Conservatory, emigrated from Russia, and lived in Paris 1923–40, and in the USA from 1941.

he wasn't the only one to turn to: there were Benois, and Gorky,[92] and Luna-charsky.[93] For God's sake, they managed to save Ziloti's library! And you could have roused your collective diplomatic brains, if you saw that my other friends were sweetly falling by the wayside!

I am very grateful to you for saving my piano, but a single page of a manu-script is dearer to me than three pianos.

Vera Miller, who had visited the devastated apartment back in the summer of 1920, tells me that until spring of 1920 it was not Jews who were living there, but some kind of very simple people from the countryside. She was told by the residential committee that in spring of 1920 these people had loaded up all the contents of the apartment on carts and transported it away to their village. I would be very grateful to you if you could determine exactly who these people where, and where they were from—in short, to find out who actually plundered the apartment.

You ask, am I planning to come to Russia? No, *merci,* for the moment I am not rushing to visit countries which are using my compositions for heating fuel.

Thanks for sending my notes on Beethoven. I received them just a few days ago. I am amazed that the second parcel of music containing *Three Oranges* has not yet reached you. In any case, the music sent by the publishing house reached your acquaintance Katzman; in addition I warned her to expect it with a registered letter, which remained unanswered, by the way. Please inquire of her what she has done with the music. To send things to you through her doesn't make any sense, since this method is apparently unreliable. If I am not mistaken, Derzhanovsky[94] already has a complete collection of my works.

The biographical information given in the article by Karatygin which you conveyed to Asafiev is correct. A complete list of my compositions is included on the cover of my songs op. 23, which just appeared in Moscow. But you do need to make a few corrections in that list: opuses 20, 21, 26, and 33 are no longer in manuscript form; *Seven, They Are Seven* is not a cantata but an incan-tation; and *The Gambler* is op. 24 and the "Classical" Symphony op. 25, and not the other way around. You could also add the information that the full score of

---

92. The Russian writer Maksim Gorky (1868–1936) was very influential in Soviet culture in the 1920s.

93. Anatoly Lunacharsky (1875–1933), the People's Commissar of Enlightenment 1917–29 and an early supporter of Prokofiev, gave him permission to leave Russia in 1918.

94. Vladimir Vladimirovich Derzhanovsky (1881–1942) was a music critic and publisher, and an early supporter of Prokofiev.

the Second Concerto was burned thanks to the negligence of the author's kind friends.

Lourié does not have the manuscript of the "Classical" Symphony: I took it with me to America, and have already conducted it in New York, Chicago, and London. The question of who has the manuscript copy of *Seven, They Are Seven* does not cause me much concern, since the thing has already been printed. I saw Lourié in passing in Berlin. He looks like he has been plucked, and generally there are few people outside Russia interested in him.

I am pleased to hear that Demchinsky remembers me. I wrote him not long ago at your address, so that you might give him the letter. Did he receive my parcels and did he have to pay a customs duty on them? They assured me at the office that it would not be necessary to pay a duty, which is why I sent them.

Accept best wishes for the new year 1923 from mama, Boris Nikolaevich, and me, and convey the same to your mama and to Vera Aleksandrovna. Boris Nikolaevich is not planning to go to Riga and has even been rather lazy in his correspondence with Riga.

Be well, write, and don't be angry at the drum beating of my letter.

Yours, S. Prokofiev

February 12, 1923
GENOA

En route to Spain, where I am playing in a few days' time, I send you greetings from Genoa. After the snows of Ettal it is pleasant to find oneself at the shore of a rather warm sea. I hope everything is splendid with you. I'll write from Spain.

S.P.

March 9, 1923
LONDON

Dear Eleonora, I am writing you from London, where I will play tomorrow and where I ended up via a concert tour through Spain, Paris, and Belgium. I received your airmail letter of February 19. I'll make inquiries about *Oranges*: if you are certain that they didn't disappear on the way from Katzman to Petrograd, then we'll find them between Riga and Berlin. Coates is returning to London from New York in only two weeks' time, and I won't wait for him, since I'm going in two days to Paris and then to Ettal. He did not reply to my letter, as usual. But don't dawdle in asking his associate about the two acts of *The Gam-*

bler—tell him you are asking on my behalf. If he answers—fine, if he doesn't answer—to hell with him, but nothing ventured, nothing gained, and there's no harm in trying.

For now, warmest greetings to you and your family.

Yours,

S. Prokofiev

I have not received any letters from Demchinsky. On my tour I received the warmest reception in Belgium, as Borodin did in his own time (see his biography).

March 31, 1923
ETTAL

Dear Eleonora,

Since I can't remember whether you celebrate your birthday according to the old or new calendar, I'm writing you after having calculated that my greetings will fall in the middle between the two. Mama and Boris Nikolaevich join me in sending you the very best wishes.

I sent you postcards from Italy, Spain, and England—from England I even sent it by messenger—and I hope you have received them [. . . .]

The question of why *Three Oranges* did not reach Riga is currently under investigation. I also saw Coates in London. He confirms that he returned the two acts of *The Gambler* to the theater library with his signature. I saw Boris Borisovich in Paris. The poet has sprouted a beard and fallen to a nonentity: he stole 37 francs from me.

I send you very best wishes, and incidentally I'm enclosing the Belgian reviews: as you can see, the people there are just beside themselves!

Yours S. Prokofiev

April 8, 1923
ETTAL

Dear Eleonora,

I'm forwarding to you the letter from the publisher regarding *Three Oranges*. Please inquire of your precious Katzman if she really did not receive them. I hadn't heard that registered parcels were disappearing between Berlin and Riga. If she really didn't receive the music, then have her let me or the publisher know immediately, so we can make the appropriate declaration at the post office.

A few days ago I wrote you by registered mail. So for now I'll remain silent, since there's been nothing new to add since then, except of course for a few more pages of the Fifth Sonata, which I'm now working on. Also the news that Balmont's new son has cut his teeth, and my invitation to give a concert in Milan, where I am going two weeks from now, and where I will write you from.

Be well and accept greetings from all of us. Write.

Yours, S. Prokofiev

June 5, 1923
ETTAL

Dear Eleonora,

Thanks for the information about the Ballade;[95] we will reprint it this summer in Berlin. Don't trouble yourself for the moment over *The Gambler*: no one is planning to stage it in the near future, and I am busy with other work—the Second Concerto and the Fifth Sonata. But if the need should arise, I'll immediately call upon your kind services.

The news of Boris Nikolaevich's wedding is highly exaggerated. It can be refuted in the simplest geographical manner, that is: Boris Nikolaevich has not ventured beyond the borders of Germany for more than a year now, while Anna Grigorevna has not gone beyond Latvia. So how can you have them combining under such circumstances?

In the month of May I was in Paris and in Milan, playing my work and listening to how Koussevitsky was playing my compositions. Paris is already an old friend; I was playing in Milan for the first time and was even amazed at the reception accorded me there, since I was hardly counting on pleasing the taste of the dear citizens of Italy. So as to revive your meager knowledge of this language, and also in order to boast a bit, I am sending you the Milan reviews.

Now I have settled in Ettal until the autumn, which makes me extremely happy. Boris Nikolaevich and I are amusing ourselves with gardening and raising chickens. Now all of our energy focuses on earthworms, manure, bulbs, incubators, and so on.

Mama is creaking and moping, her heart is acting up. She has been intending several times to write you, but recently she has been feeling bad, and yesterday we even had to take her to the sanitorium.

---

95. The Ballade for Cello and Piano, op. 15, composed 1912.

Among my compositions, the Third Concerto and the *Scythian Suite* have appeared in print, but I don't dare to send them to you until we clear up the mystery of why the previous set of music that was sent via Madame "Catsman"[96] did not reach its destination.

I am also planning to go to Stockholm in the fall, since they are offering two symphonic concerts for November. Perhaps this will allow me to squeeze your tenderly stringed paw. So keep me apprised of your foreign plans.

You asked for news of our mutual acquaintances. May God remember them . . . Boris Borisovich vanished into space and has not appeared again before my eyes; Cecilia and Boris Hansen have signed a contract for the United States; Borovsky[97] has married my acquaintance, a very interesting woman, and gone off with her to South America; Koshetz is also in South America; Alekhin is reaping international laurels on 64 different fields of competition, pursues only gray-haired ladies, and is planning to play a chess match with Capablanca for the world championship; Capablanca himself is in Havana, where he is fussing over a newborn child; Frau Ziloti broke her leg, so she and her husband are remaining in America for the summer. Who else? Well, that's enough for you for now!

I send you and yours wishes for a good summer, and hope you won't forget to write us letters.

Yours   S. Prokofiev

June 19, 1923
ETTAL

Dear Eleonora,

It's sad that you have encountered so many difficulties over my three-legged beast. Your letter has the postmarks Petrograd June 6, Moscow June 11, and Ettal June 16. So you see that Russian airplanes still don't fly any faster than trains. I am sending you the necessary certification. In Munich I don't know any Russian organizations except the Committee for Refugees, whose certification would hardly make much of an impression on any official institutions in the Russian Soviet Federated Socialist Republic, so I have decided to send you my signature as certified in our German town hall. I hope that will be the best.

96. Katzman (see note 75, above).
97. Aleksandr Konstantinovich Borovsky (1889–1968), a Russian pianist, emigrated in 1920.

Simultaneously I am sending you a telegram and hope that you will find your way as soon as possible out of all this mess created by Shcherbachev[98]—in view of your talents I think you'll be able to do that without my best wishes. Let me know how it turns out.

I wrote you on June 5 about my life. Since that time no disturbances or events have occurred in our quiet Ettal. Except for today: it snowed. On June 19—that's rather late even for the mountains, and as far as our blooming garden is concerned, it's just rotten!

You asked how I entertain myself. I am busy now with my chicks and even ordered the very latest model of electrical incubator with a capacity for 60 individuals. We walk around the surrounding villages and collect eggs from pedigreed hens, thanks to the presence in our household of an elegant and energetic rooster.

I'm sending you my opuses and would ask you, by the way, to send your photo if you have one handy. Since I last saw you I have gone bald, started wearing glasses, and now look about 45 years old. I'd be interested to see what you have become!

Yours   S. Prokofiev

I received Demchinsky's book and letter. Thank you—I'm replying to him separately. I wasn't able to send you the enclosed certification for two days in a row, because it was Sunday out there, and the town hall was locked up tight.

September 16, 1923
Ettal

Dear Eleonora,

What sort of joke is this? Where am I going to get 12 pounds sterling for you? Right now it's the end of the summer vacation, I have spent everything I earned in the spring season, and the fall season begins only a month or two from now.

And besides all that, I would like to know first of all: does the Musical Department (or Muzpred—I can't tell the difference) acknowledge that the piano belongs to me, or not? If they do not acknowledge my ownership, then why in the world should I be dragging this piano around by the ears? If they do acknowledge my ownership, then what sort of vaudeville is this: I have to send

---

98. Vladimir Vladimirovich Shcherbachev (1889–1952) was a Soviet composer and professor at Leningrad Conservatory. It seems that the difficulties Damskaya encountered in trying to preserve the piano Prokofiev won in the Rubinstein Competition in 1914 were connected with him. The relationship between Damskaya and Prokofiev noticeably cooled after her efforts on his behalf over the piano.

the money to you, and you (through Shcherbachev's stupidity and your own angelic naïveté) have to pay Muzpred, and then Muzpred will return this money to me (assuming that they acknowledge that it is in fact my piano). So wouldn't it be better for me to deal directly with the management of this institution and figure out what they are intending to do with the piano after all? And are the musical circles of Petrograd really so ignorant of my name that they don't want to help protect the piano I won as the Rubinstein Prize? Is Mayakovsky[99] in Petrograd? It seems that he has good connections in the ruling circles, and I know that his feelings about me are very affectionate. Probably he could figure out who could take care of this matter.

In short, I await a detailed explanation from you, since you have so distinguished yourself for your diplomatic talents. For the moment I cannot send money: you can't make a pound sterling out of nothing. Besides that, as it's written in *The Snow Maiden*—"if you're going to pay a fee, then you ought to know what it's for."[100]

Warmest greetings and best wishes.

Yours   S. Prokofiev

November 12, 1923
PARIS

Dear Eleonora,

I received your letter of October 8 only after a long delay, since I was on a concert tour and it was following me as I traveled. I am enclosing a letter to Lunacharsky; if this proves unsatisfactory to you, then let me know—and I will send another. Do I have his name and patronymic right?

Write me in Ettal, where I plan to be at the end of the month. Warmest greetings to B. N. Demchinsky. It's sad that he was ill, I hope he is better now. I'm writing to him separately.

I'll end this missive for the moment, since I'm rushing to send it off as soon as possible. I'll drop you a line again soon.

Best wishes—and apologies for the mountain of annoyances caused by Shcherbachev and my scoundrel of a piano.

Yours   S. Prokofiev

---

99. Vladimir Mayakovsky (1893–1930) was the leading "Poet of the Revolution," and became friendly with Prokofiev beginning around 1917. They met later in Paris.

100. *The Snow Maiden* is an opera by Rimsky-Korsakov, based on a fairy tale drama by Aleksandr Ostrovsky.

November 23, 1923
LONDON

Dear Eleonora, I send you greetings from London, where tomorrow I will play the Third Concerto. Next I'm going to Paris, Ettal and Geneva. Did you receive my letter to L. G. [Lunacharsky]? Did it help?

Yours   S. Prokofiev

December 24, 1923
PARIS

Dear Eleonora,

I send you and your entire family my greetings and best wishes for the New Year. Did you receive the business letter I sent you last month? Why haven't you written for so long?

Yours   S. P.

January 19, 1925
WARSAW

Gruss from Warsaw! I've been at the next stop from Officers' Street[101] for seven whole years now. So why has your voice been silenced? How are you? Write me at 54, route des Gardes, Bellevue, S. et O., France.

Yours   S. P.

November 3, 1925
STOCKHOLM

Dear Eleonora,

I send you greetings from Stockholm, where I have come to give three concerts. I have not yet received a reply from you to the thick registered letter that I sent you through Riga in September. There I wrote to you about a business matter: Demchinsky's libretto.[102] If you still have the same good business sense that I remember you used to have, then I hope upon my return to Paris (I'll be there in a week) to find your substantial reply.

I send you my best wishes.

Yours S. Prokofiev

---

101. Damskaya lived in Officers' Street in Leningrad.
102. Prokofiev was hoping that his literary friend Boris Demchinsky would help him with the libretto for *The Fiery Angel*, just as he had helped with the libretto for *The Gambler*.

December 3, 1925
PARIS

Dear Eleonora,

Your letter of November 25 caught me in Strasbourg. I am replying promptly, but I can only send this reply from Paris, since you didn't enclose your address, and your previous letter is lying in my desk in Paris. You know every business-minded person begins a letter by giving his own address, and only flirtatious high school girls don't follow that rule. In this case I didn't even write your address into my address book, since you wrote that you were going to be leaving Russia, and there seemed to be no reason to do so.

I made inquiries about strings for you in the two best Paris establishments: at Erard and at Pleyel. (Pleyel is well known for its chromatic harps, which Ravel is now writing for.) I have to tell you that both complained that they do not now have strings of the same high quality that they used to, but they promised to give me the best ones they had. If your address had been in your letters, then I would have sent them a telegram telling them to send you the strings right away; now I'll do that upon my return to Paris, on the evening of December 5, but since December 6 is a Sunday, the parcel will be sent to you on the 7th. As far as your finery is concerned, I'll also try to send you all of the clothes, or at least a part, but I'm afraid that I may not manage, since the stores are closed on the 6th, and we are leaving on the 7th for Amsterdam, where rehearsals begin on the 8th for the *Scythian Suite*, the Violin Concerto, and the Third Piano Concerto. You have only yourself to blame: you should have written it all out clearly right away. Don't worry about the money: it will be enough for you just to pay the customs duty.

I definitely need the telegram concerning Demchinsky before the 20th, but earlier would be even better, since 1) I have to give an answer on the 20th about when I'll be able to have the full score of *Fiery Angel* ready, and 2) apparently I'll have to leave again after the 20th and this time for a much longer period. So it's absolutely necessary to set the matter of *Fiery Angel* straight before then. But please explain to Demchinsky that this time I have to have a *firm promise*, his word of honor, so that on that basis I can enter into an obligation with the publisher and theater. Here is my telegraph address:

Prokofieff, Garritus, Paris

I will write you in Leningrad from Holland. Warm greetings to you and yours. I do not allow Sviatoslav[103] to kiss young ladies yet.

Yours   S. Prokofiev

C/o Guaranty Trust Co.
3, rue des Italiens
Paris IX, France
They will forward letters to me from this address, wherever I might be.

December 12, 1925
AMSTERDAM

Dear Eleonora, during my brief stay in Paris, I mananged to order strings and gloves for you—not much, but from the best stores. Pleyel sent you the strings on the 7th through its representative Fissor; and I ordered the gloves at Perrin on the 7th, although they probably didn't send them off until the 8th. The strings and the gloves were both sent in your name to Riga. The Dutch are giving me a good reception: over the span of ten days, they are performing me in eight concerts—six symphonic ones, and two chamber ones.

Warmest greetings.

Yours   S. Prokofiev

February 28, 1927
MOSCOW

Thanks for your assistance.

S.P.

The money order is a detachable coupon, for 118 rubles.

In Moscow I'm in the center at the Hotel Metropol. Sergei Sergeevich Prokofiev[104]

March 16, 1948
NIKOLINA GORA[105]

Kind Eleonora,

Thanks for your letter, and your promise to supply me with some photographic materials. I will have copies made and then return them to you in good condition. There's no need to send them right now, since I am planning to be in Leningrad in April, for the production of the second part of *War and Peace* at

103. Sviatoslav, Prokofiev's first son, was born in February 1924.
104. This note was written during Prokofiev's tour of Russia in early 1927.
105. Nikolina Gora was a village outside Moscow where Prokofiev lived in a dacha with his second wife, the writer Mira Mendelson. They were married in early 1948, having lived together since 1941.

Malegot. We'll get together then and I'll choose the ones I want. What's your telephone number?

I am still searching for a few photos that I don't have—for example, of Max Schmitgof and of Bashkirov.[106] But perhaps your "diplomatic talents" will lead you to trace them down . . .

I send you warmest greetings. I'm very glad that everything is going well with you.

Yours   S. Prokofiev

May 6, 1948
Nikolina Gora

Kind Eleonora,

As always happens with theaters, the opening of my opera[107] has been delayed, and I still don't know when I will end up in Leningrad.

I apologize profusely for not having yet manged to return to you the money that you spent to get the photographs. Unfortunately, I have been temporarily impoverished, but in June or July I anticipate that my situation will return to normal and I'll send you the 500 rubles to Leningrad or to your dacha—as you instruct me.

I think that it isn't worth sending the snapshots in an expensive package. I plan to be in Leningrad in any case, and if I don't manage to get them before you leave town, then I'll get them after you return from your dacha.

Warmest greetings.

Yours   S. Prokofiev

---

106. Boris Verin (see note 34, above). Prokofiev was searching for materials as he was writing his autobiography.
107. The opera was *Story of a Real Man*, based on a novel by Boris Polevoy about a Soviet fighter pilot who loses both legs in combat in World War II and struggles to return to the air. The planned production of the opera was greatly complicated by the official attacks on Prokofiev delivered at the First Congress of Soviet Composers in early 1948, which seriously undermined his political and financial position. For a while, his works were virtually banned from performance and publication, and his income dropped to almost nothing.

November 30, 1948

Kind Eleonora,

I have finally managed to get to Leningrad, and will be happy to see you. Call me at the Hotel Astoria, room 2.[108]

I hope that all is well with you and that your health is good.

I send greetings.

Yours   S. Prokofiev

February 11, 1953[109]
MOSCOW

Dear Eleonora Aleksandrovna,

Thank you for the interesting letter you sent in the autumn. I beg you to forgive me for not having gotten around to answering it before now. But most of all, I apologize for not having yet returned your two photos to you; I assure you that they are in one piece and on the way to Leningrad. It's just that I cannot decide whether to send them by registered parcel or to hand them to you in person when the opportunity arises. I thank you for Verin's photos and will be expecting them.

As for the our latest musical news—they have started rehearsing my new ballet *The Stone Flower* (based on themes from Bazhov's fairy tales of the Urals) at the Bolshoi Theater. The premiere is scheduled for this spring.[110] In Leningrad the conductor Sanderling[111] is preparing to perform my new Seventh Symphony in the near future; apparently Mravinsky then plans to take it up.[112]

---

108. Prokofiev had come to Leningrad for a closed concert performance of *Story of a Real Man* at the Kirov Theater, conducted by Boris Khaikin. He attended the performance, but not the official discussion that followed. So negative was the official reaction to the new opera that plans to produce it were scrapped. It was staged twelve years later, long after Prokofiev's death. This failure was a terrible blow to Prokofiev, who was then seriously ill.

109. This is one of the last letters Prokofiev wrote. He died three weeks later, on March 5, 1953—the same day as Stalin.

110. Prokofiev's ballet *The Stone Flower* received its premiere on February 12, 1954, in Moscow.

111. Kurt Sanderling (born 1912), a German-born conductor, emigrated to the USSR in 1936 and conducted the Orchestra of the Leningrad Philharmonic 1941–60.

112. Prokofiev's Symphony No. 7 in C-sharp Minor, op. 131, was first performed in Moscow on October 11, 1952.

The Muscovites responded to this symphony with great affection! I hope that you like it.

My wife and I send you warmest greetings. I would ask you also to convey warm greetings to "Shurik," whose patronymic I unfortunately do not know.

I assume that he is your husband, although he could be your son, or even your grandson. Oh, how quickly time flies!

Yours   S. Prokofiev

Please send the letter and snapshots to my Moscow address: 6 Moscow Art Theater Lane, Apt. 47.

CHAPTER THREE

Prokofiev and Sergei Diaghilev

Few twentieth-century composers have devoted more time and energy to composing music for ballet than Sergei Prokofiev. He spent almost forty years working with ballet impresarios, choreographers, and dancers. He wrote his first ballet, *Ala and Lolly* (later revised as the better-known *Scythian Suite*), for Sergei Diaghilev (1872–1929) in 1914 and was putting finishing touches on his last, *The Stone Flower*, the day he died in Moscow. In between came six more: *The Buffoon, The Steel Gallop, Prodigal Son, On the Dnepr, Romeo and Juliet,* and *Cinderella*. *Ala and Lolly* and *The Buffoon* were composed in wartime Petrograd; *Steel Gallop, Prodigal Son,* and *On the Dnepr* in Paris between the wars; *Romeo and Juliet, Cinderella,* and *The Stone Flower* in Stalinist Moscow.

Besides Diaghilev—who commissioned *Ala and Lolly, The Buffoon, Steel Gallop,* and *Prodigal Son*—Prokofiev's ballet collaborators included Léonide Massine (who began his career as a dancer in Diaghilev's Ballets Russes company), Leonid Lavrovsky, and Galina Ulanova. They spanned a surprisingly wide range of experience and style, from the abstract grace of the Ballets Russes to the literal and moralistic athleticism of Soviet Socialist Realism. The importance of Prokofiev's contribution to ballet—and to making ballet music a respectable and serious genre—ranks with the achievements of his countrymen Tchaikovsky and Stravinsky.

But had it not been for Diaghilev, Prokofiev might never have written ballet music at all. Despite Tchaikovsky's love for dance and his demonstration that it could accommodate significant music, Prokofiev grew up in a musical environment that still tended to condescend to ballet as a frivolous form of "applied art." Symphonies and operas were much more respectable. Prokofiev's professors at the St. Petersburg Conservatory did include several who wrote ballets themselves—notably Aleksandr Glazunov (*Raymonda, The Seasons*) and Nicolai Tcherepnin (*Le Pavillon d'Armide*)—but only Tcherepnin conveyed to Prokofiev a respect for the artistic possibilities of writing music for dance. It was through Tcherepnin, who was the first music adviser to Diaghilev, that Prokofiev first learned of Diaghilev and his activities.

But even seeing Tcherepnin work with Diaghilev did not immediately lead

Prokofiev to seek a future in ballet music. As late as 1912, after the triumphant Paris premieres of Stravinsky's *Firebird* and *Petrushka*, Prokofiev was still suspicious of dance music. "I've heard something of Stravinsky's ballets," he wrote to a friend, "but for the moment the idea of writing my own does not interest me."[1] Nor did Prokofiev's idea that ballet music was commercial and somehow lacking in substance—a mistress rather than a wife—ever completely disappear. He spent years of his long career writing operas without any promise that they would eventually be performed, while each one of his ballets was begun and completed for a specific commission.

Only after seeing the spectacularly successful Ballets Russes in Paris and London in 1913 and 1914, and meeting Diaghilev in London in the summer of 1914, did Prokofiev begin seriously to consider writing ballet music himself. Significantly, even when he met Diaghilev and his entourage for the first time, Prokofiev asked the impresario if he would be interested in an opera based on Dostoyevsky's short novel *The Gambler* rather than a ballet. Diaghilev advised Prokofiev that opera was a dying form and that the future of music for the stage lay in dance. By now, Prokofiev had seen how enthusiastically European audiences and critics responded to new Ballets Russes productions, so he did not argue when Diaghilev asked him to write a new ballet score for the company.

Ala and Lolly, never produced, was the beginning of Prokofiev's fifteen-year collaboration with Diaghilev, a collaboration marked by the same unfortunate timing and lost opportunities that plagued Prokofiev throughout his career. Diaghilev's death in 1929 and the collapse of the Ballets Russes were factors that led Prokofiev to return from Paris to Russia, where, he believed, he would find more supporters and resources. And yet the three Prokofiev ballets that Diaghilev did produce in Paris (*Buffoon* in 1921, *Steel Gallop* in 1927, and, perhaps most successfully, *Prodigal Son* in 1929) did a great deal to build and enhance Prokofiev's reputation in the West. They also taught him how to compose a dramatically effective ballet score, lessons he incorporated to brilliant effect in *Romeo and Juliet*, one of the most popular full-length ballets ever written.

The letters translated below follow the Diaghilev-Prokofiev collaboration from its beginnings in autumn 1914 to Diaghilev's death in 1929. Besides a telegram from Diaghilev to Prokofiev and four letters from Prokofiev to Diaghilev, I have included a fascinating letter about Prokofiev from Diaghilev

---

1.   This letter is in the Central State Archive of Literature and Art, Moscow.

to Stravinsky, and Prokofiev's letter to Walter Nouvel written just after Diaghilev's death. Not only do these letters shed light on Prokofiev's attitudes towards ballet and explicate Diaghilev's aesthetic guidelines; they also show just how difficult it was for Prokofiev to compete in Paris, and for Diaghilev's favor, with another Russian composer, nine years his senior, who had arrived on the scene before him: Igor Stravinsky.

(These letters appeared in Russian in *Sergei Diagilev i russkoe iskusstvo*, Vol. II, I. S. Zil'bershtein and V. A. Samkov, eds. [Moscow: Izobrazitel'noe iskusstvo, 1982]. Translated into English by Harlow Robinson with assistance from Tatiana Poliakova. Notes have been edited and modified for this volume.)

DIAGHILEV to PROKOFIEV

October 1/14, 1914 [Telegram]
FLORENCE

Could you come to Rome via Thessaloníki with a piano score of the new ballet? Would you like to play your Second Concerto in Rome? Can try to arrange it. Diaghilev.[2]

DIAGHILEV to STRAVINSKY[3]

February 23/ March 8, 1915
ROME

Dear Igor:

I have lots of news, but first of all a few words about Prokofiev. Yesterday he played with great success in the Augusteum, but this is not what I really want to tell you. What I do want to tell you is that he brought me about one-third of the score of his new ballet.[4] The libretto is merely a typical Petersburg concoction that might have been suitable for the Mariinsky Theater ten years ago, but is unacceptable for us. In Prokofiev's own words, he is not looking for Russian effects in his music. For him, it's just music in the widest sense. It is just music all right, and very bad music at that. So we'll have to start all over again, and that is why we have to treat him with kindness and keep him with us for two or three months. I am counting on your help. He is gifted, but what can you expect if the most sophisticated person in his milieu is Tcherepnin,[5] whose avant-garde swank greatly impresses him. Prokofiev is easily influenced, and nicer than he seemed after his first brusque appearance on the scene. I'll bring him to you. Either he must change totally, or we'll lose him forever.[6] [. . .]

If you can meet with us in Milan, phone me in Naples, at the Hotel Vesuvius. You could see the new studios of the Futurists. Then we would depart for

---

2.   This telegram was originally written in French. Although no reply exists, we know that Prokofiev accepted Diaghilev's offer and departed for Italy.

3.   The text used here is in *Igor Stravinsky et Robert Craft. Souvenirs et commentaires* (Paris, 1963), 126–27; published in English as Igor Stravinsky and Robert Craft, *Memories and Commentaries* (New York: Doubleday, 1960).

4.   The new ballet was *Ala and Lolly*, to a libretto by Sergei Gorodetsky.

5.   Nicolai Tcherepnin (1873–1945) was one of Prokofiev's professors at the St. Petersburg Conservatory. (See the introduction to this chapter.)

6.   Prokofiev went to Rome to introduce Diaghilev to the fragments of his ballet *Ala and Lolly* based on Scythian themes, and to perform a concert on February 22, 1915.

Montreux together. I urge you to come, since it is important for the future. I'll immediately send you some money for travel expenses. As far as Prokofiev's concert is concerned, he can do it for the benefit of the Serbs on March 20. See you soon then,

> I embrace you,
> Seryozha.

P. S. I cannot wait until you finish *Les Noces*![7] I have fallen in love with it.

PROKOFIEV to DIAGHILEV[8]

October 1, 1918
NEW YORK

Dear Sergei Pavlovich:

I hear you arrived with a small troupe in London. I am glad that you are resuming your intense activity. In Russia, which I recently left, all respectable people are very interested in your work. But they haven't heard much about you lately, except for your telegram to Karsavina, which led to heartfelt rejoicing, and Makletsova's suit against you.[9] I have written to both you and Petrushka[10] so many times, but haven't received any response from either of you. I would like to think I could blame the mail for that. From Bolm's[11] rather obscure and wordy remarks I gathered that you as well as everyone else has failed to make heads or tails of my *Buffoon*. This is a shame, although I must admit that this is entirely possible, since you once shamelessly rejected the music of my *Ala and Lolly* (just like Nouvel, who after listening to it later in an orchestral performance gave me his apologies).

Before my return to Russia, I plan to spend a few months here and would very much like to exchange some pleasant letters with you.

---

7. Stravinsky's new ballet was based on Russian folk wedding ritual; it is also known as *The Wedding*.
8. This letter is published from an original manuscript in the collection of Diaghilev's associate Serge Lifar, a dancer and choreographer.
9. Ksenia Petrovna Makletsova (1890–?) was a ballerina who performed with the Bolshoi Theater 1908–16 and with Diaghilev's Ballets Russes 1915–16. Makletsova brought charges against Diaghilev in an American court, apparently in connection with the return of ballerina Lydia Lopukhova to Diaghilev's troupe, which led to Makletsova's departure from the company.
10. Stravinsky.
11. Adolph Bolm (1884–1951), a dancer and choreographer originally from St. Petersburg, had been a member of the Ballets Russes since 1911.

What are your plans and what about the destiny of my poor *Buffoon* so traitorously buried in the secret folds of your briefcase?

Please accept my cordial regards as well as my chronic admiration. Please be so kind as to respond to this letter.

Yours,
Sergei Prokofiev

PROKOFIEV to DIAGHILEV[12]

June 26, 1922
ETTAL

Dear Sergei Pavlovich:

I was very happy to receive your telegram regarding the success of my *Buffoon.*[13] Since *The Buffoon* is being given for two extra nights, that means the season will be extended. Therefore, allow me to congratulate you on your success and wish you more of the same!

Are you planning to go to Venice as usual? If yes, let me tell you that one of the routes to Venice lies on the Munich-Innsbruck line. I would be exceedingly happy if you and Kochno could come and stay with us for a few days.[14] Our dacha is spacious, the jasmine is fragrant, and the air is wholesome with mountains and balsam!

I embrace you,
Yours, Prokofiev.

The village of Ettal is a mile and a half away from the Oberau station, which is three hours from Munich, on the Munich-Innsbruck line.

PROKOFIEV to DIAGHILEV[15]

April 19, 1928
MONTE CARLO

Dear Sergei Pavlovich:

I am leaving Monte Carlo and would like to embrace you one last time. I

---

12. This letter is published from Prokofiev's typewritten copy in the collection of Serge Lifar.
13. *The Buffoon* had received its premiere the preceding season (May 16, 1921) and was revived in the 1922 season. After that it dropped from the Ballets Russes repertoire.
14. Boris Kochno was friend and secretary to Diaghilev; he also wrote libretti for numerous ballets produced by the Ballets Russes, including Prokofiev's *Prodigal Son.*
15. This letter is published from the manuscript in the collection of Serge Lifar.

regret that last night I did not have a chance to chat with you: I had a severe attack of neuralgia.

Yours,

S. Prokofiev.

PROKOFIEV to DIAGHILEV [16]

September 21, 1928

Le château de Vetraz par Annemasse (Haute Savoie), France

Dear Sergei Pavlovich:

Without delay I'd like to thank you for your affectionate letter. Here is my detailed answer.

1. I am finishing the Third Symphony. Besides that, I've composed two big piano pieces and material for two more. I have been working on these pieces rather assiduously, and attach to them more importance than composers usually do to incidental piano pieces dashed off on the side.

2. The idea of a new ballet for you interests me greatly, as usual.[17] But I don't want to slap something together hastily, and I have no time now to do it the way I would want to. Around October 10 I intend to embark on a concert tour of the USSR that will last a month and a half. In February I am planning to go there a second time for two months to oversee a production of *The Gambler* at the Mariinsky Theater and to give concerts. If we take into consideration the concerts I'll be giving in Europe as well and the time which we'll need to spend together on preliminary discussions of the future ballet, then I would have only 2 or 2½ months to write it—which is absolutely insufficient. Maybe the alternative would be to make use of the piano pieces that I mentioned before? We could get together and try to work something up. By any chance will you be in Paris the week before October 10? There is also another option which I personally like very much: to revive *The Buffoon*.

3. *Love for Three Oranges* will be performed in October in Freiburg. *Oranges* was staged there in June right before the end of the season. I haven't seen the production, but owing to the favorable response and its success with

---

16. This letter is published from Prokofiev's typewritten manuscript in the collection of Serge Lifar.

17. The new ballet would be *Prodigal Son*, with choreography by George Balanchine. This was the last time Prokofiev and Diaghilev would collaborate. It was performed for the first time in Paris on May 21, 1929.

the public, it was decided to revive the show at the beginning of the fall season. If you wish to obtain more detailed information, telegraph Generalmusikdirektor Lindemann, Stadttheater, Freiburg in Breisgau.

4. As for my opinions about young Soviet composers, I already told you about Shostakovich, Mosolov, and Gavriil Popov, whose talents clearly stand out above the crowd. At the moment Boris Vladimirovich Asafiev (Igor Glebov) is staying with me. He is truly the most influential music writer in the USSR, the best opinion-maker and trendsetter among today's Russian (non-émigré) musicians. We discussed the significance of the "mighty three" together before I set my pen to paper to write you about them as you requested.

At present, Shostakovich seems to occupy the first position among them. His Symphony No. 1 has already been successfully conducted by Bruno Walter, and Stokowski is going to conduct it in America. This symphony was composed five years ago. Since then, Shostakovich has written a Symphony No. 2 ("To October"), which both Asafiev and Meyerhold have noted as a major step forward. His opera *The Nose* (based on Gogol) has been accepted for staging by the Leningrad Akopera.[18] In the opinion of those who have heard it, the opera is a completely new interpretation of Gogol's story. I personally have heard only a piano sonata, one of Shostakovich's earlier works—vivid, showing great talent, and even some influence of my style.[19] I have asked B. V. Asafiev to send the latest works of those composers to Paris.

In any case, I am staying in Vetraz until the first of October and expect to return to Paris early in the month.

With best regards from my wife and myself,

Yours, S. Prokofiev

PROKOFIEV to W. F. NOUVEL[20]

August 25, 1929
CHÂTEAU DE LA FLÉCHÈRE

Dear Walter Fyodorovich:

How grim an event the death of Sergei Pavlovich is! He was always so vigorous, full of life, and my impressions of him were always so vivid, that it's still

---

18. Akopera was the State Academic Theater of Opera and Ballet, later known as the Kirov. In fact, *The Nose* was performed at the Maly Opera in 1930.
19. The Piano Sonata No. 1, op. 12 (1926).
20. This letter is published from the manuscript in the collection of Serge Lifar.

impossible for me to realize that Diaghilev is no longer with us, especially since I wasn't close by at the moment of his death.

I have a lot of questions to ask you. What was the origin of the disease? Could he have been cured? How about his last minutes? Did he know that he was dying and how did he react to that fact? But I'm sure that you must be pre-occupied with other, more important matters right now. Newspapers are the only source of news in this provincial town, and I also heard a few things from Stravinsky, who lives 60 kilometers away from me.

Also, I'd like to know how this tragedy will affect your position and whether you intend to continue to run or liquidate Diaghilev's company.

Please extend my deep sympathy to Pavel Egorovich,[21] whose address I don't have, and to all of Sergei Pavlovich's colleagues and relatives when you see them.

I embrace you.

Yours,
S. Prokofiev

---

21. Pavel Egorovich Koribut-Kubitovich was Diaghilev's cousin.

CHAPTER FOUR
Letters to Vsevolod Meyerhold

VSEVOLOD EMILYEVICH MEYERHOLD (1874–1940), who studied music in his youth and briefly considered a musical career before choosing the theater, once said, "I consider my musical education the basis of my work as a director."[1] An examination of his enormously influential theoretical and practical work—throughout his long career—gives us no reason to dispute that claim. Not only did Meyerhold attempt to develop a precise musical vocabulary for the productions he directed, involving the concepts of rhythm, meter, and even "harmonic" movement.[2] Not only did he incorporate music into his productions in unusual and aggressive ways, sometimes matching the emotional mood and rhythm of the stage action, and sometimes contradicting it, in highly self-conscious counterpoint.[3] Not only did he stage numerous operas—including *Tristan and Isolde, Boris Godunov, Elektra, The Nightingale, Orpheus and Eurydice,* and *The Queen of Spades.*[4] In addition—and this, arguably, was Meyerhold's greatest contribution in the field of music—he worked closely with composers and musical figures, encouraging them to think in theatrical terms, inspiring them with his rigor, brilliance, and erudition, proposing and developing projects.

The list of composers who worked with Meyerhold at one time or another includes some of the most important Russian composers of the twentieth century: Prokofiev, Shostakovich, Asafiev, Reinhold Glière, Anatoly Liadov, Aleksandr Glazunov, Vissarion Shebalin. But sadly, Meyerhold's most cherished musical dream persistently eluded him—developing and staging a new Soviet opera that would embody his ideas on the relationship between music, narra-

---

1.   V. E. Meyerhold, *Stat'i, pis'ma, rechi, besedy,* II (Moscow, 1968), 503.
2.   "Acting is melody, directing is harmony. I discovered that not long ago, and I astonished myself, the definition was so exact. . . . Musical terminology helps us a great deal. I love it because it possesses an almost mathematical exactness." Quoted in Paul Schmidt, ed., *Meyerhold at Work* (Austin: University of Texas Press, 1980), 154.
3.   A particularly striking example was his use of Beethoven in an eccentric interpretation of Griboedov's play *Woe from Wit* (*Gore ot uma*), retitled *Woe to Wit* (*Gore umu*).
4.   Meyerhold began and ended his official career as an opera director. He worked at the Imperial Theaters for nearly ten years before the Russian Revolution, and his last job, in 1938–39, was at the Stanislavsky Opera Theater in Moscow.

tive and gesture, and prove the continuing viability of opera in the 20th century.

No composer enjoyed a longer, deeper, or more tragically frustrating artistic and personal relationship with Meyerhold than Sergei Prokofiev. Their sporadic and ill-fated collaboration, which began in 1916 and lasted until the very day of Meyerhold's arrest in June 1939, is a fascinating chapter in the careers of both artists. It provides a graphic illustration of how Russian music and culture evolved from the time of the Russian Revolution until World War II, veering from at times wild interdisciplinary experimentation to the cautious and government-enforced conservatism of Socialist Realism.

Three of Prokofiev's seven operas were influenced by his assocation with Meyerhold: *The Gambler* (particularly in its revised 1927–28 version), *Love for Three Oranges,* and *Semyon Kotko.* Meyerhold spent years preparing these operas for production in the USSR—he worked especially hard to get *The Gambler* produced—but for reasons primarily ideological and bureaucratic, he was unable to bring a single one of them to the stage. When arrested, Meyerhold was in the midst of rehearsals for the premiere of *Semyon Kotko.* Nor was their collaboration limited exclusively to opera. Prokofiev also wrote the incidental music for Meyerhold's projected production of Pushkin's historical tragedy *Boris Godunov,* similarly abandoned after several years of intensive preparation and rehearsals, between 1934 and 1936.

For nearly thirty years after Meyerhold's arrest and "disappearance," until the Thaw period of the 1960s, information on all aspects of his career—including the purely dramatic—was scarce. When Meyerhold was mentioned, he was briefly dismissed as a pernicious influence. In his 1957 biography of Prokofiev, which for many years (until the revised version appeared in 1973) remained the standard reference work and the starting point for Soviet research, Israel Nestyev made only fleeting reference to Meyerhold, minimizing and denigrating his contact with the composer.[5] The first article on their collaboration, a necessarily brief and superficial survey by Aleksandr Fevralsky, appeared in 1963. Describing the genesis of the opera *Semyon Kotko,* Prokofiev's first attempt to produce an opera specifically for a Soviet theater, Fevralsky concluded vaguely, "Meyerhold did not have the occasion to stage this opera. . . . Such were the artistic contacts between two remarkable masters of Soviet art."[6]

---

5.   Israel Nestyev, *Prokofiev,* trans. Florence Jonas (Stanford: Stanford University Press, 1960), 112.

6.   Aleksandr Fevral'skii, "Prokof'ev & Meierkol'd," in *Sergei Prokof'ev 1953–63: Stat'i & materialy,* Nest'ev and Edel'man, eds. (Moscow, 1962), 108.

Only in recent years, with the publication of the rich and detailed correspondence between Meyerhold and Prokofiev, has it become possible to grasp the full extent of the collaboration between the director and the composer he called "the new Wagner." In the late 1980s, in the liberating intellectual atmosphere of *glasnost*, information about Meyerhold's final days of torture at the hands of the KGB emerged, contributing to his already established reputation as one of the pioneer-martyrs of Soviet avant-garde culture.

As the letters translated here (spanning the years 1926–34) make clear, Prokofiev and Meyerhold held each other in the highest personal and professional regard. The correspondence dates from a period when Soviet writers, directors, and performers were still traveling quite freely between Russia and Europe—a situation that would change dramatically in the period of Stalinist isolationism that began by the mid-1930s. Meyerhold's disappearance from the scene in 1939 was a terrible blow to Prokofiev, and made him realize—perhaps for the first time—the true nature of the Soviet regime.

Meyerhold always had great hopes for Prokofiev as an operatic composer. In a speech on the role of music in staging, given January 1, 1925, almost seven years after Prokofiev had left Russia, he praised *The Gambler* as an opera of the future, and insisted that this was a composer who could revive and redefine the stagnating operatic tradition. "I am convinced that after *Aida*, *The Queen of Spades*, *Eugene Onegin* finally begin to fall into the abyss—simply because if these operas are performed 200,000 times, then all of mankind shall have heard them, and if everybody on earth hears *Eugene Onegin*, then sometime it will all end, it will be boring to hear—then the question—'What about opera?'—will arise. And then, it seems to me—I am deeply convinced of it—some new Wagner will appear—maybe his name will be Prokofiev, I don't know—who will throw out the operatic theater as such, and a new kind of opera will appear. . . . We stand on the eve of a reform."[7]

That reform never came to pass, but not for want of trying.

(What appears here is an edited version of the texts and annotations in "S. S. Prokof'ev: Pis'ma k V. E. Meierkhol'du," prepared and edited by K. N. Kirilenko and M. G. Kozlova and published in *Muzykal'noe nasledstvo: Sborniki po istorii muzykal'noi kul'tury SSSR*, Vol. II, part 2 [Moscow: Muzyka, 1968], 214–31. Translated by Geoffrey Carlson and Harlow Robinson.)

---

7.   Meyerhold, *Stat'i, pis'ma, rechi, besedy*, II, 70.

December 8, 1926
18, RUE TROYON, PARIS XVII

Highly respected Vsevolod Emilyevich,

Do you remember our conversation about *The Gambler* during your stay in Paris? You said at the time that you would take on its production if it came to the USSR. I told you that before producing it I wanted to review it in detail and revise it, and if you gave me your advice on how to improve the libretto I would appreciate it very much and would be extraordinarily grateful to you. Here's what we decided: a month before coming to Moscow I was to remind you about it, and you would read Dostoyevsky's novella and my libretto so you would be able to give me your thoughts concerning its merits and shortcomings.[8]

I plan to be in Moscow by January 20, and that's why I'm writing to you. If you don't have a piano score at hand from which you could read the libretto, I would remind you just in case that in 1916, when *The Gambler* was being prepared for production at the Mariinsky Theater, the piano score was lithographed by the library of the former Imperial Theaters. A hundred copies were made, most of which have probably remained stored in the library. You certainly shouldn't have any difficulty obtaining one of these. It's also possible that Derzhanovsky[9] or Miaskovsky has such a copy in Moscow, and Asafiev (Igor Glebov) in Leningrad.

I send you my best regards, and I'll be glad to meet you again.

Yours, *S. PRKFV*

Nov. 30, 1927
5, AVENUE FRÉMIET, PARIS XVI

Dear Vsevolod Emilyevich,

How are you? When are we performing *The Gambler*? I've already finished adapting three acts, and I'm planning to finish the fourth in January. Drop me a line.

I embrace you.   Yours, *S. PRKFV.*

---

8.   Meyerhold was one of the first to become interested in Prokofiev's opera *The Gambler*, which he first heard in autumn 1916 when the score was being completed. Meyerhold had intended to produce *The Gambler* at the Mariinsky Theater in Petrograd in 1917, but the Russian Revolution and the ensuing economic and political turmoil led to the cancellation of the production. Prokofiev thoroughly revised the opera in 1927–28.

9.   Vladimir Derzhanovsky (1881–1942) was a Soviet critic and musical figure, and a supporter of Prokofiev's music from before the 1917 Revolution. (See also chapter 2.)

December 26, 1928

1, RUE OBLIGADO, PARIS XVI, FRANCE

Dear Vsevolod Emilyevich,

I have fulfilled your commission with pleasure: the music paper, the note-books, and the pens were delivered to Olga Sossine three days ago, with a request to forward them to you through the embassy.

I was all set to go to Moscow but I was delayed by a telegram from Derzhanovsky. I'm waiting for an explanatory letter from him. Now I think I won't be able to go there before February or March, and I'm very disappointed about that, since I had quite made up my mind to go and was expecting to celebrate the New Year in Moscow. Now I'm diligently working on the ballet for Diaghilev, so that I may finish it as soon as possible and leave the spring free for my travels.[10]

Please tell me what's going on with *The Gambler*, both artistically and administratively. Don't delay in sending me some more details about your trip to Leningrad. What month is the premiere set for?

On December 14 Lina Ivanovna was happily delivered of a son. Both mother and son are in excellent condition.[11] We send you and Zinaida Nikolaevna[12] our heartfelt greetings for the New Year. I send you my embrace as well.

Yours. S. PRKFV

I read about how happy the theater was to see you on your return.[13]

January 3 [1929]

PARIS

Very interesting, but if I accept your commission, cannot finish Diaghilev's ballet, therefore must refuse.

Prokofiev[14]

---

10. The ballet was *The Prodigal Son*, with libretto by Boris Kochno and choreography by George Balanchine. It received its premiere in Paris on May 21, 1929.
11. The son was Oleg; the Prokofievs already had another son, Sviatoslav, born in 1924.
12. Meyerold's wife was a well-known Russian actress, Zinaida Raikh.
13. On December 2, 1928, Meyerhold returned to Moscow after a five-month stay abroad. He was met by the actors of his Meyerhold Theater at the Belorussia Station, and in the evening was warmly greeted by the audience gathered for the performance. His return was widely covered in the Soviet press.
14. Prokofiev's telegram was sent in response to this telegram from Meyerhold: "Telegraph agreement to write music [for] Mayakovsky's new play, scheduled for early

January 8, 1929
1, RUE OBLIGADO, PARIS XVI, FRANCE

Dear Vsevolod Emilyevich,

It seemed very appetizing to write a few musical numbers for the production of Mayakovsky's play at your theater. But this all came up too hastily—and after pondering the matter for 24 hours, I had to send you a telegram of refusal. The main reason is that I am now in the middle of working on Diaghilev's ballet. If I interrupt this job I'm afraid I'll lose my momentum. And I haven't given up the idea of coming to the USSR in February or March—and then I would surely risk not being able to finish the ballet on time. Finally, I couldn't take on a piece anyway when I haven't the slightest idea of its spirit or mood. It's too bad that during your trips to Paris neither you nor Mayakovsky explained to me the content of the play or the role music was supposed to play in it.[15]

Thank you very much for your New Year's telegram also. At first we couldn't understand what the word *Zinka* meant, and only later did it occur to us that *sinka* meant *synka* [little son]! The latter is doing fine, but his mommy is only gradually getting back to normal.

The other day I saw Diaghilev, who told me reproachfully: "That Meyerhold of yours . . ." It turns out he hasn't heard a word from you, and it's time for him to plan his spring season. Please write something to Diaghilev so he won't reproach me (but why should he anyway?).

I got a letter from the Brussels Opera with various questions regarding the nature of the production of *The Gambler*. They are now rehearsing at full speed. They wanted to know if rehearsals have also begun in Leningrad, to which I'll probably have to respond: I'll be damned if I know; no one's written me a word about it.[16]

Accept our most heartfelt greetings to you and Zina Nikolaevna. We embrace you.

Sincerely yours, S. PRKFV

February at my theater. Few musical numbers. Can royalties be paid here? If you agree I will immediately send play, noting places requiring musical numbers." (Telegram in the collection of the Central State Archive of Literature and Art, Moscow.) The play in question was Mayakovsky's *Bedbug*, a satire on life in Russia under the New Economic Policy. Shostakovich eventually wrote the incidental music.

15. Vladimir Mayakovsky (1893–1930), the "Poet of the Revolution," and Prokofiev became acquainted in 1917 at one of the poet's public readings in Petrograd. Thereafter they got to know each other better. Mayakovsky spent a good deal of time in Paris in the 1920s, like many other stars of the Soviet cultural scene. In 1928, he was in Paris

March 19 [1929]
BRUSSELS

Dear Vsevolod Emilyevich,

I send you and Zin[aida] Nik[olaevna] my greetings from Brussels and thanks for the letters. I'm rehearsing *The Gambler*—the premiere is April 29. I'm annoyed that our own ravens lost their chance at the premiere. And it looks like Meyerhold didn't do much to defend *The Gambler*! I'll be back in Paris in a few days and I'll send you more details then.[17]

Yours, S. PRKFV

March 23, 1929
1, RUE OBLIGADO, PARIS XVI, FRANCE

Dear Vsevolod Emilyevich,

First of all, let me express my deepest sympathy at the loss of your daughter. Although I didn't know her, now that I'm a father myself I can fully sympathize with your sorrow.

You probably received my postcard from Brussels, where I went to start rehearsals for *The Gambler*. Of course I was very upset about the derailment of the Leningrad production—it only made me all the more appreciative of the efforts they made in Brussels, and of their punctuality: at least they assured me that the premiere would take place on April 29 and not a half hour later. [. . .]

However, this isn't the end of my afflictions: those turtles still won't have things ready by the very beginning of next season, and in November I'll be leaving for America, where I'll stay until March. So they'll have to present the production without me.

Derzhanovksy writes that the Bolshoi Theater was asking him about the scores and conditions for a production of *The Steel Gallop*.[18] In view of the fact

---

from October 15 to December 3, and worked on *The Bedbug*. (See also chapter 2, n. 99.)

16. The projected production of *The Gambler* to be directed by Meyerhold never took place.

17. *The Gambler* received its world premiere in Brussels on April 29, 1929, at the Théâtre Royal de la Monnaie, where it was well received by the audience and critics.

18. *The Steel Gallop* (*Stal'noi skok*), also known under its French title *Le Pas d'acier*, was written for Diaghilev's Ballets Russes, which gave its premiere in Paris on June 7, 1927. With a libretto by Prokofiev and Georgii Yakoulov, the ballet portrayed the new life of Bolshevik Russia in an avant-garde Futurist-Constructivist style that irritated the increasingly conservative Soviet cultural establishment.

that currency conditions in the USSR are really difficult right now, and especially in view of the nature of *The Steel Gallop,* the publishers and I have decided to make an exception in this case and agree to payment in *chervontsy.*[19] Do you know anything about this proposed production? By the way, I am also conducting negotiations about a production of *The Steel Gallop* in New York.[20] If you have a chance to announce this in Moscow, this would provide a good pretext for quoting the Paris and London reviews of *The Steel Gallop* again, as you were so kind as to do once already.

I saw Mayakovsky in passing, and he told me about the success of *The Bedbug*—I congratulate you and shake your hand.[21] Thank you for the reviews and the amusing announcements about it. I wish you success with "The Commandarme 2"; let me know how it goes.

I send you my best regards, and I kiss Zinaida Nikolaevna's hand. Both Lina Ivanovna and I thank her very much for her letter. Although my wife is not a writer, she'll be dashing off a few lines in the near future. Please remind Zinaida Nikolaevna to send me the "new little journal," where they tore me to pieces.[22]

Sincerely yours, S. PRKFV

May 4, 1929
1, RUE OBLIGADO, PARIS XVI, FRANCE

Dear Vsevolod Emilyevich,

I'm writing to you on my return from Brussels, where I spent a week directing the final rehearsals for *The Gambler,* and its first performance. Considering the capabilities of this theater, *The Gambler* was performed fairly well; especially valuable was the goodwill with which everything was accomplished. From

---

19. *Chervontsy* were ten-ruble banknotes; Prokofiev had many difficulties arranging performances of his works in the Soviet Union because of the shortage of "hard" (foreign) currency there, which was needed to rent the parts from Prokofiev's Western publishers, Koussevitsky's firm Editions Russes.

20. *The Steel Gallop* was performed at the Metropolitan Opera in New York in 1931, with the Philadelphia Orchestra conducted by Leopold Stokowski. Natalia Goncharova designed the production, using "emblems of Soviet daily life" such as the hammer and sickle and red flags.

21. Mayakovsky was abroad in 1929 from February 14 to May 2. He and Prokofiev met at a reception at the Soviet embassy in Paris during this period. *The Bedbug* received its premiere in Moscow at the Meyerhold Theater on February 13, 1929.

22. The "new little journal" was *Proletarian Musician (Proletarskii muzykant),* the organ of the Association of Proletarian Musicians, which was published 1929–32 in Moscow. In the first issue Prokofiev's works were harshly criticized.

a musical standpoint it was first rate, and the male singers weren't bad; the female singers weren't as good, but they were all good actors, good material for a real director to mold successfully, but this director was ordinary, everyday, doing everything by the book, but failing to create anything new. At the same time, he knew his place, and when I told him about you, he answered dreamily that he'd love to go to Leningrad in the fall and see how you were producing it. The scenery was weak, but the costumes weren't bad. The opera was tremendously successful, and at the end the entire audience called me to the front, turning their backs to the stage and their faces to my box. It turned out that each act inspired more interest than the previous one. On the one hand, this shows that the libretto is well structured, but on the other hand, it doesn't say much for Act I. For that reason I've actually inserted a short scene that will interrupt the excessively lengthy explanation between Aleksei and Polina and that will liven up the flow of this act.

In the near future I'll send you something from the reviews, but in the meantime I'm enclosing the interview I gave on the day of the performance. It appeared on the front page of the leading Brussels newspaper. The interviewer garbled a lot of what I told him, so don't be surprised by some of the absurdities and inaccuracies. But this isn't important; what's important is what I said about our theaters, conservatories, directors, and composers—and if you have the opportunity, it would be good if you could publicize this in the Moscow press.

When Mayakovsky was in Paris, he read me some excerpts from *The Bedbug* and told me you were planning to bring it here in the spring.[23] How are your travel plans going? Will we have the pleasure of seeing you and Zinaida Nikolaevna soon? Diaghilev's season will begin on May 21 with *The Prodigal Son*. Diaghilev came to the premiere of *The Gambler* and praised it, especially the roulette scene, but mentioned in passing that he didn't like the operatic-declamatory style.[24] Thank you for the little magazine you sent. What a pitiful copy: full of malicious stupidity and stupid malice, on which it is likely to choke.

We send you and Zina Nikolaevna our heartfelt greetings. I embrace you.

Yours, S. PRKFV

---

23. In April 1929, during another of his trips to Paris, Mayakovsky read passages from *The Bedbug* at a private party. Mayakovsky commited suicide in Moscow in 1930. The Meyerhold Theater took a European tour in spring and summer of 1930, but did not perform *The Bedbug*.

24. Diaghilev died just a few months later—on August 19, 1929.

May 25, 1929

1, RUE OBLIGADO, PARIS XVI, FRANCE

Dear Vsevolod Emilyevich,

Did you receive my letter of May 4—about *The Gambler*? Since then I've been so busy running around with the production of *The Prodigal Son* and the performance of my Third Symphony that it was only today that I was able to grab some articles about *The Gambler*, which I'm sending to you.[25] In addition, in a few days Asafiev will send you a clipping from an illustrated Brussels magazine, about the characters in *The Gambler*.

Diaghilev's season opened on the 21st with my *Prodigal Son* and Stravinsky's *Renard*. We both conducted. The social parade was frightful and the success enormous. The tickets were sold out several days before the performance. Despite the success, I wasn't particularly satisfied with the choreography, although Rouault's scenery was first-class.

Why haven't I heard anything from you? Are you coming? With the theater troupe? Without the theater troupe? Be sure to write. I embrace you and ask you to kiss Zinaida Nikolaevna's little hand for me. My wife sends her regards to both of you.

Yours, *S. PRKFV*

October 23, 1929

6, RUE BASSANO, PARIS XVI, FRANCE

Dear Vsevolod Emilyevich,

Two joyful pieces of news: the first—that you are interested in producing *The Steel Gallop* (I'm sure no one else can see this piece the way you can!); the second—that I'll be able to see you soon in Moscow, where I'll probably arrive on October 30 or 31. Call Nik[olai] Yak[ovlevich] Miaskovsky on the evening of the 29th; by that time he'll have a telegram from me, and he'll know where I'll be staying.[26]

In the meantime I embrace you, and kiss Zinaida Nikolaevna's little hands. Warmest greetings to you both from Ptashka; she'll be staying in Paris.[27]

Yours, *S. PRKFV*

---

25. Prokofiev's Third Symphony, using music originally written for the opera *Fiery Angel*, had its first performance in Paris on May 17, 1929, conducted by Pierre Monteux.

26. Prokofiev was in the USSR from October 30 to November 19, 1929.

27. Ptashka was Prokofiev's favorite nickname for his wife Lina; in Russian it means something like "little bird."

December 2, 1929

6, RUE BASSANO, PARIS XVI, FRANCE

Dear Vsevolod Emilyevich,

It's been ten days since I got back to Paris, but I can still see myself at your house on Bryusovsky, where I spent so many delightful hours.[28] When I told my wife about the hospitality I received from you and Zinaida Nikolaevna and about all the interesting things I saw and heard during my visit, her mouth watered, and she exclaimed that she would definitely come with me in the spring.

The other day I was in Brussels, and while I was watching *The Gambler*, I was again reminded of you. The scene I inserted and the cuts made were just right, by the way. But the director still did only a quarter of what was required, and *The Gambler* is still waiting for a true production—yours. I came up with the following idea: *The Gambler*, whose action takes place in a constant flow of words, is more suitable for small stages than for large ones. Probably it could still be given successfully at the Mariinsky Theater, but I'm afraid that at the Bolshoi too many details would disappear into the immense space of the theater—and without the details this opera would lose too much.

Esenin's books are complete and bound, and in a few days I'll pick them up so I can bring them to Zinaida Nikolaevna in April.[29]

So far I haven't heard any news about my relatives, and I'm beginning to worry. I'll be very grateful to you if you can somehow write to me.[30] We're taking off for America on December 24, and I hope to get a letter from you before then. Or could it be that all our conversations have led to nothing?

I kiss Zinaida Nikolaevna's hand and your forehead. Ptashka sends both of you her most heartfelt regards and gratitude for the gifts. The little box and the tray were a great success. She was also pleased with my fur coat.

Affectionately yours, S. *PRKFV*

---

28. Meyerhold's apartment was at 12 Bryusovsky Lane (later renamed Nezhdanova St.), not far from Red Square.

29. Sergei Esenin (1895–1925) was the most prominent of the Russian "peasant writers." In 1923 he married Isadora Duncan and spent some months with her on a scandalous American tour. He committed suicide in 1925, but not before writing a last poem in his own blood. Many of his poems were set to music by popular and serious composers.

30. Although Prokofiev's mother also left Russia soon after the Russian Revolution, her sister (Prokofiev's aunt) Ekaterina Ignatievna (1857–1929) remained in the USSR, along with her daughter. In addition, Prokofiev had another cousin in Russia, Alek-

Feb[ruary] 4, 1930

[NEW YORK]

Dear Meyerhold,

Here at the Metropolitan they have gotten very interested in *The Fiery Angel* and *The Steel Gallop*. So your name has often been on people's lips.[31]

I'm sending you my interview about Soviet composers, as well as Burlyuk's gossip about you and me.[32]

Thank you for writing so often, but so far not one of your letters has reached me.

Did Pyotr Leonov come to you for the jacket I left at your place?[33] If he comes and shows you a letter from me, give it to him.

I embrace you warmly.

I kiss Zinaida Nikolaevna's little hand.

Yours, S. PRKFV

September 24, 1930

VILLA STEVENS, LA NAZE, PAR VALMONDOIS (SEINE ET OISE), FRANCE

Dear Meyerhold,

When I got back from my trip to Alsace and Vosges I went to your hotel, but they told me you'd apparently already left for Moscow. I thought you were still in Paris, since on my way from Vosges I read Lunacharsky's interview about how you and he went to the theater together.[34] The publishing house told me that before you left you picked up a copy of *Choses en soi* and the Divertisse-

---

sandr Raevsky (1887–1942). Apparently because Raevsky had studied at the St. Petersburg Lyceum, a privileged college for the nobility, he was arrested by the Soviet government in the 1920s. Beginning with his first trip back to the USSR in 1927, Prokofiev made many attempts to get him released. It seems that Prokofiev had asked Meyerhold to help him in this regard.

31. Negotiations with the Metropolitan for a production of *Fiery Angel* were unsuccessful.

32. This article was published in the Russian émigré newspaper *Russkii golos* (Russian Voice) in New York on January 8, 1930, in connection with Prokofiev's concert at Town Hall.

33. In a letter to Meyerhold written on January 25, 1930, Prokofiev instructed him to give a blue suit he had left behind in Moscow to a certain Pyotr Fyodorovich Leonov.

34. Anatoly Lunacharsky (1875–1933) was the People's Commissar of Enlightenment and a literary and cultural critic. (See also chapter 2, n. 93).

ment there; I was very glad to hear about that.[35] You are the very first person who has purchased the Divertissement, and got to see it in published form even before the composer did. Esenin's books in their festive bindings are not only at the publisher's but kept in a fireproof safe for protection. In a word, they are so well concealed that people have even forgotten that they exist.

As far as Moscow is concerned, I'm gradually changing my plans: it seems that now that I've started working on my ballet, it would be better to try to finish it, and go to Moscow in January or the beginning of February.[36] [. . .]

What are your plans? How did your children receive you? Your apartment? The theater? Moscow? The Paris newspapers mention that Oborin has signed a contract with the American impresario Hurok for next season. I was very pleased to hear this, but I just hope Levushka doesn't get caught in some form of servitude. If anything is unclear to him, have him ask me about it—I've had many years of experience in concert matters with America.[37]

I send heartfelt greetings to both of you from my wife and myself. Lina Ivanovna will write to Zinaida Nikolaevna in a few days.

Yours, S. PRKFV

January 24, 1931

5, RUE VALENTIN HAÜY, PARIS XV, FRANCE

Dear Meyerhold,

I wrote to you three months ago, but I haven't heard anything from you.

I read the account of your speech in Leningrad in which, among other things, you objected to the attacks on Prokofiev printed in *Contemporary Theater*. Which Prokofiev is this? What sort of attacks? And what is this *Contemporary Theater*? In view of the fact that there were no initials before the name Prokofiev, many people might mistake him for me, so I would like to know whether it was sufficiently clear in the artistic circles of the USSR that this was

---

35. Both of these works were published in Paris by Editions Russes, *Choses en soi* in 1928, and the Divertissement in 1930.
36. Prokofiev did not make a trip to the USSR in 1931.
37. Russian-born American impresario Sol Hurok (1888–1974) was one of the first to attempt to bring Soviet performers on tour to the United States. In the summer of 1930, it was announced that Hurok had signed a two-year contract with the Soviet government engaging numerous dancers and musicians, including the pianist Lev Oborin. The terms of the contract were never fulfilled, however, and none of the specified performers traveled to the United States at this time.

someone else. By the way, please send me this article from *Contemporary Theater*—I'd be interested in looking at it.[38]

The Paris newspapers mentioned that you had been given a better venue in which to stage your plays, and that your troupe would be celebrating its tenth anniversary in the near future.[39]

I've finished composing my ballet for the Grand Opéra, and now I'm finishing writing out the orchestration. The premiere is set for April.

I send my best regards to you and Zinaida Nikolaevna, and my wife does the same.

Yours, S. PRKFV

[January 27, 1933][40]
[CHICAGO]

Dearest Meyerhold, many greetings from Chicago. Three concerts here, including *The Gambler, The Buffoon,* and the Fifth Concerto—then I'll turn around and head eastwards, until I reach Moscow and your tender embraces.[41]

A *bientôt*
S. PRKFV

Sept. 13, 1933
VILLA FLORIANA, SAINTE-MAXIME, VAR

Dear Vsevolod Emilyevich,

Alas, alas, we are nowhere near Paris, but at the Mediterranean Sea, and will not be returning until the 25th. Let me know if we will still find you and Zin[aida] Nik[olaevna] there. I'm very disappointed. There is some consolation: at the beginning of October I'll be leaving for the USSR (with stops in Lithuania, Latvia, and Poland), where I will remain until Oct. 18. One way or

---

38. Prokofiev did not have all the information here; in fact the article was written by a certain S. I. Prokofiev, and was published in the journal *Soviet Theater*. It had nothing to do with the composer Prokofiev or his music, but Prokofiev's concern shows how sensitive he was about how he was portrayed in the Soviet press at this time.

39. Meyerhold's theater celebrated its tenth anniversary in 1931 but did not receive a new venue. Instead, the Meyerhold Theater was closed for renovations and moved into a temporary home.

40. This information was taken from the postmark.

41. Prokofiev left the USSR on December 17, 1932, then traveled to Chicago. He returned to Paris in February 1933, where he stayed until April, when he returned to the USSR for a two-month stay.

another we'll see each other soon, but I hope it will be in Paris, since we could have a good time there together.

I embrace you and kiss Zin[aida] Nik[olaevna]'s little hand.

Yours, S.P.

Write me at the address given above.

Why didn't you write me sooner, you so-and-so! You know I was in Paris until Aug.[42]

Sept. 8, 1934

MAISON SADOUL, STE. MAXIME, VAR, FRANCE

Dear Vsev[olod] Em[ilyevich],

I wanted to reply to you while you were in Carlsbad, but it turns out that I was too late.[43] I believe you're already in Moscow. I was very disturbed by your claim that I'd promised to write music for your "Boris." On the other hand, the project does sound interesting, if I could figure out how to approach it. So far I haven't figured that out, and especially with all your instruments I'm not sure how to proceed—I don't know how they would sound.[44] Drop me a line here. I embrace you and Zin[aida] Nik[olaevna].

Yours S. PRKFV

---

42. From August until October 1933, Meyerhold toured England, France, Switzerland, Austria, and Poland. Prokofiev was in the USSR from October 19 through mid-November 1933.

43. Meyerhold received medical treatment in Carlsbad in August 1934.

44. In 1936 Prokofiev did write a great deal of music for a projected production of Pushkin's historical tragedy *Boris Godunov* at Meyerhold's theater. Owing to Meyerhold's increasingly difficult political and personal problems with the Soviet cultural establishment, however, the production was never staged.

CHAPTER FIVE

Letters to Boris Asafiev

WHILE LITTLE KNOWN OUTSIDE OF RUSSIA, the composer-musicologist Boris Vladimirovich Asafiev (1884–1949) is one of the central figures in the history of Soviet music. Like Prokofiev, he was drawn to the theater from the very beginning of his career. As a composer, he was the prolific creator of no fewer than twenty-seven ballets, almost single-handedly furnishing the bulk of the repertoire to Soviet ballet companies for many decades. Probably the best known and most highly regarded of these is *The Fountain of Bakhchisarai* (1932–34), set to a libretto by Nikolai Volkov, who would later write the libretti for Prokofiev's *Cinderella* and Khachaturian's *Spartacus*. Based on an early poem by Aleksandr Pushkin, *The Fountain of Bakhchisarai* is set in an exotic Crimean kingdom and tells the story of the Khan Girei's passionate love for a Polish princess he abducts from her homeland. Saturated with the pseudo-oriental style Asafiev admired in such earlier Russian composers as Aleksandr Borodin, *The Fountain of Bakhchisarai* was one of the most popular of all Soviet ballets. Asafiev wrote several other ballets based on Pushkin: *Prisoner of the Caucasus, The Peasant Girl, The Stone Guest, Count Nulin, The Coffin Maker,* and *A Cottage in Kolomna.*

Before composing his ballets, Asafiev drew on his musicological expertise to conduct extensive research into the popular music of a particular era or locale. *The Flames of Paris* (produced at the Kirov in 1932), set in France in the period immediately following the French Revolution, includes music from the "Marseillaise," as well as fragments from the music of Lully, Gluck, Grétry, Cherubini, and others. As is evident from several of the letters translated below, Prokofiev even helped Asafiev locate relevant materials in French libraries when he was working on the ballet.

As a critic and historian of music (particularly Russian) Asafiev was no less prolific, and probably more highly regarded in the Russian musical community. Among his many books are one of the first important studies of the music of Stravinsky. *Book about Stravinsky* (1929), as well as *Russian Music from the Beginning of the Nineteenth Century* (1930) and *Musical Form as a Process*

(1930), a volume that has been described as "the single major influence on con-temporary Soviet musicological vocabulary and methodology."[1] Born and edu-cated in St. Petersburg during one of the most glorious periods in its artistic and musical history, Asafiev (often writing under his literary pseudonym, Igor Glebov) also edited and wrote for an amazing number of important journals, becoming one of the most widely respected critics of his time.

Asafiev and Prokofiev knew each other from a very early age. They studied together at St. Petersburg Conservatory, from which Asafiev graduated in 1910, having already completed his university degree. In his early days as a critic, Asafiev-Glebov was one of the first and most enthusiastic champions of Prokofiev's music. In his review of the first performance of Prokofiev's *Ugly Duckling* in 1915, Asafiev wrote insightfully: "For many people, Prokofiev is himself an ugly duckling. And who knows, perhaps that's why the ending of the tale is unsuccessful, because his transformation into a swan—the complete unfolding of his rich talent and self-knowledge—is still to come.[2]

Like others who knew Asafiev well, Prokofiev sometimes accused him of excessive fluency and dilettantism, especially as a composer. And yet Prokofiev had great respect for Asafiev and his opinions, and urged him—unfortunately unsuccessfully—to write the same sort of study of his music that he had writ-ten about Stravinsky. Asafiev followed Prokofiev's career closely, even after Prokofiev left the USSR in 1918, and continued to write about him in the Soviet press. The two composers began to correspond regularly in 1920. Well aware of Asafiev's influence in the Soviet musical establishment, Prokofiev sent him detailed, entertaining, and witty letters providing information on his own cre-ative activity and gossipy news of the musical scene in Europe and America.

A frequent traveler to Europe, Asafiev came to visit Prokofiev in France in the summer of 1928, along with Moscow Conservatory professor Pavel Lamm. Since Prokofiev and his wife Lina were living in a château near the Swiss bor-der, they took drives together to Chamonix, Lausanne, Montreux, Bern, Zurich, and Lugano. Lina later described their excursions: "Sometimes the road went through high mountain passes where we met St. Bernards with little barrels attached to their collars. Sometimes we would descend into valleys as wonder-ful as a fairy tale, then rise up again to the glaciers of the Rhone. We would

---

1.   Stanley Dale Krebs, *Soviet Composers and the Development of Soviet Music* (London: George Allen and Unwin, 1970), 88.

2.   *S. S. Prokof'ev: Materialy, dokumenty, vospominaniia*, S. I. Shlifstein, ed. (Moscow, 1961), 318.

spend the night in the most diverse spots—once on a high summit in a little hut that opened onto a magnificent view."[3]

After Prokofiev returned to Russia permanently in 1936, he and Asafiev (now a professor at Moscow and Leningrad Conservatories and the only musician named to full membership in the Soviet Academy of Sciences) remained on friendly terms. Despite the increasingly intolerant climate in Soviet culture and criticism, Asafiev continued to defend the music of Prokofiev, Miaskovsky, and Shostakovich, as well as the work of European modernists like Stravinsky and Berg.

But not even the highly respected Asafiev could escape some degree of involvement in the official assault launched on Soviet music in 1948. Already ailing and frail, Asafiev was conspicuously absent at the three-day meeting called by Stalin's cultural commissar Andrei Zhdanov in January 1948, which inaugurated a series of resolutions and conferences focusing on the "deviations" of Soviet composers. Significantly, Asafiev's name was not among those composers accused of "formalism": Shostakovich, Prokofiev, Khachaturian, and Miaskovsky. And when the First All-Union Congress of Composers was held in Moscow in April 1948, Asafiev was named to and accepted the position of Chairman of the Union of Composers. He also wrote a statement read at the Congress which has been widely considered to be a cowardly capitulation to Zhdanov's campaign of intimidation, slander, and threats. It was an unfortunate end to what had been a distinguished career, although it is difficult to know exactly how much was done in Asafiev's name without his knowledge, since he was seriously ill at the time. He died less than a year later, on January 27, 1949. Asafiev's disappearance from the scene helped to facilitate the rise of Tikhon Khrennikov, who had been named General Secretary of the Composers Union.

His ambiguous behavior in 1948 notwithstanding, Asafiev left behind a solid body of music and writings that have secured his place in Soviet culture. His advocacy of Prokofiev's challenging, bumptious music is one of the accomplishments he will always be remembered for.

(These letters were published as "Pism'a S. S. Prokof'eva-B. V. Asaf'evu [1920–1944]," a publication of M. Kozlova, in *Iz proshlogo sovetskoi muzykal'noi kul'tury*, Vol. 2 [Moscow: Sovetskii kompozitor, 1976], 4–54. Here the letters and accompanying notes have been edited. Translated into English by Eileen Fisher, Geoffrey Carlson, and Harlow Robinson.)

---

3.   Lina Prokofieva, "Iz vospominanii," *Sergei Prokof'ev 1953–63: Stat'i & materialy*, Nest'ev and Edel'man, eds. (Moscow, 1962), 184.

Sept. 1, 1920
[PARIS]

Dear Borenka,

Koussevitsky told me that you and Miaskovsky are alive and well. Pyotr Petrovich[4] is in Sofia, Nina Pavlovna[5] is on her way to New York. I'm in France and in two weeks I'll be going back to America until January. They're presenting my opera *Love for Three Oranges*[6] with considerable pomp. Write to me C/o Mlle. Jung, Conservatory, Riga. Have the papers and music in my apartment at No. 4 Pervaya Rota really perished? I had a score of my Second Concerto[7] there and masses of all sorts of letters and notebooks. If *Seven, They Are Seven* has been published as Koussevitsky said, then send me a copy. I send you kisses, my dear friend, and remember you tenderly.

Affectionately, Sergei Prokofiev

November 7, 1922
ETTAL, OBERBAYERN, DEUTSCHLAND

Dear Boris Vladimirovich,

Please answer the following two questions for me.

First: Are the manuscripts I left in my apartment on Pervaya Rota still in one piece? According to some people I know, including Eleonora Damskaya, the apartment was left empty and deserted, and the people who moved in apparently used the manuscripts as fuel with which to fry eggs. According to others (Lourié, Souvchinsky), you got to the apartment in time and carried them off in an official manner to be preserved. Which of the two stories should I believe? If the second is correct, which manuscripts do you have?

---

4.   The music critic Pyotr Souvchinsky was a publisher in 1917–18, and with Asafiev the editor of the journal anthology *Melos* in Petrograd; he emigrated in 1920. In the published letters Prokofiev often refers to him as Petya.

5.   The Russian émigré singer Nina Koshetz; Prokofiev dedicated a song cycle to her— five songs without words for voice and piano, op. 35 (1920), first performed by her and the composer in New York on March 27, 1921. (See also chapter 7.)

6.   *Love for Three Oranges,* op. 33, an opera by Prokofiev, libretto by the composer, based on a divertissement by K. A. Vogak, V. E. Meyerhold, and V. M. Solovyov after the commedia dell'arte tale of the same name by Carlo Gozzi, was first performed (after some delay) at the Chicago Opera on December 30, 1921, with the composer conducting.

7.   The original score of the Second Concerto for Piano and Orchestra in G Minor, op. 16, written in 1913, was lost. When rewriting the score in 1923, Prokofiev produced a new edition of the Second Concerto, which premiered in Paris on May 8, 1924, performed by the composer under the direction of Serge Koussevitsky.

My second question:

Would I be able to get the score of *The Gambler* from the Mariinsky Theater Library? This score is the property of the theater. The original manuscript seems to have been destroyed during the civil unrest, or, if it wasn't destroyed, God knows where it ended up. In the meantime I've used the piano score to plan a number of substantial changes in the opera, and would very much like to get to work on them. I don't think the Mariinsky Theater has any basis for refusing to give me my score, and in any case I'll do everything I can to make sure *The Gambler* does not get produced in the original version—that would only cause harm to the project.[8] So the sooner I could start making these changes to the score, the better. Souvchinsky discussed this topic with E. A. Cooper in Berlin, and he replied that he didn't have anything against giving me the score, but that it all somehow depended on you and on Ekskuzovich.[9] So: can I get it or not? If Cooper needs any scores from Koussevitsky's publishing house, I'd be glad to get them in exchange for the score of *The Gambler*. It should be delivered to Berlin or to Souvchinsky:

Herrn P. Suwtschinsky, bei Frau Kriwan,

Potsdamerstrasse 23, Portal 5, BERLIN Sudende.

Or to:

Russicher Musikverlag, Dessauerstr. 17, Berlin, SW.

But it must not get lost on the way, so it must be sent either with someone you trust or by diplomatic courier.

Please let me know your answer, because my plans for future work depend on the "gambling" question.

I greatly enjoyed reading your new book,[10] which Eleonora Damskaya sent

---

8. *The Gambler*, op. 24, an opera by Prokofiev, libretto by the composer, is based on the novella of the same name by Fyodor Dostoyevsky. The opera was written at the request of the Mariinsky Theater, where preparations for its production began in October 1916. After the February Revolution of 1917, budget and administrative difficulties in the theater led to a decision to produce the opera without scenery. However, this project was not realized either, and in May 1917 *The Gambler* was removed from the theater's repertory plans.

9. E. A. Cooper was the chief director of the Mariinsky State Academic Theater of Opera and Ballet 1919–21, and in 1921 he became the artistic director of the Petrograd Philharmonic as well (he emigrated in 1924); Asafiev managed a theater library where the piano score and the full score of *The Gambler* were kept. I. V. Ekskuzovich was the director of the Petrograd (after 1924, Leningrad) Academic Theaters 1918–28.

10. B. V. Asafiev (I. Glebov), *Symphonic Etudes* (St. Petersburg, 1922).

me, and I was glad to hear from her that *The Buffoon* was to your liking.[11] I hope you've already received the second part of the work, which I sent to Eleonora via Riga. I've recently been in correspondence with Derzhanovsky, who seems to be rising together with his *Music*.[12] He sent me a package of Miaskovsky's compositions, but I haven't had a chance to look at them. I'll be staying in Bavaria for the winter, and the above address is good until spring. I hope you'll drop me a line, and in the meantime, I send you hugs and kisses and hope you're in the best of health.

Affectionately, S. Prokofiev

July 9, 1924
VILLA BÉTHANIE, ST. GILLES-SUR-VIE, VENDÉE, FRANCE

Dear Boris Vladimirovich,

I got a long business letter from Gauk dealing with the production of *The Gambler* and *The Buffoon*.[13] I'm enclosing my response to him. Please read it and send it on to Gauk. What I've written in this letter about *The Buffoon* is the official version. Privately, I'm adding the following for you.

I've written a suite from *The Buffoon* which incorporates three-fourths of the ballet music. The suite consists of 12 movements and lasts 35 minutes. The Mariinsky Theater could produce an excellent ballet with this suite; they'd have to change the plot a little, since there will be some pieces missing, but I have nothing against such a change, especially if the choreographer is sensitive and talented. The score of the suite has been published, the material has been lithographed, and both can be rented from my publisher. You need to apply to Eberg at the address I gave in my letter to Gauk. This Eberg, who is my repre-

---

11. *Tale of a Fool Who Outsmarted Seven Others* (*The Buffoon*), op. 21, was a ballet by Prokofiev, revised in 1920 (first edition, 1915), with a libretto by the composer, and based on two tales from *Collection of Russian Tales* by A. N. Afanasyev. The ballet was written at the request of Diaghilev. In 1922 the author wrote a twelve-movement symphonic suite from *The Buffoon*, op. 21-bis.

12. V. V. Derzhanovsky, critic and musician, was the editor and publisher of the magazine *Music* (*Muzyka*), published in Moscow 1910–16; from 1924 until 1929 Derzhanovksy was the editor of the magazine *Contemporary Music* (*Sovremennaia Muzyka*). (See also chapter 2, n. 9.)

13. At the initiative of director A. V. Gauk, negotiations were renewed for productions of *The Gambler* and *The Buffoon* at the Mariinsky State Theater of Opera and Ballet, but they were unsuccessful.

sentative,[14] can arrange the conditions of my author's fee with the theater, thus leaving me out of the matter. In view of my contract with Diaghilev, I can't write any of this officially, but I'm telling you as a friend, counting on your diplomatic abilities.

Please tell Gruber I got his letter with his description of the concert of my compositions, and I'll answer him soon. Right now I'm sitting in the country at the seashore and working on a short ballet, which B. Romanov[15] will produce this fall in Paris. I'm writing the ballet for an orchestra of five musicians: oboe, clarinet, violin, viola, and double bass. It could also be performed at chamber concerts as a quintet, since it consists of six totally complete movements, one of them a theme with variations.[16] So far none of my other compositions has been published; as soon as anything does come out, I'll send it to you right away. Koussevitsky performed *Seven, They Are Seven* in Paris in May, and *they* were very successful.[17]

I send you a big kiss. I hope you'll write me soon. Thanks for the notice about the concert of my music (in *New Music*).[18] I enjoyed it very much.

Affectionately, S. Prokofiev.

Dec. 2, 1924
54, ROUTE DES GARDES, BELLEVUE, SEINE ET OISE, FRANCE
Dear Boris Vladimirovich,

Your custom of writing to me only once a year is rather capricious and not very nice. I yield to it reluctantly, but nevertheless I would remind you that it's already been nearly a year since your last letter, so be true at least to yourself

---

14. E. A. Eberg was the director of Editions Russes and Gutheil publishers until 1925.
15. Boris Romanov, who emigrated in 1921, was a dancer and ballet master of the Mariinsky Theater 1909–21; in 1924 he headed the "Romantic Theater," a small touring ballet troupe.
16. *Trapeze* was the name of a ballet produced by Boris Romanov to music by Prokofiev, who included it in the list of his compositions as a Quintet for Oboe, Clarinet, Violin, Viola, and Double Bass in G Minor, op. 39. In addition to the music of the Quintet, Prokofiev wrote two other numbers for the ballet.
17. The premiere of *Seven, They Are Seven* took place on May 29, 1924.
18. A brochure was published for the "New Music" concert series, organized by the Russian Institute of Art History; one of these concerts (May 16, 1924) consisted of works by Prokofiev. This brochure contained concert programs and articles by Asafiev: *New Music*, Leningrad, 1924, 1st ed.

and take your pen between your fingers. No, seriously, my dear friend, I'm very sad that you indulge me so rarely with your letters—Miaskovsky is better than you; he and I correspond regularly. Do you want the very latest news, which you may not even know? He's writing his Fourth Sonata in three movements.

As for me, I'm tinkering with a symphony; I've already finished most of the music, and I plan to sit down and orchestrate it soon.[19] My publisher hasn't published any new works of mine for a long time, but by New Year's they'll publish my Fifth Sonata[20] and the pocket orchestral scores of the *Buffoon* suite, which I'll send you as soon as I get the author's copies.

Gauk wrote to me this summer that the Mariinsky Theater is planning to produce *The Gambler*. For this reason I sent him a long explanation on September 26, dealing mostly with how to settle affairs with my publisher. I never got an answer to this letter; either it got lost, or Gauk's response got lost, or they decided not to produce *The Gambler*, but in that case they should have informed me. [. . .]

I send you a big kiss and I hope to receive a missive from you, otherwise I'll have to get news of you secondhand: either through Souvchinsky or through *Musical Culture*, where I read your articles[21]—I've found many valuable ideas in them, but my, how densely expressed!

Affectionately, S. Prokofiev.

Feb. 8, 1925
54, ROUTE DES GARDES, BELLEVUE, S. ET O., FRANCE

Dear Boris Vladimirovich,

I'm sending you my Fifth Sonata, which just came out. I look forward to hearing what you think of it. Thank you for your December letter. You answered me so quickly then that I thought it wasn't a response, but simply that our letters had crossed somewhere around Verzhbolov.

Stravinsky's concerto[22] is a continuation of the line he adopted in the finale of his Octet—that is, a stylization in imitation of Bach—which I don't approve

---

19. Prokofiev refers to his two-movement Second Symphony in D Minor, op. 40, first performed in Paris on June 6, 1925, conducted by Koussevitsky.

20. Fifth Sonata for Piano in C Major, op. 38, written by Prokofiev in 1923.

21. *Musical Culture* (*Muzykal'naia Kul'tura*) was a monthly journal that appeared in Moscow in 1924.

22. Concerto for Piano and Wind Instruments, written by Stravinsky in 1923–24, was first performed by the composer under the direction of Koussevitsky in Paris on May 22, 1924.

of, because even though I love Bach and think it's not a bad idea to compose according to his principles, it's not a good idea to produce a stylized version of his style. Therefore I don't regard this concerto as highly as, say, *Les Noces* or *The Rite of Spring*; and in general, I don't think very highly of things like *Pulcinella* or even my own "Classical" Symphony (sorry, I wasn't thinking of this when I dedicated it to you), which are written "under the influence" of something else. Unfortunately, Stravinsky thinks otherwise; he doesn't see this as a case of "monkey see, monkey do," and now he's written a piano sonata in the same style.[23] He even thinks this will create a new era. It looks like the sonata will be coming out soon; I'll send it to you then, and you can write and tell me your impressions of it, of Stravinsky's concerto, the Octet finale and in general of the aesthetic line Stravinsky has adopted.

So, what has happened with *The Gambler*? And really, how about it—my original manuscript of the score is lying around somewhere in the state theater library. It's my property, after all, and I'd like to have it, but of course would not want to trust it to the mails. but would like to have it delivered by someone who's coming here in person. Is this possible, and is the management inclined to give it to me? How did the December 11 concert go, the one at which my compositions were performed? Why, for example, didn't Gruber write to me about it? When Gruber was visiting me, he took great pains to express his enthusiasm for my music, but when it came to writing, he couldn't tell me about anything that really interested me! I'm working on the orchestration of the symphony; I'm working as hard as I can, but because of the complexity, it's going at a snail's pace. You write, "But the main thing is, how is *The Fiery Angel* coming along?"[24] It's exactly for the sake of that "main thing" that I'd now like to coerce you a bit. If you think *The Fiery Angel* is to some extent the main thing, then I need a certain favor from you.

The Fiery Angel has been completed, but not yet orchestrated. The reason is, I'd like to clean up a few spots in the piano score beforehand, where I'm not totally sure from the dramatic point of view. Remembering what brilliant service Demchinsky rendered to me when writing the libretto of the roulette scene in *The Gambler* (he has a wonderful dramatic sense), I sent him my libretto of *The Fiery Angel* so he could take a look at it. Demchinsky swore and promised that he'd be "delighted" to make a few changes, especially since he had a lot of

23. Prokofiev refers to the Sonata for Piano written by Stravinsky in 1924.
24. *The Fiery Angel*, op. 37, is an opera in five acts by Prokofiev (1919–27), libretto by the composer, based on the novel of the same name by Valery Bryusov.

material on medieval subject matter. But it's been a year and a half already, I've bombarded him with letters and still I haven't gotten any response—so I still haven't begun the orchestration. Demchinsky is a complex person: his indisputably Christian soul is not without its Mephistophelean nooks and crannies. It seems that he can't forgive me for my successes, thinking they don't correspond with the rather petty soul I possess. Perhaps you don't totally agree; if that's the case, please go to Demchinsky, talk to him and find out whether he intends to make the promised changes and why he hasn't given me an answer to my interrogations—although he knew I needed one. You met him at my place, and even though you two didn't talk much, I know he gets along well with you. I also know you're a mimosa and it will be very difficult for you to do this, but for the sake of *The Fiery Angel*, please do it anyway! His name is Boris Nikolaevich; his address: Mozhaiskaya, 7, Apt. 6. As soon as I get the corrections from him, which I'm sure will be quite inventive, I'll get down to finishing and orchestrating *The Fiery Angel*, and if Demchinsky doesn't take too long, my opera will get off the ground by autumn. The next move is yours.

I'm expecting *Love for Three Oranges* to be performed on March 14 in Cologne, and it looks like it will be produced with great pomp. They were supposed to produce it on Christmas, but it turned out to be more complex than they expected. I saw Souvchinsky in Berlin. He's planning to part with Deutschland and move to Bellevue, and of course I'm very happy about that.

I send you hugs and kisses. I look forward to your answer. Remember: 1) the Fifth Sonata, 2) *The Gambler*, 3) *The Fiery Angel*. Look at how I'm exploiting your busy time! Don't be angry and forgive me.

Affectionately, S. Prokofiev

March 21, 1925
54, ROUTE DES GARDES, BELLEVUE, S. ET O., FRANCE

Dear Boris Vladimirovich,

The other day I returned from Cologne, where the premiere of *Three Oranges* took place on March 14. In general the Rhiners outdid themselves and staged a fine production: both the director and the producer worked with a great deal of love and talent. The public received it well, but the press received it even better, especially the Berlin press, which came to Cologne for the premiere; it was full of praise and demands that my operas be produced in Berlin.

Here the questions again arise about *The Fiery Angel* and *The Gambler*, about which I wrote to you in my previous registered letter (February 8), and to which I still haven't gotten a response. I'm waiting for your answer, and you can understand how important this is to me. Have you seen Demchinsky? Did you find out what he thinks about sending the libretto of *The Fiery Angel* back to me? You must understand: I don't want to send just anyone to Demchinsky, for example someone like Gruber or Damskaya; I need someone to talk to him who is intelligent and subtle and who sincerely believes in the significance of what I'm doing. Demchinsky promised a long time ago to make corrections, additions, and embellishments to my libretto, but it's been over a year already and there's no way I can find out from him why he hasn't sent me anything. If you manage to speak with him, his reply might be quite unexpected, such as: "Prokofiev is too cerebral and rigid, I can't force myself to work with him." Or: "Prokofiev is nothing but bravura; let him suffer." Maybe he'll just turn out to be a very appealing lazybones and spin out a pile of strange details for you concerning black magic of the sixteenth century. You ask me why I have focused particularly upon him? Because I remember our collaboration on the roulette scene in *The Gambler*, work in which he proved himself to be a great expert, an ingenious individual gifted with deep analytical powers. So in memory of that very successful roulette scene, I'd like to finish my *The Fiery Angel* libretto with him now as well.

Since I haven't gotten a yes or no from him, I'm asking you to go to him and find out how I am to understand his silence: if yes, then when? If no, then I'll be very disappointed and I'll have to do something else—but it's time to get *The Fiery Angel* off the ground. So the sooner you see Demchinsky and send me his answer, the more grateful I'll be to you.

The second question: has the management of the Mariinsky Theater agreed to give me my manuscript of the full score of *The Gambler*, a manuscript that is my personal property and ended up in the theater library only by chance? (The theater has its own copy, which was made in 1916.) I've been trying to attain this goal for three years, both through you and through Gauk, who claimed to be the head of the library, but then fell silent. Then I made a request through someone else, but I still can't get an answer. Be a friend, find out and let me know. If yes, I'll try to arrange it so you can have it delivered by someone who's coming this way.

I'm sure I can count on your help in these two matters, and that your good intentions towards my music and towards me are not just limited to sometimes playing my compositions on the piano! Be sure to write to me. I've also ordered a pocket score of the orchestral suite from *The Buffoon* to be sent to you. It will probably clear up some of the spots that seem ridiculous in the ballet's piano score. By the way, Monteux will be going to Moscow soon, and he'll give you the suite.[25]

I send you hugs and kisses. I very much look forward to your letter.

Yours, S. Prokofiev

By the way, I suggested to Demchinsky that he specify a fee for adapting the libretto, but he hasn't given me any response to this proposal.

April 30, 1925
BELLEVUE

Dear Boris Vladimirovich,

Demchinsky has agreed to get to work on *The Fiery Angel* immediately, and I was extremely pleased about this. I believe this was the work of your hands, and therefore I'm very grateful to you. Thank you also for the article about the Third Concerto[26]—I fear that my symphony won't measure up to the high standards you have prescribed for me. And why haven't you written me about the Fifth Sonata? After all, wasn't the article "Seconds" in the same issue written by you? How cleverly that fellow managed to squirm out of evaluating the finale! Now I'm working like a madman on my symphony, which I hope to finish soon.

I send you kisses. Yours, S. Prok[ofiev]

May 23, 1925
BELLEVUE

Dear Boris Vladimirovich,

I got your letters of May 7 and 12, and I was extremely pleased by your praise for my Third Concerto, Fifth Sonata, and *The Buffoon*. I finished my symphony the other day, to my great relief, and it will be performed on June 6 in Paris under Koussevitsky. Unlike my Third Concerto, it is chromatic and ponderous, but this doesn't mean that I've bid farewell to diatonic music for the future. In its form the symphony is similar to the last sonata of Beethoven: a somber first

25. The first performances of Prokofiev's symphonic suite *The Buffoon* took place in Moscow on February 21 and in Leningrad on March 3, 1926; they were directed by the French conductor Pierre Monteux, who was touring in the USSR.

26. The Third Concerto for Piano and Orchestra in C Major, op. 26, was written by Prokofiev in 1917–21. The article by Asafiev appeared in *Contemporary Music*, No. 19 (1925), pp. 57–63.

movement, and a theme and variations for the second and final movements. I have my "Classical" Symphony with me for proofreading, and the piano score of my Second Concerto is being engraved, but none of this will be finished before autumn. Stravinsky's sonata will be out any day now, and I'll send it to you then. I'll send you my report on the new music in a month, as there will be a series of new pieces coming out in late May and June: piano concertos by Honegger and Tailleferre, some American pieces, Auric's ballet *Les Matelots*, and *Zéphire et Flore* by Dukelsky,[27] an extremely talented Russian composer "discovered" by Diaghilev, etc.

I would be extremely pleased if you wrote a book about me, and I'm certain that my publishing house would be glad to publish it, probably even with translations into other languages. But I wouldn't feel very comfortable suggesting a book about myself, so I entrusted Souvchinsky—who is here now—to discuss this with Koussevitsky and Eberg, presenting the matter as though you had written to him (Souvchinsky) about this. For your part, write to Ernest Aleksandrovich Eberg immediately, without delay, while Koussevitsky is still in Paris, because in the final analysis, they will make the ultimate decision. [. . .]

Affectionately, S. Prokofiev

I'll be publishing my Sinfonietta[28] and *Autumnal*,[29] but not right away, because I still have my symphony, the orchestral suite from *Oranges*, the orchestral score of my Second Concerto, my quintet, etc. waiting in line. At this rate my *Dreams*[30] will be published as an *oeuvre posthum* or in my old age, by which time I will have nothing left to write, and nothing left to publish!

I'll be leaving Bellevue on June 1, so write to this address:

Serge Prokofieff
C/o Guaranty Trust Co.,
3, rue des Italiens, Paris IX.

---

27. The ballets *Les Matelots* by the French composer Georges Auric and *Zéphire et Flore* by the Russian émigré composer V. A. Dukelsky (Vernon Duke) were performed by Diaghilev's company in 1925; the premiere of the latter took place in Monte Carlo on January 31, 1925.

28. The Sinfonietta in A Major was written by Prokofiev in 1909; in 1914–15 the composer wrote a new edition, and the Sinfonietta was included in his list of compositions as op. 5; in 1929 the third edition appeared with substantial changes and the addition of a new opus number, 48.

29. *Autumnal*, a symphonic sketch for small orchestra, op. 8, was written in 1910; Prokofiev returned to it twice, writing a second edition in 1915 and a third in 1934.

30. *Dreams*, a symphonic portrait for large orchestra, op. 6, was written by Prokofiev in 1910.

June 6, 1925
32, RUE CASSETTE, PARIS VI

Dear Boris Vladimirovich,

I didn't get your airmail letter until the 4th; part of the problem was that I'm no longer in Bellevue, but in Paris, at the above address, where I'll be staying until July 1. I was sincerely delighted with your offer to perform *Oranges*. I fully agree that *Oranges* should be performed, rather than *The Gambler*. Give my regards to Dranishnikov;[31] I remember him with love and would be glad if he would drop me a line. I met Radlov fifteen years ago at a chess tournament. Yesterday I sent you a telegram with a summary of my conditions. I would like a thousand dollars for a season. [. . .]

I am also now writing to the Berlin office of our publishing house, asking them to send the piano score of *Oranges* to you personally, free of charge. I hope that this production will really come off; your artistic leadership should guarantee that these *Oranges* would be performed marvelously. Who has been chosen to design the scenery? I send you a big kiss and thank you for your concern about my offspring.[32] Today my symphony is being performed for the first time. But I'll tell you about that in my next letter.

Affectionately, S. Prokofiev

I sent you a registered letter on May 23. Have you really still been unable to get hold of Demchinsky?!

June 24, 1925
32, RUE CASSETTE, PARIS VI

Dear Boris Vladimirovich,

Your opinion is the most important thing to me, and therefore if you recommend that I accept these conditions [for production of *Love for Three Oranges*], then I accept them. [. . .]

But who will be designing the scenery? Give Dranishnikov my thanks for his long letter. I'll answer him in a week or two, as soon as I can get a little time off

---

31. Vladimir Aleksandrovich Dranishnikov (1893–1939) was appointed chief conductor at the Mariinsky Theater in 1925.

32. Negotiations for the production of Prokofiev's opera *Love for Three Oranges* at the State Academic Theater of Opera and Ballet (now known as the Kirov) were successful. The producer was S. E. Radlov, the designer was V. V. Dmitriev, the conductor was V. A. Dranishnikov; the premiere took place on February 18, 1926.

from my business matters. At the same time I'll send you a review of the new pieces I've heard this spring. The most interesting one for me was Dukelsky's ballet *Zéphire et Flore*, performed by Diaghilev. Diaghilev commissioned a second ballet from him for next season.[33] I will also be writing a ballet for Diaghilev.[34] Most people were horrified by my symphony, although there are a number of ardent admirers; other admirers are bemoaning my demise. In any case the piece is cumbersome and complex.

As for my biography for the small anthology,[35] you probably have my early biography, and the first half of my biography of my years abroad appeared in Derzhanovsky's magazine *Toward New Shores* in May 1923 in the form of my letter to the editor;[36] you know about the latest events from your correspondence with me. Do I need to give you all this material again? Tell me more precisely what you would like from me. As for the large book, Souvchinsky conducted successful negotiations with Eberg and should have written to you or will be writing to you in a few days. If you want to send him a letter, you would do better to send it in care of my name.

Demchinsky is unbearable. What an unbalanced person he is! The Berlin State Opera[37] offered to perform *The Fiery Angel*, but because Demchinsky didn't respond, I couldn't sign the contract. This was quite a nuisance, although I will try to force *Oranges* through instead of *Fiery Angel*. I sincerely respect your busy schedule, but the first time you have a free evening, please find the time to talk with this person. Forgive me for my importunity, but there's no one who can do this better than you. Stravinsky's sonata will be coming out in a few days, and I'll send it to you then. I don't like it. [. . .]

I send you hugs and kisses. Forgive me for the telegraphic style of this letter.
                              Affectionately, S. Prokofiev

---

33. Diaghilev's company performed only one ballet by V. A. Dukelsky—*Zéphire et Flore*.
34. In 1925, at Diaghilev's commission, Prokofiev wrote his ballet *The Steel Gallop*, op. 41, libretto by G. B. Yakoulov and the composer. It was performed by Diaghilev's theater company and the premiere took place in Paris on June 7, 1927.
35. "Sergei Prokofiev," an essay by Igor Glebov (Asafiev) in the *Contemporary Composers* series, was published in 1927 by the Tritone Publishing House, Leningrad.
36. *Toward New Shores*, No. 2 (1923).
37. The state opera—*Staatsoper* in German; in the following letters Prokofiev writes "*Staatsoper*" in Cyrillic.

8/14/1925
BOURRON-MARLOTTE, SEINE ET MARNE, FRANCE

Dear Boris Vladimirovich,

I didn't answer your letter of July 17th right away because I was waiting for the *Oranges* contract for the Mariinsky Theater to be signed so that I could tell you about it; I was also waiting for a letter from Demchinsky. However, Demchinsky has not written, and the contract has still not been signed. You know, Ekskuzovich and I met up in Paris. He was pleasant, affectionate, even lyrical, and at times melodramatic. He said that the matter of the staging of *Oranges* at the Mariinsky Theater had been definitely resolved, and even that another production of it was possible at the Bolshoi Theater[38] this year. Above all, he was very interested in *The Buffoon* and *The Gambler*. He himself began the discussion about *The Gambler*, asking whether I would be very distressed if he presented it in its first version. I replied that it would be regrettable to present the opera in a bad light when it is possible to present it in a good one; in this case our interests coincide, since the revision has been focused on eliminating the rough edges in the vocal parts, harmony, and orchestration. He then promised that upon his return to Leningrad, he would search out with you the piano score of *The Gambler* and send it to me through the embassy, with the condition that I promise the first production of the opera to the Mariinsky Theater for the 1926–1927 season. This conversation seemed to considerably widen the scope of my possible dealings with the academic theaters. What kind of antireligious minstrelry in *The Buffoon* are you talking about? Of course I have no intention of tolerating any such insertions or tendencies. Ekskuzovich also agrees that they are unnecessary. Regarding *Oranges* he said that the contract would probably be signed soon in Berlin, where a branch of my publisher is empowered to sign both for the publisher and for me.

Allow me to thank you again for making possible the arrangements for "Oranges à la Leningrad," since I am fully aware that 99 percent of the effort and propaganda was your doing. I hope that his matter can be called decisively settled, since I don't see how anything could now prevent the signing of the contract. And so, I give you a big hug for *Oranges*, but have to berate you for *Fiery Angel*.

You write that Demchinsky is a lunatic. Agreed. But what about you, are you any better? I asked Demchinsky to work on the libretto more than a year ago

---

38. Prokofiev's opera *Love for Three Oranges* was first performed at the Bolshoi Theater in Moscow on May 19, 1927.

but he zigzags around it. Yet I also asked you to go and see Demchinsky almost a year ago. He's not a beast, but a courteous fellow human, a charmer, in fact a fan of yours to boot. But you also zigzag around. Instead of simply going to his place on Mozhaiskaya Street and resolving the matter in a snap, after much evasion you finally decide to crouch in the corner and throw stones. I have no doubt that your letter was a heavy stone, but don't forget, the heavier the stone, the more likely it is to miss the target. You yourself admitted that you barely know Demchinsky, and for that reason could not write to him freely. The result is this: I have not heard a word from him. Have you?

I already wrote that this foot-dragging has managed to sink the proposed production of *Fiery Angel* at the *Staatsoper* in Berlin, where it was being considered for the upcoming season. Fortunately, I managed to insert *Oranges* in place of *Fiery Angel*—and now *they* have been accepted. This is a great victory, especially since the *Staatsoper* promised to take *Fiery Angel* for next season if *Oranges* is successful. But can it really be possible that this accursed libretto problem has not moved along even a single step? Or will I get a letter: "Dear Seryozha, while I sincerely love your music and am particularly interested in *Fiery Angel*, I am still avoiding any discussion with Demchinsky." Yet if you realize the total Jesuit-ness of a letter like that, then how long will you still feed me these sweet evasions, which have left me licking my chops for more than a year now?

I'm sending you an overview of the Paris spring season.[39] Derzhanovsky asked me about it, too. Could you send him a copy? Or write him an article yourself on the basis of my material? I would prefer the latter, because otherwise I would have to send him the material not as an article, but just as anonymous material for somebody else's article. In any case, I won't send anything until I hear from you. I'm also sending you an outline of my musical life since the *Autobiography*; it appeared in *New Shores* and you can use it for your brochure. As far as the book about me is concerned, you yourself understand that I am uncomfortable talking about this with Eberg myself, so I fobbed it off on Souvchinsky, who now lives in Paris: 42, rue Mazarine, Paris VI, France. He spoke with Eberg, got him interested, and then wrote to you. Did you get his letter? Since you haven't written anything about it, and since Souvchinsky wrote to you at the beginning of July, I worry that it got lost. So I ask you to write to Souvchinsky immediately concerning this matter. I very much want your book to be written and published.

---

39. Prokofiev's survey "Paris, Spring Season 1925" was published in the collection *De Musica* (Leningrad, 1925).

Are you in possession of Stravinsky's Octet? If not, then I will send it to you. Along with it I will send Auric's *Les Matelots*. Dukelsky's *Zéphire* will be printed by our publisher, and therefore will not be out very soon. My Second Concerto, which I will also send, will come out in September.

I am now writing a new ballet commissioned by Diaghilev. Romanov is now rehearsing a chamber ballet, a quintet in six parts to which two parts will have to be added to make a complete ballet. [. . .] Romanov will present my chamber ballet (the name is still under discussion) in Berlin, then will tour Germany and Switzerland with it, and show it in Paris in the springtime. My Second Symphony has not yet been published; I want to hear it through one more time. Dorliak never came to me. I saw B. B. Krasin,[40] who wants me for ten concerts, three in Leningrad, three in Moscow, two in Kharkov, and two in Rostov, and who promised various passport conveniences, such as entrance and exit visas—guaranteeing the latter without any difficulties. I am very drawn to Russia, but it is unlikely that this will take place any earlier than autumn of next year.[41] [. . .]

Affectionately, S. Prokofiev

9/12/1925

BOURRON-MARLOTTE, SEINE ET MARNE, FRANCE

Dear Boris Vladimirovich,

Yesterday I once again had a talk with the publisher, a definitive discussion of your book about me. The house wants to print it, paying you a fee rather than a percentage, and now awaits your word as to the size of the work and your fee. The publisher also asked me to tell you that it is interested in your work in general, and that if you had anything else in mind you wish to publish, you should let them know. (If you like, you can do this through me.)

My Second Symphony was raked over the coals at length by the French press, although they admitted that they couldn't understand it at all. Now a detailed and flattering article by Marnold[42] has appeared, who borrowed my piano score and sat analyzing it for two weeks. If you need this article for your research, I will send it to you.

Hugs and kisses. Write!

Affectionately, S. Prkfv.

---

40. B. B. Krasin headed the musical department of Narkompros of the Russian Soviet Republic and in 1925 directed the Russian Philharmonic Society.

41. Prokofiev's first trip to the USSR after his departure from Russia in 1918 was in 1927 (January 18–March 20).

42. Marnold's article appeared in the French weekly *Mercure de France* on September 5, 1925.

Jan. 18, 1926
SAN FRANCISCO

Dear B[oris] V[ladimirovich], as you can see, I've made it to the end of the world,[43] playing my own compositions and something of Miaskovsky,[44] in whom they are beginning to show some interest here, especially after the success of his Fifth Symphony in New York.[45] I plan on sending you a long letter in the near future; in the meantime, I send you hugs and kisses.

SP

March 26, 1926
FRANKFURT

Dear Boris Vladimirovich,

On my way through Paris I received your two letters. I was incredibly happy over the success of *Oranges* and thank you for your labors. I've waited ten years to see my opera on the Mariinsky Theater stage, and when it was finally produced, the fates decreed that I should be on the other side of the globe. I also received Dranishnikov's dispatch, and will answer him tomorrow. But accounts of a different nature have also been leaking out to me: it seems that many do not find *Oranges* entirely to their liking, and that they even want to remove it from the repertory altogether. How much truth is there in this? The brochure about *Oranges* was very nice; there was only one thing that was bad and which astonished me—my completely insolent tone in my autobiography; I was ashamed to read it.[46]

The publisher has sent or will soon send you the "Classical" Symphony, a proofread copy, it seems. They request that, for heaven's sake, you not give it to anyone to copy and that you not let it out of your sight. I also sent you Dukelsky's concerto. It is earlier than *Zéphire*, and not as good, but it is interesting all the same. I'll send you *Zéphire* soon, as well as Stravinsky's Serenade for

43. In January and February 1926 Prokofiev toured the United States.

44. On his solo tour of America in 1926 Prokofiev performed, along with his own compositions, Miaskovsky's piano pieces nos. 1, 4, 5, and 6 from the cycle *Caprices*.

45. Miaskovsky's Fifth Symphony in D Minor, op. 18, was performed in New York by the Philadelphia Orchestra conducted by Leopold Stokowski on January 5, 1926, and in Philadelphia on January 2 and 4.

46. The publisher Academia of the State Institute of Art History published a brochure called "Sergei Prokofiev and His Opera *Love for Three Oranges*" in 1926.

P[ia]n[o]. I have not heard anything about a pocket score of the new edition of *Firebird*, in any event it is not being done by our publisher, but when I see Stravinsky I will ask him about it and write to you or send it to you. No interesting music books have popped into view lately. No interesting American composers are in sight either. The Americ[an] press wrote frivolously about me, nothing worth sending to you. [. . .]

I send you a big kiss. Write to me at Paris, as in the past.

Yours, S. Prokofiev

Apr. 5, 1926
ROME

Dear Boris Vladimirovich,

I'm sending you my holiday greetings from Rome, where I am performing on the seventh and ninth. I received the proposal for your book—I thank you and send hugs.

Yours, S. Prkfv.

May 28, 1926
[PARIS]

Dear Boris Vladimirovich,

I received your letters of Apr. 26 and May 10, forgive me for sending such a short answer—I'm horribly busy. Mid-June I move to the dacha outside Fontainebleau; then I will have a little free time. The Cl[assical] Symphony, as it turns out, has still not been sent to you—there were no available copies, but now they've got a batch, and will send it soon, albeit on bad paper. The publisher requests that I remind you that this is exclusively for your own personal use, and that you are not to let it be copied or even to let it out of your house. Along with the symphony, they are sending you Dukelsky's *Zéphire* and Stravinsky's Serenade for P[ia]n[o]. The suite from *Firebird* really does exist, but at an English publishing house. I will get it and send it, and will also write to Vienna so that they send something of Rieti's. [. . .]

Diaghilev has postponed my ballet until next season. He put on ballets by Rieti and the Englishman Lambert.[47] The first was nice, although a little like Rossini; the second was bad—even Russian influence could not rescue it. My Second Symphony was performed in Paris on May 6 after seven rehearsals. It

47. Prokofiev was referring to the ballets *Barabau* by the Italian composer Vittorio Rieti and *Romeo and Juliet* by Constant Lambert.

came out more clearly, but there still hasn't been an authentic performance. Nonetheless, many musicians did bow and scrape before me, atoning to some extent for their lack of understanding last year. I decided to make a few more repairs and send it out to be printed.

Those who've arrived from Russia—Monteux, Marsheks, Milhaud, Venier—have praised the production of *Oranges*. The last two were in ecstasy over you in particular; they say you are the most interesting person of all those they saw in the USSR. Yavorsky and Meyerhold are in Paris and are urging me to come to Russia—and I feel like going myself. I'm planning, vaguely, perhaps on doing that in January or February. Sabaneyev is hanging around; he tried making the rounds to see me, Koussevitsky, and Souvchinsky, but without much success; he looks quite pitiful.[48]

I send warm hugs. Write to me at Guaranty Trust. What do you think of Dukelsky's concerto?

Affectionately, S. Prokofiev

August 9, 1926
SAMOREAU, SEINE ET MARNE, FRANCE

Dear Boris Vladimirovich,

I received your postcard of June 22 and your letter of July 13. Excuse me for not writing for so long, I have been very busy of late with the finishing touches and orchestration of my opera, and writing an overture commissioned by an American chamber orchestra. The orchestra consists of seventeen players: flute, oboe, two clarinets, bassoon, two trumpets, trombone, percussion, celesta, two harps, two pianos, cello, and two double basses.[49]

It was very interesting to read through your comments on contemporary music, although, it seems, you give it more significance than it deserves. In Italy, for example, there is no one besides Rieti, absolutely nobody, and even Rieti turned out to be highly insignificant in his new ballet, *Barabau*, which was produced by Diaghilev this season. In England there is absolutely nothing to speak of, but at least Diaghilev with his keen sense of smell managed to sniff out the young Lambert, although he has turned out to be a pitiful rehash of

---

48. Leonid Sabaneyev (1881–1968) was a musicologist, composer, and critic who emigrated from Russia in 1926. In 1916 he became notorious for writing a negative review of a performance of Prokofiev's *Scythian Suite* that had been scheduled but never took place.

49. Overture for Chamber Orchestra in B Minor, op. 42, written by Prokofiev in 1926; in 1928 he created a version for symphony orchestra.

Pulcinella. I know very little of Hindemith, I heard his Concerto for Orchestra conducted by Koussevitsky in June—the music was forceful and intentionally devoid of beauty. But then one "listen" is not enough. Concerning Sasha Tcherepnin, you are right in the sense that he does overindulge in pouring material from one empty vessel into another, but not long ago I saw his piece for violin, flute and small orchestra, and it seemed very interesting to me. I'll send it to you if I have the opportunity. I think you have undervalued Dukelsky. His ballet is undoubtedly superior to the concerto; after all, it was written later. And of course Auric's influence played no role whatsoever here. I'll send you Stravinsky's Serenade. I admit that I have still have not figured out what motivated him to write it the way he did. I am wary about taking him to task, since Stravinsky has so often deceived us, and what seems ugly at first glance has become interesting with the passage of time. But the paucity of melody is obvious immediately.

I will send you some notes about my pre-American period under separate cover in the near future. Did you finally get the contract from Paichadze, the new director at the publishing house? According to the plans we have worked out, these pieces should be coming out first: my quintet, in full score, parts, and piano score; then your book about me; and then the full score of my Second Symphony. The full score for the Quintet has already gone to press; next in line now is your book.

I received a very dry and official invitation from the Leningrad Philharmonic, signed by Klimov; so now I am corresponding with him. He has invited me to play and conduct among other things two performances of *Oranges*, but I must decline conducting, since I have not even picked up a baton for four years now. As for my coming as a pianist, that depends on Moscow, but it is possible that I really will be in the USSR in January–February for five or six weeks. [. . .]

I send a big hug, and will be very happy if you write back soon. I am in the country, at the above address, until October.

Affectionately, S. Prkfv.

September 18, 1926
Samoreau

Dear Boris Vladimirovich,

I am sending you the autobiographical information from my pre-American period. Forgive me for holding it up, but at least the assignment was carried out conscientiously. I beseech you, and here and now set it forth as a condition, that you will not insert my version into your book the way I wrote it. For heaven's sake, don't keep it in the first person, but rework it, and adapt it in your own way. There is already more than enough of my relaxed American style of writing around! It would be very desirable for you to rework the post-American section as well for the second edition of the *Oranges* brochure. After all, what I sent you was merely an outline, and you put it in without changes. The tone came across very badly, and some newspapers made fun of it—and rightly so. [. . .]

Drop me a line at my Paris address.

Affectionately, S. Prkfv.

Oct. 10, 1926
BERLIN

Dear Boris Vladimirovich,

I received your postcard and registered letter. I will start book shipments to you as soon as I return to Paris. I am having preliminary talks with Prunières, a major specialist on Rameau, Lully, and so on. They staged *Oranges* here at the *Staatsoper* yesterday—truth be told, it was ponderous, done in a very Prussian manner. I can't wait to see how it's done in Leningrad.

I send you a big hug.

Yours, S. Prkfv.

11/23/1926
18, RUE TROYON, PARIS, XVII

Dear Boris Vladimirovich,

Have you received my Quintet which I sent recently? The full orchestral score and parts will come off the press in the near future, and will be available for sale, but not for rent. [. . .]

I saw A. N. Benois, who praised the musical presentation of the production of *Oranges*, but he roundly denounced the sets and the director's desire to constantly make the audience laugh at any cost. He is living in a hotel now and will probably move out soon, so if you want to write to him, it would be better to do so through me.[50]

As before, I am planning to come to Russia, and the first Moscow concert is slated for January 24. But it is very difficult for me to figure out which agencies

---

50. Aleksandr Nikolaevich Benois (1870–1960) was a Russian painter and stage designer. (See chapter 2, n. 81.)

I should be dealing with, and which ones I should not. I have now temporarily ceased responding to any invitations, until I determine exactly what responsibility Rosfil [Russian Philharmonic Society] is taking. If you could provide some sort of clarification, it would be invaluable to me.

I am at work on *Fiery Angel*. Three acts are finished and orchestrated, but there are still two left to go. Demchinsky held things up for a long time, but in the end the mountain gave birth to a mouse and I hardly even used his suggestions for the libretto. I will try to bring the orchestral score of the Second Symphony with me to Russia. If you can, send me the program for the concert where they played the "Classical" Symphony. [. . .]

With a big hug,

Yours,

S. Prkfv.

12/17/1926

18, RUE TROYON, PARIS, XVII

[. . .] Is it good or bad that Malko is now the manager of the Philharmonic?[51] Has he become any more agreeable than before? Miaskovsky's Sixth Symphony was met with great success and good press when performed in New York and Philadelphia. In general, America is making some progress. Miaskovsky's Sixth Symphony and my *Scythian Suite* were the only pieces played at these American concerts—nothing else.[52] Except for Moscow, I can't imagine any other cities which would have undertaken such a program.

I hope to bring the published orchestral score and parts for the Quintet with me. So it's not worth copying the parts out, especially since I cleaned up the whole piece before it was printed.

I send hugs and kisses, and heartfelt holiday greetings.

Yours, S. Prkfv.

---

51. N. A. Malko, from 1925 to 1928 the head conductor of the Leningrad Philharmonic, in 1927 also became its manager, replacing M. G. Klimov, whom Prokofiev mentions in his letter of August 9, 1926.

52. The Sixth Symphony, op. 23 (1921–1923), by Miaskovsky was first performed in America in Philadelphia on November 26, 1926, conducted by Leopold Stokowski; it was also performed in New York on November 30, conducted by Artur Rodzinski. *Ala and Lolly* was also performed at those concerts (*Scythian Suite* for large orchestra, op. 20, written by Prokofiev in 1914).

Feb. 5, 1927
Moscow

Dear Boris Vladimirovich,

It's a shame you didn't come: we[53] were expecting you and reserved a seat for you at the concert. Thank you for the telegram. We arrive on Wednesday the ninth on the express train (arriving at 10:00 A.M.), and have already picked up our train tickets. It will be great to hear *Oranges* on the tenth. It would be nice if there was a piano in the hotel room, and a private bath if you can manage it.

I send you a kiss. Greetings from both of us.

Yours, S.P.

Mar. 7, 1927
[IN RUSSIA]

Dear Boris Vladimirovich,

I'm writing to you on the train. I saw Meyerhold twice. There was much he didn't say, but apparently we are in agreement regarding our future work.[54] Ekskuzovich has still not given him the piano score, so I gave him mine. We return to Moscow from Odessa on the 18th. On the 20th during the day is our farewell concert with Persimfans (the "Classical," Second Concerto, and the *Scythian*), and on the 22nd at five o'clock we depart for the West, assuming we get all the formalities taken care of. When are you coming to Moscow? I'm sorry you missed the Quintet; they played it briskly, and it sounded marvelous.[55] Bring me a piano score to replace the one I gave Meyerhold, and of course an orchestral score of *The Gambler*. Meyerhold said he opposes the idea of putting *The Gambler* on together in the same evening with *Buffoon*.

I am so worn out; the two days at Detskoye were the only days off. I send hugs and kisses. Lina Ivanovna sends greetings to you both, and I kiss Irina Stepanovna's little hand.

Yours, S.P.

4/15/1927
5, AVE. FRÉMIET, PARIS XVI

Dear Boris Vladimirovich,

Three days ago they played the Quintet here, but they didn't learn it properly. Although there were also shortcomings in the Moscow performance, they

---

53. Prokofiev and his first wife, Lina.
54. It was planned that V. E. Meyerhold would stage the production of Prokofiev's *The Gambler* at the Leningrad Opera and Ballet Theater.
55. The first performance of the Quintet in Moscow took place on March 6, 1927.

somehow managed to play it with a certain brilliance, while here they fudged some spots. But the Quintet was received well, especially among musicians; Marnold, Prunières, and others. [. . .]

Did you get my postcard from Monte Carlo? I was there at Diaghilev's summons in order to get rehearsals of my new so-called Soviet ballet op[us] 41 rolling. There is a plan afoot to call it *The Steel Gallop*, but this is strictly between you and me. By the way, I was able to incline Diaghilev favorably towards the idea of allowing performances of this new ballet in the USSR starting January 1, 1928. Diaghilev said he would agree if Lunacharsky himself made the request. He hasn't gone back on his word yet, especially since he has already taken a bribe from me: an additional dance. So if the Mariinsky or Moscow Bolshoi Theater were to decide after all to present an entire evening of my ballets, then *Buffoon, Scythian,* and this new ballet would make a complete evening. The Diaghilev ballet could be staged in Diaghilev's production, with sets by Yakoulov, as I discussed with Ekskuzovich in the train. He seemed to like the idea. [. . .]

Affectionately, S. Prkfv.

5/2/1927
5, AVE. FRÉMIET, PARIS XVI

Dear Boris Vladimirovich,

I am sending you a ballet by the American composer Carpenter called *Skyscrapers,* which I believe I mentioned to you.[56] The ballet was written for Diaghilev, but not accepted by him; it was then performed by the Metropolitan in New York and is now going to Munich. I cannot say that this is a first-rate work, but from the standpoint of what is being produced in American music it is worth taking a look at. Besides, it could be interesting for the USSR, since it features various scenes of construction, workers, Negroes, amusement parks, etc. The ballet was orchestrated well, in imitation of Stravinsky and the French composers.

Hugs and kisses.

Yours, S. Prkfv.

---

56. The American composer John Alden Carpenter (1876–1951) wrote his ballet *Skyscrapers* on a commission from Diaghilev in 1923–24 and called it "a ballet of modern American life." It had its premiere at the Metropolitan Opera on February 19, 1926. The instrumentation includes three saxophones, tenor banjo, two red traffic lights controlled by a keyboard in the wings, and a chorus of six tenors and six sopranos onstage.

5/5/1927

5, AVE. FRÉMIET, PARIS XVI

Dear Boris Vladimirovich,

[. . .] What is the situation on bringing *Oranges* to Paris? Please keep me informed on all the details.[57] The premiere of my new ballet, which has in fact definitely received the title *The Steel Gallop* (*Le Pas d'acier*), has been set for June 7 in Paris. Diaghilev proposed that I conduct, but I refused, suggesting in turn that Dranishnikov conduct, a suggestion which Diaghilev graciously accepted.[58] [. . .]

Yours, S. Prkfv.

5/21/1927

5, AVE. FRÉMIET, PARIS XVI

Dear Boris Vladimirovich,

An idea just came to me: why don't you come visit me in France? To do that, you would need to obtain a business passport and get yourself a French visa. I would more than happily pay for your transportation here and back, and in Paris you could stay with me. At the end of June we are going to a dacha which I rented near Royan, a stone's throw from the Atlantic Ocean. There is a room waiting for you at the dacha, and you could stay with us a month or however long you like without causing any inconvenience whatsoever to anyone; on the contrary, it would give us enormous pleasure to have you there.

Of course, it would make the most sense if you came along with the Mariinsky Theater troupe when they bring *Three Oranges* to Paris. But your own mysterious silence concerning this upcoming event, and the total lack of information about it in Parisian musical circles, makes me adopt a sceptical attitude towards the possibility of *Oranges* appearing in Paris. If that is the case, then why don't you try to come for the premiere of *The Steel Gallop* on June 7? [. . .]

I send you a big kiss. I hope we will be meeting soon. Heartfelt greetings to everyone from both of us.

Yours, S. Prkfv.

---

57. The planned tour of the Leningrad Theater of Opera and Ballet to Paris never occurred.
58. V. A. Dranishnikov wasn't able to take advantage of Diaghilev's invitation because he was busy with a production of Alban Berg's *Wozzeck*; after the departure of Albert Coates, he controlled the entire opera repertory of the Leningrad State Theater of Opera and Ballet.

August 29, 1929

CHÂTEAU DE LA FLÉCHÈRE, CULOZ (AIN) FRANCE

Dear Boris Vladimirovich,

You can understand what a terrible impact the news of Diaghilev's death has made on me. He died of a boil—something he had always feared—in Venice after remaining unconscious for a day and a half at the end. He had gone there after the London season. His death affected me not so much in terms of our musical relationship, since in recent days it had seemed to me that this relationship had run its course with the completion of *Prodigal Son*, [59] and not even in terms of our personal relations, since the image of Diaghilev is still so distinct and alive that I still find it impossible to conceive of him having left us. No, what amazed me most was the disappearance of an enormous and unquestionably unique figure, whose scope continues to grow the further it recedes from us. It seems an attempt will be made to continue Diaghilev's work under the supervision of Nouvel, Kochno, and Grigoriev, but it remains to be seen if this fragmentation could achieve any success. I hear that Diaghilev left no will.

This summer I worked on cleaning up my old Sinfonietta. As usually happens in such cases, the "cleaning up" turned into a job of complete rewriting that took me a good two months. At the same time, what will emerge is a really fine piece, akin to the "Classical" Symphony. Four movements are already completed; I'm hoping that the fifth won't take me too much longer.

Besides work and corrections, I sometimes see my neighbors: Nina Koshetz, who is still wondering how you couldn't have seen her last year;[60] Stravinsky, who came to visit me with his sons, and to whom I then went with Petya[61] to listen to his new piano concerto. I liked this last one a lot better than his works from the preceding period, and more than his first concerto. It seems to me that it is composed less in imitation of others, although in the finale the rhythms of military marches do pop up, with very special chords in thirds and fourths. [. . .]

I send you a big hug. Greetings from the inhabitants of our château. I hope you are in good spirits. I'll send you some photos of our home life in the next letter—they are being developed in Aix.

Lovingly, S. Prkfv.

---

59. *Prodigal Son*, op. 46, libretto by Boris Kochno, written in 1928 at Diaghilev's request, was choreographed by George Balanchine. Prokofiev conducted at the premiere on May 21, 1928.

60. In September 1928, at Prokofiev's invitation, Asafiev lived with him in Vétraz (Savoie).

61. Petya is P. P. Souvchinsky; see no. 4, above.

October 8, 1929
Château de la Fléchère, Culoz (Ain) France

Dear Boris Vladimirovich,

It's been a long time since your postcard from Moscow; you did not answer my registered letter of August 29, and although by now I am used to the unexpected interruptions in our correspondence, I am all the same beginning to worry since you complained of poor health in your postcard and mentioned going away for a rest. Please write. We are leaving here tomorrow, and because we gave up our Paris apartment, it's best to write me c/o my publisher.

Having finished the Sinfonietta, which I turned into an entirely new piece, I finished orchestrating the Divertissement in four parts;[62] the very lively number that you liked so much in Vétraz went into it. I did not add the numbers from the Quintet, but rather composed new music, including a larghetto which I am sure you will love, and which turns out to be a continuation of the mood and lyricism of *Prodigal Son*.

I have many concerts coming up in W[estern] Europe and America this winter. My concert season begins in the second half of November and continues until late spring. At the end of October I plan to take a trip of about two weeks to the USSR; this will be finalized upon my return to Paris.

I send hugs and await your letter.

Yours, S. Prkfv.

November 9, 1929
Moscow

Dear Boris Vladimirovich,

I am very sorry that we did not manage to see one another or at least to talk properly on the phone before my departure. Having arrived in Moscow, I have checked into the Grand Hotel (formerly the Grand Moscow Hotel), on Revolution Square, where I ask that you forward Lina Ivanovna's letters. Come to Moscow not on the 16th but on the 15th without fail; everyone with whom you need to talk will be at Meyerhold's on the evening of the 15th. Just imagine, no one from the conservatory appeared to take my compositions. So, I brought them here and will give them to the Moscow Conservatory.

Hugs, Yours, S. Prkfv.

---

62. Divertissement for Orchestra, op. 43, by Prokofiev, was first performed on December 22, 1929, in Paris, conducted by the composer. An arrangement for piano (op. 43-bis) was completed in 1938.

December 9, 1929
6, RUE BASSANO, PARIS XVI, FRANCE

[. . .] We leave for America on the 24th. On the 22nd, before my departure, a symphonic concert of my works is being held at which, by the way, I will conduct the Divertissement for the first time. Tomorrow I go to Holland to perform my Second Concerto with Monteux. The publisher has still not received an offer from the Leningrad Akopera to renew the *Oranges* contract. They started to make some noise, but then fell asleep again.

I send hugs. Greetings to you and yours from Lina Ivanovna. She appeared in concert last night after a long hiatus—and was accorded a very respectable reception. I will send you some photos. Write soon.

Yours, S. Prkfv.

December 17, 1929
6, RUE BASSANO, PARIS XVI, FRANCE

Dear Boris Vladimirovich,

[. . .] I rehearsed the Divertissement with an orchestra for the first time today. It came out clearly and nicely. I heard Stravinsky's new Capriccio for Piano and Orchestra. The writing contains hints of a return to his old manner. Overall I liked the first half the most, but there are some technical blunders; that is, for example, during moments of musical climax, the p[iano] does not climax, but instead is played with what sounds like a single finger. I believe that in concertos, the musical climax must occur simultaneously in the orchestra and in the solo instrument. The finale, on the other hand, is technically outstanding, but the material is a little frivolous, and in places even flimsy, especially where Stravinsky dashes into fairly blunt ninth chords and 4–3 chords. The Capriccio was very successful with the public. Another novelty is *Aubades* by Poulenc: a piano concerto accompanied by an ensemble of (it seems) eighteen players;[63] it's one of Poulenc's successful pieces, although it does not venture beyond the limit of his capabilities. By the way, Les Six is celebrating its tenth anniversary with two concerts. The first was held while I was in Holland, but I will attend the second in a few days' time, and will send you the program with various illustrations and article.

I set off for America on the 24th, and will arrive on the 30th. I count on

---

63. *Aubades* is a "Morning Serenade" Concerto-Ballet for piano and ensemble of eighteen instruments by the French composer and pianist Francis Poulenc.

receiving a letter from you before I leave, and my American address is as follows:

Serge Prokofieff
C/o Haensel & Jones
113 West 57th Street
New York, New York
U.S.A.

I send a big hug. I hope you received my letter of December 9. Akopera did not contact the publisher for the music of *Oranges*.

Yours, S. Prkfv.

Jan. 11, 1930
CLEVELAND

Dear B[oris] V[ladimirovich], I am conducting *S[teel] Gallop* here; the orchestra is very good and very large; of course there are Russians among the musicians. The city is an incredible colossus, studded with skyscrapers; it stretches for 33 kilometers along the banks of Lake Erie! America is altogether an unbelievable place. Don't forget to write me at my New York address. I send you a big kiss.

Warm greetings to Ir[ina] Step[anovna].

Yours, S. Prkfv.

Jan. 25, 1930
[NEW YORK]

[. . .] My concerts are proceeding successfully; five down, twenty to go. I'm conducting negotiations about productions for the coming season, mainly *Fiery Angel* and *Steel Gallop*.[64] How is my concert grand?[65] Is *Oranges* running? Or did they lie about it to my face?

Hugs and kisses.

Yours, S. Prkfv.

---

64. Discussions of a production of *Fiery Angel* at the Metropolitan Opera in New York proved unsuccessful; a performance of the ballet *The Steel Gallop* was conducted on April 21, 1931, by Leopold Stokowski.

65. Prokofiev is referring to the piano he won for being the best student in his piano class at graduation from the St. Petersburg Conservatory in 1914. That piano, by certification of Prokofiev, was located in storage at Eleonora Damskaya's house; but in 1929, a new certification and proof of property rights were demanded, so Asafiev testified to Prokofiev's ownership of the piano. (See also chapter 2.)

March 3, 1930
DETROIT

Dear Bor[is] Vl[adimirovich], it seems I haven't written to you in a long time, but then, you have been as silent as "a frozen fish." After New York, Philadelphia, and Boston, we went through New Orleans and along the Texas-Mexico border to California, then turned around and came back via Chicago and Detroit. We were received well everywhere; America has grown up in these past four years, or maybe has simply learned my name. I return to France on Apr. 3. I foresee being in the USSR in the beginning of May, but this is still unclear, especially when friends don't write.

Hugs and kisses.

S. Prkfv.

March 15, 1930
[CUBA]

Dear Boris Vladimirovich,

I'm writing to you in the train, on the way out of Havana, where we went for two concerts. Cuba has a lovely tropical climate, not too hot this time of year. The palm trees, the moon at its zenith, the southern sea—all this is astonishingly beautiful, but all the same I have a northern heart, and I wouldn't want to live here for long. In terms of music, there are some interesting groups thirsting for contemporaneity and publishing some respectable periodicals, and I would like to match you up with them as well. [. . .]

I received your postcard and was very saddened by the news of your illness. I hope you're better now. I was sorry you didn't write more about the theaters, especially the Bolshoi, since neither Meyerhold nor Gusman has written me a word about it.[66] I was thinking of coming to the USSR at the beginning of May, but it's hard for me to plan my musical affairs if not a single living soul writes to me. Would it be worth it for me to give one concert apiece in Moscow and Leningrad? After 25 concerts, I'm in good shape now.

I'll be returning to Europe on April 3 or 4, so write to me at the publishing house. It seems, though, that I'll have to spend all of April traveling around Europe giving concerts, but the publishing house will forward letters to me quickly.

66. The production of *The Steel Gallop* that Meyerhold was planning to direct at the Bolshoi Theater did not take place. At that time Gusman was the head of the production staff of the Bolshoi Theater.

I embrace you cordially.

Yours, S. Prkfv.

I've begun my String Quartet;[67] it was commissioned by the Washington Library, where the manuscript will also be kept.

May 18, 1930
5, RUE VALENTIN HAÜY, PARIS XV, FRANCE

Dear Boris Vladimirovich,

I received both your letters, from April 4 (the one describing nature) and May 4. I'm sorry for not writing, but my journeying didn't stop with my return from America—I underwent another six concerts. Three of them were "Prokofiev Festivals" in Brussels (the Third Symphony, the Divertissement, etc.). And after that, two concerts in Italy and in Monte Carlo. I saw Meyerhold only yesterday; once again he's putting high hopes in the Bolshoi Theater. [. . .]

Your book about Stravinsky,[68] or rather some of the ideas expressed in it, made quite an impression on many people. Now I've obtained my own copy through Petya Schloezer.

Send me your chapters about me for my approval as soon as possible[69] at the above address: this is my permanent address now. [. . .] What happened with my prize-winning piano? Did they give you the necessary certificate? Glazunov was received with indulgent respect in America. Now he's in Paris; he just went to Poland and Prague.

In musical news: Rieti has written a horrifying violin concerto; Vierne has composed some Negro trash; Honegger's violin concerto contains some very tender, bright moments, but a lot of it is rubbish; Nabokov's symphony was very successful, and you can tell he's made a lot of progress since his *Ode*. All these pieces were performed by Monteux in his May concerts. Dukelsky's Second Symphony was successfully performed by Koussevitsky in Boston. Stravinsky's Capriccio was published with a million misprints. As soon as the director of the publishing house returns to Paris, I'll ask him to send you a copy. Now Stravin-

---

67. Prokofiev's Quartet for Two Violins, Viola, and Cello in B Minor, op. 50, was first performed in Washington on April 25, 1931. The andante from the Quartet (the third movement) was transcribed by the composer for string orchestra and exists as an independent composition—op. 50-bis.

68. *Book about Stravinsky* by Igor Glebov (Asafiev's pseudonym) was published in 1929 by the Tritone Publishing House in Leningrad.

69. This refers to a book about Prokofiev, an unrealized project of Asafiev.

sky is writing a two-movement symphony for orchestra and chorus based on texts from the Psalms.

Well, I send you my love—get well soon and keep your spirits up. You praise me for my good spirits, but you know where I got them from!

Yours, S. Prkfv.

How did Deshevov's opera go?[70] And Shostakovich's *Nose*?[71]

Apr. 2, 1931
VIENNA

Dear Bor[is] Vl[adimirovich], I send you a hug from Vienna: yesterday I debuted here with my Second Concerto, and the response was *ausgezeichnet* ["excellent"]. When I was in Paris and Belgium I looked for the book you asked for as well as information about Salvador; so far I haven't had any luck, but when I return I'll renew my searches. Write to me. I've written a quartet (for strings) and a new ballet for the Gr[and] Opéra—it will be performed by Lifar in May.[72] I embrace you cordially.

Yours, S. Prkfv.

September 14, 1931
LA CROIX BASQUE, CIBOURE (BASSES PYRÉNÉES), FRANCE

Dear Boris Vladimirovich,

During the past week I received two letters from you—dated August 14 and September 4. I'm sorry to hear you've been feeling so awful. But between the lines I can clearly see that this is the result of a momentary condition and you're aware of that; once you reach that stage, it isn't far to recovery!

I'm glad the music I sent reached you and that you enjoyed it. Thank you for your *Musical Form*[73] and for Kamensky's book.[74] Your work on form is a very complex work; I've looked through it but haven't studied it carefully, so let me

---

70. The opera *Ice and Steel* by Vladimir Deshevov (1889–1955) was produced at the Leningrad State Academic Theater of Opera and Ballet on May 17, 1930.

71. Shostakovich's opera *The Nose* (based on Gogol's story of the same name) was produced at the Maly Opera Theater in Leningrad on January 18, 1930.

72. Prokofiev's ballet *On the Dnepr* (*Sur le Borysthène*), op. 51, was produced by Serge Lifar at the Grand Opéra; the premiere took place on December 16, 1932.

73. Igor Glebov [Asafiev], *Musical Form as a Process* [Moscow, 1930].

74. V. V. Kamensky, *The Way of the Enthusiast* [Moscow, 1931].

give you my opinion later. The general mood of Kamensky's book is nice, but if everything in it is as garbled as the section about me, then what value does it have?

This summer we stayed in Paris until the end of July, and then I drove around France for a couple of weeks by automobile, first towards Geneva and Savoie, then diagonally to Toulouse and Biarritz. There are a lot of interesting things in central France. There are bleak, uninhabited areas as well as phenomenal grottoes! Now we're spending the rest of the summer by the Atlantic Ocean, seven kilometers from the Spanish border. The country is beautiful here: the Pyrénées on one side, the warm ocean on the other. I've learned how to swim and dive.

Among my works, I've finished a F[orte]p[iano] Concerto for One Hand as a commission for the one-armed pianist Wittgenstein. It's already called my Fourth Concerto, and probably in about four years, when my contract with Wittgenstein expires, it will turn into a concerto for two hands (incidentally, I'm keeping quiet about that for now, so as not to offend my customer).[75] Afterwards I made six transcriptions for piano from some of my orchestral and chamber compositions.[76] Some genuine piano pieces have emerged as a result, not at all like arrangements. They have already been engraved, and they'll go on sale in October. The publisher intends to send copies out to leading pianists; among the Leningrad pianists I'd like to send copies to Kamensky, Nikolayev, and Yudina—please let me know their addresses. Would it be worth sending one to the conservatory library as well? They treated me like pigs in 1929, but directors and librarians change with time, and this is no reason for young people not to know my works. The real question is this: what sort of political line are they taking now, and do they really want to have my compositions or not?

[. . .] The publishers are very reluctant to give out copies of *The Gambler*; somehow I managed to persuade them to send some to the directors of the two leading Soviet theaters. I wasn't very worried about you, since you have a manuscript copy—and your desire to possess a printed copy is merely a bibliographical whim. But if you really want one, I'll send you a copy when I return to Paris. I've just outlined a suite from *The Gambler* in five parts: 1) Aleksei, 2)

---

75. Fourth Concerto for Piano and Orchestra in B-flat Major (for left hand), op. 53; Prokofiev's plans to transcribe the concerto for two hands were not carried out. Paul Wittgenstein was an Austrian pianist.

76. Six Pieces for Piano, op. 52, were first performed by the composer in Moscow on May 27, 1932.

Grandma, 3) The General, 4) Polina, and 5) Dénouement. It wasn't easy to put together, and I had to compose some new music to connect some of the parts, but generally I seem to have succeeded, and the condensed version has actually brought the characters' personalities into sharper focus. However, all the pieces have to be orchestrated all over again—quite a sizeable amount of work.

My ballet is called *Borysthène*, because "Dnepr" doesn't sound nice in French; the Russian title is *U Dnepra* [*On the Dnepr*]. The plot is lyrical and has no special significance; when I was planning this ballet with Lifar, we began with the choreographic and musical structure, considering the ballet's plot to be of secondary importance. And so for a Soviet theater this plot might need to be modified, in comparison with what the Paris Opéra wants. As a result of this approach, we were hoping to achieve a greater sense of musical and choreographical structure. That's why I was surprised that you weren't satisfied with the ending. This is probably because you were expecting an apotheosis like the one in *Prodigal Son*—but here, the dénouement is laconic in nature.

I wish you success in your work on your ballet.[77] Since you didn't say it was a secret, I shared your plans with my friends, who were very interested. Get well soon, keep your spirits up—and write to me. We'll be at the above address until October 7, and after that in Paris.

Greetings to yours from both of us.

With love, *S. Prkfv*

November 14, 1931
5, RUE VALENTIN HAÜY, PARIS XV, FRANCE

Dear Boris Vladimirovich,

I'm still looking for dances and songs from the time of the French Revolution, both Parisian and provincial, but it isn't so easy because you want street music, not theatrical music or music of official celebrations.[78] The opinion I expressed to you in my last letter [on October 31] was supported by many knowledgeable Frenchmen: music that seemed so cheerful and robust in comparison to the Gluck that preceded it doesn't seem robust at all to us—actually, it sounds rather formal.

Poulenc introduced me to a well-educated seller of used books who recom-

---

77. *The Flames of Paris.*
78. Prokofiev was helping Asafiev with research into French popular music of the period just after the French Revolution for his new ballet, *The Flames of Paris*, which was first produced in 1932 in Leningrad.

mended a thick collection of 2,000 French songs that was first published in 1807 and thus covers exactly the era you need. It goes by the comical title *La Clé du Caveau* [*The Key to the Vault*]. With some of the texts it's possible to tell whether the song comes from this or that region, which may be of use to you. Along with this volume I'm sending you a little brochure with texts of songs from the time of the French Revolution, a bibliographical rarity. It indicates to which motive this or that song was sung, and then you can find the motive in *La Clé du Caveau*. Let me know whether the volumes I'm sending are suitable for you, and in the meantime I'll see if I can find anything else.

I looked through the list of works by Constant Pierre, may he rest in peace, but didn't find any work on music of the Revolution of 1848. They say he often promised books to people and then didn't publish them.

I embrace you warmly.

Yours, S. Prkfv

November 28, 1931
PARIS

Dear Boris Vladimirovich,

I just received your letter of November 28, and I'm glad you were satisfied with the materials I sent. Yesterday I sent you Tiersot's book about music at the time of the French Revolution—it was also hard to get, since it's *épuisé* [out of print]. I didn't get a chance to look at it, but they say it's very serious material. At the Paris Conservatory they're teaching harmony with the Reber-Dubois textbook, which is highly praised. Nonetheless, a new textbook by Caussade will be coming out soon, and it will probably be used in the conservatory as well, since Caussade is a professor there. Among the non-French authors, they're praising the Belgian Paul Gilson and the German Rischbieter. You're so busy with your own affairs that you haven't even written me a word about the Andante op. 50—and it's one of my greatest successes.

I embrace you. Yours, S. Prkfv.

February 6, 1932
5, RUE VALENTIN HAÜY, PARIS XV, FRANCE

Dear Boris Vladimirovich,

Thank you for sending your book about Russian music.[79] I took it with me on my concert tour and read it on the train. I felt as if I were actually speaking

---

79. I. Glebov (Asafiev), *The Russian Romance: An Experiment in Intonational Analysis* (Moscow and Leningrad, 1930).

with you, the whole book was so characteristic of you. You successfully contrasted the different worldviews of Borodin and Mussorgsky as reflected in both composers' works, especially in the area of folk music. This reflection is easier to follow in lyrical music, but easier to see in the crowd scenes, so your analysis is especially interesting. I also liked the triangle made up of Tchaikovsky, Mussorgsky, and Borodin. Of course you idolize Tchaikovsky's romances, but this part of the book leaves me colder because despite the merits of some of these romances, they were thrown together in a hurry; and I can't avoid a sense of awkwardness when I look at these collections. You flattered me when you referred to my *Scythian* while talking about Borodin or Rimsky; I felt like a child seated at the table with adults. But in the chapter on romances, I believe you offended Miaskovsky and me. His "Circles"[80] is more important than any Selinovs or Steingbergers or others, to each of whom you've devoted a page. And you could have found something besides "elegant irony" in my *Ugly Duckling* or Akhmatova.[81]

While reading it, I noticed a few errors in the text, not particularly substantial, but I'll tell you about them anyway. [. . .]

The other day I sent you a book about Bizet. Before that I sent you Stravinsky's Violin Concerto and Ferroud's symphony; the latter was interested in your opinion. I don't know this symphony, but it's been played in America and France, and Florent Schmitt was ecstatic. Next week I'll send Ravel's new concerto as well as my Quartet, which will be coming out in a few days.

Did you finish your ballet, and when will it be performed? I wrote a note about it in *Comoedia*. Derzhanovsky wrote that the Mikhailovsky Theater has "definitely" decided to perform *The Gambler* in the fall, and he conveyed Kanin and Kaplan's request that I give them a little information. I decided to act *en bon garçon* and wrote to the Mikhailovsky Theater. Let's hope they don't betray us.[82] Between my trips to various cities, I've almost finished the rough draft of my new piano concerto, which, by the way, I want to call "Music for Piano and

---

80. "Circles" ("I remember the two of us"), No. 3 in Miaskovsky's song cycle "From Z. Gippius," op. 5, composed 1905–08.

81. *The Ugly Duckling* (based on Andersen's fairy tale) for voice and piano, op. 18, was written by Prokofiev in 1914; "Akhmatova" is what Prokofiev calls his 1916 composition "Five Poems of Anna Akhmatova" for voice and piano, op. 27.

82. Negotiations for the production of *The Gambler* at Malegot (at the Mikhailovsky Theater, later called the Maly Opera Theater) were not successful. A. I. Kanin and E. I. Kaplan were the directors of the Malegot in 1932.

Orchestra"[83]—what do you think about this? I've also brought two piano sonatinas into being.[84]

I send you hugs and kisses, and I hope you're feeling in better spirits and you'll send me a long letter soon.

Yours, S. Prkfv.

April 9, 1932
5, RUE VALENTIN HAÜY, PARIS XV, FRANCE

Dear Boris Vladimirovich,

I was glad to receive your letter of April 2. The other letter, the long one of February 12, also arrived in a timely manner. Congratulations on finishing the score of your ballet. Let's hope the theater doesn't take too long to produce it. As for my *Dnepr*, I've been waiting a whole year already, but the Paris Grand Opéra wasn't up to any new productions; the French government hasn't been providing enough of a subsidy, and the director was tired of adding money from his own pocket, so he sent in his resignation. As it turned out, he had signed all the contracts in his own name, not in the name of the theater (that is, the state), and this caused considerable alarm among the employees at the Grand Opéra. Now the question of subsidies has been resolved, and we'll have to hope my *Dnepr* will be performed soon. The choreography has already been set by Lifar—in my opinion, successfully.

As soon as you know that the premiere of your ballet is coming up, send me some factual information about it—what kind of a ballet is it, what's the story, how is it made up, in short, everything you want people to know—and I'll translate it into French and publish it in the papers here. By the way, the Mikhailovsky Theater still hasn't answered my letter. What is this, have they nailed the coffin on *The Gambler* again, or not quite?

I was very touched by your praise of my Quartet and even embarrassed, because in my opinion, it was more than the piece deserved. I've finished two sonatinas and I'll be playing one of them on the 18th on London Radio, and later I'll send both of them to the publishers. The "Music for Piano and Orches-

---

83. Prokofiev's idea for "Music for Piano and Orchestra" turned into the Fifth Concerto for Piano and Orchestra in G Major, op. 55; it was first performed in Berlin on October 31, 1932; the soloist was the composer, and the conductor was Wilhelm Furtwängler.

84. Two Sonatinas for Piano in E Minor and G Major, op. 54 (1931–32), first performed by Prokofiev on April 17, 1932, in London.

tra" is coming along, but unfortunately it's turning out to be rather difficult for the pianist; I had been hoping to come up with a piece that was easy but effective. This summer I'll have to do a lot of cramming, because the first performance will take place in October with the Berlin Philharmonic conducted by Furtwängler; that means I'll have to push myself.

I'd say Ravel's Concerto is rather dry, but still superbly written. I say "superbly" with the caveat that he doesn't follow any of the requirements of a concerto; this is simply a piece in which the piano has solo passages on an equal level with the piccolo or the bassoon. The French critics, including your idolized Prunières, consider it their patriotic duty to call it a *chef d'œuvre*, but in Germany, for example, the concerto was not successful.[85]

Ferroud is a capable representative of the younger generation in France, and his symphony is certainly better than his strange undertaking on a story by Chekhov.[86] I read him your reviews of his symphony, leaving out the parts where you snap at him. He listened with great interest, almost greedily, and he asked if you might be able to have his symphony performed in Leningrad. Actually, if you don't find it too awful, maybe you could show it to one of the conductors.

I heard a symphony of Roussel that was written last year. Of course Roussel is not a first-rate composer, but within the limits of his abilities the symphony is successful, cheerful, clear, and in any case better than his ballet *Bacchus*,[87] which was produced by Lifar at the Grand Opéra.

In news of Russian composers, I happened to notice Dukelsky's *Epitaph* for chorus and orchestra dedicated to the memory of Diaghilev. I wasn't able to form an opinion, but Koussevitsky praised it and decided to perform it this spring in Boston. Medtner performed his new sonata, op. 53, called "The Stormcloud" (what a name!)—it was dreadfully boring and unnecessary. Rachmaninov performed some long *Variations on a Theme of Corelli*, written with the proper ordinariness; at the end a tender lyrical passage shone forth, but only as a reflection of the good old days of the Second Concerto.

The suite from *The Gambler* was performed recently in Paris. In form it is not just a suite, but a series of symphonic character portraits made out of material assembled from the entire opera and then created anew. It was well

85. Ravel's Piano Concerto in G Major was completed in 1931, the same year as his Piano Concerto in D Minor for Left Hand.

86. Pierre-Octave Ferroud's comic opera *Chirugie*, based on a story by Chekhov, was written in 1928 and performed in Monte Carlo.

87. The Roussel compositions Prokofiev refers to are the Third Symphony (1930) and the ballet *Bacchus and Ariadne*.

received. My Sinfonietta was very successful in Paris.[88] In general nowadays the critics in Paris have nothing but praise for me, and the same has been true in Berlin since my Third Concerto was performed. Stokowski performed my Third Symphony in America, first in Philadelphia,[89] where it was a failure, and later in New York—where it was an extraordinary success: there people found it to be one of my most significant compositions, and declared that they had finally seen the serious side of Prokofiev. [. . .]

D'Indy died honorably and imperceptibly.[90] Villa-Lobos lived in Paris for a while, and in 1929 he even used my piano to demonstrate his compositions to Diaghilev, who, by the way, didn't approve, believing that Lobos didn't know what he wanted. Now the latter has gone into hiding somewhere in the wilds of his native Brazil.

I embrace you warmly. Lina Ivanovna sends her best regards to you and Irina Stepanovna. Write to me.

Yours, S. Prkfv.

June 8, 1932
5, RUE VALENTIN HAÜY, PARIS XV, FRANCE

Dear Boris Vladimirovich,

Thank you for your letter of May 28. I was very interested to hear how your ballet was going. In my previous letter of April 9 (I couldn't tell from your lines whether you received it) I asked you to send me some short notes about your ballet, which I could print in the Paris newspapers. We could also do it this way: as soon as it is performed, send some explanatory notes from the program or a newspaper article appearing in advance of the premiere, and I'll put it together here and translate it into French.

It's too bad you're getting along so poorly with your own health; it's as if you'd never read a single book about it, or if you did read one, didn't understand anything.[91] I really want to see you, and I'm definitely counting on being in the USSR in mid-November, if only for three weeks. By the way, I've finished my

---

88. The first performance of Prokofiev's third edition of his Sinfonietta (with a new opus no. 48) took place in Paris on January 23, 1932.

89. The concerts in Philadelphia, where Prokofiev's Third Symphony was performed, took place on January 8 and 9, 1929.

90. The French composer Vincent d'Indy had died recently, on December 2, 1931.

91. Prokofiev is referring to his belief in Christian Science, of which he often spoke to friends and colleagues.

new piano concerto ("Music for Piano and Orchestra," op. 55), and now I'm orchestrating it, and at the same time I'm learning the piano part. If things work out well, I'm planning to play it in Moscow and Leningrad.[92] [. . .]

They celebrated Glazunov's fiftieth birthday here the other day, but the event was rather pale, and ignored by French musical circles. Markevich composed a piano concerto (Partita), a rather energetic piece, but I don't see any further development since the previous one, and he's just now at the age when one should be developing.[93] Petya, his enthusiastic admirer, has disappeared somewhere beyond the horizon. Rieti has given us a sinfonietta for small orchestra, a pleasant, joyful piece in the Italian style, but not always pure in the sense of grasping some higher good. Stravinsky is writing a suite for violin and piano, in which, according to him, the thoughts are compressed and concentrated "like a diamond," he explains. Lina Ivanovna sang *Ugly Duckling* with orchestra—successfully, and the orchestration was also well received.[94] My new sonatinas will be out in about two weeks; yesterday I sent Miaskovsky a copy of the proofs—the sonatinas are light ones, just right for his repertoire.

I wish you success with the production of your ballet, I look forward to hearing more news about it, and I embrace you warmly.

Yours, S. Prkfv.

July 31, 1932
5, RUE VALENTIN HAÜY, PARIS XV, FRANCE

Dear Boris Vladimirovich,

I'm writing you a few quick words before I leave for southern France. I received your letter of July 12 and thank you for it. I'm glad the sonatinas were to your liking, but I don't understand why the "lyricization" of my music could be unconvincing for Soviet musicians. After all, melody is the basic element—

---

92. Prokofiev performed his Fifth Concerto for Piano and Orchestra at a concert in Moscow on November 25, 1932 (conducted by N. S. Golovanov), and in Leningrad on December 1 of the same year (conducted by Dranishnikov); at the same concerts his "Four Portraits and Dénouement from *The Gambler*" were performed for the first time in the USSR.

93. Igor Markevich was a French composer and conductor who emigrated from Russia; his Partita for Piano and Orchestra was written in 1931, when he was nineteen.

94. The performance of the orchestral version of *Ugly Duckling* referred to by Prokofiev took place in Paris on May 19, 1932.

the most accessible and most desirable thing. Those who don't understand this must be taught.

I'm sending you a clipping from *Comoedia*, where a notice about your ballet appeared on the front page, but for some reason Leningrad was not allowed to be called Leningrad; furthermore, the ballet itself was not named. The newspaper is not at fault, but instead my absent-minded correspondent, who never once mentioned the name of his own composition.

I'm planning to come to Moscow on November 21 for about two weeks. I've already received an invitation from the Leningrad Philharmonic for December 1, and they promise to write to me from Moscow also. I communicated with Breitkopf about your notes. I embrace you warmly. I'm glad you've become less sour; I hope the success of your ballet and the Kislovodsk sun will do the rest.

Yours, S. Prkfv.

Write to me at my Paris address.

December 14, 1932

5, RUE VALENTIN HAÜY, PARIS XV, FRANCE

Dear Boris Vladimirovich,

I'm sending you Romain Rolland's book *Histoire de l'opéra en Europe avant Lully et Scarlatti*. The *Mémoires de Louise Michel* were published in 1886 and sold out. I left instructions to look for it at the used bookstores, and if anyone finds it, to send it to you even after I leave for America. I had no more luck with the third book, *La vierge rouge, Irma Boyer*, since its publisher went bankrupt and his property was seized. So I can't get this book at the moment either, but when the case is resolved one way or another, they'll send it to you.

On my way through Berlin I left instructions to make a payment to Breitkopf and Härtel and tell them the next payment will be made in a few months.

Prunières is worried about the publication of your book about Russian history. He's asking you to write to him without delay. The thing could be quite voluminous.[95] I composed an article about *The Flames of Paris* which will appear in *Comoedia*, in *Petit Marseillais* (so there's your marching "Marseillaise"!), and also, apparently, in some Dutch and American newspapers. By the way, I've already run across one article, or rather a reprint from the Soviet papers; I'm enclosing it.

---

95. The negotiations between Asafiev and Prunières, the editor and publisher of *La Revue Musicale*, were not successful.

Tell Popov that his Septet will be played in Paris in May, but have him tell me who is supposed to send me the score; otherwise we'll have the material, but no score. Also, don't forget that you promised to send the Sov[iet] romances to Lina Ivanovna.

The Parisian public and critics were enthusiastic about the Fifth Concerto. At the moment we're spending some time on the *Dnepr*, and, as usual in such situations, not everything is going well yet. It will be performed on the 16th, and on the 17th I'm getting on an ocean liner. I'm waiting for the moment when I can breathe a little fresh air and play a few games of chess. Do you remember our conversations about this noble game? I believe that if you devoted your leisure time to it and even joined a chess club, it would not harm your scholarly works.

I hope to receive a letter from you at my Paris address, where they'll forward it to me, or you can write to me directly in America:

Serge Prokofieff
c/o Haensel & Jones
113 West 57th Street,
New York, N.Y.
U.S.A.

I embrace you warmly.

Yours, S. Prkfv.

January 2, 1933
BOSTON

Dear Boris Vladimirovich,

I'm sending you my interview about the USSR, in which there are also a few words about your ballet.[96] Before leaving Paris I prepared an entire article about it based on materials from the Soviet newspapers: it will appear (rather, it already appeared) in *Comoedia* and in *Petit Marseillais*[97] (a major Marseilles newspaper, despite the diminutive title) and a few Dutch papers; I left instructions to send them to you; if they haven't sent them, I'll do it when I get back to Paris.

96. Prokofiev's interview was published in the *Boston Evening Transcript* on December 31, 1932.

97. A few copies of Prokofiev's article from the newspaper *Le Petit Marseillais*, January 3, 1933, were attached to his letter of March 4, 1933; the often-mentioned article in *Comoedia* has not been found.

The Boston [Symphony] Orchestra accompanied my Fifth Concerto[98] with extraordinary brilliance: this was the best performance; the public and the press also received it warmly. Now I'm sitting outside the city, almost in the country; I'm resting for a few days, and then I'll begin my New York season.

I'm very interested in your plans—for composition, moving around, etc. Write to me at my Paris address, and they'll forward it to me right away. Did the material for *Oranges* arrive? When is the revival taking place?

I embrace you warmly.

Yours, S. Prkfv.

March 4, 1933

5, RUE VALENTIN HAÜY, PARIS XV, FRANCE

Dear Boris Vladimirovich,

When I returned from America, I found two letters of yours, from January 28 and February 6. I'm sending you two of my interviews, which I gave before I left for America, in which I talk about *The Flames of Paris*. The text of the second, based on what appeared in Soviet newspapers at the time of production, I sent to Olin Downes in New York, who promised to print it in the *New York Times*. In addition, Downes was interested in resuming his correspondence with you, and I gave him your address—or more exactly, I even wrote it on an envelope so that it would arrive at the proper destination. I performed in twenty symphony concerts in America: the Fifth Concerto, the Third, the *Buffoon* Suite, *Portraits*, the "Classical" Symphony. It looks like the Americans are beginning to take me seriously, the way they should—because you know in the past they were rather like savages who would burst out laughing if you played (for example) Beethoven's Ninth for them on a record player. That's the good old Yankees for you: if they don't understand something, that means the author is doing it for fun or out of spite. Now they're gradually beginning to investigate the seriousness of my intentions.

I heard Shostakovich's Third performed by Stokowski, but I was disappointed by it. As always, there were interesting ideas, but the whole piece didn't hold together well; it was awkward, not flowing; there was a lot of counterpoint, and counterpoint is justified only when there is a tendency towards melody, and

---

98 The performance of the Fifth Concerto referred to by Prokofiev took place in Boston on December 30 and 31, 1933, conducted by Serge Koussevitsky.

this is precisely where Shostakovich is weak. The New Yorkers listened attentively, but most of the musicians share my impression.[99]

I came back from America on a large Italian steamship which made its way through the Azores and Gibraltar and let me off in Nice. We went through Gibraltar late in the evening, under the moon. The impression was incredible: both shores were outlined; the European coast was closer, mountainous, and in the distance was the African coast, which also had some hills. The Fort of Gibraltar itself, on a separate high rock, is located beyond the strait, in the Mediterranean Sea; it also created an extraordinary effect, totally covered with lights.

I'm glad the material for *Oranges* has arrived. On your advice I wrote to Radlov;[100] to Dranishnikov I sent a postcard while I was still in America. Popov has been looking for the score of the Septet for some time; he can stop looking because the "Serenade" society in Paris, which will be performing the Septet in June and to which I sent the parts, found a score in Leipzig. Soviet composers in general don't seem to make much effort to supply me with chamber music to be performed by ensembles abroad—almost as if it didn't concern them. I arranged to have Shostakovich's Octet performed at Triton in May. If you want to send something else, I could accommodate other authors as well; I've already discussed this topic with the chamber music societies of New York, Boston, and Chicago, and now I'm negotiating with those in Italy. [. . .]

I embrace you warmly. I'm definitely planning to be in the Soviet Union in April and May. I'll probably get to Moscow around April 10. What is the Leningrad Philharmonic thinking about, with those heavy brains of theirs? Write to me at my Paris address.

Yours, S. Prkfv.

November 20, 1933
Moscow

Dear Boris Vladimirovich,

I was very distressed not to see you at any of my concerts. At first they explained that you had locked yourself up at home and didn't want to see anyone (which seemed to be confirmed by the fact that you didn't tell anyone when you were in Moscow), but yesterday, just before I left Leningrad, I heard a rumor that you were in poor health—I was distressed to hear this.

---

99. Shostakovich's Symphony No. 3 ("First of May"), op. 20, was completed in 1929.

100. Sergei Radlov (1892–1958) was an avant-garde director with whom Prokofiev later would collaborate on *Romeo and Juliet*.

I'll be coming back to Leningrad November 28–30. Write to me at the Astoria by the 28th and let me know how you are and whether I can see you.

I embrace you warmly. S.

December 28, 1933
5, RUE VALENTIN HAÜY, PARIS XV, FRANCE

Dear Boris Vladimirovich,

After saying good-bye to you, I spent the day in Moscow and left for Rome in frightful cold; freezing Miaskovsky saw me off. In Rome, on the other hand, it's warm, cloudy, rainy, and sometimes the sun breaks through, and at those times they sell flowers on the sunny side of the street. My Third Symphony and Miaskovsky's Sinfonietta were played magnificently.[101] Just think: ten rehearsals! In other words, this was a completely different performance from that given by the Leningrad Philharmonic,[102] and that's why it became immediately accessible to the public as well. When I left Rome, I visited my youngest son briefly, who's living with his grandmother in Cannes, and then I returned to Paris for only three weeks, as I'll be starting some more concert tours on January 2.

I've hardly seen anyone or heard anything in Paris. I did hear Glazunov's rather modest Quartet for Four Saxophones, which, surprisingly, was written harmonically rather than contrapuntally (by the way, by using a contrapuntal and orchestral approach to the saxophone, you can get some curious sounds!), and also Poulenc's mixed-up Sextet, which wasn't very interesting—his dilettantism shines through, and there's no new material. I'm spending most of my time at home, hurrying to finish the music for Tairov's *Egyptian Nights*.[103]

In April they're planning a symphonic concert of Soviet music here. I'd like the program to include Popov's symphony. He was in such a hurry, he didn't give me his address, so I ask you not to delay in talking it over with him. [. . .]

The organizers of the concert are planning to ask you to give them a few notes about the Soviet composers who will be performed. You won't need to do

---

101. The concert in Rome, at which these compositions were performed, took place on December 10, 1933, and was conducted by Bernardino Molinari.

102. The performance of Prokofiev's Third Symphony took place at the Leningrad Philharmonic on April 21, 1933, under the direction of Dranishnikov.

103. At the request of Aleksandr Tairov, Prokofiev wrote music for the play *Egyptian Nights* (based on Shaw, Shakespeare, and Pushkin), which was being produced at Tairov's Moscow Chamber Theater; in 1934 the composer used this music to create a symphonic suite in seven movements, op. 61.

any special work for these notes; all they need is some biographical information, a list of compositions, and a few words of description. But I'll tell you more about that later.

Although I'll be on tour all through January, you (and Popov) can write to me at my Paris address, and my letters will be forwarded from there immediately. By the way, I can already tell you definitely that from January 9 to 13 I'll be in Milan. My address:

Ufficio Concerti Moltrasio & Luzzatto,
pour Serge Prokofieff,
Via T. Grossi 7,
Milano (101),
Italie.

I embrace you warmly. How is your work going? What is the layout of your apartment? I won't ask about your health; I'm sure it's in good shape and your headaches aren't interfering with your reading and study. Best regards from Lina Ivanovna to Irina Stepanovna and you.

Yours, S. Prkfv.

Jan. 23, 1934
TARVISIO

Dear Boris Vladimirovich,

I have three days free between concerts, so I've decided to hole up in this little place, in the mountains in northern Italy, or rather in the part of Italy reconquered from Austria. There's a lot of white snow around here (just like whipped cream) and the temperature is right at zero. How are you? I wrote to you at the end of December, and I hope to hear from you when I get back to Paris. I embrace you warmly.

S.P.

April 17, 1934
MOSCOW, HOTEL NATIONAL, ROOM 406

Dear Boris Vladimirovich,

There's nothing worse than Leningrad friends! I haven't heard a word from you since the creation of the world. Not a living soul has written to me about the new production of *Oranges*, and I didn't find out about it until I got to Moscow. I sent a telegraph to Dranishnikov on the 10th and to Radlov on the 14th, asking them to tell me the dates so I could plan my trip accordingly—but it was like talking to a brick wall; not one of them answered me.

I'm going to Ukraine on the 24th. I might get to Leningrad around May 5 or 6 and stay until the 10th or 11th. Is there any chance that *Oranges* can be stuck in during this time? Please be a decent person at least once in your life and write to me right away at the National.

I embrace you. Yours, S.P.

April 26, 1934
KHARKOV

Dear Boris Vladimirovich,

I was very happy about your decision to go to the Ukraine with me and on the 24th waited for you. After that I figured out that like a professor out of Jules Verne, you had probably mixed up the months!

At least one normal person has shown up in Leningrad: Iokhelson. He shook up Bukhshtein[104] and, with the signatures of both, sent this information: *Oranges* will be given on May 12. So you say you have cast off lyricism; from this point of view your letter was very appealing.

And so, from Odessa I go directly to Leningrad, where I arrive on the 6th in the afternoon, and will stay until the 13th. Come by the Astoria on the same day.

Warm hugs, Your S.P.

June 5, 1934
MOSCOW

Dear Boris Vladimirovich,

I was planning to leave Moscow for Ufa on the 3rd, but bad weather and bad steamships delayed my departure. I'll be leaving on the *Jaurès* on the 6th by myself: Afinogenov and Gusman have let me down.[105] It's a shame you've let me down also, although you referred to it only vaguely. In her letter, Lina Ivanovna joins me in saying: "I still hope Asafiev will come along."

I spent a week at Konchalovsky's dacha, three h[ours] from Moscow. It's beautiful there; I'd never walked through the forests outside Moscow before. He drew an excellent portrait of me at my full height, in the garden, in an arm-

---

104. B. S. Bukhshtein was the director of the Leningrad Academic Theaters in 1934; V. E. Iokhelson was the head of the literary and repertory department of Malegot.

105. The writer A. N. Afinogenov and Gusman had offered to accompany Prokofiev on his journey through the Five Rivers region.

chair, while I was orchestrating the "Hebrew Overture"[106] and making a suite out of *Kije*.[107]

I'll be coming back to Moscow around the 19th or 20th for a few days. Drop me a line at the National around that time.

I embrace you warmly. I've been reading the magazines you gave me, which are very interesting and useful.

Yours, S. Prkfv.

July 12, 1934
BERLIN

Dear Boris Vladimirovich,

I received your letter just before my departure, and I'm responding from Germany, on my way to Paris. During my last evening I saw Volkov at Meyerhold's, and I talked with him about you and your new ballet.[108] I congratulate you on your interesting work; I'll try to print something about it in the French newspapers—Volkov told me it was no secret. But Miaskovsky is a real rogue: he played his Fifteenth for you and even convinced you of its virtues, but he ignobly concealed it from me. That is, I knew he was planning a new symphony, but I gathered from his words that it was all still up in the air.[109] This was probably because I was so rough on the finale of his Fourteenth. [. . .]

In August and September I'm planning to spend some time in Paris and some time in Biarritz. Write to me at my Paris address. I wrote to you at the beginning of June, just before my cruise to Ufa through the Five Rivers region.

I embrace you warmly—get some rest and gather your strength. I've read through the magazines you sent me several times.

Yours, S. Prkfv.

---

106. The Overture on Hebrew Themes for clarinet, two violins, viola, cello, and piano in C Minor, op. 34, was written by Prokofiev in 1919; in 1934 he created a version for symphonic orchestra—op. 34-bis.

107. The symphonic suite *Lieutenant Kije*, op. 60, was constructed by Prokofiev out of music he wrote for the 1934 film of the same name. The artist who painted Prokofiev's portrait was Pyotr Konchalovsky (1876–1956).

108. In 1934 Asafiev wrote a ballet, *The Fountain of Bakhchisarai*, with a libretto by N. D. Volkov, based on Pushkin; it was first performed at the Kirov Theater of Opera and Ballet in Leningrad on September 28, 1934.

109. Miaskovsky's Fifteenth Symphony in D Minor, op. 38, was composed between May and October 1934, and the orchestration was completed on November 29, 1934. When Prokofiev was in Moscow, there were only sketches for the first two movements of the symphony.

Sept. 6, 1934
MAISON SADOUL, STE. MAXIME, VAR, FRANCE

Dear Boris Vladimirovich,

In July, on my way from Moscow to Paris, I wrote a letter to you in the Caucasus. Did you get it? I haven't gotten anything from you. At the moment we're at the Mediterranean Sea at Sadoul's dacha, where we were also two years ago. Petya and I came from Paris by automobile and visited Stravinsky, who is writing a concerto for two f[orte]p[ianos] without orc[hestra] and a book about himself.[110] When I asked him which was the best book about him so far, he answered: Glebov's.[111]

I embrace you. S.P.

February 9, 1935
PARIS

Dear Boris Vladimirovich,

Why haven't you written to me? Yesterday your *Flames* was praised by Herriot, who said that such a piece might be of interest in Paris. I was pleased to note that he even pronounced your name correctly, with the right stress.

But you are a fine gentleman! I'm prepared for the fact that Shapiro hasn't written to me as he promised, but it's really shameful that you've turned out to be unreliable!

I read Dos Passos: it's interesting, but not much material. I'll have to come back to this idea next autumn, when I will be going to America and could work out this subject with the author.[112]

---

110. Stravinsky's *Chronicle of My Life* was originally published in French: *Igor Strawinsky. Chroniques de ma vie* (Paris: Danoël Steele, 1935). It was translated into English as *An Autobiography* (New York: Simon and Schuster, 1936).

111. In a letter to Miaskovsky dated October 26, 1931, Asafiev wrote: "Did I mention that my book about Stravinsky was very much to his liking? He was amazed at how, without knowing him personally and without any correspondence or 'interviews,' I was able to figure out his creative method (or rather, his creative process)." (State Archive of Literature and Art, fund 2040, collection no. 1, item no. 97, p. 28.)

112. Asafiev suggested that Prokofiev use the novel *1919* by the American writer John Dos Passos (which appeared in a Russian translation in 1933) as the subject for an opera libretto. Apparently Prokofiev did not return to this subject either in the fall of 1936, as he had intended to, or any time later, since no other references to this project have been found.

I wrote to Iokhelson to tell him to talk with Shapiro about my affairs (the old opera, the new ballet).[113] Write to me anyway, if you have any vestiges of conscience left. I plan to be in the USSR on March 10.

Yours, S.P.

Mar. 16, 1935
Moscow

Dear Boris Vladimirovich,

Here I am back in Moscow, but so far I'm still outside the musical field—I'm playing in a chess tournament.[114] How is life treating you? Why haven't you sent me a line in three months? Write to me at this address, at the Hotel National, as soon as possible, so I'll receive it by the 21st. On the evening of the 21st I'll be going to Sverdlovsk for three concerts;[115] my future plans are still uncertain. L[ina] I[vanovna] is planning to come here April 5–10. I embrace you warmly.

Yours, S.P.

If you think that your letter may not reach me by the 21st, then address it to N. Ya. M[iaskovsky], and he'll forward it to Sverdlovsk.

July 25, 1944
[NEAR IVANOVO]

Dear Boris Vladimirovich,

From the silent fields of the composers' state poultry farm[116] I extend both

---

113. This refers to Prokofiev's negotiations with R. A. Shapiro, the director of the Kirov Theater of Opera and Ballet in Leningrad, regarding the production of his works there.

114. The Second International Chess Tournament took place in Moscow from February 15 to March 15, 1935. Prokofiev attended the final rounds of this tournament as a spectator and a fan.

115. Prokofiev was invited to Sverdlovsk by the concert bureau of the opera theater to participate in lectures and concerts—on March 25 at the University of Musical Culture at the Uralmash industrial complex, a *klavierabend* at the Lunacharsky Theater, and on March 26 at the House of Literature and Art.

116. "The composers' state poultry farm" is what Prokofiev calls the sanitorium operated by the Composers Union near the site of a large state poultry farm close to the city of Ivanovo. During the difficult war years, many Soviet composers lived and worked here. Prokofiev spent the summer and fall of 1944 and 1945 at the sanitorium.

my arms towards you to congratulate you with all my heart on your jubilee birthday.[117] May you enjoy greater health, greater strength, greater compositions and work!

I embrace you warmly.

Yours, S. Prkfv.

117. June 29, 1944, was Asafiev's 60th birthday.

CHAPTER SIX

Letters to Vernon Duke

KNOWN TO MILLIONS as the American composer of such popular song hits as "Autumn in New York," "April in Paris," and "Taking a Chance on Love" (from his score to the Broadway hit *Cabin in the Sky*), Vernon Duke (1903–69) was also another composer: as Vladimir Dukelsky (his real name), he composed respectable "classical" ballets, symphonies, concerti, sonatas, oratorios, and chamber music. Born in Russia and educated at the Kiev Conservatory, Dukelsky came to the United States in 1921. For the rest of his life, Dukelsky/Duke led a double creative life, writing "serious" music for such imposing impresarios as Serge Koussevitsky and Sergei Diaghilev with one hand, and collaborating with Ira Gershwin, Bob Hope, and the Ziegfeld Follies with the other.

Duke had admired Prokofiev (twelve years his senior) long before he finally got to meet him. In his charming memoir *Passport to Paris*, Duke describes how he first saw Prokofiev in Kiev in the autumn of 1916, when Prokofiev went there to play his First Piano Concerto under the direction of the composer Reinhold Glière. Glière was one of the many people Prokofiev and Duke had in common—childhood tutor to Prokofiev, Glière was also Duke's professor at the Kiev Conservatory. Prokofiev's Kiev performance made a huge impression on the future song-and-dance man, not least for its visual intensity and theatricality:

> He had white-blond hair, a small head with a large mouth and very thick lips [. . .] and very long, awkwardly dangling arms, terminating in a bruiser's powerful hands. Prokofiev wore dazzlingly elegant tails, a beautifully cut waistcoat, and flashing black pumps. The strangely gauche manner in which he traversed the stage was no indication of what was to follow; after sitting down and adjusting the piano stool with an abrupt jerk, Prokofiev let go with an unrelenting muscular exhibition of a completely novel kind of piano playing. [. . .] This young man's music and his performance of it reminded me of the onrushing forwards in my one unfortunate soccer experience; there was no sentiment, no sweetness there—nothing but unrelenting energy and athletic joy of living [. . .] there was frenetic applause and no less than six flower horseshoes were

handed to Prokofiev, who was now greeted with astonished laughter. He bowed clumsily, dropping his head almost to his knees and recovering with a yank.[1]

It was another shared mentor, Sergei Diaghilev, who finally brought Prokofiev and Duke together. They met while Duke was in Paris to work on his first ballet for the Ballets Russes, *Zéphire et Flore*. A recreation of a 1796 ballet staged by the legendary Charles-Louis Didelot, *Zéphire et Flore* received its premiere in Monte Carlo on April 28, 1925, with choreography by Léonide Massine. But for Duke, the date of his meeting with Prokofiev—June 17, 1924—was almost more important, since "a great and durable friendship began on that day."[2]

Similarly irreverent and fond of practical jokes and crude humor, Prokofiev and Dukelsky took to each other immediately. Until 1938, after which time Prokofiev was no longer able to leave the USSR, he and Duke maintained a lively and witty personal and creative friendship. Occasionally sharing billing in Paris appearances, they encouraged and criticized each other, argued about music, and took motor trips along with Prokofiev's wife Lina. In the spring of 1928, it was Duke who brought George Gershwin to Prokofiev's Paris apartment, where the American composer "played his head off," impressing Prokofiev with his facility, although Gershwin's enjoyment of "dollars and dinners"—a vice shared by Duke—made him wary.[3]

As time went on, the creative paths Prokofiev and Duke followed came to diverge more and more. Duke followed up the commercial success of his 1932 "April in Paris" (written for the show *Walk a Little Faster*) in 1934 with another standard, "Autumn in New York" (written for the show *Thumbs Up*). In 1940 he produced the music for one of the first Broadway shows with an all-black cast, *Cabin in the Sky*, later made into a feature film starring Ethel Waters. Although he continued to compose "classical" works, Duke became known primarily as a "popular" composer, an identity he did not attempt to cast off.

In the letters Prokofiev wrote to Duke during the frequent periods when they were in different places, the issue of "popular" versus "classical" music often arises. Prokofiev jokingly chides Duke for having been seduced by the lure of money and fame into writing what he dismissed as "tra-la-la." In a letter to Nikolai Miaskovsky (May 22, 1931), Prokofiev expressed disappointment over

1.   Vernon Duke, *Passport to Paris* (Boston: Little, Brown, 1955), 25.
2.   Ibid., 120.
3.   Ibid., 209.

the direction Duke's career had taken: "Dukelsky, who now lives in New York, sent me his latest manuscripts, but his inspiration has somehow just completely dried up. It's a pity, for he had a lot of promise." Even so, Prokofiev continued to energetically promote Duke's classical compositions, attempting to persuade Soviet conductors to program them and urging Koussevitsky to maintain his support of their fellow Russian.

Prokofiev's decision to return to the USSR permanently came as something of a surprise to Duke, and eventually brought an end to their friendship and correspondence. In the letters he wrote to Duke in the late 1930s from Russia, Prokofiev began to write in French, in an apparent attempt to make them more difficult for the censors to read. He also advised Duke to avoid mentioning money matters, since he did not want Soviet officials to know all the details of his dealings in foreign currency. Nor was Prokofiev especially complimentary in assessing his new Soviet composer colleagues.

Duke and Prokofiev met for the last time in New York early in 1938, on Prokofiev's last foreign tour. Not long before he was scheduled to leave for Europe in the last days of March, Prokofiev received an intriguing offer from Duke's Hollywood agent to write music for the movies at $2500 a week.

> I showed Serge the telegram exultantly; there was a flicker of interest for a mere instant, then, his face set, his oversize lips petulant, he said gruffly: "That's nice bait, but I won't swallow it. I've got to go back to Moscow, to my music and my children. And now that that's settled, will you come to Macy's with me? I've got to buy a whole roomful of things you can't get in Russia—just look at Lina's list."
>
> The list was imposing, and we went to Macy's department store, another sample of capitalistic bait designed by the lackeys of Wall Street to be swallowed by oppressed workers. Although he wouldn't admit it, Serge enjoyed himself hugely in the store—he loved gadgets and trinkets of every description. Suddenly he turned to me, his eyes peculiarly moist, his voice even gruffer than usual: "You know, Dima, it occurred to me that I may not be back for quite some time. . . . I don't suppose it would be wise for you to come to Russia, would it?" "No, I don't suppose it would," I answered, smiling bravely, my happiness abruptly gone. I never saw Prokofiev again.[4]

(These letters are in the Music Division of the Library of Congress. They were published in the original Russian in the USSR as Nest'ev, I., ed. "Neizvest-

---

4.   Ibid., 367.

nye materialy o Prokof'eve: Ob odnoi prervannoi druzhbe," *Istoriia i sovremen-nost': Sbornik statei* [Leningrad: Sovetskii kompozitor, 1981], 239–60. Translated by Harlow Robinson. I have edited and abbreviated the letters here.)

April 6, 1930
PALACE HOTEL, BRUSSELS

Dear Dima,

I spent only a few hours in Paris; I saw Gege,[5] who said that your songs and
Dushenka[6] were sent to the printer a month ago, and therefore the proofs
should be at the publisher's within a few days.

It's a pity that you didn't find the time to give me your handwritten instructions: now Paichadze is leaving for London, and I'm off to Italy, and I won't see
him before the end of April.

My festivals here are proceeding in fine fashion. There were already two
symphonic concerts, at which Ansermet conducted the Third Symphony, the
Divertissement, *Buffoon*, and the Third Piano Concerto. The public responded
marvelously. All that's remaining now is my recital.

With a hug, I remain yours, SP

November 9, 1930
5, RUE VALENTIN HAÜY, PARIS XV, FRANCE

Dear Dima,

The touching story about young maidens who take up prostitution in order
to feed their mothers has been known from time immemorial. In Karamzin's
time it even brought many people to tears.[7] But gradually they began to understand that if a young maiden actually enjoys lying on her back, then she will try
to disguise her desire behind some charitable-sounding pretext. If she doesn't
enjoy lying on her back, then she'll find a different means of feeding dear
mommy. Incidentally, the latter will most likely not find bread earned in such a
fashion so very tasty anyway.

No matter how you might pretend and prevaricate, the fact is that you like
your half-respectable bread. You can't hide the excitement you feel because

---

5. Gavriil Grigorevich Paichadze was director of the Editions Russes de Musique in
    Paris.
6. *Dushenka* is a duet for women's voices and chamber orchestra, to texts by Hyppolite
    Bogdanovich, completed in 1927.
7. Nikolai Mikhailovich Karamzin (1766–1826) was a Russian writer of the Sentimental-
    ist movement, most famous for his story "Poor Liza" (1792), a tale of a lower-class girl
    taken advantage of by an artistocrat who later abandons her, leading her to commit
    suicide.

your lousy record is number one in sales.⁸ But if I were to ask you what you have accomplished in the last year in the field of *real* music, then aside from two rather dry piano pieces you couldn't show me a single thing.⁹ The dryness of these pieces very accurately reflects your present situation: when, after a long hiatus, you decide to take up "serious" music once again, you're very fearful to display some sign of the "operetta-ness" that has now become (even though you haven't noticed it) your very flesh and blood. Russian music has already seen a precedent for such a phenomenon, and, strangely enough, in the person of Rachmaninoff. After all, at one time he was also considered to be twice as talented as many others, and although he never lowered himself to can-cans, he did still let himself wallow in excessively syrupy songs. When musicians expressed their indignation, he tried to put on a serious face, but started turning out such dried-up stuff that it quickly disappeared from the stage. And so he remained a composer of "songs for the broad public."

Let's look forward to the year 1931, and hope that you will succeed in rehabilitating your name, which is now half-forgotten in Europe.

I will be happy to promote your Second Symphony.¹⁰ The first step was to read to Paichadze some excerpts from your letter, and to persuade him to prepare a copy of the orchestral score so that it can be passed around from one conductor to another. And so it has been decided that the score will be given to a copyist in the coming days. In October I was in Berlin, when the Radio gave a symphonic concert of my compositions. The concert went well, which gave me the opportunity to recommend your Second Symphony to the director of the Radio. He was favorably disposed, and said he would be happy to put it on the program, and asked to have the score sent to their conductor, Zeidler-Winkler, which Paichadze has done. I will be in Berlin again on November 18, and will find out the results. Besides that, I will go to Warsaw and Brussels, and there I will also tell them about your symphony. As for Paris, Paichadze is counting on Ansermet. If nothing happens with Ansermet in a month's time, then I will have a serious talk with Monteux. On December 18 in the Salle Pleyel under his direction there will be a festival of my music (Fourth Sym-

---

8. Duke's song "I'm Only Human after All," with lyrics by E. "Yip" Harburg and Ira Gershwin, written in 1930 for *The Garrick Gaieties* (1930) on Broadway, was his first popular success as a songwriter.

9. Prokofiev is referring to Dukelsky's "2 Pieces" for piano, completed in 1930.

10. Dukelsky worked on his Second Symphony from 1928 to 1930. It received its first performance in Boston on April 25, 1930.

phony, Second Piano Concerto, and other works)—and that will be a convenient moment to nudge Monteux in the direction of your symphony.

Your songs came out a long time ago already, but I like them much less than
the ones to the texts by Bogdanovich.[11] The "dried-up pieces" were given to the
printer and will appear at any moment. Paichadze took your address and will
send the songs and the pieces there. They have promised to perform *Dushenka*
in London. Oh yes, *Dushenka* also came out, but without the dedication.
Merci.[12]

If you aren't annoyed with me again , then please write and tell me how my
Fourth goes with Kusi.[13] I have asked his secretary to send me the reviews, but
first of all it's not clear whether she will, and secondly the most interesting
thing is the general atmosphere surrounding the performance. I would also like
to know your opinion.

My new compositions? After the quartet I wrote a ballet that will be staged
in May at the Opéra by Lifar, with sets by Larionov and costumes by Goncharova. Right now I'm doing the orchestration and have already finished
nearly half of the full score. Those who have heard the ballet's music (Nouvel,
Souvchinsky, Lifar) praise it and consider that it represents the next step after
Prodigal Son.[14]

My family and I send you a big hug. We now have a new permanent apartment, which is gradually being furnished thanks to the considerable efforts of
Lina Ivanovna. But hurrah, I now have a real desk, a real "extension" bookcase,
and soon there will be a real divan!

Yours,

SPRKFV

Write to me at the above address.

June 3, 1932

5, RUE VALENTIN HAÜY, PARIS XV, FRANCE

Dear Dima,

Thanks for your plump letter. Nineteen pages—that has to be a record! But
what I found most touching was something to which you probably paid little
attention—a certain youthful freshness of your style, a quality lost long ago by

---

11.   "Poésies de Hyppolite Bogdanovitch (and Pushkin)," completed 1930.
12.   It seems that Dukelsky had promised to dedicate the score to Prokofiev.
13.   One of Prokofiev's nicknames for Koussevitsky.
14.   The new ballet was *On the Dnepr* (*Sur le Borysthène*).

all those Markeviches and Nabokovs in their Parisian struggle for existence.[15] You have managed to preserve it somehow, even amidst your perpetual pandering to the scum of New York music.

Before composing this response, I paid a call on Paichadze to find out from him what useful information I could convey to you concerning your publishing affairs. Paichadze replied that the most important thing is to ask you to get married as soon as possible to a rich American, since in this case you had promised to give a percentage to the publishing house, which would come in very handy in these difficult times. Secondly, you did a very superficial job of correcting the proofs of your *Printemps 1931* and the trio, so that during the checking of the second proofs many questions were raised.[16] Paichadze asks you to return the manuscripts of these pieces as soon as possible, so that the questionable spots can be checked—and then he'll release both pieces immediately. He also asks if it wouldn't be possible in the trio to indicate that the flute and bassoon can be replaced by violin and cello. G. G. showed the trio to some string players, who found that it would be entirely acceptable in that combination. Paichadze thinks that such doubling would lead to greater sales and more frequent performances. There are precedents in both Mozart and Haydn.

I held the manuscript of the *Epitaph* in my hands in passing at the publishing house a few months ago, when you sent it to have the voices written in. But when I saw that it was written on jazz paper, I was overcome by a feeling of disgust and put it aside. Koussevitsky regards the *Epitaph* with a kind of well-meaning encouragement, so if you really give it so much significance, then I'll look at it more attentively.[17] But what sort of decadent idea is it to write a monumental piece about dying Petersburg! There I can see the influence of your fraternizing with the fading emigration, this branch ripped from its trunk, which dreams in its decline about the lush springtimes of the past. If you want to write something like that, then why not *Leningrad* or *Dneprostroi*?[18]

If you have decided to throw caution to the winds and spend money on your

---

15.   Prokofiev refers to Russian émigré composers Igor Markevich (see n. 31, below) and Nicolas Nabokov.

16.   *Printemps* for piano solo (1931); Trio (Variations) for Flute, Bassoon, and Piano (1930).

17.   *Epitaph* (on the death of Diaghilev) for soprano solo, chorus, and orchestra was given its premiere by the Boston Symphony on April 15, 1932.

18.   Prokofiev is referring to Dukelsky's *The End of St. Petersburg*, an oratorio. Leningrad was the name given to St. Petersburg in 1924, after Vladimir Lenin's death. Dneprostroi was one of the enormous new Soviet industrial complexes that symbolized the Soviet Union's nascent socialist economy.

own festival in Paris, then I would advise you to take a different approach. A festival is expensive to put on, and can take place with a half-filled hall. It's much cheaper to provide (even through a third party) a small sum to some orchestra or other, for the extra expenses of hiring a chorus or additional instruments. More orchestras appear in Paris with each passing year, and they are more and more impoverished, so that if you were to go to them with a thousand or two thousand franc note in your hand, it wouldn't be difficult to arrange for them to include some work or other of yours in their program. Proceeding this way, you could have several performances at different concerts instead of just one festival, which would give you a wider public and press, and would in the end cost less. It won't be difficult to set up the performance of your chamber pieces for next season, either under the auspices of Serenade, or in Cortot's concerts,[19] which he conducts with a chamber orchestra and programs of contemporary music, or in the new chamber society for the performance of contemporary music that is now being formed. I will be a member of the jury.

It was very pleasant for me to find out that you liked my Third Symphony. I also believe that it has a lot of real material, and I couldn't understand why it has been so slow to win people over. The *Prodigal Son* Suite was made from the left-over material that didn't go into the Fourth Symphony. So it's no wonder that it does not include the best numbers, for example the A-minor rondo or the concluding andante. They make up the two middle movements of the symphony, which the treasured representative of our tribe, Couscous,[20] so unfairly buried in Boston. I hope that after the success of the Third Symphony someone will take it into his head to rehabilitate the Fourth, which is infinitely more significant than the suite, which Walter[21] performed, and which I had put together "just in case," so that the remaining material of the ballet would not go to waste. I didn't foresee that Walter would get so fixated on the suite.

Among my new pieces which are unknown to you, the String Quartet has appeared in print, as well as six piano pieces arranged from various orchestra

19. The French pianist Alfred Cortot (1877–1962) established the Association des Concerts A. Cortot in 1902.

20. This nickname for Serge Koussevitsky demonstrates Prokofiev's love of puns and wordplay.

21. Bruno Walter (1876–1962), the German conductor of the Gewandhaus Orchestra in Leipzig 1929–33, emigrated from Germany in 1933 and moved to the United States in 1939.

and chamber works; two sonatinas will also soon appear.[22] I promise to send them along soon. My ballet *On the Dnepr* has been marinating for two seasons already at the Paris Grand Opéra, which is now afflicted with marasmus and has almost closed down altogether. Also marinating is my "Handless" Concerto, since the pianist who commissioned it cannot seem to figure it out at all.[23] Even so, I have finished yet another concerto; incidentally, it will bear the title "Music for Piano and Orchestra," op. 55—not because the work isn't concerto-ish enough, but so as not to run up too many numbers. I will perform it for the first time on October 30 with Furtwängler and the Berlin Philharmonic, on December 30 in Boston, and then in New York.[24]

In fact, the entire autumn, beginning with the second half of October, I will be traveling around central Europe with opus 55, and then I'll proceed to Moscow, and in the second half of December I'll set off for America, where I'll spend January and February. August and September we will probably spend in the south of France—either in Saint Jean de Luz or near Cannes.

Fitelberg did not perform your symphony in Warsaw: he had a difficult season, the orchestra was impoverished and he had lost some of his influence.[25] It seems that the prospects look better for autumn; Fitelberg is coming to Paris at the end of June—I'll speak to him again about it, since he likes your symphony—he called it "nice fresh music." This year the Russian Opera has gone from bread to kvas, and there's no hint of repeating the brilliance and regularity of last season. By the way, the Opéra Comique has invited them now to give a series of performances with Chaliapin. The performances have been proceeding with considerable pomp, but there are few of them, and it's not clear what will happen at the end of this engagement.

So there, I have also responded on a grand scale to your long letter. I send you a big hug, Lina Ivanovna sends her greetings and is planning to write you. She really did sing your music in London on the radio and will be singing it again in the coming days on the Paris radio. If the Sudeikins[26] have divorced

---

22. String Quartet No. 1, op. 50 (1930); Six Pieces for piano, op. 52 (1930–31); Two Sonatinas, op. 54 (1931–32).
23. Piano Concerto No. 4 in B flat for the left hand, op. 53 (1931).
24. This work eventually became the Piano Concerto No. 5 in G.
25. Gregor Fitelberg (1879–1953), a Polish conductor, violinist, composer, and pedagogue.
26. Prokofiev refers to the divorce of Sergei and Vera Sudeikin. Vera later married Igor Stravinsky.

there where you are, then here so have the Souvchinskys and the Tansmans[27]—
and all of them have disappeared from the horizon.

Yours, SPRKFV

March 23, 1933
5, RUE VALENTIN HAÜY, PARIS, XV, FRANCE

Dear Dima,

I promised to write you concerning the calendar of my geographical where-
abouts for the spring and autumn, but for the moment not all the details are yet
in place. On the sixth I'm leaving for the USSR, where I plan to stay until the
beginning of June. Lina Ivanovna will stay in Paris until about April 25th, and
then she'll also join me in Moscow. It looks like we'll spend some time in Paris
in June, but what will happen after that is not yet clear.

Triton is playing your trio in Paris on April 28.[28] In view of the fact that the
program includes other pieces for string ensemble, they want to play your trio
with violin and cello. In my opinion, it would be better to let them play it like
that than not to play it at all. But the idea of replacing the strings with flute and
bassoon was inspired exclusively by financial concerns. If you want to send fifteen dollars (you could send it to Paichadze or to Lina Ivanonva), then that
would suffice to engage a flutist and bassoonist.

I spoke to Count Sanmartino about your Second Symphony. He expressed
interest in it and asked to be reminded to include it in the program of symphonic concerts that takes place in Rome at the Augusteum; he is the official
representative of that series. That would of course be for next season, whose
programs will be set up in May–June. Molinari conducts these concerts.[29]

And so, how are you doing and why don't you write? Lina Ivanovna sends
you her heartfelt greetings; she will be singing you on April 2 at the American
Club in Paris. I send you a hug.

Yours, SPRKFV

Please find out from Kochanski what has prevented him from sending me the
score of my Sonata for Two Violins.[30]

27. Alexandre Tansman (1897–1986) was a Polish composer, conductor, and pianist who
    lived in Paris after 1919; he was close to the French composers known as Les Six.
28. Triton was a Paris concert organization on whose jury Prokofiev served. It included
    several members of Les Six—Poulenc, Honegger, and Milhaud—and presented per-
    formances of chamber music.
29. Bernardino Molinari (1880–1962) was a conductor and music director of the Augus-
    teum.
30. Pawel Kochanski (1887–1934) was a Polish violinist who lived in Russia 1913–19. The

August 14, 1933
5, RUE VALENTIN HAÜY, PARIS, XV, FRANCE

Dear Dima,

[. . .] These are my plans for the near future: having sent Lina Ivanovna off to Geneva for vacation, and the children to their grandmother on the Riviera, I stayed in Paris for about three weeks, so I could settle down and get to work. At the end of August I'll go by car to get Lina Ivanovna and then together we will head down to the Mediterranean to do some swimming. Around September 15–20 we'll return to Paris, and in early October I'll leave first for Riga and Warsaw, and then to the USSR until December. From there I'll go directly to Italy. I'm telling you all this in case you should be dropping in to Paris and counting on my presence there.

As usual, it was very interesting in the USSR, not only in Moscow and Leningrad, but also in the Caucasus, right up to Mt. Ararat, at whose base I gave a concert, in Erevan. In October I want to take a few of your compositions with me, so they could be placed in the library of the Composers Union in Moscow.

Remember in New York you told me about your links with a very cultured society of contemporary music in Mexico, and I told you about my project to set up various exchanges for Soviet music. Combining both these ideas, it occurred to me that maybe in Mexico they would like to receive some interesting scores (both orchestral and chamber) by contemporary Muscovites and Leningraders so that they could be performed in Mexico. In return, they could send works of their own composers, whose performance I could guarantee *réciproquement* in Moscow or Leningrad. I have succeeded in establishing this sort of "property exchange" between Moscow and many large European cities, and this exchange has stimulated lots of excitement. Perhaps Mexico would also be interested in such a project, but don't just do it casually, any old way—enter into discussions with them in a businesslike and tactful manner.

I don't remember if I informed you that Fitelberg wrote me the following: Dukelsky's symphony had a good success and good reviews.

I squeeze your hand, write me in Russian: You're not Markevich, who can't string together two words in his native language without stumbling.[31]

Yours, SPRKFV

Sonata for Two Violins in C Major was composed in 1932 and first performed in Moscow on November 27, 1932.

31. Igor Markevich (born 1912) was a conductor and composer prominent in Paris musical circles; he wrote the ballet *Rebus* in 1931. He was Diaghilev's last lover.

September 29, 1935
POLENOVO

My dear Vernon [these words only in English],[32]

[. . .] I had been planning to go to America this winter, but after Bruno Walter failed to sign his contract, I lost my engagement in New York, and besides that my new four-act ballet (*Romeo and Juliet*, based on Shakespeare), which I have just completed and am now orchestrating, will be put on in the winter at the Bolshoi Theater and at the Mariinsky. So an extended absence at this particular moment wasn't exactly music to my heart.[33]

I'm spending the summer at an estate that belongs to the Bolshoi Theater, near Serpukhov. It's a marvelous little spot, a bit noisy when ¾ of the Bolshoi Theater troupe comes here on vacation, but it's actually fun, especially since I have a separate little cottage with a Blüthner [piano] and a terrace overlooking the Oka River, where it is very quiet and very conducive to good work. Lina Ivanovna and the children also came here in August; everyone made a great fuss over the boys and spoiled them to pieces. Now all the opera and ballet people have gone away, and I'm sitting over the score up to eight hours a day. Besides the ballet, I have written a Second Violin Concerto, two symphonic suites, two opuses for piano (one of them is called *Thoughts*), and an album for children. [. . .][34]

In a month I plan to be in Paris for the first performance of the Violin Concerto, and in December I'll go to Africa.[35]

Shostakovich is talented, but a sort of unprincipled fellow, and like some of our other friends, lacks the gift of melody. They make too much of him here, by the way. Kabalevsky and Zhelobinsky *sont des zéro-virgule-zéro*.[36] I am flattered that you consider several of my works to be "beyond time." Perhaps that is pre-

---

32. The entire letter is written with most vowels omitted, in a kind of shorthand.

33. The production of *Romeo and Juliet* was delayed for several seasons. It received its world premiere in Brno on December 30, 1938, and its Russian premiere at the Kirov Theater in Leningrad on January 11, 1940.

34. Concerto No. 2 for Violin and Orchestra in G Minor, op. 63; *Thoughts* (three pieces for piano), op. 62; "Music for Children, Twelve Easy Pieces for Piano," op. 65.

35. The premiere of the Second Violin Concerto took place not in Paris but in Madrid, on December 1, 1935.

36. Dmitri Borisovich Kabalevsky (1904–87), a Soviet composer and professor at the Moscow Conservatory, was an influential and active member of the Soviet Composers Union. Valery Viktorovich Zhelobinsky (1913–46) was a Soviet composer, pianist, and pedagogue who wrote several operas, including *Mother* (1938), based on Gorky's politically correct novel of the same name.

cisely one of the reasons why people who are too much confined within time often fail to understand my musical language. The rumors of my friendship with Poulenc and with Igor [Stravinsky] are very much exaggerated, and half-Igor[37] I can hardly bear.

I send you a hug, don't forget in the future your acts of generosity, and if you publish something that is *not* in the realm of tra-la-la, then send it along.

Yours, S. PRKFV

January 24 [?] 1937
AUDITORIUM HOTEL, CHICAGO[38]

Dima, thank you for your missive. [. . .] For the moment I'm still in the dark as to when I'll be going to New York, and even when I'll be leaving for Europe.

Chicago has given me a pleasant reception. The orchestra was attentive and played well, and even during a daytime concert the old ladies applauded heartily, risking their white gloves. To my disappointment, it turns out that Stock is on vacation, so that I could discuss your works only with his deputy Lange and the manager Voegeli, whom I immediately defeated at chess, as proof of my enthusiasm for your music.[39]

On Tuesday P.M. I'm moving on to St. Louis, where I'll be staying at the Hotel Coronado. Don't fail to send me a line there about what's up in New York, and tell me how Stravigor[40] does with his second program. [. . .] I leave St.Louis on the 31st in the morning and arrive in New York on the morning of the first. I'll be at the St. Moritz.

I send you a hug, SP

February 28, 1937
PARIS

Dear Dima,

I have been detained in Paris longer than I had anticipated (we're leaving tomorrow for Moscow), and this gave me the opportunity to do some serious work on behalf of your "musics." You already know about the symphonies: the

37. Igor Markevich.
38. This letter is labeled "copy" and is not in Prokofiev's handwriting.
39. Frederick Stock (1872–1942) became the conductor of the Chicago Symphony in 1905, and was a longtime supporter of the music of Prokofiev and Miaskovsky.
40. Igor Stravinsky.

first will be performed on March 14th by Lamoureux, the second on March 20th by Pasdeloup.[41] I received your money ($200 = 4276 francs) and gave it to the publisher, where Astrov (Mikhail Fyodorovich)[42] will take charge of the matter under Paichadze's supervision. I have promised 2000 francs to each of the orchestras, and Astrov will use the remaining 276 francs for expenses. I also told him that for his work you will pay him another 200–250 francs. Among his duties I instructed him to search for the analyses of both of your symphonies that appeared in the programs in Boston (the ones from previous years are either in the cellar of the publishing house or in American libraries) and to send them to musical journals and to the programs for the Paris performances; and then to cut out the reviews of the Paris performances and to send them to you right away. Astrov is awaiting the score of the First Symphony so he can give it to Bigot[43] (a serious person, *avec métier*, but he won't be setting the world on fire); Wolff[44] already has the Second Symphony. [. . .]

So there. I send you a big hug as I go off to get my bags together. You can write me in Moscow by registered mail (Zemlyanoi val 14, apt. 14) either in French or in English. If you write about my business affairs, it's all right to give figures, but don't put the word "dollars" or "$" next to them, so that it will not be clear what sort of foreign currency it is.[45] Lina Ivanovna remembers you affectionately and sends you her greetings.

Yours

PRKFV

---

41. The Lamoureux Concerts (Société des Nouveaux-Concerts) were named after Charles Lamoureux (1834–99), the Pasdeloup Concerts after Jules Etienne Pasdeloup (1819–87).

42. Mikhail Astrov was Prokofiev's personal secretary in Paris.

43. Eugène Bigot (1888–1965) was a French conductor, musical director of the Théâtre des Champs Elysées (1925–27), and director of the Lamoureux Concerts (1935–50).

44. Albert Wolff (1884–1970) was a French composer and conductor, president (1934–40) and second conductor (from 1925) of the Pasdeloup Concerts, and president of the Lamoureux Concerts (1928–34).

45. Soviet laws regarding the possession of foreign currency were very strict and harshly enforced. Prokofiev was obviously sensitive about attracting attention to the income he earned abroad. He had moved into a new apartment with his family at Zemlyanoi val in 1936. It was a luxurious building by Soviet standards, and was intended especially for prominent figures in Soviet culture and science.

June 19, 1937
ZEMLYANOI VAL 14, APT. 14, MOSCOW 64, USSR

Mr. Vernon Duke
315 West 57th St.
New York City

Cher Ami,[46]

Thank you for your letter of April 20, which gave me great pleasure. I received it a month ago—I have delayed in replying to you while waiting for the promised score of your oratorio, which has still not arrived.

Everything is fine here, and I have just finished the sketches for a cantata celebrating the twentieth anniversary of the USSR—a huge machine for orchestra, two choruses, military band, percussion orchestra, and an accordion ensemble.[47] When I think about the quantity of notes that I'll have to put down on paper in order to orchestrate all of that, I'm seized with terror! The first suite from *Romeo and Juliet* is being printed, and the second suite—which was played and well received in the two capitals upon my return from America—will follow right after its premiere.

The automobile has arrived, and—with a good chauffeur—makes life much easier, especially when spring comes and one has the opportunity to go out *ins grüne*.[48] The radio-phonograph sounds marvelous, actually I should say the phonograph part, since I haven't yet been able to install the antenna on our roof so that the radio can operate. All our furniture from Paris has also arrived, and among my books I rediscovered the manuscripts of your two melodies ("*Loin du bruit*". . .) I'll have them copied and send you one.

[. . .] Have they played your oratorio in Paris?[49] Do you have any firm projects with the Boston Symphony? You probably know that the performance of

---

46. Prokofiev had this letter typed in French, apparently to make it more difficult for the Soviet censors to read it.

47. *Cantata for the Twentieth Anniversary of October*, op. 74, for symphonic orchestra, military orchestra, orchestra of accordions, orchestra of percussion instruments, and two choruses, using texts by Marx, Lenin, and Stalin. One of Prokofiev's most curious creations, it failed to win the favor of the Soviet cultural authorities and received its premiere only after Prokofiev's death.

48. During his 1937 tour of the United States, Prokofiev purchased a new blue Ford which he shipped back to Moscow for his personal use. At the time, very few private Soviet citizens owned cars. *Ins grüne* is German for "into the countryside."

49. The oratorio *The End of St. Petersburg* received its premiere in New York on January 12, 1938.

my *Russian Overture*—planned for Boston this past April—has been buried, since our friend Gabriel[50] didn't provide the music in time. Yesterday I had a visit from Burgin,[51] who assured me that my engagement in Boston for next winter is still valid. Burgin is here for a brief stay, getting acquainted with Soviet works with the aim of performing them in Boston.

So there, cher Ami, don't forget to "drop me a line"[52] from time to time. I retain a very pleasant memory of the time we spent together in New York. My family also sends a friendly wave in your direction. I ordered the Hindemith flute sonata—it is very good, especially the end is *bien ausgedacht*.

Bien à toi

Serge Prokofieff

January 14, 1938

HOTEL ASTOR, 11 RUE D'ASTORG, PARIS 8

Dear Dima,

Forgive me for not writing you for so long. In September, when I was in the Caucasus, I received a very interesting letter from you, and I confirmed its receipt with a telegram, in which I expressed my joy over your successes, even though they might be in the realm of prostitution.[53]

Today Lina Ivanovna and I arrived in Paris from Moscow, alas, only for two days; then Prague, London, and on the 29th, to the USA on the *Normandie*. We will fall into your tender embraces on February 3, *natürlich* if you will be in New York at this time.

Unfortunately, for the moment it has not been possible to play your *Leningrad* in the USSR; the time isn't right: they're playing the classics, and of

50. Gavriil Paichadze.

51. Richard Burgin (1892–1981) was a Polish-born American violinist and conductor, concertmaster of the Boston Symphony, and appointed in 1927 as assistant conductor of the BSO by Koussevitsky.

52. Prokofiev writes this phrase in French (*faire tomber une ligne*), even though he knows it is an English idiom.

53. By early 1938, Duke had become a very popular Broadway songwriter. His "Autumn in New York" was written for the 1934 show *Thumbs Up* (with Duke's lyrics and music), and he wrote "I Can't Get Started" (sung by Bob Hope and Eve Arden) and several other songs for *Ziegfeld Follies of 1936*.

contemporary composers only Soviet ones. Miaskovsky looked over the score and praised it.[54]

I'd be very happy to see you, but for now send you a big hug.

SPRKFV

April 5, 1940
Снкацоvsкаіа 14, арт. 14, Moscow 64, USSR[55]

Mon cher Ami,[56]

It's been an age since I've had any news of you. I was counting on coming to America in February, but there's fighting going on in Europe—so I had to "*postponer*" that pleasure. Even so, I just read in the *Musical Courier* that you were present at a reception, therefore all must be fine with you and I am happy to learn that.

So, *vieux bonhomme*, what's new? What have you composed 1) in the way of music, 2) in the way of tra-la-la? Is the tra-la-la still paying well? Have you gotten married, or are you still on the prowl for *des petites demoiselles*?

This summer I completed an opera in five acts to a rather lively novella by Katayev, *I Am a Son of the Working People* (I'm looking for another title). It's being rehearsed in Moscow right now and the premiere is expected in two or three weeks.[57] My ballet *Romeo and Juliet* was produced at the Leningrad Opera in January with great pomp and our best dancers. The dancers were rather mistrustful at the start, but when they were called out for 15 curtain calls at the premiere, they decided that new forms can be accepted after all. I have finished a big piano sonata (25 minutes) which I will send you as soon as it is published.

So, I send you a hug, *mon vieux. Drop me a line*,[58] preferably by registered mail.

---

54. Prokofiev seems to be referring to Dukelsky's oratorio *The End of St. Petersburg*. Obviously, Dukelsky's status as a Russian émigré living in the United States made him anathema to Soviet cultural officials—as did the title of his oratorio. The tour that Prokofiev and Lina made of the United States in early 1938 was Prokofiev's last trip outside the USSR.

55. The name of the street on which Prokofiev's apartment was located had been changed to honor the Soviet pilot Valery Chkalov.

56. This letter is handwritten in French.

57. The opera received its premiere on June 23, 1940, under the title *Semyon Kotko*.

58. Prokofiev wrote this phrase in English.

Bien à toi

Serge Prokofieff

P.S. Best greetings, Duckie, dear. LP. [written in English in Lina's hand][59]

---

59. At this time, Prokofiev was already involved with Mira Mendelson, a young Soviet writer. He would leave Lina for Mira in early 1941.

CHAPTER SEVEN

American Trio:
Letters to Nina Koshetz,
Nicolas Slonimsky, and Jascha Heifetz

SERGEI PROKOFIEV lived in the United States from 1918 to 1922. And even after his move to Europe that year, he continued to tour the United States regularly as a composer and pianist until 1938. During these twenty years, he developed relationships with many musicians—including other Russian émigrés who had sought refuge from the turmoil of the Russian Revolution. Among these were the soprano Nina Koshetz (1891–1965), the musicologist Nicolas Slonimsky (1894–1995), and the violinist Jascha Heifetz (1901–87). All members of his Russian artistic generation, the three settled permanently and firmly in the United States, making significant contributions to musical life here.

Koshetz and Prokofiev knew each other in Russia before the Russian Revolution. In a letter to Eleonora Damskaya (August 1, 1917) from the Caucasus resort of Essentuki, Prokofiev mentions spending time with Koshetz, who "prayed with her head on my shoulder that heaven would send me even a single drop of love for her. She must be a great sinner because heaven has so far turned a deaf ear to her prayers, and she is leaving tomorrow." A few years later, in 1920, Prokofiev helped Koshetz leave Russia via Constantinople and introduced her to his American managers, Haensel and Jones.

Before emigrating, Koshetz had established herself as a serious and well-regarded operatic soprano. Both her parents had starred at the Imperial Opera in Moscow, and her father, Pavel, a tenor, was the first Russian Siegfried. Following in their footsteps, she studied at the Moscow Conservatory, mastering the piano before she went on to focus on singing. Koshetz studied with many of the greatest pedagogues of the day, and even took acting lessons from Konstantin Stanislavsky. In 1913 she made her debut as Tatiana in Tchaikovsky's *Eugene Onegin* with the prestigious private Zimin Opera Company. Her success led to roles in many other operas, including *The Queen of Spades*, *Don Giovanni*, *Otello*, *Aida*, and *Faust*. Soon she was discovered by Serge Koussevitsky, who took her on tour to the Russian provinces with his orchestra and called her "A Chaliapin in petticoats." In 1915 Koshetz met Sergei Rachmaninoff. They began giving joint recitals, and even conducted a clandestine extramarital affair (for both parties) in the summer of 1916. Koshetz and Prokofiev also gave recitals together.

It took little time for Koshetz to establish herself in the United States after she left the new USSR. On December 31, 1920, she made her debut as a soloist with the Detroit Symphony, conducted by another recent Russian émigré, Osip Gabrilovich. Prokofiev also helped her find work: she took the leading role of the witch Fata Morgana in the world premiere production of his opera *Love for Three Oranges* at the Chicago Opera in late 1921. It was Koshetz, too, who gave the premiere of The Songs without Words, op. 35, with Prokofiev at the piano. And in Paris on June 14, 1928, Koshetz sang the demanding role of Renata in the world premiere of excerpts (from Act II) of *The Fiery Angel*, in a concert performance conducted by Koussevitsky. Besides her appearances with Prokofiev, she was invited to sing with Stokowski, Klemperer, and Rodzinski.

By the early 1930s Koshetz had settled in southern California. Soon the movie business was using her to dub voices and to take character roles, like the obese, languid Tania in the Charles Boyer film *Algiers*.

Always very fond of food ("My principal hobbies are eating and drinking," she once said) and good living, Koshetz turned to the restaurant business as her voice passed its prime. When the business failed two years later, her old flame Rachmaninoff (now living nearby in Beverly Hills) came to the rescue. For the rest of her life, Koshetz devoted herself to teaching (her prize student was her own daughter, Marina) and (according to critic Edward Hagelin Pearson in his notes to a recently released collection of Koshetz's recordings) "being the centre of attention at heavily attended barbecue suppers. There, with a sumptuous buffet cart at her side and a large glass of vodka in her hand, she could relate such tales as the night she sang before the Czar and to 32,000 people in an opera square in Mexico City."

A somewhat less flamboyant, but no less eccentric, member of the Russian expatriate community in Los Angeles was Nicolas Slonimsky. He moved there in 1964, having already excelled in several different careers. Born in St. Petersburg to a distinguished intellectual family, he studied piano at the conservatory there. By 1921 he was in Paris, working as a rehearsal pianist for Koussevitsky, who brought him to Boston in 1925 as his assistant. In Boston he also started writing about music for several newspapers and magazines, as well as conducting his Chamber Orchestra of Boston. Eventually, however, Slonimsky returned to academia, teaching at Harvard and UCLA.

The author of numerous books, Slonimsky achieved his greatest fame in the unlikely position of editor—beginning in 1958—of *Baker's Biographical Dictionary of Musicians*. He was also noted for party tricks and for his friendship with the rock musician Frank Zappa, among many other strange and varied accomplishments.

Like Koshetz and Slonimsky, violinist extraordinaire Jascha Heifetz chose to live in the mild climate of southern California. He left Russia early in 1917, just days after sharing billing with Prokofiev in a literary-musical evening at a chic St. Petersburg gallery. A student of the legendary Leopold Auer at St. Petersburg Conservatory, a soloist with the world's greatest orchestras and conductors, and a very successful recording artist, "Mr. Violin" gave famous master classes at the University of Southern California.

(These letters are in the Music Division of the Library of Congress and were written in Russian unless otherwise indicated. Translated by Harlow Robinson. I have edited and abbreviated the letters here.)

I. Letters to Nina Koshetz

April 8, 1920
NEW YORK

Dear Nina,

I'm sending you a contract from Haensel and Jones, my impresarios, and also the impresarios for Godowsky.[1] I recommend them to you as impeccably honest people and irreproachable gentlemen, who won't try to squeeze you. The contract doesn't give you any guarantees, but they'll set up better engagements for you here than you could get from across the ocean. That was the case with me, and it was the case with Rachmaninoff, who is making the rounds here with unbelievable success, playing his polkas. I looked over the contract carefully, and it's perfectly fine, the percentages that go to the managers are average, even lower than average. But for America, you must write your name with an *e* (Koshetz), and not with an *i* (Koshits), since if you write it with an *i*, it would evoke undesirable associations.

I'm leaving soon for England and France, and will return to America in the fall. Write to me at the following address:

Serge Prokofieff
C/o Mr. M. O. Kling
11 Great Marlborough Street
London, W   England

If your letter doesn't reach me in London, then they'll forward it to me.

In Constantinople please make inquiries in the Russian Embassy about my mother, Maria Grigorevna Prokofieva, who was evacuated with other Russian refugees to the Prince Islands. She has nearly gone blind from anxiety and fear. Please give her assistance in any way you can. For my part, I'm doing everything I can to get her to Paris. Most likely I'll succeed in bringing mama to Italy or Marseilles, and will meet her there.[2]

---

1.   Leopold Godowsky (1870–1938) was a Polish pianist, pedagogue, and composer. He lived and worked in the USA after 1914.

2.   Prokofiev's mother, whose political sympathies were with the anti-Bolshevik forces, had stayed behind in Russia when he left in May 1918. Neither of them realized how difficult life would become during the civil war period, and how difficult it would become to leave the USSR. Many Russians fled from Black Sea ports to Constantinople during these years.

I embrace you. *Bon voyage*.

Seryozha

The contract is being sent in three copies, in three different letters, just to be sure. This letter is being taken by hand to France, and will be mailed to you from there.

December 11, 1920
OVERLAND LIMITED [USA]

Nina,

I'm writing you from the *clubcar* [in English] on my way west. I received your two letters: the nice one, and the one with the reprimand. The latter was dated December 30, but I think you should have crossed out the zero. I wrote you ten days ago, and I hope you received the letter, and before my departure I sent you four songs.[3] Write about them in detail to me in San Francisco:

> C/o Mrs. Jessica Colbert
> 619 Hearst Building
> San Francisco, Calif.

I'll be in California until either January 2 or 13, depending on whether I get any additional concerts. I know that you are engaged for the New Year by Gabrilovich.[4] And how is Gatti?[5] In recent days I've been tearing around Chicago quite a bit, but without particular taste. My opera will not be staged this season.[6]

I send you a kiss and will write you soon from San Francisco.

Seryozha

---

3.   During 1920 Prokofiev was writing the Five Songs without Words for voice and piano. (See note 7, below.)

4.   Osip Gabrilovich (1878–1936), a Russian-born pianist, conductor, and composer who left Russia in 1914, became the conductor of the Detroit Symphony in 1918. It was with him and the Detroit Symphony that Koshetz made her official American debut as a soloist on December 31, 1920.

5.   Giulio Gatti-Casazza (1869–1940) was the general manager of the Metropolitan Opera in New York 1910–35.

6.   Prokofiev had been expecting to have *Love for Three Oranges* produced, but it was postponed for one year.

December 31, 1920
HOTEL CLARK, LOS ANGELES

Nina,

Aleksei Fyodorovich Kal will tell you how I am faring in California and will also give you the fifth song.[7] Reward him for this with dinner and show him the Akhmatki.[8] A.F. is writing a big article about me for Paris, and he should get to know these songs.

I embrace you and send you New Year's greetings.

Seryozha

July 11, 1922
ETTAL

Nina,

Thanks for the letter, the programs, and for singing my songs. It's nice to know that after two years of performing in America, you have finally wised up and starting singing Prokofiev, even if together with Saminsky.[9] But what gave me really the most pleasure was the news that the instrumentation of the second song sounds good.[10] I forgive the dedication to Akhmatova, but don't let it be repeated.

Our life here is flowing in an amazingly carefree manner. I'm writing *Fiery Angel* and have the proofs of *Three Oranges*, which will be published in August. I doubt that I'll be coming this winter to America, since I have some engagements in Europe, and besides that, the house in Ettal—a winterized one—has been rented for the year, and abiding by German-style economy, I can sit here, calmly passing the time and writing thick opuses.

Haensel, who was touring Germany, dropped in to see me, but it seems he hasn't managed to set up many concerts for me, and my so-called friends who are on kissing terms with Gabrilovich, Monteux,[11] and other American scoundrels have also limited themselves to pretty words and ephemeral pathos.

7.   The Five Songs without Words for voice and piano, op. 35. Koshetz gave the premiere of this cycle in New York on March 27, 1921.

8.   The "Five Poems of Anna Akhmatova" for voice and piano, op. 27, composed in 1916.

9.   Lazare Saminsky (1882–1959) was a composer and a graduate of the St. Petersburg Conservatory who emigrated to the United States in 1920.

10. Prokofiev arranged the second of the Five Songs without Words for orchestra as op. 35-bis, and also arranged all five songs as Five Melodies for violin and piano, op. 35-bis.

11. Pierre Monteux (1875–1964) conducted the Boston Symphony 1919–24.

By the way, Miss Beirne, whom we discussed at your place over dinner on the eve of my departure from New York, has sent me a signed contract for a production of *Three Oranges*, along with a letter portraying the undertaking as extravagantly funded and in general highly recommended. But the matter ended there, and they all seem to have succeeded in expiring without ever having given birth to anything. [. . .]

On the other hand, Europe is smiling on me: Paris greeted *The Buffoon* with terrific excitement, London did the same to the Third Concerto, Berlin is planning an entire symphonic concert devoted to me—in a word, if I do have to crawl beyond the cozy confines of Ettal, it's somehow easier in Europe than with the Yankees.

I congratulate you on your successes and hope that you have settled in well for the summer and are successfully aiming at next season. I received a very touching letter from Asafiev. His address: Petrograd, Bolshaya Konyushennaya 25, apt. 12. I'm in frequent correspondence with Souvchinsky.

I embrace you and Aleksandr Aleksandrovich. Whom did Salima run away with?

Yours,
SPRKFV

Are you composing anything?

[Undated; probably around 1920–21]
HOTEL BREVOORT, NEW YORK

Madame Nina Koshetz
Room 1
Nina,

I got home at 10, and am so wrung out that I'm going to bed. Tomorrow morning at 9:30 I'll come to have coffee.

With a kiss, S.

II. Letters to Nicolas Slonimsky

December 6, 1926

18, RUE TROYON, PARIS XVII

Respected Nikolai Leonidovich,

I received your letter, and also the several packets of programs and reviews; thank you very much for sending them. I hope that you will continue to send them in the future. The tone taken by the Boston newspaper people after the performance of the suite from *Three Oranges* is truly remarkable. "How could the poor ugly duckling have dreamed of such happiness!" In counterbalance to Boston, London is adopting a reserved attitude: not long ago the same suite was performed by Bruno Walter, and in response came a deluge of the same old complaints about a lack of melody, an absence of profundity and even one that the brass took over the first violin part. Incidentally, Sergei Aleksandrovich[12] is not in London; he would surely and insistently have driven my nails into the tough brains of the Englishmen . . .

We are planning to move to Moscow about the tenth of January. I'll be happy to send you any sort of materials for the American press. You could already report that in anticipation of my arrival, Moscow has announced five symphonic festivals of my works. You had asked me to obtain some scores in Moscow for the Boston library. Please let me know exactly what you have in mind, and how much money I could spend on them.

I give your hand a good squeeze. Please give my warmest greetings to Natalia Konstantinovna and to Sergei Aleksandrovich.[13]

Yours,

SPRKFV

September 2, 1930

VILLA STEVENS, LA NAZE, PAR VALMONDOIS, SEINE-ET-OISE, FRANCE

Respected Nikolai Leonidovich,

Of course I have never done any kind of transcription of the Overture on Hebrew Themes, and I don't understand what sort of obtuse people could have found it necessary to reorchestrate it, since it was conceived for a sextet and doesn't need any kind of reworking.[14] If you have the gramophone recording on hand, then send it to me, but it's not worth buying specially.

---

12. Serge Koussevitsky.
13. Serge and Natalia Koussevitsky
14. In fact, in 1934 Prokofiev did write an orchestral transcription of the Overture on Hebrew Themes, op. 34-bis.

The Boston library (if you mean the big Boston Public Library) could obtain the orchestral score of the "Classical" Symphony. To do this, they would have to write to the Paris office of my publisher and provide an official pledge that the score would not be allowed to circulate either for performance or to be copied. It seems that the score would cost about 75 dollars. As for the signed title page, I would of course be happy to give it to them, if they make a personal request to me.

I send you greetings and best wishes, and thank you for thinking of me.

Yours,

SPRKFV

May 28, 1931

5, RUE VALENTIN HAÜY, PARIS XV

Respected Nikolai Leonidovich,

Thanks for the tickets. I am leaving for Biarritz for a week on Sunday, and therefore I'm not sure whether I'll be back by the sixth. But if I do return in time, then I'll probably come to the second concert. I'll pass the ticket on to Nabokov.[15]

I liked your article, although it's a pity that you didn't mention my most recent period, for I consider it the most significant. In addition, it represents the best synthesis of the contradictions of the preceding periods. By the way, this latest period doesn't have that "absolute predominance" of measures in 4/4 meter, something for which you pricked me in passing. Here are some other more trivial corrections: *Seven, They Are Seven* is a Chaldean inscription, not Babylonian, which makes it more ancient; and you can add to the list of recording excerpts from *Buffoon* and the *Three Oranges* Suite, which was recorded in full by Poulet.[16]

Since you didn't ask me to return the galley proofs of the article, I will keep them for my files. If I have incorrectly understood you, then let me know by Saturday.

I squeeze your hand and wish you success in the concerts.

Yours

SPRKFV

---

15.   The Russian émigré composer Nicolas Nabokov.
16.   Gaston Poulet (1892–1974) was a French violinist and conductor; he ran the Poulet Concerts at the Sarah Bernhardt Théâtre in Paris 1927–35.

February 9th, 1939
ULIZA TCHKALOVA 14, AP. 14, MOSCOW 64, U.S.S.R.

Dear Mr. Slonimsky,[17]

I expected to come to the states around this time but, inasmuch as my tour is postponed until next season, I send you herewith the informations you wanted about my compositions—so that you may use them for the next edition of your book.

Unfortunately, I could not give you some of the dates (1st concerto, Ugly Duckling, Classical Symphony, 3rd Symphony, etc.) as I have no material at hand, but I hope to be able to do this later.

With kind regards,

Sincerely yours,
Serge Prokofieff

III. Letter to Jascha Heifetz

February 24, 1938
200 CHERRY STREET, DENVER, COLORADO

Dear Jascha,

When you see my publisher in Paris, ask him to show you the full score and piano score of *The Steel Gallop*. There is one dance there—the Dance of the Sailor and the Female Worker—that I think would come out well on the violin. In any case, I've wanted to arrange it for violin for a long time now.[18]

I wish you *bon voyage* and send my greetings.

Yours,
SPRKFV

---

17. This letter was written in English, as were most of Prokofiev's letters sent abroad from Moscow after his return to the USSR in 1936. The spelling is Prokofiev's.

18. It does not appear that Prokofiev ever did arrange this dance for violin and piano.

CHAPTER EIGHT

Letters to Serge and Natalia Koussevitsky

THE TWO SERGEIS—Prokofiev and Koussevitsky—had known each other well in Russia before the 1917 Revolution. Koussevitsky (or Kusi, or Kuskin, or even Couscous, as he was called by friends) had helped to introduce Prokofiev's raucous and startling music to the conservative Russian public, both as a conductor and publisher. Gutheil, one of the music publishers Koussevitsky owned in Russia, was among the first to print Prokofiev's works.

Prokofiev's departure from the USSR in 1918 for a time separated the two musicians. But then Koussevitsky abandoned Russia, too, settling first in Paris (where he ran his important Editions Russes de Musique, which continued to publish Prokofiev's music) and then moving to Boston in 1924 to become the conductor of the Boston Symphony Orchestra. At the time still a young organization, the BSO would climb into the ranks of the world's great orchestras under Koussevitsky's inspired musical and administrative leadership.

During Koussevitsky's twenty-five-year tenure in Boston, he raised the standard of the orchestra, established the Tanglewood Festival in western Massachusetts, and introduced an amazing number of new works by some of the many composers of all nationalities whom he knew and supported, including numerous Russians: Stravinsky, Miaskovsky, Vernon Duke, and Prokofiev. Both in Boston and in Paris, where he often appeared in the 1920s, Koussevitsky did a great deal to promote Prokofiev's new compositions. He introduced the world to *The Fiery Angel* and the Symphony No. 4 (commissioned by the Boston Symphony), and regularly invited Prokofiev to Boston to perform his piano concerti and to conduct.

Seventeen years Prokofiev's senior, Koussevitsky acted as father figure and artistic advisor to the often willful and obstreperous composer. In rather formal, businesslike letters, very different from those he wrote to Vernon Duke or Nikolai Miaskovsky, Prokofiev kept Koussevitsky informed of his activities wherever his endless travels took him.

Because Koussevitsky was not noted for his verbal skills, the letters he wrote back to Prokofiev were usually composed either by his wife Natalia or by one of his assistants. Nicolas Slonimsky, who served as Koussevitsky's assistant in the mid-1920s, loved to joke about his employer's limited command of any language but Russian:

> Koussevitzky's English was peculiar. He would ask a rhetorical question and supply a rhetorical answer, "You hev? Mek!" Deciphered, it meant, "You have it in the music? Then make it!" When a player tried to say something during a rehearsal, Koussevitzky would cut him short with the unequivocal order, "Me talk, you no speak." In Russian, a scale is a "gamma," and Koussevitzky thought that in English it was "game." Occasionally he indulged in whimsicalities. Whenever he was dissatisfied with the way the double-basses played he would say: "Bassi, you play like bassi auf vitch the price is five cents!"[1]

Prokofiev's letters to Koussevitsky show that he was competing for the conductor's attention with many other composers, and that he sometimes became impatient with what he regarded as insufficient promotion of his music. And yet no single person with the exception of Diaghilev did more than Koussevitsky to familiarize audiences with Prokofiev's work. Even after Prokofiev had returned permanently to the USSR (a decision the conductor found difficult to understand), Koussevitsky continued to play his music in Boston and elsewhere.

(These letters are in the collection of the Music Division of the Library of Congress. The versions here have been edited and abbreviated and were translated by Harlow Robinson.)

---

1.   Nicolas Slonimsky, *Perfect Pitch: A Life Story* (Oxford: Oxford University Press, 1988), 97.

September 5, 1920

12 Quai de la Tour, Mantes-sur-Seine, S. et O., France

Dear Sergei Aleksandrovich,

Thanks for the interesting news, and also for having taken care of my suitcase. I didn't reply to you before now because I kept planning to appear to you personally in Aix-les-Bains. It seems that I'll manage to do this in the coming days, so I would ask you please to send me a little telegram upon receiving this letter, to tell me if you're still in Aix and if you have any plans to come to Paris in the near future. Once I receive it, I'll quickly pack my suitcase and take a jaunt to Aix for a day or two. It will be fine to see you and to chat a bit about Russia. It's also extremely important to clarify the matter of the further publication of my works. This is now a painful issue for me, since I don't want to be published in any of these foreign "shops." On the other hand, none of my compositions are now available either on the American or the European market, and they probably won't be in the near future, since all the original printing materials—both those done by Jurgenson and by your firm—were prepared in Russia.[2]

Something else has also happened: my American impresario, who has set up an American tour for me for October (eight concerts with a guarantee of $3,400), now sent me a telegram that the tour is being postponed to December 4, so that a hole is going to appear in my so-called budget. I'll need to fill it, perhaps by selling my new piano pieces. So I'd like also to talk with you about this matter: would Editions Russes buy them or not?

For the moment I send you my warmest greetings and hope that we'll be meeting soon.

Your faithful servant,

SPRKFV[3]

---

2.   Jurgenson was the largest music publishing business in Russia in the late nineteenth century. The firm published some of Prokofiev's early works before the Revolution. In 1918 the firm was nationalized and became part of the Soviet State Publishing House. Koussevitsky began his activity as a music publisher in Russia in 1909, when he established the Russian Music Publishing House. In 1914, he acquired another publisher, Gutheil. After leaving Russia for Paris, Koussevitsky transferred his music publishing activities there, to the Editions Russes de Musique, which published many of Prokofiev's works and those of other Russian composers. This company was acquired by Boosey & Hawkes in 1947.

3.   Prokofiev often signed his letters only with the consonants of his names. He often wrote letters this way, too, omitting vowels, in a kind of shorthand.

February 17, 1921
LONDON

Dear Sergei Aleksandrovich,

Here's some quick extra information for you:

1) The *Tales of an Old Grandmother* should be printed and bound together, in a single volume.[4]

2) The Four Dances, op. 32, can be published in four separate sheets.[5]

3) In the "Minuet," on the second page, you'll find a variant written in pencil. It should be crossed out.

4) My permanent address: Serge Prokofieff, c/o American Express, rue Scribe, Paris, 9e.

Besides that, I wish you bon voyage, send you a hug, and kiss Natalia Konstantinovna's hands.

They sent me a visa from Paris, but for Pierre Prokofieff instead of Serge, and the consul doesn't want to give me a visa. I can't figure it out![6]

Yours, SP

July 21, 1921
ST. BRÉVIN-LES-PINS, LOIRE-INFÉRIEURE, FRANCE

Dear Natalia Konstantinovna,

I hope that you have rid yourselves of your friends from Warsaw and that you are now resting in the shade of a cool resort. Is it true that Sergei Aleksandrovich is leaving to conduct in America? If so, then I congratulate him heartily. Who is his manager and what orchestra is it?[7]

I'm continuing to work on the Third Concerto and would be feeling fine except that my bicycle broke underneath me and I was carried home with a face transformed into a cutlet. Now I'm trying to get better.

I kiss your little hands and send warm greetings to Sergei Aleksandrovich.

With sincere respect,
SPRKFV

---

4. *Tales of an Old Grandmother*, four pieces for piano, op. 31, composed in 1918.
5. Eventually published under the title Four Pieces, composed in 1918.
6. At this time Prokofiev was traveling on a Nansen passport; they were issued to foreign residents in Western Europe after the First World War.
7. Koussevitsky would be appointed conductor of the Boston Symphony in 1924.

August 30, 1921
St. Brévin-les-Pins

Dear Natalia Konstantinovna,

Your doubts concerning the likelihood of my trip to Dinar seem to have found justification: I have become more and more settled in St. Brévin-les-Pins. The main reason is this damned concerto, which has turned out to be so long that I keep on orchestrating and orchestrating and still can't see an end to it. On top of that, I've been suffocating under a load of proofs to be corrected, and since I want to be responsible, I've been sitting over them several hours a day. And finally, I've been invited to conduct *Three Oranges* in Chicago and New York, so that now I have to do some cramming to learn my own orchestral score. I didn't count on this, and wrote something terribly difficult; now I have to pay in time and tears.[8]

I'm planning to be in Paris around October 1, and in America around the 15th. Can it be that you really won't be in Paris at that time?

In February, when you arrive in America, as it happens I will be in New York and *Oranges* will be running; if, of course, the Americans can still stand them by then. So then we can do some real carousing in a skyscraper.

I kiss your little hands and am very sorry that the trip to Dinar isn't going to work out. I send a hug to Sergei Aleksandrovich. I hope that we'll see each other in Paris.

Your faithful servant,
SPRKFV

October 18, 1921
On board Cunard RMS *Aquitania*

Dear Sergei Alexandrovich,

I send you and Natalia Konstantinovna greetings from the *Aquitania* en route to New York. So far the trip is going very well; I'm cramming to learn *Three Oranges* and I'm playing chess (there's a tournament, and I have a chance of winning first prize).[9]

---

8. Prokofiev worked on the Third Piano Concerto from 1917 to 1921, and played the solo part in its world premiere with the Chicago Symphony on December 16, 1921. For *Love for Three Oranges,* see chapter 5, note 6. The Chicago production was given in New York for a single performance on February 14, 1922.

9. A chess player of nearly professional caliber, Prokofiev enjoyed participating in tournaments wherever he traveled.

Once again, I regret that we did not have the chance to see each other before my departure. And besides that, we didn't clarify something important: how will I receive the orchestral score and materials of the *Scythian Suite* in New York, where it will be performed in February or March? The best thing would be for you to send it to me by courier immediately after your performance. There's little hope of receiving it promptly through the mail or commercial transport: two years ago my manager sent something that way from America to London, to Coates,[10] and it took 3½ months. We were already convinced that it had perished.

And so, immediately send me just one word, telling me what you plan to do with it, so that I'll stop worrying. The address to which that "one word" and the *Oranges* Suite should be sent:

> Haensel & Jones
> 33 West 42nd St.
> New York

I send you a hug. I kiss Natalia Konstantinovna's little hands.

> Yours,
> SPRKF

> December 6, 1921
> AUDITORIUM HOTEL, CHICAGO

Dear Natalia Konstantinovna,

Last week I transferred into Sergei Aleksandrovich's account in London 57 pounds and 14 shillings. Thanks again for your help and I kiss your little hands.[11]

They are giving the premiere of *Three Oranges* on December 23 instead of November 28. After 12 rehearsals the orchestra is ready, along with the soloists and chorus, and staged rehearsals begin tomorrow, for the moment with piano. The work atmosphere is superb and the production promises to be spectacular.

My Third Concerto has turned out to be so devilishly difficult that I have not yet managed to learn it, but even so I'll have to play it in ten days' time. I'm nervous and cramming at the piano three hours a day.

---

10. Albert Coates (1882–1953), an English conductor and composer who was principal conductor at the Mariinsky Theater 1911–19, later introduced Prokofiev's Third Concerto in Britain, with the composer as soloist.

11. The generous Koussevitsky often lent money to the composers whose music he published, including Prokofiev.

Rumors are circulating that Sergei Aleksandrovich will soon become the conductor of the Boston Symphony. Now that would be just terrific!

I saw Rachmaninoff once, at the time of his recital in Chicago. He played a most atrocious program excellently. Ever since he had his hemorrhoids surgically removed, he has become noticeably more cheerful.[12]

Oh, but it seems I'm starting to write letters inappropriate for ladies. So I'd better withdraw, kiss your little hands and send a hug to Sergei Aleksandrovich.

With love,

SPRKFV

P.S. How did the changes in *Scythian Suite* turn out? I'm making a suite from *Three Oranges*.[13]

January 2, 1921 [1922]

AUDITORIUM HOTEL, CHICAGO

Dear Sergei Aleksandrovich,

I'm still worried whether you have sent to America the orchestral score and parts of *Scythian Suite*. When I sent it two years ago through commerical transport from New York to London, it took 2½ months. The New York Symphony Orchestra is scheduled to perform it on March 10, so that the materials should be here by March 1. If it has not yet gone, then you should send it by personal courier to Haensel & Jones, 33 West 42nd St., New York. If you try to send it by mail or commercial transport, then it now may not arrive in time. Just in case, I should tell you that I have had photocopies made from the full score, but without the new changes.

Why haven't you yet written me about how these changes turned out? I thank you for the tickets that you sent to mama. According to her, *Scythian Suite* had a great success; according to the Paris newspapers, the audience responded with catcalls and whistles.[14]

---

12. Sergei Rachmaninoff (1873–1943) left Russia in December 1917 and never returned. He divided his time between Europe and the United States, performing as a pianist and continuing to compose, although much more slowly than earlier in his career. He died in Los Angeles.

13. Prokofiev's Suite from *Love for Three Oranges,* completed in 1924, became one of his most popular compositions, especially its ironic "March."

14. Prokofiev's mother, Maria Grigorevna, emigrated from Russia after considerable difficulties in early 1920. She lived with him and his wife in Europe until her death near Paris in 1924.

The Americans, on the other hand, are a more appealing people: they received *Love for Three Oranges* with such ovations that you couldn't ask for anything better. Actually, *Oranges* has been declared the hit of the season. The Third Concerto was also received well, but the "Classical" Symphony did even better.

I have read in the newspapers about your triumphs in Paris, and take great pleasure in them. It will be interesting to hear how *The Snow Maiden* goes in Barcelona. In Chicago it has been postponed until next season (with Roerich, Koshetz, Baklanov); the sixteen orchestral rehearsals devoted to my *Oranges* gobbled up that production. *Snow Maiden* will be staged in New York (at the Metropolitan) in January.[15]

I wish a Happy New Year to you and to Natalia Konstantinovna, and send you my very warmest greetings.

With a big hug, Yours,
SPRKFV

P.S. If you do write, then write care of Haensel & Jones, as indicated above for the sending of the suite.

I have received a certification from your London bank that my check has arrived there. Thanks once again for the money you lent me for my trip. SP

March 21, 1922
HOTEL MOLTKE, BERLIN

Dear Natalia Konstantinovna,

I received through Russicher Musikverlag[16] the commission to send to Sergei Aleksandrovich the orchestral score of the Third Concerto as soon as possible. What was our young and talented maestro thinking of when I was at his house in Paris?! Right now I'm doing a *klavierauszug*[17] of the Concerto, and in a few days will begin rehearsing it for a performance, so that I cannot possibly send the score (which exists in a single copy); I'll bring it with me to Paris several days before the concert. But the maestro musn't worry: this is no

---

15. *The Snow Maiden,* an opera by Nikolai Rimsky-Korsakov, was based on a fairy tale play by Aleksandr Ostrovsky. It exists in two versions, one completed in 1880–81 and the other in 1895.
16. Russian Music Publishers (German).
17. Piano score (German).

Stravinsky symphony, there are no complicated meters, no dirty tricks, it can be conducted without preliminary cramming—it's difficult for the orchestra, but not for the conductor. So please let me know as soon as possible when I will be playing in Paris, on the 20th or the 27th, and also, when in London—that is, if they haven't finally canceled my performance.

I kiss your little hands, and send a hug to Sergei Aleksandrovich. If you write, then address the letter in care of the publisher.

With love,
SPRKFV

July 8, 1923
ETTAL[18]

Dear Natalia Konstantinovna,

It's entirely unfair to look askance at my long silence, for even if I haven't been writing, I have often remembered you, and in the most diverse connections: both while reading reviews of Sergei Aleksandrovich's performance of *Scythian Suite* and while fussing over the hens in my Ettal poultry enterprise. Let me tell you some news: I have purchased an electric incubator for 60 "individuals," which has been in operation for 14 days now, and which has among its population both Plymouth Rock hens from the poultry farms at the monastery nearby, and others from Oberammergau, and finally 22 eggs from our own cock, who is strolling in our garden with his eight lady friends. And just think: upon examining the eggs after seven days, it turned out that of those 22 eggs all 22 were successfully fertilized by our cock. We are terrible proud of our 100% rooster, and at a general gathering granted him eternal life plus a pound of oats.

Passing from poultry to the piano, I must say that during these two months I have not been working very energetically, giving my faulty heart a chance to rest, and it seems that my health has settled down.[19] Even so, I revised and orchestrated two movements of the Second Concerto, and now I'm orchestrat-

---

18. Prokofiev and Lina Llubera, a singer of Spanish and Slavic background whom he had met in the United States, were married in the Bavarian village of Ettal on September 29, 1923, where they had been living together since early 1922.

19. In April 1919, while living in the United States and working frantically to finish the commissioned opera *Love for Three Oranges*, Prokofiev fell ill with scarlet fever and diphtheria. These illnesses apparently left him with a weak heart for some time afterward.

ing—with great enthusiasm—a vocal suite from *The Fiery Angel*.[20] Leipzig continues to shower me with proofs to be corrected, and if I can show some courage, then it seems that I can work this summer with admirable energy. [...]

And how is your health? How does the maestro feel, worn out from his rhythmic exercises and his plaudits? Where are you now and where are you planning to spend the summer: will you be cooling yourselves on some mountain summit, or baking somewhere in the south of the European map, or will you be dipping your toes on the shore of some lake? Do write, it would give me great pleasure. For a long while Ettal treated us to rain and cold, but now the sun is smiling, and the sun always makes it look enchanting. It's a pity there's no place to swim. I don't have the heart to crawl into the pond, where there are more frogs than liquid.

I throw down at your feet with a crash a pile of greetings, and I send the maestro a hug.

> Your faithful servant,
> S Prokofiev

> November 1, 1923
> [ETTAL?][21]

Dear Sergei Aleksandrovich,

When I was writing my two letters to Zederbaum (on September 7 and 17), I had the impression that you had ceased to take any interest either in me or in my music.[22] So I did not think that the harsh words I used in my letters would touch you in any way. But having now discovered that you took these sharp

---

20. Because the original manuscript score of the Second Concerto, completed in Russia in 1913, was lost with some of Prokofiev's other papers remaining in his apartment after he left the USSR in 1918, he had to reconstruct it later. It seems Prokofiev never finished this "vocal suite" from *The Fiery Angel*—instead, he continued working on the opera itself until 1927.
21. Handwritten letter without return address.
22. Prokofiev is referring to two letters he wrote (on September 7 and 17) to Vladimir Zederbaum, Koussevitsky's secretary and assistant, in which he complained bitterly about the cancellation of a performance of *Seven, They Are Seven* planned for November. "I place much more value on this composition than on all my numerous concertos performed together, and believe that for me—and perhaps also for Russian music—it is extremely important that *Seven* be performed as soon as possible. For God's sake, it has already been lying around for six years now without someone to perform it. . . . I am also entirely aware of the friendly attitude Sergei Aleksandrovich has towards me, but as a friend he has even less right to break the promise he made to

words so much to heart, I am hastening to assure you that I had no intention of offending you (maybe I just wanted to annoy you a little) and I beg you to turn your anger into kindness, for I sincerely love you and have always greatly admired your work. I thought that with the growth in your fame you had become very arrogant, but Natalia Konstantinovna says this is not the case. Therefore, if you are no longer angry with me, then allow me to give you a big hug and repeat once more that I had no intention of offending, insulting, or distressing you. I thought you would simply say: "Well, the composer is calling me names—they're all like that!" It goes without saying that I would never have uttered the words I did if I had received an accurate explanation of the matter.

Love,
SProkofiev

[A drawing by Prokofiev depicting how Zederbaum is trying to undermine Prokofiev's friendship with Koussevitsky follows at the bottom of the page.]

August 26, 1924
Villa Béthanie, St. Gilles-sur-Vie, Vendée, France

Dear Sergei Aleksandrovich,

Thank you for the affectionate letter, which I value all the more because I know what torture it is for you to write letters. In America you should buy yourself a dictaphone and on your free evenings, reclining comfortably in your armchair, you could sing letters onto recordings for your friends, and then send them the recordings as *échantillon sans valeur* (if the thoughts you express are frivolous) or *échantillon à valeur déclarée* (if the thoughts you express are profound). It goes without saying that you'll have to give each of your correspondents a gramophone so they can listen to what you send them. The recorded letters would go something like this: "Dear Seryozha. Exclamation mark. I am very happy . . . Please edit out that phrase. I am very unhappy, comma, that you . . ." and so on.

I have finally brought my quintet to a conclusion: I wrote out the full score, made a *klavierauszug* for piano two-hands, and sent all of that off to the copyist. Now I'm sitting over my symphony, but cannnot get it to come out right. I'd like, as you say, for it to be a hit, but when you set such goals for yourself no

---

me" (Prokofiev's letter of September 17, 1923). Prokofiev was so annoyed that he even canceled a planned performance of the Second Piano Concerto with Koussevitsky on October 25.

matter what you write seems either bad or insufficiently good. As a way of loosening up, I started with the variations and have already completed two of them.[23]

So as not to interrupt my work, I think I will not travel to Paris, although I would very much like to see you. As far as my American concerts for next season are concerned, I don't even know what to tell you: I am relying implicitly on you and am sure that whatever you'll set up will be the best thing possible. (Just don't do it like they did this year in Spain!) It would be good if you could manage to get some businesslike and energetic manager interested in me.[24] Up until now I have been represented by F. Haensel, 33 West 42nd St., New York, the one whom you liked so much when he came to you in Paris with his proposals. I have no contracts with him; our agreements have been oral, which requires an even greater degree of scrupulousness. At the same time, I feel justified in leaving him, since he has been unable to set up a single decent concert for me during the last three years. What makes leaving him difficult, though, is that I owe him a little more than $1000, which of course I would have to pay if we parted ways. I am telling you these details because in America there is a strict code of behavior among managers: none of them has the right to make a proposal to an artist if that artist is still working with another manager—otherwise the one who makes the new proposal can be thrown out of the association.

If you were to bring me together with a new manager, therefore, it would be important for you to know what my relations are with Haensel. Haensel has been taking 15% of my concert fees. For America that is reasonable: some managers take 25%. But 25% is a lot, especially when you consider that out of the remaining 75% you have to pay for transportation from Europe, living expenses, taxes, and so on.

Forgive me please for writing all this boring stuff to you. Right now none of this may be of interest to you, but it will be essential if you succeed in setting up some sort of business arrangement for me. So I ask you please to retain this letter and to take it along with you to America.

The Cologne Opera has apparently taken a serious interest in staging a production of *Love for Three Oranges*. They sent me a contract accompanied by a

---

23. The Symphony No. 2 in D Minor, op. 40, was composed in 1924–25 on a commission from Koussevitsky and first performed by him in Paris on June 6, 1925. It has two movements, scored for oversized orchestra; the second movement is a theme and variations.

24. Koussevitsky, having recently become the conductor of the Boston Symphony, lived most of the year in Boston.

letter from the musical director Szenkar[25] in which he goes to great lengths to describe his love for my *Love*. [. . .]

Have you read the colossal article about you by Olin Downes in the *New York Times* of July 15, which was later reprinted in the *Boston Evening Transcript*? It describes in detail your last Paris concert. There are many funny remarks about *Seven, They Are Seven*. By the way, Miaskovsky writes that in Moscow, *Seven, They Are Seven* has been banned owing to its "religious" content, and that the score has been removed from the store windows at the State Publishing House—and may be removed from circulation altogether. Miaskovsky has finished his Eighth Symphony. Universal Edition has undertaken to publish his scores and has already accpted the Sixth Symphony and the symphonic poem *Silence*.

My financial affairs are more or less in order. Romanov has begun to make payments to me for the ballet-quintet I wrote for him.[26] He delayed in starting to pay me, but apparently is ready to do so. Besides that, Eberg and I dragged $250 out of New York for an illegal performance of *The Buffoon*, and the Cologne Opera is promising to pay me 8% of the box office receipts.[27] Of the checks you gave me I have already consumed one in the amount of $2,000 and will probably consume that other in September (also for $2,000). If it isn't too inconvenient for you, could you give me one more, for $3,000, for October, and then I hope I won't be needing to bother you any further, since in November I'm expecting further payments from Romanov, as well as some concerts.

Congratulate Natalia Konstantinovna on my behalf for having lost 8 kilos and kiss her little hand for me; I send you a big hug, and will be following your American triumphs with the greatest interest. What a delight to be able to put all these Damrosches, Bodanzkys, and others in their place![28] Ptashka sends you both her warmest greeting and is writing to Natalia Konstantinovna separately.

Love, SProkofiev

---

25. Hungarian conductor Eugene Szenkar (1891–1977).

26. Boris Romanov (1891–1957) was a Russian dancer, choreographer, and director who emigrated from Russia in 1921 and founded the Russian Romantic Ballet, for which Prokofiev wrote a ballet, *Trapeze*, which was also adapted as his Quintet, op. 39.

27. Ernest Aleksandrovich Eberg (died 1925) was the director of Koussevitsky's Editions Russes and Gutheil publishers.

28. Polish-born Walter Damrosch (1862–1950) had conducted at the Metropolitan Opera and New York Philharmonic, and later led the NBC Symphony Orchestra. Artur Bodanzky (1877–1943) was an Austrian who conducted at many major opera houses, including the Metropolitan Opera.

My permanent address:
    Serge Prokofieff
    c/o Guaranty Trust Co.
    3, rue des Italiens
    Paris IX
For telegrams:
    Prokofieff, Garritus, Paris

September 25, 1924
St. Gilles [France]

Dear Sergei Aleksandrovich,

First of all, isn't today your name day?[29] If it is, I send you a big hug. And even if it isn't, I still send you a big hug. Secondly, accept my congratulations on having been named a member of the Legion.[30] You could say that the French have showered you with honors. I can even imagine how you and Damrosch, taking each other by the arm, and donning your venerable Legion medals, could walk slowly along Fifth Avenue in New York, and how the amazed Americans would make way for you, whispering reverently: "There go two of our best conductors! . . ."

The symphony is moving along: I have finished the sketches for the first movement, it came out very severe, and have sketched five of the variations. But probably I won't limit myself to two movements—I must write a finale. Send me please the trombone manuals that you saw at Milhaud's place, and if you come across similar manuals for any other instruments, I would very much like them as well. But please don't put off sending the package, for they will be most useful for orchestrating the symphony.

Don't be amazed if a young man comes to you with a letter of recommendation from me, with the purpose of insuring your life against death or mutilation (and in fact it would always be possible, carried away by an *accelerando,* for you to fly right off the stage). This young man's name is Gottlieb, he is my Chicago acquaintance, and he has done a great deal to propagandize my music, insofar as his modest situation as an insurance agent allows him to do. So I could not refuse to give him a letter of recommendation to you when he asked for one. Of

---

29. According to Russian Orthodox tradition, the name day is the day on which the saint after which a person has been named is honored. It is almost more important than a birthday in Russia.
30. Koussevitky had been named a chevalier of the French Legion of Honor.

course you are not in any way obliged: I know very well that you don't have anyone to worry about, for your two sons—Gutheil and Editions Russes—are
already flourishing from the sale of Stravinsky, Prokofiev, and gypsy songs. In a
word, if you were not intending to get insurance, then please show him the
door, but if you were, then you would do well to insure yourself with him, and
not with someone else.[31]

I have now been swamped with proofs to correct, of the orchestral score and
parts of the Violin Concerto.[32] [. . .] I'm now swallowing 25 pages a day, not
counting the composition of the variations.

I send you a big hug, I kiss Natalia Konstantinovna's palms and thank her for
the postcard from the *Aquitania*. Mama, Ptashka, and Sviatoslav Sergeevich
send you numerous greetings. I'm not sure how much longer we will remain in
St. Gilles, so send the manuals to my permanent address: c/o Guaranty Trust
Co., 3, rue des Italiens, Paris IX.

With love,
SProkofiev

November 28, 1924
54, ROUTE DES GARDES, BELLEVUE, S. ET O., FRANCE

Dear Sergei Aleksandrovich,

I very much appreciated—in the midst of your successes and drudgery—
that you managed to find the time to send me a long letter. The typewriter on
which it was typed is an excellent one, the typeface is very pretty, and I was
especially impressed that it apparently has both Cyrillic and Latin alphabets.
But do tell Vladimir Nikolaevich[33] to leave a wider and straighter margin on the
left side of the page, and to leave three spaces after a period. Good taste
requires that.

Thanks once again for the propaganda you are doing on my behalf in America. The success of the *Scythian Suite* has really given me a lift. Zederbaum
wrote me that he spoke with Brennan, who is ready to take on my management
for next season. In reply, I sent Zederbaum a precise description of the techni-

---

31. Prokofiev met Ephraim Gottlieb on one of his early trips to Chicago and remained in
correspondence with him for many years.

32. Koussevitsky was publishing the Violin Concerto No. 1, op. 19. Although composed
simultaneously with the "Classical" Symphony in 1916–17, it was not performed until
October 18, 1923, in Paris, by Koussevitsky, with violinist Marcel Darrieux.

33. Vladimir Nikolaevich Zederbaum, Koussevitsky's secretary and assistant.

cal details involved with my move from one manager to another. Meanwhile another letter arrived from Vladimir Nikolaevich with the information not only that Brennan is willing to take me on, but that he's also prepared to pay my debts to my former manager in order to free me of any obligation to him. This is really a big step forward and indicates that the matter really is moving ahead on track.

Of course I understand very well that I am obliged above all to you for this "track," and that without your support Zederbaum could not have managed to accomplish even a quarter of what he has. On the other hand I see clearly that you have absolutely no time to concern yourself with the technical side of the matter, and that perhaps it would not be entirely appropriate for you to descend from the conductor's pedestal in order to enter into the details. So probably it is very good that Vladimir Nikolaevich has taken upon himself the initiative for transferring me from Haensel to Brennan, and the arrangement of my upcoming tour. I would only ask you to keep track of things and to be a sort of supreme commander; I'm sure that Vladimir Nikolaevich will take good care of all the technical twists and turns. Please convey to him my gratitude for his efforts and tell him that I will write him in a few days to answer all the questions he raised in his letter of November 9.

I'm working on your symphony every morning, but it is progressing rather slowly, first of all because the structure is complicated and secondly because I don't want to just drag it along, but to make each separate moment good. I still have to finish three more variations, including the big concluding one, and then I can start on the instrumentation. When is the last concert of your season?

I thank you for your useful advice to dedicate the symphony to the Boston Symphony and its leader. It seems to me, however, that for a composer to make dedications for the sake of his career is just as wrong as for a woman to have sex for the sake of promoting her business affairs. I am very well aware that this would help my American career, but even so, if I am writing this symphony for you, then such a dedication does not sit well with me. Of course we could still do some flirting, and I would ask you when you have the opportunity to let it be known to the members of Boston Symphony that I am writing this symphony with the intent that they be the first to perform it, and that I had no other orchestra in mind, and that while orchestrating I am imagining only their sound and no other, and that I am in ecstasy over all of them, beginning with the tam-tam players and ending with the extra bassoon, and that I adore Boston, and Symphony Hall, and their music stands, even the spit that they pour out of their trombones—and yet their leader is even more dear to me, and that it is precisely to him, and not to some collective body, that I wish to dedicate this symphony. [. . .]

Write and tell me what I should do with the suite from *Three Oranges*. Do you want to be the first to perform it, or can I give it to someone else? (I still don't have anyone in mind, and have not shown it to anyone.) Of course this suite has less musical significance than the suite that I want to make from *The Fiery Angel* (of five movements, three movements for soprano and orchestra and two for orchestra alone). But I'm still not entirely sure that this suite will be ready by May. If it were finished by then, and you were to play it here in May, then a good soprano soloist would be Nina Koshetz, who by the way is now in Paris. Write me what you think about this. And do please send me the manual for trombones that you promised, and similar manuals (if there are any) for other instruments, e.g. saxophones and other wind instruments.

[. . .] Diaghilev has commissioned new ballets from Auric and (it seems) Dukelsky, a rather capable fellow out of whom he apparently plans to mold a new star. He isn't putting on my *Buffoon* at all: it seems that if someone finds shelter under Koussevitsky's wing, then he also earns Diaghilev's curse. And is it true that Medtner[34] had a smashing success in America? So will the publishing house once again have to take him back into the tender fold?!

I'm in ecstasy that Natalia Konstantinovna is driving an automobile. When she takes me for a drive in the spring, I'll take the symphony with me: so if we hit a post, then we'll all perish together! My housemates are flourishing. Sviatoslav is getting smarter and is trying to crawl.[35] We all send you and Natalia Konstantinovna warmest greetings, and on top of that I send you a big kiss. Natalia Konstantinovna is probably less busy than you are. It would be very nice if she could write me somehow.

With love,

SProkofiev

Please convey my respects to Vladimir Nikolaevich.

---

34. Nikolai Medtner (1880–1951) was a Russian pianist and composer who left Russia in 1921 and eventually settled in England.
35. Prokofiev's son Sviatoslav was born in February 1924.

December 23, 1924
54, ROUTE DES GARDES, BELLEVUE, S. ET O., FRANCE

Dear Natalia Konstantinovna,

I wish you and dear Sergei Aleksandrovich happy holidays and hope that in the New Year in your household you will eat laurel soup for dinner every day!

Ptashka joins me in sending holiday greetings and best wishes to you and Sergei Alexandrovich. We are not planning to observe Christmas at all, since we are still in mourning: my mama died from a heart attack. Her health was completely undermined by the events in Russia. Last winter she was seriously ill; she felt much better this summer, but that turned out to be the last flicker. We buried her here in Bellevue.[36] After this sad event we would like to move to another place—the house in which all this transpired no longer appeals to us, but we have a contract with the landlord here until May, so we will have to stay.

Please tell the maestro that I am still waiting to receive from him the American manuals on wind instruments—I need them for the orchestration of the symphony, which I have now started to do.

I kiss your little hands and would be extremely happy to get some news from you. You have been very silent until now. I send Sergei Aleksandrovich a big hug.

With love,
SProkofiev

Please convey my best wishes for the New Year to Vladimir Nikolaevich.

February 10, 1925
BELLEVUE

Dear Natalia Konstantinovna,

I was very happy to receive your letter of January 7, and thank you for it. It took you a long time to get around to writing it, but when you did, you wrote quite tenderly. I am in ecstasy that you will be taking on my management: that means that I'll get a good contract. I know very well how splendid you are at bargaining.

I am anxiously awaiting news about the performance of the Violin Concerto. Did you take a look at how the score was printed? I think they did a good job.

---

36. Maria Grigorevna Prokofieva died of a heart attack on December 13, 1924, at the age of sixty-nine. An accomplished amateur pianist, she was very instrumental to Prokofiev's success, having encouraged him from an early age to fulfill his musical talent. She also secured his entrance into the St. Petersburg Conservatory.

But here's what is bad: the publisher has completely stopped printing my music. The Fifth Sonata (22 pages) was released a few days ago, but now there is nothing else in the works—except for a few lousy old songs that are being reprinted at a lazy pace. And meanwhile here's what I have waiting to be published: 1) the "Classical" Symphony, 2) the piano score of the Second Piano Concerto, 3) the full score of the Second Concerto, 4) the symphonic suite from *Three Oranges*, 5) the Quintet—and in a few months: 6) The Second Symphony and 7) the orchestral suite from *The Fiery Angel*.

[. . .] I'm working on the symphony and it is moving forward, but not very fast—the knowledge that my compositions are not being published is very demoralizing to me and decreases my desire to work.

[. . .] Ptashka and Sviatoslav are in good health and send you a thousand greetings. And when can we expect to see you in Paris? I've already been missing both you and the maestro, although the latter has completely forgotten about me; he never sent the trombone manual and has replied not even with a single word concerning the suite from *Oranges*. He must already be enjoying very great success!

I kiss your little hands and beg you not to get angry at me for carrying on like this. But for one thing, emaciated Gutheil is really behaving indecently towards me, and for another, if I sprinkle a bit of pepper in your laurel soup, the soup will not be spoiled.

With love, SProkofiev

January 2, 1925 [1926]
GREAT NORTHERN HOTEL, 109 W. 56TH ST., NEW YORK
Dear Sergei Aleksandrovich,

Yesterday we arrived safely in New York and send you and Natalia Konstantinovna our best wishes for a Happy New Year. [. . .] Since you are arriving in New York most likely on the 6th or 7th, unfortunately I probably will not see you, because we leave on the 5th for the western states (St. Paul, Portland, etc.) for five recitals.

[. . .] And here's another matter: the society Pro Arte, which set up the five recitals in the West for me and my wife, wants us to perform under their auspices in New York on January 26, in a closed concert in a private apartment, without critics. I replied that I could not accept their invitation without your permission. So I ask you please to immediately send me a telegram and tell me if I can play for them or not. They would not pay very much, so that this per-formance is not important in the financial sense; if we do perform for them, it would be exclusively in gratitude for the tour they set up in the western states. If you do give me permission to play, and the concert does take place, then I would leave for Boston in the evening on the day of the concert, the 26th.

For now I send you a big hug and ask you to kiss Natalia Konstantinovna's little hand. My wife sends her warmest greeting to you both. I'm very happy that I'll soon see you in Boston, and thank you once again for coaxing me to America.

Sincerely, SPRKFV

March 6, 1926
ON BOARD S.S. FRANCE

Dear Sergei Aleksandrovich,

We have set sail on the *France* and are heading to France. I left the "Classical" Symphony with the doorman at the artists' entrance at Carnegie Hall for you to pick it up. Klemperer has proposed performing it in New York next season but I proposed to him instead that he perform the suite from *The Buffoon*.[37] They didn't manage to return the materials of the Third Concerto to me in Syracuse, since I left immediately after the concert. Therefore I told them to send the materials to you in Boston, along with a check for the rental of the music. Did you read the notice in *Musical Courier* about our New York concert of February 4? They wrote that you played excerpts from *Oranges*, which they liked better than my concerto. Just like Sabaneyev![38]

And then please let me thank you one more time for my trip to America, and to send you a big hug. My wife sends her greetings to you both. I kiss Natalia Konstantinovna's little hands. We drank the port while smacking our lips.

Yours, SPRKFV

---

37. Otto Klemperer (1885–1973), the German conductor.
38. In 1916, Russian critic Leonid Sabaneyev published a scathing review of a scheduled Moscow performance of Prokofiev's *Scythian Suite*, even though the piece was replaced by another at the last minute. The New York reviewer mentioned here did the same thing, describing a performance of excerpts from *Love for Three Oranges* that never took place.

November 18, 1926
18, RUE TROYON, PARIS XVII

Dear Sergei Aleksandrovich,

I feel very guilty that I haven't written either to you or to Natalia Konstanti-novna until now. By the way, after your departure we more than once took advantage of your hospitality by using your house here, spending the night there when we would come to Paris looking for apartments to rent. While we were making the final move from the country to the city, we lived at your place for four entire days, when we were waiting to settle in somewhere. Ksyusha was very attentive, and even after we had settled into the hotel several days we foisted Sviatoslav off on her, until he broke his nose and Ksyusha in horror refused to take on such a responsibility again.[39]

People interested in renting your house came to look at it quite often. They praised its cleanliness and artistic atmosphere but complained that there was nothing to sit on. As far as our own search for an apartment is concerned, we still didn't find anything good, so we have temporarily given up on the idea of an unfurnished apartment and have now moved into a furnished one: it is a sort of funny mansard with a terrace on the roof. All this searching and vegetating in temporary residences has really interfered with my work and although I am now on page 400 of the orchestral score of *Fiery Angel*, the end is still not any-where in sight.

Please let me thank you for your frequent performances of the *Buffoon* suite and for your intention to perform the suite from *Oranges*, and the "Classical" Symphony. It seems that this year you have decided to beat America into sub-mission with my opuses. Gavriil Grigorevich gave me the telegram about your success.[40] I also received the programs and press clippings sent by Slonimsky, but it seems to me that the reviews were rather cool—but I'm thankful even for that from America.

Oranges was staged very well in Berlin and has been performed there five times already. The conductor Blech[41] studied and learned the music extremely conscientiously, but this conscientiousness even made me sick: it was all too slow and boring. Overall, they put on this Italian fairy tale in a German style, but people say that's why it was a success; if they had staged it in an Italian

---

39. Apparently, Ksyusha took care of the Koussevitsky's Paris home.
40. Gavriil Grigorevich Paichadze (1879–1976) was director of the Editions Russes de Musique in Paris.
41. Leo Blech (1871–1958) was the conductor at the Staatsoper 1926–37.

style, then the Berliners would not have appreciated it. *Oranges* has now been accepted for Kharkov, Kiev, and Odessa. Malko will conduct and the same production will be staged in all three cities: the cast will change in the course of the season.

My negotiations with Russia are continuing and I already have permission to receive a certificate allowing me to travel: these are documents that I will use only during my stay in the USSR. When I leave, I can again become a subject of Doctor Nansen. Persimfans is arranging five symphonic concerts of my music, and actually everything would be going very well if not for the terrible bickering between the various concert organizations in Moscow and Leningrad.[42] At first the Leningrad Philharmonic Society—a state-sponsored institution—invited me, but then Rosfil, a joint-stock company that had temporarily closed down, revived. But then I was warned that Rosfil's owners were to gobble up the Philharmonic Society in Leningrad, even though it's a state-sponsored organization. Next, another state-sponsored institution with more clout—Glavnauka—sent me the information that I didn't have the right to sign an agreement with anyone except Rosfil or Persimfans. And from a private source I was told that Glavnauka itself is about to be reorganized in the near future. So just try to figure what the hell is going on!

Your music store continues to flourish. Rabenek, Gavriil Grigorevich's new assistant, is a very nice person. But the publishing house still doesn't want to publish me, apparently planning to turn our relationship into a historical anecdote. At one time I banged my head against the wall persuading the publishing house to print the "Classical" Symphony and the suite from *Oranges,* and now they are making money on them. The same thing is happening again now with my new things.

Ptashka and I send you and Natalia Konstantinovna our warmest greetings. Ptashka will write separately to Natalia Konstantinovna in a few days. It would be very nice if you could somehow plan to dictate a letter to Slonimsky for me and tell me about your triumphs. After all, you once said that you respond to business letters with a mathematical accuracy—so here then, maybe you can scrape together a few minutes to write a personal letter.

With a kiss,

Love, SPRKFV

---

42. Persimfans is a Russian acronym for *Pervyi simfonicheskii ansambl'* (First Symphonic Ensemble). This quirky collective without a conductor was organized in Moscow in 1922 by violinist Lev Tseitlin (1881–1952); it concertized actively from 1922 to 1932.

LINA PROKOFIEVA to
NATALIA KONSTANTINOVNA KOUSSEVITSKY

December 31, 1926
Paris

Dear Natalia Konstantinovna,

We send you and Sergei Aleksandrovich warmest wishes for the holidays and the New Year.

I hope that everything is fine with you and that Sergei Alexandrovich's successes will grow with each passing day.

We are now getting ready to go on our trip. We are planning to leave around the 13th, since we will have a concert on the way in Riga.

We were not able to find an unfurnished apartment. We lived for two months in a furnished one and now are faced with the prospect of packing up all our belongings in trunks and boxes, which we will leave with Pleyel.

Sviatoslav is growing and his *vocabulaire* is increasing in both Russian and French. He has fallen in love with the little farm you gave him, and drags it from one room to the other; he even took the farmer's wife to bed with him even though she is wooden and hard.

I see Vera Vasilievna Paichadze rather often; she is very nice.

Seryozha is learning to drive in the same school where Stravinsky learned, and will take the test in a few days. We have been teasing him that he'll fail just like Tansman did.[43] I will also learn to drive, but I have put it off until after our return from Moscow, when I'll have more free time and the weather will be warmer. We have subfreezing weather here now, which is preparing us for the Moscow climate.

I wrote down the things you asked me to do in Moscow, and if it's possible I will try to carry them out.

They also asked me to sing a *liederabend* of Seryozha's songs in Moscow at the Association for Contemporary Music, but I don't know if I will accept the invitation, considering how tiring our trip will be, how different the climate will be, and most of all, because of the strong emotions involved.

I send you a big kiss and warmest wishes for the New Year. We both send greetings to Sergei Aleksandrovich, and Seryozha kisses your little hands.

Your faithful servant
Lina Prokofieva

Prokofiev performed often with the orchestra during his first trips back to the USSR in the late 1920s.

43. The Polish-born composer Alexandre Tansman (born 1897) lived in Paris after 1919 and was acquainted with the Prokofievs.

January 18, 1927
RIGA

As we depart for Eurasia-land, we send you our warmest greetings.
L. and S. Prokofiev

March 29, 1927
VICTORIA PALACE HOTEL, PARIS

Dear Natalia Koussevitsky,

Here we are in Paris again. We are very pleased with our trip to the USSRia: they received us there very affectionately, those in power behaved properly, and we left with a feeling of regret.[44] Altogether I gave 23 concerts, including some in Kharkov, Kiev, and Odessa. I sent you the reviews right away. I saw *Oranges* at the Mariinsky Theater, where it was staged very cheerfully; in June they will bring it to Paris—the arrangements have already been made. But the Bolshoi Theater is planning to stage "them" even more extravagantly, and now there is a struggle going on over which of the two theaters should go to Paris.[45] You and Sergei Aleksandrovich were often remembered [in the USSR]; Tseitlin, Tabakov, and many others send you their respects.[46] Sergei Aleksandrovich's library is still together and has not been broken up. I went past your large house: what a marvelously handsome little place! As far as your instructions to Ptashka are concerned, she spoke with Rybnikova and with Grishin. She will write you about the details separately, but there were no positive results.

Gavriil Grigorevich told me how much S. A. has been playing me this season. I am touched and amazed, and was never counting on such a large quantity of performances!

In a week I will set off for a few days to Monte Carlo, where Diaghilev is beginning rehearsals of my new ballet; its premiere is scheduled for May 29 in

---

44. Prokofiev and his wife were in the USSR from January 19 until March 23. It was Prokofiev's first trip back to Russia since he had left in May 1918. He was greeted with such enthusiasm there that he began to think of returning permanently to the USSR, which he did in 1936, after nine years of increasingly frequent visits. "USSRia" is a word Prokofiev invented.

45. Neither of these planned tours to Paris took place.

46. Mikhail Tabakov (1877–1956) was a Soviet trumpeter and teacher. A member of Koussevitsky's orchestra in Russia before the Revolution, he was one of the original founders of Persimfans.

Paris.[47] Stravinsky is completing a two-act opera written in Latin—*Oedipus*; he's working on it with Cocteau.[48] *The Gambler* and *The Buffoon* will be put on next season at the Mariinsky Theater. I managed to get hold of the full score of *The Gambler* and will revise it. They would very much like me to return to the USSR next year and are already offering me contracts. In any case I would like to go there for the production of *The Gambler*.[49] Borovsky is in Moscow and came to see us the day we left. His debut there was accompanied by great success.[50] Medtner is not doing so well there; he's driving the audience away. I heard Miaskovsky's Eighth Symphony—it's a very good piece.

We are awaiting you in Paris. I kiss your little hands and send a big hug to the dear maestro. Ptashka sends her warm respects to you both. Sviatoslav is flourishing—the absence of his parents seems to have done him good. In response to Slonimsky's request, I arranged to have two copies of *Seven, They Are Seven* sent from Moscow for your library. Did you receive them? I paid about 12 rubles for these, which comes out to $6; let the library pay it.

Sincerely,
SPRKFV

November 29, 1927
5, AVENUE FRÉMIET, PARIS XVI

Dear Natalia Konstantinovna,

Thank you very much for the parcel containing the programs for the Boston performance of *Steel Gallop* and for the parcel with the reviews. Did *Steel Gallop* really have such a limited success that Sergei Aleksandrovich didn't play it anywhere else? After all, in Chicago he played the "Classical." So what's the story? Can it really be that Americans have not yet seen through C Major music and weren't able to understand a single melody? Or is this piece simply unsuitable for a concert performance?

---

47. The new ballet for Diaghilev was *The Steel Gallop* (*Stal'noi skok*). It received its premiere in Paris on June 7, 1927.

48. Stravinsky completed his opera-oratorio in two acts, *Oedipus Rex,* in May 1927, and it was first performed in a concert version in Paris on May 30, 1927.

49. Because of intractable political and administrative problems, none of these projected productions of Prokofiev's ballets or of *The Gambler* took place in Russia at this time.

50. Aleksandr Borovsky (1889–1968) was a Russian pianist who emigrated in 1920; he lived in the United States after 1941.

I worked all autumn on the revision of *The Gambler*. I did a fundamental reworking of the score, and in some places left no stone unturned; besides that I reorchestrated all of it. Now, thank God, I have finished Act III and only Act IV remains. I'll start to work on that as soon as we return from London, where Ptashka and I are going in a few days to spend a week, doing two radio concerts and also to record for Duo-Art. It still isn't clear if *The Gambler* will be staged at the Mariinsky this spring, but in any case I focused so completely on my work on it that I got very behind in checking the proofs of the Second Symphony. Now it is perfectly obvious that the symphony won't be in print before May.

Will Sergei Aleksandrovich play the symphony in America? I'm asking this question not in order to burden him, but so I will know how I should plan to use what is still the only manuscript copy of the symphony; Persimfans has requested it from Moscow. If Sergei Aleksandrovich is likely to play the symphony, then we will refuse Persimfans' request; if he isn't likely to play it, then I would ask him to please write me, since Persimfans is waiting for an answer in order to make definite plans for their programs. I have not yet decided whether I will travel to Russia, but the decision will most likely depend on the production of *The Gambler* at the Mariinsky Theater, since I would like to go to Russia this time as a composer unavailable for playing the piano. Last time they wore me out so completely that I didn't even have a chance to look around.

[. . .] And so, my dear Natalia Konstantinovna, I'm waiting for a long letter from you. For the time being we are staying in the same apartment, since its owner has gotten waylaid in Germany. All of Paris is talking about Sergei Aleksandrovich's benefit concert for students: that was really a phenomenal hit. Long live Koussevitsky! Sviatoslav is flourishing, and Ptashka is preparing intensively for London, where she has been asked to sing in English, so she is cramming English texts and cursing the way they constrain the voice when they are sung. My Haensel has not written me anything further and is apparently entirely satisfied with having proposed 1½ concerts for me for this season.

We both send big hugs to you and to Sergei Aleksandrovich and send you our best wishes. I kiss your little hands.

Love,
SPRKFV

January 31, 1928
5, AVENUE FRÉMIET, PARIS XVI

Dear Natalia Konstantinovna,

We are both very appreciative of your affectionate letter, and the promptness of your reply.

[. . .] We were not very happy with our trip to London: we ended up in a nasty fog and Ptashka got laryngitis and could not sing. Ansermet conducted the Second Concerto almost without preparation and I did not play so well.[51] Besides that, during the last movement the sound from another studio intruded into ours, and so somebody was heard loudly giving the weather forecast for tomorrow to the accompaniment of my music. But we did fly back from London by airplane—and it was thrilling. In London we saw Dukelsky, although he could not come to the first concert because that evening he was giving a bath to a maiden of questionable virtue. But he has written a symphony that isn't bad at all—much more vivid than his Sonata with Orchestra.[52] His symphony is well-crafted and not especially long (15–20 minutes). He is now orchestrating it and I promised as much as possible to give him my suggestions, for orchestration is not his strong suit.

[. . .] I am now completing the revision of *The Gambler,* which has turned into a completely new composition. There is a hope that it will be staged in April at the Mariinsky Theater, and then Ptashka and I would go to see the production. But I have refused all offers of concerts in Russia, since all my days have been going to *The Gambler,* and it's imposssible simultaneously to compose and practice the piano the way I should. And I couldn't show up in Russia with last year's program.

[. . .] Is it true that Koshetz had barely arrived in America before she landed in Boston? How could that have happened? I saw the program of her New York recital in the newspapers—it was really inexcusable trash.

I kiss your little hands. I send a hug to Sergei Aleksandrovich. Ptashka embraces you both. Sviatoslav sends his respectful greetings.

Love,
Yours, SPRKFV

---

51. Ernest Ansermet (1883–1969), a Swiss conductor, often worked with Diaghilev's Ballets Russes.

52. Prokofiev seems to be referring to Dukelsky's Piano Concerto (1924), disparaging it by calling it a Sonata with Orchestra. Dukelsky finished the first of his three symphonies in 1928.

October 15, 1928
C/O EDITIONS RUSSES, PARIS

Dear Natalia Konstantinovna,

[. . .] We returned not long ago to Paris; we lost our old apartment and have not yet found a new one. In September Ptashka, Asafiev, Lamm,[53] and I traveled to Chamonix, rode up by cable car to Planpraz, spent the night there, and then the men (we left Ptashka in a chalet) climbed the Col de Brévent, where I showed them the road that Sergei Aleksandrovich and I traversed together. On the return trip we surveyed the Gorges de Diosaz, which are just amazingly interesting. It's a real pity that Sergei Aleksandrovich and I didn't get to this ravine on our trip. At the end of September the same group of us traveled for five days in Switzerland: we skirted Lake Geneva, Thunersee, Brienzersee, crossed the Furkapass and Passo di San Gottardo, spent some time in Lugano and returned home via the Rhône Valley. Both the automobile and Ptashka emerged from these exertions quite well, while Lamm and Asafiev were just ecstatic over the trip. Asafiev did not have a visa, so we took him over the border at night by motorcycle.

Ptashka also made the trip from the dacha to Paris by car (she really is crazy!). Actually, she bore up quite well during the trip,[54] but in Paris because of an automobile show all the rooms were taken. We would have slipped into your place, but Ksyusha wouldn't let us in because we did not have a letter from Fiedler. Only towards evening did we finally get into a small hotel near the Porte d'Auteuil. We are now looking for an apartment, so if you do bestow a letter upon us, then send it for now to the publishing house. The production of *The Gambler*, and my trip to Russia connected with it, will likely take place at the end of December or in January. I'll finish the Third Symphony in a few days.

Ptashka and I send you both big hugs. We hope that you traveled home safely, and that Sergei Aleksandrovich is now supplied with good health for the new season, just as the Leiden Dike is stocked with electricity.

Love, SPRKFV

---

53. Pavel Aleksandrovich Lamm (1882–1951), a musicologist and pianist, later copied many of Prokofiev's works from detailed piano scores into orchestral scores. He visited Prokofiev in France in 1928 with Boris Asafiev.
54. Lina was six months pregnant with their second child, Oleg, who was born on December 14, 1928.

December 26, 1928
1, RUE OBLIGADO, PARIS XVI

Dear Natalia Konstantinovna,

I received both of your telegrams, one without a joke, and the other with a joke, as well as a long letter. In the end, I am right back where I started, on that same spot at which Sergei Aleksandrovich has been flinging mud for five years in a row now. But there is nothing to be done, I'll try to lick the mud off bravely—and enter into negotiations with Haensel. I am very grateful to Sergei Aleksandrovich for writing the letters to conductors. Let's hope the letters will succeed in rousing these deaf posts.

My trip to the USSR has been postponed, since no assurance was given that I could receive permission to convert Soviet banknotes into foreign currency. They are promising to obtain that permission in the course of January, which would mean I would go in February or March. Meanwhile, I have nearly finished a new ballet for Diaghilev, and am now orchestrating it. The ballet is turning out to be simple, clear, melodic—in other words, just right for Brooklyn.[55]

On December 14 Ptashka brought into the world a second son, who has been given the name Oleg. Things could not have gone better, and the day after tomorrow I will bring him home from the clinic. We both send you warmest wishes for a Happy New Year. I send Sergei Aleksandrovich a hug and kiss your little hands.

Love,
SPRKFV

November 25, 1929
6, RUE BASSANO, PARIS XVI

Dear Sergei Aleksandrovich,

I am writing you having just returned from Russia, where I spent three weeks. Of course I am full of the most varied emotions. Life has become more difficult there than it was at the time of my previous trip, but even so a lot of interesting things are happening. The attitude towards me there was extremely cautious, so I am planning to go again in the spring, and even to take Ptashka with me. I did not give any concerts—my hand was still aching a bit from the car accident—but I did oversee a revival of *Three Oranges* at the Bolshoi

55. The new ballet was *Prodigal Son*, to a libretto by Boris Kochno and with choreography by George Balanchine. Diaghilev's Ballets Russes gave the premiere in Paris on May 21, 1929.

Theater, whose first performances attracted full houses. I conducted several pieces for a concert of my music on the radio. Radio is now playing an important educational role, which is completely understandable when you think of all the godforsaken places to which the radio sprays new ideas, which the people there would never have dreamed of before. This radio station is located in a huge new building on Tverskaya and is staffed by rather cultured people with whom it is possible to work. By the way, they asked me to be their permanent advisor on foreign repertoire.

This same concert featured the first performance of my Sinfonietta, which I completely revised once again during the summer.[56] I ended up with an easily accessible piece, something like the "Classical" Symphony. I think it would be very good if you could put it in the program of the concerts in which I will be participating. I could bring the music with me. You will play the Third Symphony even before my arrival, I hope.

Upon my return to Paris I found a contract from the Boston trustees with a "commission" for my Fourth Symphony. I hasten to thank you for this, since I detect your efforts here. But the good Americans have mixed up something. Because as far as I can remember, you and I had said this: touched by the long-standing attention of the Boston Symphony to me and my music, I would delay for a year the premiere of this symphony, so it would take place on their anniversary. Brought to ecstasy by this symphony, they would then pay me $1,000 for the manuscript for their library. They got mixed up and sent me a contract for a commission. For you know, you could commission a symphony from Lazar or Tansman for $1,000,[57] but it would be awkward for me to accept such a commission. Prokofiev gets three to five thousand dollars for a commissioned symphony, or simply for the right to announce that "we commissioned this from him." So I believe it would be best to go back to our first idea: like a good gentleman, I give them the right to play the first performance, and they (like good gentlemen) buy the manuscript from me. In any case, of course I'll do as you advise me—the best thing would be for us to talk about this when we meet. For now I will not reply to them, and you could indicate that I am in Russia, and therefore out of reach by mail.

Now let me trouble you concerning another matter: on what piano will I be

---

56. The Sinfonietta in A Major, op. 48, was a third reworking of the Sinfonietta in A Major, op. 5, originally composed in 1909 and revised in 1914–15.

57. Filip Lazar (1894–1936) was a Romanian composer and, in 1928, a founding member of the modern music society Triton.

playing in America? Have you spoken with Mason and Hamlin?[58] Because that could add a significant sum to my fees. I ask you please to resolve this issue and to write Haensel about it.

Now that I have returned from Russia I am devoting myself entirely to preparing for the American tour, as is Ptashka, since she will be performing in most of my recitals.

I send you a big hug and kiss Natalia Konstantinovna's little hands. I will be very happy to see you both.

With love,

SPRKFV

January 15, 1930

GREAT NORTHERN HOTEL, NEW YORK CITY

Dear Sergei Aleksandrovich,

Reviving the conversation we were having at the Savoy Plaza, I would like to ask you once again to try to give in New York an entire program of my compositions. This is especially important *pour me poser bien à New York*, where it is so difficult to find a niche. And if you are devoting so much energy to Glazunov, then you could think at least a little bit about me, damn it all![59] The Boston Symphony has not played anything of mine for almost a year (yes, 11 months) now, and if after that the orchestra will get away with playing only my Second Concerto (along perhaps with some other old piece), then that will be just shameful! I know that it is very hard because you have to put together a program for your provincial tour, but please make an effort on my behalf, I beg you. It's very important for me.

I send you a hug, and kiss Natalia Konstantinovna's little hands.

Yours, SPRKFV

---

58. Mason and Hamlin was a prominent piano manufacturer and trademark. Prokofiev sometimes endorsed pianos in advertisements.

59. Aleksandr Glazunov (1865–1936) was a Russian composer, and director of the St. Petersburg Conservatory 1905–28. He was one of Prokofiev's teachers there. Prokofiev rejected Glazunov's conservative symphonic style, but they maintained collegial relations after Glazunov moved to Paris in 1928. In this letter, Prokofiev is expressing his frustration that Koussevitsky had recently organized a Glazunov Festival with the Boston Symphony.

February 10, 1930
ON BOARD THE SUNSET LIMITED [USA]

Dear Natalia Konstantinovna,

When we parted, you promised to ask Maxwell about the fees for the rental of the opera materials. Since this issue is very important for my operatic negotiations, please let me give you a little written explanation.

According to my agreement with the publishing house, I will conclude an independent contract with the theater, and the publishing house will independently loan out the materials for rental. According to established tradition, the author gets 10% of the box office receipts or a sum approximately equal to that percentage. The publishing house (such was the case in Germany, Belgium, and the USSR) loans the material for the entire season, without concerning itself over the number of performances that will be given during that season.

What I would like to know is the sum that the publishing house intends to charge for an annual rental from 1) the Metropolitan Opera House, 2) the American Opera Company, 3) the Chicago Opera, and 4) the San Francisco Opera.

I ask you please to write me an answer in Chicago, Congress Hotel, where I will be staying from February 24 to 28, and where I will perhaps be talking things over with the Chicago Opera.

Remind Maxwell that during the three years of his reign he hasn't lifted a finger to get my operas staged. So now, when things are starting to come together for me, he has the obligation to behave decently and meet me halfway—and not to create obstacles. At least that is what common decency requires.

I kiss your little hands and apologize for bothering you. I send the conservative maestro a hug and thank him once again for the marvelous performance of my Scythian old lady.

Yours, SPRKFV

February 28, 1930
CONGRESS HOTEL, CHICAGO

Dear Natalia Konstantinovna,

I'm sending you the photo taken in Boston. It seems to me that you and I are having a marvelous conversation.

Did you send off the Third Symphony, the full score and the other materials? Please, it's very urgent! You told me that one of the parts was missing or had been inserted into the full score? Please tell Paichadze about this so that he can restore it; otherwise there will be a misunderstanding at the rehearsal. Because I'm going to get to Brussels just in time for the dress rehearsal.

I kiss your little hands. I send a hug to the Doctor.

Yours, SPRKFV

We'll be in New York from the 4th to the 7th, and then Havana.

March 18, 1930

GREAT NORTHERN HOTEL, NEW YORK

Dear Sergei Aleksandrovich,

I was with Engel yesterday so we could come to a final agreement about the commission for the quartet.[60] I took advantage of the opportunity to ask him if he would take on the representation of our publishing house. In doing this, I explained that I was posing the question as a private individual, on my own behalf, since during my travels through different American cities I had become convinced that Maxwell's policies have done real harm to my compositions. Without thinking, Engel answered, "I would take it on with pleasure, both for location and for sale." He is definitely staying with Schirmer's.

His answer made me very happy. It seems to me that we should not lose the opportunity to appoint a real gentleman as the representative of our publishing house—instead of some sort of buffoon who gets into arguments with all the orchestras. I assure you, it was most unpleasant for me when in one orchestra someone said that "Koussevitsky has intentionally appointed this Cerberus so that no one will play his editions and so that he will be the sole benefactor to his composers . . ." I know that this is not true and that on the contrary, you yourself set up performances for me with all the orchestras—but that's the sort of reputation Maxwell has.

Gatti-Casazza[61] said that the subject of *The Fiery Angel* does not suit him, and that he prefers the subject of *The Gambler*. So *Angel* has gone to the devil, but tomorrow Serafin[62] has invited me to play *The Gambler* for him. Rosing

---

60. Prokofiev had received a commission from the Library of Congress to write a string quartet; this became his String Quartet No. 1 in B Minor, op. 50. It was completed in 1930 and first performed in Washington, D.C., on April 25, 1931.

61. Giulio Gatti-Casazza (1869–1940) was the general manager of the Metropolitan Opera in New York 1910–35.

62. Tullio Serafin (1878–1968) was principal conductor at the Metropolitan Opera 1924–34.

doesn't want to take *Fiery Angel* for the American Opera Company.[63] The information Maxwell provided on their finances turns out to be incorrect: Hoover has paid some attention to them; they got some money and they are now making their way again.

I was at two rehearsals of Toscanini.[64] Very interesting: he broke his baton and shouted "*Vergogna*"—"Shame"! He spoke with me and immediately said that he is going to play the Sinfonietta next season. But while "Simfonini gets ready to play the Toscanetta," you should really perform it in Boston, as you promised: the time has come to realize that it really is a good piece.

Stokowski suddenly invited us to his box today and then for breakfast at his place ("so you can see my new apartment").[65] We won't go to the box because we are leaving, and as for having breakfast—we did already. We also talked about music: in three weeks he will play the Overture, op. 42, in Philadelphia and New York. Since you have no interest in this piece, let him play it; otherwise the Overture has been sitting around like an old maid.

I leave for Montreal on the 19th, then for Chicago, where Ptashka and I will give two concerts. On the 26th we will be in New York again, and on the 28th at 5 P.M. we sail on the *Ile de France*.

I give you both a big kiss. Thank you for all your help.

Yours, SPRKFV

October 11, 1930
5, RUE VALENTIN HAÜY, PARIS XV

Dear Sergei Aleksandrovich,

I want to give you some information about the Fourth Symphony, so you can write a program note about it. The symphony was begun in 1929, and finished on June 23, 1930. In several places in the symphony I used music that was included in the ballet *Prodigal Son*. But this does not mean that the symphony was written from material from *Prodigal Son*, or that *Prodigal Son* was written from material from the symphony. In the symphony I had the opportunity to

---

63. Vladimir Rosing was a Russian singer who organized the American Opera Company at the Eastman School of Music in Rochester, N.Y.

64. Arturo Toscanini (1867–1957) was at this time conductor of the New York Philharmonic.

65. Leopold Stokowski (1882–1977) was at this time conductor of the Philadelphia Orchestra.

develop symphonically what the form of a ballet would not permit me to do. You can find precedents for such an approach in Beethoven, in his ballet *Prometheus* and in his Third Symphony.

This should be indicated with as much precision as possible in the program, since a lack of caution in the writing of program notes can give rise to various unnecessary judgments in the press after the performance.

We both send warmest greetings to Natalia Konstantinovna, and also wish you the greatest successes. Please also convey our greetings to your niece and ask her to send me the program and reviews after the symphony.

I hug you.

Yours, SPRKFV

SERGE KOUSSEVITSKY to PROKOFIEV

December 20, 1932

[Boston]

Dear Seryozha,

Natalia Konstantinovna and I are impatiently awaiting your arrival in Boston and insist that you stay with us. On Saturday, the 24th, Drolka will be lighting the Christmas tree and wants very much for you to be there. We share his sentiments and will be very happy if you will join us on Saturday.

With a warm embrace, [S. Koussevitsky unsigned]

ANDREI GROMYKO to KOUSSEVITSKY

November 8 [1941?]

[TELEGRAM IN ENGLISH, FROM WASHINGTON, D.C.]

Serge Koussevitzky

Boston Symphony Orchestra

It is regretted that it would not be safe to depend on Serge Prokoffiev's [sic] coming to the United States due to war situation

Andrei Gromyko Chargé d'Affaires

[Embassy of USSR in Washington, D.C.]

October 20, 1943
Moscow

Dear Sergei Aleksandrovich,

I am taking advantage of the opportunity to send you a deeply felt greeting and to express my joy that you are as robust and active and productive in your work as ever. We were all happy to learn that you had become the head of the Musical Commission of the National Council for American-Soviet Friendship, and we look forward to creative artistic contact from this initiative.

It's very nice that you are planning to perform my Second Concerto with Horowitz. The orchestral score is now being copied and will be sent to you in a few days. For my part, I wish you could tell me if you have the orchestral score of my cello concerto: after the manuscript was sent to the publisher I was left without a duplicate, and we have been unable for several years now to perform this concerto.[66]

I send you my very warmest wishes.

Sincerely, SPRKFV

[telegram in English]

November 6, 1945
Moscow

Happy you conducting American premiere my Fifth Symphony. Work very close to my heart. Sending sincere friendly greetings you and all members your magnificent orchestra.

Serge Prokofieff

---

66. The Concerto for Cello and Orchestra in E Minor, op. 58, was composed 1933–38 and first performed in Moscow on November 26, 1938. Material from this work was later used in the Sinfonia Concertante for Cello and Orchestra, op. 125.

CHAPTER NINE

Prokofiev and Sergei Eisenstein

Music has played an unusually important role in the Soviet film tradition. "Serious" composers have collaborated with filmmakers since the earliest days of the Soviet film industry. Dmitri Shostakovich (1906–75) wrote music for more than thirty films (both silent and sound), among them masterpieces such as Grigory Kozintsev's *King Lear* and *Hamlet*; Sergei Prokofiev wrote music for eight films, including *Aleksandr Nevsky* and *Ivan the Terrible* by Sergei Eisenstein; Aram Khachaturian also produced numerous film scores, including one for the notoriously anti-American *The Russian Question*. Today, "serious" Russian composers such as Alfred Shnittke and Sofia Gubaidulina have continued that tradition. In America, composers who write for film are for the most part branded "popular" or "commercial." With a very few exceptions, "film composers" and "serious composers" have inhabited separate spheres. Soviet composers who worked in film suffered much less from such categorization.

There are several reasons for this. One was Lenin's belief (shared by the Soviet cultural bureaucrats) in the supreme importance of film among all the arts. Another was the fact that the birth of Soviet (post-1917) culture, including music, happened to coincide almost exactly with the worldwide explosion of the film industry. (The poor young Shostakovich worked as a movie-hall pianist in the 1920s, accompanying silent films.) Soviet music and Soviet film developed side by side, and it was natural that Soviet composers would work in this new "proletarian" medium. And finally, several of the pioneer Soviet film directors—Sergei Eisenstein (1898–1948) especially—possessed a high degree of musical sophistication and conceived of the role of music in film in new and highly theoretical terms. Their intellectual approach to the film score as an art, and their willingness to respect the composer as a collaborator on equal terms, led "serious" composers to view film music as a worthwhile and unique genre.

Of these composers, Prokofiev was probably the most successful in understanding the possibilities of film as a medium. He was able to write scores that could simultaneously illustrate a film's subject matter and style and stand on their own as significant and interesting music. Prokofiev did not feel constrained by the visual and technical limitations placed on a film composer; instead, he exploited them to artistic advantage. Never one to waste a note, Prokofiev was able to recycle two of his film scores into concert pieces. Both of them—the *Lieutenant Kije* Suite and the *Aleksandr Nevsky* Cantata—were destined to rank among the composer's most popular compositions.

All of Prokofiev's eight film scores were produced for Soviet film studios between 1932 and 1946. At the beginning of this period, Prokofiev was still living in Paris and was only beginning to establish his identity as a "Soviet" composer; by 1945 he had lived in the Soviet Union for almost ten years and was considered one of the country's most important cultural figures. Prokofiev's work in film played an important role in establishing him as a truly "national" composer, thereby soothing some of the resentment the official Soviet cultural establishment felt towards him for the many years he had spent abroad.

Prokofiev's work with Sergei Eisenstein on two films was without question the most significant of his film career. Both critics and audiences consider their two joint projects (*Aleksandr Nevsky*, released in 1939, and *Ivan the Terrible*, filmed during World War II and released in two parts) among the greatest achievements in combining music with the moving image.

Prokofiev and Eisenstein had apparently first met in Paris in the 1920s. Personally and socially, they had a great deal in common. Only seven years apart in age, both came from the pre-Revolutionary educated middle-class (though Eisenstein, unlike Prokofiev, was a Jew), both had come of artistic age during the Revolution, both worked with antirealist director Vsevolod Meyerhold, both had traveled widely outside Russia (and were therefore regarded with suspicion by the provincial Soviet cultural bureaucrats).

Of special note is their shared experience of Hollywood. During the 1930s both Prokofiev and Eisenstein had the opportunity to view firsthand the enormous technological and creative possibilities of the burgeoning American movie industry.

Already world-famous for his early silent films (*Battleship Potemkin*, *Strike*, *October*), Eisenstein arrived in Los Angeles in May 1930, having signed a contract with Paramount to make a series of films over the next few years. Eisenstein's working relationship with the studio quickly soured, however, and the contract was canceled after only five months. To the rescue came the American writer Upton Sinclair, with whom Eisenstein embarked on a complex venture to make a film about Mexico. But this project almost immediately ran into serious difficulties and was never completed. Eisenstein returned to Moscow in the spring of 1932 with little to show for his American sojourn except a better (and somewhat bitter) understanding of how filmmaking was done in a capitalist economy.

Prokofiev had been making frequent visits to Los Angeles for many years, but not until his last American tour, in 1938, did he become more closely acquainted with the Hollywood community. Having already seen and admired *Snow White and the Seven Dwarfs*, Prokofiev met Walt Disney. They shared a fascination with technology and the possibilities of recorded sound, as well as a special talent to create art that children loved and understood. One can only regret that they never had the chance to work together, especially considering Disney's later work with "serious" music, such as *Fantasia*.

Prokofiev's visit to Hollywood, and the chance to see the advanced technology of the American film industry, was an important event in his life. Like so many things in Prokofiev's career, however, it came at the wrong moment. He was now firmly established in Soviet musical and cultural life, and his home and family were in Moscow. He must have been sorely tempted by the brilliant world of American movies, by the huge financial and artistic possibilities, by the sophistication and élan. But it was too late to make such a major change. For Prokofiev, and for Eisenstein, Hollywood would remain in the realm of fantasy.

Soon after Prokofiev returned from the United States in the spring of 1938, he and Eisenstein began their first collaboration, on the medieval nationalistic epic *Aleksandr Nevsky*. The film was an enormous popular, critical, and political success, although its ferociously anti-German sentiments proved temporarily inappropriate during the several years (1939–1941) of the Stalin-Hitler pact.

As the letters translated here demonstrate, *Nevsky* brought Prokofiev and Eisenstein together both personally and professionally. They remained close friends and creative colleagues until Eisenstein's death on February 11, 1948.

(These letters were published in Russian as "Iz perepiski S. S. Prokof'eva i S. M. Eisenshteina," edited by P. M. Atasheva and M. G. Kozlova, *Sergei Prokof'ev 1953–1963: Stat'i i materialy* [Moscow: Sovetskii kompozitor, 1962], 277–89. Translated and edited by Harlow Robinson.)

EISENSTEIN to PROKOFIEV

July 26, 1939
Moscow

Dear Sergei Sergeevich:

I hope that you're luxuriating and enjoying yourself thoroughly in the Caucasus. Our trip to Central Asia was crowned with complete success—we will make a very big and complicated film[1] that is slated to be released in May 1940. I could never imagine undertaking such a project without you, which is why I have "taken the liberty" of sending you this expanded libretto which has already been approved as a basis for the film by the Committee and the Studio. I don't envision that there will be any major revisions, and I have used it to sketch an outline of the material with which, I hope, you will brighten my days. As I see it, *the stuff*[2] will be devilishly interesting and maybe even just great.

Deadlines: I think that in September or October you ought to fly here to where we are, so that we could take a look at Samarkand and Bukhara (which are very interesting) and take in a bit of the *couleur local*[3] of Uzbekistan. The bulk of the work will fall in December–January, when we are planning to bring in Parts II and III in nearly finished form, and when we'll have to prepare the material for Part I . . . Then in April will come the finishing touches, the final alterations and adjustments.

Now to the matter at hand: the notes in the margins, I think, are clear enough, and since you know me "a teeny bit," no doubt you'll grasp immediately what I have in mind.

The basic theme is, of course, the "water theme."

It appears four times:

1) Menacing (Timur), destructive.
2) Lyrical (the small irrigation ditch of Tokhtasyn and the daughter's dance).
3) Menacing (the uprising of the poor people), destructive (in a sense different from No. 1).

---

1.   The project in question was *The Great Fergana Canal*, to a screenplay by P. A. Pavlenko and Eisenstein, which was never made because of production problems. Eisenstein's directorial screenplay was published in the journal *Isskustvo kino* (*The Art of the Cinema*), in issue No. 9 for 1939.
2.   Eisenstein wrote these words in English, a language both he and Prokofiev knew well.
3.   Eisenstein wrote this expression in French, another language that both he and Prokofiev knew well. He apparently forgot that *couleur* is feminine.

4) Victorious-joyful (the inauguration of the canal. Probably, No. 2 brought to the point of pathos—with elements of No. 1 and No. 3 added to it).

The second theme is a very peculiar one—the theme of the sand. When the sand, that bastard, marches through the dunes in the desert at night, it sings! A special ringing rustling sound. And a very creepy kind of perpetual motion (*perpetuum mobile*).

The duel between the water and the sand (with the sand's victory) should also come out very nicely.

The "sand theme" appears in the following ways:

1) The city dying of thirst (this is where the theme is introduced).
2) The victory of the sand (the finale of Part I).
3) The attack of the sand (through Part II and especially in the finale: the girl's death. N.B.—The theme should also be in the background during her dance).

The third group is the song of Tokhtasyn and, of course, a "work" theme in Part III that is somehow connected with it.

In general, Part III should be made in the same way as our battle[4]—two or three musical knots, and as for the rest . . . Volsky,[5] who, of course, will again be working with us.

So there, briefly, are *mes désirs à ce sujet.*[6]

I beg you please to write me immediately and tell me what you think about all this, since I'll be flying off to the building site of the Fergana Canal in early August, around the tenth.

I embrace you warmly and eagerly await your letter.

Yours, Ser. Eisenstein.

Moscow, Potylikha, 54-b, Apt. 7. Write soon.

---

4. Eisenstein refers to "The Battle on the Ice," a fragment from the film *Aleksandr Nevsky*, on which Eisenstein and Prokofiev collaborated in 1938.
5. Boris Alekseevich Volsky was the sound technician who had collaborated with Eisenstein and Prokofiev in their work on *Aleksandr Nevsky* and later also worked with them on *Ivan the Terrible*.
6. In French: "my wishes on this subject."

PROKOFIEV to EISENSTEIN

July 30, 1939
KISLOVODSK[7]

Dear Sergei Mikhailovich,

Lo, how it brought me unspeakable joy to see a marvelous American envelope with "Sergei M. Eisenstein" on it, but, having read its contents my spirits drooped, since apparently it is not in the cards that I should work with you this time. At the moment I'm up to my ears in the opera, and they've already started to learn their parts.[8] As soon as I finish it, rehearsals will start, and simultaneously there's the production of *Romeo and Juliet* in Leningrad, and the planned arrival of the Leningrad troupe in Moscow. So to take on a large project like the one you're describing is impossible: I can't divide my energies that way, I wouldn't be able to concentrate.

Don't be surprised that I've switched over to opera. I continue to consider the cinema the most contemporary art, but precisely because of its newness, people here have still not learned to fully appreciate its various components, and consider the music as some kind of little ditty off to the side, undeserving of special attention. And you know, to compose something like the themes for sand and water that you describe would take a great deal of effort. So that's why I've taken up opera in my old-fashioned way—at least there the music receives the sort of recognition that it should. There's less uncertainty involved.

By the way, after the catastrophe with M. [Meyerhold],[9] who was supposed to stage my opera, my first thought was to throw myself in pursuit of you and beg you to take on this production. The theater was also very receptive to the suggestion, but you were in Asia and it seemed you would be busy there for some time—so I had to abandon my dream.

---

7.   Prokofiev liked to spend part of the summer in Kislovodsk, a resort and spa in the northern Caucasus. He met Mira Mendelson there.

8.   The opera in question was Prokofiev's *Semyon Kotko* (to a libretto by Prokofiev, based on Valentin Kataev's novella *I Am a Son of the Working People*), whose premiere took place at the Stanislavsky Opera Theater in Moscow on June 23, 1940.

9.   The original director for the first production of *Semyon Kotko* was Vsevolod Meyerhold, the brilliant avant-garde stage director with whom Prokofiev had been linked personally and professionally since 1916, when they collaborated on a projected production of his opera *The Gambler*. On June 20, 1939, in the midst of rehearsals for *Kotko*, Meyerhold, who had remained outspoken and defiant despite the growing pressure to conform with Stalin's increasing regimentation of Soviet culture, was arrested. He died in prison several months later, after being brutally tortured. (See also chapter 4.)

I retain the timid hope that you won't wash your hands of me in response to this letter, or, that if you do, then not for very long, and that we will meet in the not-so-very-distant future, whether it be in a film or in an opera. Somehow, I continue to believe *a prior-i-ly* in Eisenstein the opera director![10]

I embrace you tenderly and wish you huge success.

Yours. S. Prkfv.

EISENSTEIN to PROKOFIEV

July 23, 1941

Dear friend Sergei Sergeevich!

I'll write quickly: Director Petrov[11] is leaving for Tbilisi today and bringing you this message.[12] I didn't write to you by mail—I didn't count on it reaching you. The facts: *Ivan the Terrible*[13] will be filmed. Evidently I'll be starting at the end of winter. Now I'm finishing the scenes, and I'll send them to you at the next opportunity. We can start getting together at the beginning of next year to work out the details, etc.

I've come up with a two-part film, which is very entertaining.

The composer is presented with great opportunities in all directions.

How are you two doing? We're managing fairly well. As far as the filming is concerned, it looks like we'll be filming in various locations, not excluding Moscow!

I look forward to hearing from you.

My address: Alma-Ata, United Film Studio.

---

10. Eisenstein was very knowledgeable about opera and opera staging; he would direct a very famous and controversial production of *Die Walküre* at the Bolshoi Theater in November 1940.

11. Vladimir Mikhailovich Petrov was a film director.

12. Soon after the Nazi invasion of the USSR in June 1941, most leading Soviet cultural figures were evacuated from Moscow. Prokofiev went with Mira Mendelson and many others to the Caucasus, first to Nalchik and then to Tbilisi, where he lived during the winter and spring of 1941–42 before traveling to Alma-Ata, in Kazakhstan, to work with Eisenstein.

13. The two-part film *Ivan the Terrible* was written and produced by Eisenstein and cameramen A. N. Moskvin and E. K. Tisse, with music by Prokofiev. Part I was completed in 1944, Part II in 1945. Part I was released in 1946, but Part II did not appear on the screen until 1958 (see n. 37, below).

Petrov will give you a colorful account of the peripetiae of the journey and of life here. I embrace you from my heart. Best regards to your companion in life.[14]

Yours always, Ser. Eisenstein.

EISENSTEIN to PROKOFIEV

March 3, 1942
ALMA-ATA

Dear Sergei Sergeevich!

Nikolai Mironovich[15] is coming to Tbilisi to work on *Ivan the Terrible*, and he promised to see you and show you the script. I hope you like it!

You can begin working on the music whenever you like. I'll begin filming by the end of the summer. You can start in the spring, the summer, the fall, or even the winter—whenever is most convenient for you.

You can make all the arrangements with Nikolai Mironovich. If you need money, you can speed up the agreement.

Let me know how you're doing.

I heard you finished *War and Peace*[16]—I'm curious to hear about that.

I embrace you warmly.

Yours always, Ser. Eisenstein.

Best regards to the family.

PROKOFIEV to EISENSTEIN

General Delivery, March 29, 1942
TBILISI, COMMUNICATIONS CENTER

Dear Sergei Mikhailovich,

Nikolai Mironovich brought me your letter just in time: I'm finishing the last measures of *War and Peace,* and consequently I'll be able to fall under your yoke in the near future. Inasmuch as Sliozberg is planning to return at the end of April, Mira and I hope to go with him. He promises to deliver the script to me one of these days—I'll be very interested to see them. [. . .]

---

14. Mira Mendelson would become Prokofiev's second wife in 1948.
15. N. M. Sliozberg was the producer of the film crew for *Ivan the Terrible*.
16. *War and Peace* was an opera by Prokofiev (libretto by Prokofiev and Mira Mendelson, based on Tolstoy's novel of the same name). The first edition was completed in 1943, the second in 1952.

I "look forward" warmly to our collaboration and send you a big hug.

Yours, S. Prkfv.

[. . .] Petrov carried your December letter for three whole months and didn't deliver it until after the March one.

PROKOFIEV to EISENSTEIN

Dec. 4, 1942

SEMIPALATINSK

Dear Sergei Mikhailovich,

I'm sending you a list of the first seven scenes of *War and Peace*. I'll send the rest tomorrow. Tomorrow we're planning to move to Moscow, as I've finished working on the film.

I embrace you. Mirochka sends her best regards.

Yours, S.P.

Please ask Sveshnikov[17] whether he gave back the books I left at the Library.

EISENSTEIN to PROKOFIEV

December 7, 1942

[ALMA-ATA]

Dear Sergei Sergeevich!

I'm sending you my heartfelt greetings on the tenderest rosy paper available in Alma-Ata, in addition to my article about you.[18] If there's anything you don't like, cross it out mercilessly.

Best regards *à madame*,[19]

Toujours à vous

Ser. Eisenstein

---

17. Boris Aleksandrovich Sveshnikov worked on the crew for *Ivan the Terrible*.

18. Eisenstein's article "PRKFV" was first published in edited form as a preface to *Sergei Prokofiev: His Musical Life* by Israel V. Nestyev (New York: Alfred A. Knopf, 1946). The article appears in its entirety in the collection *S. M. Eisenstein: Collected Articles* (Moscow: Iskusstvo, 1956).

19. In fact, Prokofiev and Mira Mendelson were not married at this time. Lina, Prokofiev's first wife, refused to grant him a divorce. Mira and Prokofiev finally married in 1948, with the reasoning that Soviet law never recognized the German marriage of Prokofiev and Lina in 1923.

Telegram from EISENSTEIN to PROKOFIEV

[January 4, 1943]

Cordial greetings. Hugs. Confirm that you have received the article. Await your arrival. Eisenstein.

Telegram from PROKOFIEV to EISENSTEIN

[January 20, 1943]

Received brilliant article. Thanks for telegram. Samosud intends to produce opera in spring.[20] Plan to leave for Alma-Ata 19th. Hugs. Prokofiev.

EISENSTEIN to PROKOFIEV

[July 9, 1943]

Dear Sergei Sergeevich!

Please, please don't abandon these environs until the recording of the Oprichniks' chorus has been done;[21] without you the chorus is sure to mess it up (*if you know what I mean!*).[22] At rehearsals they clearly still don't know what they're doing, and therefore it would be far, far preferable to plan your departure not for Monday, but for the next possible departure date. For my part I will put on the pressure to help you out.

I await your answer. *Yours sincerely.* Ser. Eisenstein.

Telegram from EISENSTEIN to PROKOFIEV

[October 7, 1943]

Telegraphed Perm. Please come to Alma-Ata late October. I'm waiting. Hug you both. Sergei Eisenstein.

---

20. The first concert performance of the first edition of Prokofiev's opera *War and Peace* took place in Moscow in the Great Hall of the Conservatory on June 7, 1945, performed by artists of the Bolshoi Theater, the Philharmonic, and the Radio, conducted by S. A. Samosud (see n. 23, below).
21. "The Oprichniks' Oath" is a fragment from Part II of *Ivan the Terrible*.
22. Written in English.

PROKOFIEV to EISENSTEIN

November 17, 1943

Moscow, P. O. Box 25, General Delivery

Dear Sergei Mikhailovich,

I hope you aren't too angry at me for not coming to Alma-Ata. I wasn't able [. . .]

And now we're beginning preparations for two symphonic concerts: the first one, *War and Peace* with artists of the Bolshoi Theater under Samosud's direction,[23] the second made up of some of my other new compositions. Both will take place in December.

I'm sending you "The Furnace Play"[24] and would greatly appreciate it if you would 1) send me details of the pieces I can finish before your arrival, and 2) telegraph and let me know exactly when you'll need me in January. Because the Kirov Theater will be starting rehearsals of *Cinderella* and *Duenya*,[25] and I will have to go to Perm. I will arrange my time according to your telegram. [. . .]

We would both like very much to see you, we look forward to your arrival, we're dying to behold *Ivan* and we send you hugs and kisses.

Yours, S. Prkfv.

Telegram from EISENSTEIN to PROKOFIEV

[January 16, 1944]

Soundtrack recording moved to second half of March. Greetings. Eisenstein.

PROKOFIEV to EISENSTEIN [*rough draft handwritten by Mira Mendelson*]

March 7, 1944

[Moscow]

to Eisenstein, Alma-Ata

Dear Ser[gei] Mikh[ailovich],

I haven't heard from you in a long time. How is your work going? Will you and your entire entourage be coming to Moscow soon? I haven't heard much

---

23. Samuil Samosud (1884–1964) was head conductor at the Bolshoi Theater 1936–43.

24. "The Furnace Play" is a fragment from Part I of *Ivan the Terrible*. It is based on a liturgical mystery play frequently performed in Russian Orthodox churches during the reign of Ivan the Terrible.

25. *Cinderella* is a ballet by Prokofiev (libretto by N. D. Volkov); *Duenya* (*Betrothal in a Monastery*) is a lyric comic opera by Prokofiev (libretto by Prokofiev and Mira Mendelson); these works were performed at the Kirov Opera and Ballet Theater in Leningrad in 1946.

news about your work, but what I've heard has only been good. Owing to the change in the artistic management of the Bolshoi Theater, *War and Peace* has been postponed for a while, since Pazovsky is supposed to enliven the classical repertoire with a few classical operas.[26] To make it up to me, they are putting on *Cinderella*,[27] for which they'll be starting rehearsals this month so it can open at the beginning of the fall season. [. . .]

Send me a note, but not to Moscow 9, but rather 159; this is located in the Hotel Moscow where I live, but I prefer to receive letters addressed to general delivery and not to my room number, since I may be asked to move out on some not-so-lovely day.[28] Mirochka and I remember you often, and we miss the lovely evenings we spent with you in Alma-Ata.

I embrace you.

[S. Prokofiev]

Telegram from EISENSTEIN to PROKOFIEV

[July 30, 1944]

Your presence categorically required now. Counted on your agreement to arrive before me, deadlines established. Two-week delay will throw off all my plans for release of both parts. Please come now. Sergei Eisenstein.

PROKOFIEV to EISENSTEIN
To Eisenstein, Moscow

July 31, 1944
IVANOVO

Dear Ser[gei] Mikh[ailovich],

It gives me joy to welcome you back to Moscow. I expected you to call me at the beginning of July and expected the promised materials from Idenbom[29] at

---

26. In 1943 Samosud was replaced as head conductor at the Bolshoi Theater by Arii Pazovsky (1887–1953). This greatly complicated the fate of Prokofiev's opera *War and Peace*, which Samosud had been planning to produce at the Bolshoi.

27. The premiere of Prokofiev's ballet *Cinderella* took place at the Bolshoi Theater on November 21, 1945, later than originally planned.

28. Built in the 1930s, the Hotel Moscow was right off Red Square and considered the height of Soviet hotel luxury. Rooms in all Moscow hotels were very hard to find during the war years, and even famous cultural figures were often forced to move around.

29. Lev Aronovich Idenbom was the assistant director of *Ivan the Terrible*.

the end of July. Now I'm busy with work on my Fifth Symphony,[30] and my composition is flowing along in such a way that I can't interrupt and switch over to *Ivan the Terrible*. I'm sure you'll understand me. On August 15 I'll be in Moscow, and I'll devote myself entirely to our film—I'll work quickly and precisely.

At the same time as this I'm writing to Idenbom that our agreement expired in 1943, and I'm asking him to draw up the terms of our collaboration again. Support me in this effort.

I embrace you warmly. Best regards from M[ira] A[leksandrovna].

Yours, [S. Prokofiev]

EISENSTEIN to PROKOFIEV

[September 22, 1944]

Dear S[ergei] S[ergeevich]!

I'm sending you "Kazan"[31] marked with indications of timings and with notes to help you remember what's happening and, where necessary, what kind of music is required.

Hugs, Ser. Eisenstein

EISENSTEIN to PROKOFIEV

Feb. 8, 1945
BARVIKHA

My dear and beloved Sergei Sergeevich,

I was very concerned to hear that you aren't feeling better yet. I know and fully share your "Molièrean" view of doctors, but you still have to see them.[32] I've been here a week—it's very nice in Barvikha now; everything's been rebuilt as it was before the war. Why don't you and Mira Aleksandrovna arrange to

---

30. Prokofiev's Fifth Symphony, op. 100, written in 1944, was first performed in Moscow on January 13, 1945, under the direction of the composer. This would be Prokofiev's last public appearance as a conductor.

31. "Kazan" is a fragment from Part I of *Ivan the Terrible*.

32. Shortly after he conducted the premiere of his Fifth Symphony in Moscow on January 13, 1945, Prokofiev had a dizzy spell, fell downstairs, and suffered a brain concussion. He never again entirely regained his health and often suffered from severe headaches and high blood pressure. Eisenstein knew that Prokofiev did not have much faith in the medical profession; in fact, the composer was powerfully drawn to the ideas of Christian Science.

come here—Khrapchenko could do this (Okhlopkov and Ruben Simonov are here); Bolshakov, as far as I know, is ill himself, otherwise you could arrange it through him. I've been sick with the flu all week; that's why I don't go for walks *and do not enjoy life as much as it is possible to do it here.*[33]

I look forward to hearing from you and hope the news will be good.

I send you hugs and kisses.

Your devoted Ser. Eisenstein

EISENSTEIN to PROKOFIEV

August 1, 1945
Moscow

Dear Sergei Sergeevich!

I'm writing *in a great hurry*, so forgive me for writing in pencil. Besides the *hurry*,[34] I'm writing with great anxiety—both for your health and for our common task. You must be in very bad health, because I can't imagine any other reason to change our schedule from the beginning of August to October; I'm so used to believing your promises. This change will have a catastrophic effect on my work; based on your promise to write the dance music,[35] we've built scenery and moved up all our plans and the actors' schedules for the filming. Now everything will get so mixed up that we won't know which end is up!

I implore you, if there's even the slightest possibility that you could work on this dance, please do it now—it won't take more than a day or two, and postponing it to October could make it impossible to release the film this year and would destroy all our future work.

Let me know, and I'll hurry to you right away.

For now I send you hugs and kisses and hope your health will improve.

Yours, Ser. Eisenstein.

Best regards to Mira Aleksandrovna.

---

33. In English.
34. In English.
35. This refers to "The Oprichniks' Oath" (see n. 21, above).

MIRA MENDELSON to EISENSTEIN

August 3, 1945

Dear Sergei Mikhailovich,

I'm terribly sorry, but I must confirm that there's no way Sergei Sergeevich can write the music to Part Two.[36] He's been trying to work, but he recently had several nosebleeds, which worried the Moscow professor treating him, N. A. Popova, with whom we are in contact by telephone. She has strictly prohibited him from doing any sort of work at all at this time. Sergei Sergeevich very much wants to write the dance he promised you, but he is very unlikely to get started on it soon, especially since the character of this dance would require intense effort.

Sergei Sergeevich embraces you warmly; he himself longs to work, and he can hardly endure this forced idleness.

I send you my best regards.

Mira Mendelson

PROKOFIEV to EISENSTEIN

F. 20, 1946

Dear Sergei Mikhailovich,

Why are they punishing you like this? I often go to the clinic (for "electrification" and "toothification") and would really like to visit you, but apparently the granting of visiting hours isn't up to you.

I embrace you warmly. I hope you feel better. Everyone is praising *Ivan*.[37]

Yours, S.P.

---

36. To help complete the music to Part II of the film *Ivan the Terrible*, Prokofiev recommended using the composer Gavriil Popov, who had written scores for many Soviet films. When he felt somewhat better, Prokofiev completed the work himself.

37. Part I of the film *Ivan the Terrible* was released in 1946 to great acclaim. But Part II was withheld from distribution because Soviet cultural officials found its portrayal of Ivan's psychological decline too disturbing and negative. It was not released in the USSR until 1958. Originally, Eisenstein had planned to make a third part, but the official failure of Part II and his declining health made that impossible.

EISENSTEIN to PROKOFIEV

[February 23, 1946]

Dear Sergei Sergeevich!

I was very glad to get your note.

I very much want to see you, but because of the flu epidemic in the city, no one is allowed to visit us.

As soon as they lift the quarantine, I'll ask someone to get in touch with you, and I'll be very happy to see you.

It looks like I'll have to stay in bed for a long time. *Funny to say it,*[38] but I almost died from my heart attack on February 2, and strictly speaking, it was quite by chance and unexpectedly that I survived.[39]

I'm enclosing a present; it was among the magazines I received from some kind people so I wouldn't get bored.

Regards to Mira Aleksandrovna.

> I embrace you warmly, yours.
> Ser. Eisenstein.

---

38. In English.
39. Eisenstein lived for two more years but never recovered his health; he died on February 11, 1948.

CHAPTER TEN
Letters to Nikolai Miaskovsky

EMPATHY AND COMPASSION were never strong traits in Prokofiev's character. Understandably, Soviet biographers ignored this fact in their attempts to portray him as a good socialist artist profoundly concerned over the fate of his fellow man. In his student years in St. Petersburg, Prokofiev used to enjoy watching family arguments in first-floor and basement apartments; on his way home from the conservatory, he would even squat down on the sidewalk for a better view. Such voyeurism suggests a highly theatrical nature, but also a lack of human sympathy. According to Nicolai Tcherepnin, Prokofiev's professor of conducting, the adolescent Seryozha would sit on the staircase at the conservatory and make fun of students as they entered. Another favorite pastime was keeping track of his fellow students' grades and distributing the information.

These habits did not disappear with age. When he visited Russia in 1927 after a nine-year absence, Prokofiev made little attempt to censor his egotistical behavior. Olga Lamm, the daughter of the musicologist Pavel Lamm, recalled that "many Moscow musicians and other artistic figures couldn't excuse Sergei Sergeevich for his cockiness and his mocking tone, his inability to spare the self-esteem of others."[1]

Prokofiev's caustic, mocking manner did not make it easy for him to form lasting intimate and reciprocal friendships. While he had many acquaintances and professional associates, as an adult, he had almost no close friends. The prime exception was the Soviet composer Nikolai Miaskovsky (1881–1950). Their relationship began in the fall of 1906, when Miaskovsky joined Prokofiev in Anatoly Liadov's composition theory class at the St. Petersburg Conservatory, and lasted until Miaskovsky died in 1950. Even Prokofiev's absence from Russia between 1918 and 1927 did not prove an obstacle; after 1923, they were in nearly constant communication through letters.

While Prokofiev was younger than most of his fellow students at the conservatory, Miaskovsky was older: he was already twenty-five years old when he

1. Olga Lamm, "Druz'ia Pavla Aleksandrovicha Lamma i uchastniki muzykal'nykh vecherov v ego dome (20-e gody XX veka)," *Iz proshlogo sovetskoi muzykal'noi kul'tury*, Vol. I., T. N. Livanova, ed. (Moscow, 1975), 84.

entered, almost exactly ten years older than Prokofiev. Like Nikolai Rimsky-Korsakov, Miaskovsky had remained for a long while in the military service—where he received training as an engineer—before turning to music professionally. In fact, he was still a soldier during his first year at the conservatory, before entering the reserves. (During World War I he worked on defense construction projects.) When Miaskovsky did finally make the decision to study music, however, he proceeded with gravity and thoroughness.

By the time they met, Miaskovsky had composed considerably less than Prokofiev: songs to poems by Konstantin Balmont, Evgeny Baratynsky, and Zinaida Gippius, plus some piano pieces. Eventually, however, Miaskovsky became the "greatest Soviet symphonist," completing twenty-seven symphonies. Reserved, shy, melancholic, pessimistic, sedentary, and given to depressions, Miaskovsky was in many ways Prokofiev's opposite—which is, perhaps, why they developed such a long and close relationship.

In the many letters he wrote to Prokofiev, Miaskovsky, who never married, marvels at his younger friend's boundless optimism, energy, and enthusiasm. For his part, Prokofiev seemed to find in Miaskovsky a source of quiet stability and advice, the older brother that he never had. Miaskovsky's opinion came to carry great weight with Prokofiev, even after he had become a celebrity in the West, although Miaskovsky's music does not seem to have strongly affected Prokofiev's.

It was Miaskovsky's respect for Prokofiev's enormous natural talent that first drew him to his precocious and often irritating classmate. They also shared an ambivalent attitude towards Liadov, whom Miaskovsky later said he remembered "with admiration, gratitude, but also with horror." When he discovered that Prokofiev was an excellent pianist and sight reader, he proposed that they start reading through piano arrangements of scores he wanted to learn, such as Beethoven's symphonies, Rimsky-Korsakov's *Sheherazade*, and Max Reger's *Serenade*. Their sessions of piano four-hands became an established tradition that continued throughout their relationship.

Prokofiev and Miaskovsky began exchanging detailed letters by the summer of 1907, with critiques of the music each was composing. It was the start of a very long and intense correspondence, extending with a few breaks (notably between 1918 and 1923) for more than forty years, from 1907 to 1950. After they resumed epistolary contact in 1923, Miaskovsky became a lifeline for Prokofiev to the Soviet musical world, while Prokofiev wrote fascinating and detailed descriptions of the music he was hearing in Paris (including the works of

Stravinsky) and on his world travels as a touring pianist. Unlike the peripatetic and globe-trotting Prokofiev, Miaskovsky disliked travel and made only two trips abroad, both in the 1920s, to nearby Warsaw and Vienna. Miaskovsky even declined to accept Prokofiev's repeated and insistent invitations to visit him (at Prokofiev's expense) in France in the 1920s.

Patient and soft-spoken, Miaskovsky was a born teacher and devoted much of his energy to his pedagogical work at the Moscow Conservatory. Prokofiev, on the other hand, never enjoyed teaching and did very little of it during his career. But he had great respect for Miaskovsky's opinions about his music, as the Soviet composer Dmitri Kabalevsky (1904–87), who knew both men well, observed in his introduction to the 1977 Russian-language edition of their correspondence. "Throughout his entire life, even when he had already achieved renown as one of the foremost composers of his era, Prokofiev would hardly have finished the final measure of his next new composition before he would immediately show it to Miaskovsky, whose opinion was for him unusually important and cherished. And Miaskovsky was the only one whose critical suggestions would force Prokofiev sometimes to rewrite his music."[2]

Miaskovsky's aesthetic views were conservative and even isolationist. He was harshly critical of new trends in European music and completely rejected the "New Viennese" school and serialism. Most of Stravinsky's works left him cold. His favorite genre was the symphony, already considered a dead form by most progressive Western composers. Nor did Miaskovsky exhibit interest in writing for the theater, either ballets or operas—although he eagerly awaited each of Prokofiev's works for the stage.

During the 1920s and 1930s, Prokofiev was a very loyal friend to Miaskovsky in the West. He lost no opportunity to promote his music with the conductors and impresarios he knew, including Sergei Diaghilev, Serge Koussevitsky, and Leopold Stokowski. Although he occasionally accused Miaskovsky of being old-fashioned and indulging in "Glazunovism," he believed in his creativity and music until the very end.

Prokofiev's friendship with Miaskovsky was surely one of the factors that led him to return to the USSR permanently in 1936. He had no such loyal colleagues in Paris, where he was overshadowed by Stravinsky and alienated by the constant pursuit of the fashionable. For Prokofiev, Miaskovsky symbolized the

---

2.   Dmitri Kabalevsky, "Chudesnaia druzhba," *S. S. Prokof'ev & N. Ia. Miaskovskii: Perepiska* (Moscow: Sovetskii kompozitor, 1977), 10.

familiar values of his childhood and youth, which eventually would pull him back to Russia.

But soon after returning to the USSR in 1936, Prokofiev discovered that life had changed there much more than he had anticipated. Even Miaskovsky could not spare him the pain of seeing colleagues arrested and executed. And in 1948, when Stalin and Zhdanov decided to turn their wrathful attention to Soviet composers, both Prokofiev and Miaskovsky found themselves attacked as "formalists" deviating from the proper path of Soviet music. Already frail from the physical ordeal they had endured during World War II, both composers were unable to recover from this final blow. Prokofiev was too ill—both physically and spiritually—to attend Miaskovsky's funeral in August 1950.

The hundreds of letters they wrote to each other have immortalized the unlikely friendship between Prokofiev and Miaskovsky. Prokofiev loved to use affectionate nicknames for Miaskovsky in the salutations of his letters, especially as they came to know each other better: *Lieber Kola*, Nice Little Kolyechka, Dear Little Angel, Dear Little Nyamusya (from the initials of Miaskovsky's name). Miaskovsky responded with Dear Sergusha, My Sweetest Serzhyonka, Golden Seryozha. Only when Prokofiev was living abroad in the 1920s and 1930s did their correspondence for a while take on a more formal tone, with the use of the first name and patronymic. But eventually Prokofiev abbreviated Nikolai Yakovlevich to the snappier Nik Yak, and by the late 1940s, when they had reestablished their youthful intimacy, they returned to the affectionate nicknames they had used decades before.

Not only a monument to a marvelous creative and personal friendship, these letters are an invaluble chronicle of a turbulent and exciting era in the history of Russian and world music. The editors of the Soviet edition of the Prokofiev-Miaskovsky correspondence performed heroic work in preparing it for publication. The result is a model of scrupulous and passionate scholarship, and my translations of Prokofiev's letters would have been impossible without their efforts.

(Prokofiev's letters to Miaskovsky were published in S. S. *Prokof'ev & N. Ia. Miaskovskii: Perepiska* [Moscow: Sovetskii kompozitor, 1977]. Introduction by Dmitri Kabalevsky, preparation of the text by M. G. Kozlova and N. Ia. Iatsenko, notes by V. A. Kiselev, and preface and index by M. G. Kozlova. Translation by Harlow Robinson. Both the letters and the notes have been edited.)

June 26, 1907
S<small>ONTSOVKA</small>

Dear Nikolai Yakovlevich (My dear friend Kolyechka! . . .):

I am sending you along with this letter my 2 piano "puppies" which I wrote for you. When you study them, please pay special attention to the rhythms, as they play a very important role. Also try to think up names for them, particularly for the second piece: it seems that I expressed the idea clearly, but failed to give it an appropriate name. Of course I expect you to comment pointedly, as usual, on the nuances which you are so keen in detecting. [3]

How is your poem for orchestra on a "very good" theme coming along?[4] I have finished the first movement of my sonata which I showed you during our exams. It seems that I won't add the second, third, and fourth movements to it at all. Let it remain *à la Miaskowsky* in one movement that is efficient, amusing, and pretty.[5] I have recently and rather unexpectedly written a new sonatina in two movements.[6] It was exciting to work on it. I was trying to make it as simple as possible, and it came out lively. At present I am finishing work on the fourth act of *Undine,* which you saw in May.[7]

You should not have run away from the final exam! Kankarovich and I waited another 5–10 minutes and were rewarded for our patience by getting into the director's office, where Liadov showed us our corrected assignments.[8] Where you have parallel fifths they are marked wrong of course, but you don't have any other serious mistakes except for a few rough places here and there. Zakharov's octaves are all marked in red; everyone else wrote the five-voice fugue smoothly. My three-voice fugue turned out worse, though with no serious mistakes, and the stretto is fine. In general, only Asafiev passed according to the rules, for in

---

3.   The manuscripts of the early piano pieces that Prokofiev called his "puppies" have not survived. Prokofiev was spending the summer at Sontsovka, the estate that his father managed in Ukraine.

4.   This could be the kernel of the symphonic parable *Silence,* inspired by Edgar Allan Poe, composed in 1909.

5.   The sonata for piano in F Minor in one movement was completed in 1909 and revised and published in 1911 as the Sonata No. 1, op. 1. Prokofiev uses the Western spelling of Miaskovsky.

6.   The manuscript of this sonatina has not survived.

7.   *Undine,* an opera to a libretto by the amateur poet Maria Kilshtett, was begun by Prokofiev in 1904; Acts III and IV exist in manuscript.

8.   The composer Anatoly Liadov (1855–1914) was one of Prokofiev's professors at the St. Petersburg Conservatory.

order to pass one must receive a perfect 4 which nobody else managed to get:[9]

	5-voice fugue	3-voice fugue
Asafiev	4	4
Miaskovsky	3.5	4
Zakharov	3.5	4
Prokofiev	4	3
Kankarovich	3	3.5
Saminsky	3	3
El'kan	3	3
Chefranov	3	3

The five of us received a 4 as a final grade (even Kankarovich! . . .) It seems that the rest will have to repeat counterpoint.

Now it's your turn to write some "puppies."

Of course, you have forgotten my address:

Ekat[erinoslavskaia] province, Bakhmutsk[ii] region, P.O. Andreevka.

Faithfully yours, S. Prokofiev.

August 12, 1908
SONTSOVKA

Dear Nikolai Yakovlevich:

Just imagine: I forgot to enclose with my last letter the new little themelets which I had prepared in advance. No sooner had I suddenly found them when I received your letter of August 7. Your letter deeply moved me with your sincere concern for my "baby."

I am not neglecting my "baby," which is due in the fall. I have all the themes already. I just need to finish up the reprise and the coda in the finale and to finish and orchestrate the second movement. I have just coped with one place where five or six themes merge. Only the devil knows why they merged like that. It's not because of any mastery of counterpoint. But the way I structured it all on the background of the expanded second concluding theme makes it come out very forcefully.[10]

---

9. Miaskovsky and Boris Asafiev both went on to have distinguished careers as composers. Under the pseudonym Igor Glebov, Asafiev also wrote prolifically as a critic and music historian (see also chapter 5). Boris Zakharov (1887–1942) became a pianist.

10. Prokofiev was composing a symphony, inspired by the example of Miaskovsky, who completed his Symphony No. 1, op. 3, during the summer of 1908.

I heard you were terrified by the news that I would become a piano composer. Calm down! I got annoyed with the symphony because I find it tedious to write long abstract pieces when I enjoy program music so much. That's all there is to it. But now that my "sweet darling" is almost finished, my anger has vanished.

Regarding the symphony, your question about Liadov amazes me. Why on earth show it to him? Why don't we get together, meet Glazunov some place in the hallway and tell him that we've written something that we would like to show him. He will be pleasantly surprised.[11]

Your *largo* did not enrage me at all: I do like it very much. It evokes a melancholy mood and might have been even better if it had been free from the chains that Liadov had managed to put on you as well.

Did you receive my letter of August 4? I will be back in Petersburg in the second half of September.

Faithfully yours,
S. Prokofiev.

September 15, 1908
Sontsovka

Dear Nikolai Yakovlevich:

Today I have finished my symphony. It turned out to be 131 (57 + 19 + 55) pages long and lasts 28 minutes, just a little longer than I wanted. Because of the cholera epidemic we are planning to depart later. My family is afraid of the disease and we will leave as soon as it abates. Did you finish work on your symphony? If not, get it done. If yes, don't show it to anyone until I come. And don't even mention anything to Liadov, for it makes no sense whatsoever to show it to him. Glazunov may help us with arranging its performance, while Liadov will only criticize us. If there is still cholera in St. Petersburg, we won't plan on going for a while yet, so drop me a line.

Yours,
S. P—v.

---

11. The composer Aleksandr Glazunov (1865–1936) was one of Prokofiev's professors at the St. Petersburg Conservatory. He lived abroad after 1928. Although conservative in his own compositional style, Glazunov was a devoted teacher and mentor.

October 31, 1908
St. Petersburg

By decree of the fates tomorrow night (Saturday) I happen to be free and will be home alone. Regardless of whether you can or cannot, I urge you to come over. I'll be happy beyond words. Bring:

1) Miaskovsky's *Quartet*,

2) Wagner, *Faust*,

3) Glazunov's V,[12] and anything else you wish to play.

Yours,

S. P—v.

December 19, 1908
St. Petersburg

Well, first of all let me tell you that Mrs. Yemtsova also got sick, therefore seven pieces were omitted.[13] As it turned out, your music was played last. Karatygin was accompanying in your music.[14] In all fairness to him, he played brilliantly, especially the last two pieces. Demidova also sang quite well.[15] In my opinion, they took "The Moon and the Mist" too fast; by the way, I am sure now that this romance is a bit too long and taken at a slow tempo it would sound monotonous. Furthermore, the accompaniment should have been a little more gentle, a bit more "misty." I am not very familiar with the song "Contradiction" and refrain from judging it. The only comment I would like to make is that I liked its ending very much. The audience was somewhat perplexed by it and did not start to applaud for a few moments, apparently waiting for the song to continue. They performed "Blood" very well and I derived great pleasure from listening to it. As far as I could tell, the audience liked it less than the other pieces. By the way, the audience belched out applause at the end of each song. I'll tell you the singer's opinion. She said that your romances were written for a machine and not for a human voice.

12. Prokofiev means Glazunov's Fifth Symphony.
13. On the preceding evening, December 18, Prokofiev performed for the first time in public, at one of the highly regarded Evenings of Contemporary Music. He played several of his own piano pieces from manuscript (including "*Suggestion diabolique*"). At the same concert, three songs by Miaskovsky (his op. 4) to verses of Zinaida Gippius were performed.
14. Viacheslav Karatygin (1875–1925) was a music critic, composer, teacher, and one of the founders (in 1901) of the Evenings of Contemporary Music series, in which he actively participated until 1912.
15. Sophia Demidova was the performer.

A few words about myself. I played much better than I did at home. Both the concert organizers and Winkler liked my playing.[16] The moment I stepped on the stage, the audience burst into applause and then applauded after every piece (with the exception of "Snow"), and especially loudly at the end. The most successful pieces were: "Reminiscences," "Despair," and *"Suggestion diabolique."* To sum it up, now we'll hear the castigating voices of the critics (I think I saw six of them).

Get well soon, then! I am awfully sorry that your disease is contagious, as you say, and I cannot come to see you.

Yours,

S. Prokofiev

As for composers, only Chesnokov was there.[17]

January 24, 1909

St. Petersburg

Dear Nikolai Yakovlevich:

Instead of coming on Sunday, thrill me by appearing on Tuesday evening. Won't it be better this way? It's impossible to make out *Ecstasy.*[18]. . . I get headaches.

Yours,

S. P—v.

March 6, 1910

St. Petersburg

Lieber Kola:

Come over on Sunday night to bang on the pianoforte. A few ne'er-do-well friends have also promised to be there. Don't you dare to be a ne'er-do-well.

P—v

---

16. Aleksandr Winkler (1865–1935) was a pianist, composer, critic, and teacher at the St. Petersburg Conservatory.

17. Aleksandr Chesnokov (1880–?) was a composer who emigrated from Russia in the 1920s.

18. *Poem of Ecstasy (Le poème d'extase)* by Aleksandr Scriabin was completed in 1908.

[between April 4 and 9, 1910]
ST. PETERSBURG

My darling Kolyechka:

Let's go see *Gotterdämmerung* tonight.[19] This is a most marvelous opera! I beg you not to refuse. Seat # 401, row 15, at 7:30 P.M. If you do refuse, I'll be very upset with you. Because *Gotterdämmerung* is really worth listening to. As far as I know, you haven't heard anything by Wagner for quite some time. Just think of all those wonderful bugles and the beautiful ending. Well, it's decided then, we'll go. Your refusal is not acceptable.

Truly yours,
S. Prkfv

July 2/15, 1910
TERIOKI

My dear little chick:

On July 8 I'll be in Petersburg and on the 9th I will be coming back to Terioki. Drop me a line at my Bronnitskaya address and we'll go together on the 9th, but not too late. I have no doubts that you will be able to make it and I'm glad about that.

So, see you on the 9th! *Dreams* will be given in concert in Moscow with Cooper conducting.[20] And when I see you, you will get a scolding from me for not working on your Second Symphony.

P–v

August 5, 1910
SONTSOVKA

Lieber Kola:

As you probably know already from *Novoye vremia [New Time]* my father died on July 23. We had the funeral on July 27, on the 30th I went to Terioki one more time, on August 1st we left Petersburg and on the third arrived here. I have no news for you, save for the fact that Boryechka[21] called me just a few minutes

19. Wagner's opera *Gotterdämmerung* was performed at the Mariinsky Theater on April 4, 7, and 9, 1910.
20. The premiere of Prokofiev's symphonic tableau *Dreams* took place in Moscow a year later, on July 1, 1911, conducted by Konstantin Saradzhev, not Emil Cooper.
21. Boryechka was an affectionate nickname for Boris Zakharov.

before my departure from Petersburg. He said that Ziloti[22] had sent him my *Dreams* and in an accompanying letter mentioned that he was looking forward to seeing my subsequent works and said he thought of me as a talented composer, and so on and so forth. But of course he won't perform my *Dreams*. What a fool! Now I am trying to persuade Mr. Cooper, and Borusya has started to do a four-hand piano arrangement of *Dreams*.

My best regards.

Write soon!

Yours S. Prkfv

P.O. Andreevka, Yekaterinoslavskaia Province.

August 19, 1910

SONTSOVKA

Lieber Kola,

In a day or two I will finish and send you the score of my new piece, about the same size as *Dreams* but with less elaborate scoring. I am not even sure if you'll like it or not, but the piece is very simple and "unpretentious." I don't even have a name for it yet. What would you suggest?[23] You shouldn't have "heralded," as you put it, my new concerto. So far I have done nothing. I am afraid that as soon as I am done with this orchestral piece, I'll start working on some other nasty thing and put the concerto off until fall. Anything can be expected of me, you know.

Please try to be on good terms with Koussevitsky. We need him not only as a performer, but as a publisher.

I am glad you finished your quartet and are now going to write orchestral music. But you really shouldn't have sent all three quartets to the competition at once; those two would win the prize by themselves. You should have kept "Edvard" for next year's competition.[24]

---

22. Aleksandr Ziloti (1863–1945) was a pianist, conductor, and concert organizer who left Russia in 1920 and later taught at the Juilliard School.

23. The new piece was *Autumnal*, a symphonic sketch for small orchestra, op. 8.

24. These quartets were later revised by Miaskovsky as op. 67, no. 1; op. 33, no. 4, and op. 33, no. 3. None of Miaskovsky's quartets received prizes at this competition. "Edvard" refers to the second movement of what became op. 33, no. 3, which is a theme with variations based on the theme from "Lullaby" for piano, op. 66, no. 7, by Edvard Grieg.

On September 1 I am leaving for the Caucasus (my address there: Sukhumi, Smetsky's dacha). Try to write to me while I am still here, but mail your review of my "thing" to the Caucasus.

I embrace you. Borusya went to the competition four days—I guess you weren't there.

Yours, S.P.

I am studying Beethoven's *Aurora*. Why is it called "Aurora?"

August 17, 1912
KISLOVODSK

Dear Kolyechka:

The weather is really not bad at all here in Kislovodsk: warm and sunny. Every morning I go to the pharmacy to work. The piano is decent, the room is cozy, nobody bothers me, and it does not smell of medicine there at all. In the composition department my choice has fallen on Sonata opus 14, which is coming along well and even acquiring a fifth movement.[25] In order to get a sure reply from you I have chosen a coercive means of correspondence. So write back!

Serge

June 3/16, 1913
PARIS

Nice Kolyechka:

I have arrived in Paris today and am deriving great pleasure from being here. I used to think of Paris either as a dot on the map of Europe, or as the city with the Eiffel Tower in its center. In reality Paris is much more exciting.

My regards.
SP.

The postcard was bought in Germany. Owing to the 25th birthday anniversary of the emperor, on every corner they are selling cards with Wilhelm's photo.

---

25. The Sonata No. 2 for piano in D Minor, op. 14, in four movements was completed by August 28, 1912.

June 11/24, 1913
LONDON

Nice Kolyechka:

I have been to see Diaghilev's ballets in Paris and would like to share my opinions with you. *Petrushka* is truly entertaining, vivacious, witty, cheerful, and exciting.[26] The music—dynamic, with lots of movement and exclamation and illustrating the tiniest features of what is happening on stage (just as the scenic design perfectly illustrates the tiniest musical phrases in the orchestra). The orchestration is excellent, even amusing when necessary. But now a few words about a more important question, whether this can be called music or not. Yes and no. Of course the music in many parts of the ballet is simply great, but a large part of it is nothing more than modernistic filler. Next question: when does he use filler? And a broader one: when is filler acceptable (if it is acceptable at all)? It seems that filler works fine in episodes of secondary importance or in boring parts resulting from a flawed libretto. But what does Stravinsky do? For the most exciting moments and the most dynamic scenes he writes something that isn't music but which brilliantly illustrates the scene. You couldn't call this anything else but filler. And if for the most important episodes he cannot compose music, but just sticks in whatever is handy, then he is musically bankrupt. And even if we agree that Stravinsky is trying to open a new door, then he is opening it with the tiny, very sharp knife of the quotidian, and not with the big axe that might earn him the status of a titan.

I haven't heard *Firebird* and *Narcisse*. *Daphnis* is boring and amorphous—it makes you sleepy when it's being poetic and makes you laugh when there's drama and movement. If it does have some success with the public, then it's owing to its remarkable design and staging. Florent Schmitt with his *Tragédie de Salomé* is just vulgar. *Sheherazade* is staged with grandeur, in perfect harmony with the music. The production of *Carnaval* is rather dull and unimaginative. The orchestration produces a comic effect and is well done overall except for some weak spots in the piano playing. The Polovetsian dances from *Igor* are always nice to listen to.[27]

26. Stravinsky's ballet *Petrushka* received its first performance in Paris on June 13, 1911, staged by Diaghilev's Ballets Russes with choreography by Mikhail Fokine.
27. In Paris in June 1913 Prokofiev saw the Ballets Russes productions of Stravinsky's *Firebird* and *Petrushka*; Nicolai Tcherepnin's *Narcisse*; Ravel's *Daphnis et Chloé*; Schmitt's *Tragédie de Salomé*; Rimsky-Korsakov's *Sheherazade*; Schumann's *Carnaval*; and the Polovetsian dances from Borodin's opera *Prince Igor*.

Well, my angel, that's all. I am in London for five days to explore the capital of Great Britain. I would be happy to receive a letter from you when I come back. It seems that my letters from here are eventually reaching you in your "mosquito-infested swamp" after all; I was about to write to your Sadovaya address. I'm ashamed and grieved to admit that I haven't started to work on the concerto yet, but at the beginning of next week I'll definitely set down to work zestfully .[28]

Best wishes,

Write to Boulevarde Malesherbes.

Yours,

S.P.

June 20/July 3, 1913

Royat

Sweet little Kolyechka,

You'll receive this letter when your symphony is being performed.[29] Once again it is being performed at the end of June, and once again I am in a distant corner of the world and will have to be satisfied with hearing only reactions to the performance, and not the performance itself. I regret it very much and ask you to tell me in detail how everything turned out, and how the public and the press reacted. At the moment I am stuck in Royat where I found a piano and have plunged into work on my G Minor Concerto. I decided to learn it by heart all at once. It seems that I shall succeed in this endeavor, for I have been sitting at the piano no fewer than 4 hours a day, and the intervals have started to come out right.

I'd like to ask a big favor of you. My angel, could you please on your way to or from Pavlovsk go and ask my doorman (Pervaya Rota 4, the entrance by the eye clinic) if there is any mail for me or my mother. Then put the letters (if any) in an envelope and send them to me. (Don't send any ads like the ones the shops usually send out, of course.) My address: France. Auvergne. Royat. Grand Hôtel des Sources.

Have you received my "special opinion" about the ballets I saw in Paris? If you wrote to my address c/o Mme. Guyonnet, don't worry, even though I am no longer there, she'll forward my mail to me.

---

28. Prokofiev means his work on learning his Concerto No. 2 for piano, op. 16, which he would play later in the summer for the first time in public at Pavlovsk.

29. Miaskovsky's Second Symphony was performed at Pavlovsk on June 28, 1913.

I embrace you and apologize for my importunate request, which will make you modulate from poetic C-sharp Minor into the prosaic eye clinic.

Yours,

S. Prkfv

July 9/22, 1913

GENEVA

Sweet little Kolyenka,

Overwhelmed by backbreaking toil, I am seeking repose in a weeklong trip across beautiful Helvetia. Soon I will come back to Pervaya Rota and embrace you at last.

SP.

June 6/19, 1914

CHRISTIANA [OSLO]

Dear Nyamochka:[30]

I have passed through Stockholm, Gotland Channel, Trollhattan Falls and arrived in Christiania. I like Grieg's birthplace as much as I like his compatriots. Tomorrow I will cross the mountains and will set sail for England. We won't see land for 24 hours.

I embrace you.

S.

June 12/25, 1914

LONDON

Sweet little Nyamusya:

You shouldn't reproach me. I didn't write to you because I was en route to London till the 9th of June. During the first week of my stay here I didn't really have a chance to see anything or get to know anyone, and so it is only now, during my second week here, that I finally have something to write you about.

The news of the coming season of Diagilev's ballets is two productions: Stravinsky's *Les Noces*[31] and my ballet. Our friends at the Evenings of Contemporary Music must have been working on him: when Nouvel introduced me to him, Diaghilev right away started to talk about a ballet.[32] I tried in vain to switch

---

30. Nyamochka was one of Prokofiev's favorite nicknames for Miaskovsky; it was derived from his initials: Nikolai Yakovlevich Miaskovsky.

31. Stravinsky's ballet *Les Noces* was completed and staged much later, in 1923.

32. Walter Nouvel (1871–1949) was a close friend and artistic advisor to Diaghilev.

the topic to opera and *The Gambler*, but nothing came of it. He didn't like *Maddalena*'s libretto.[33] So, I am still working on the Sinfonietta until the end of August, and meanwhile waiting for the libretto of a new ballet on a Russian theme.[34] A draft of the piano score is due at the end of November, and the complete score in March. However, Nijinsky, who will be doing the choreography, may go off to America for Christmas, in which case he would not have enough time to stage the dances and work with the dancers. That is why there is an option to postpone working on the new ballet until the 1916 season. For 1915 we could make a ballet based on an orchestral arrangement of a suite of some of my piano pieces, which I would orchestrate in the winter. Finally, there is a third option, very typical of Diaghilev—to use my Second Concerto, which sends him into rapture. However, it is difficult to find a plot that would suit the music. But as a last resort, I am ready for the third alternative, since it would launch me on a dazzling career as a pianist. In a day or two Nijinsky will be coming here and the three of us will decide what to do. Owing to these negotiations I have free passes to all the ballet performances; otherwise, tickets are hard to get, for the ballets are having an enormous success with the public.

A few words about the *Cockerel*.[35] In a few places the effect of a perfect illusion is attained (word and gesture). But as soon as you take a look at the singers standing by the side of the stage dressed in red caftans, this illusion instantly vanishes. Ballet is introduced at every turn (the ladies-in-waiting dance while Dodon is asleep, as do the guards of the Queen of Shemakha during her aria, and there is a lot of dancing in Act III). Maybe that is a good thing, for if Dodon was lying down and the queen standing still, it would be more boring. The costumes are fancy, but the procession is staged in a very commonplace manner. As far as the music is concerned, the whole seduction scene is terribly dull, cold, and unimaginative. Karsavina dances all the time, performing miracles on the stage, but still fails to excite the drowsy audience.[36] At the end the chorus does a good job of howling. I would rate my impressions of the ballet as a 4-minus.

33. *Maddalena*, op. 13, was an opera completed in 1913 to a libretto by Magda Liven and Prokofiev. The composer orchestrated only the first scene.

34. Prokofiev's Sinfonietta, op. 5, was originally composed in 1909, but the composer revised it in 1914–15.

35. Rimsky-Korsakov's opera *The Golden Cockerel* was staged as a ballet with singing in Paris by the Ballets Russes on May 21, 1914, with choreography by Mikhail Fokine. Prokofiev saw the production in London.

36. Tamara Karsavina (1885–1978) was one of the leading ballerinas of the Ballets Russes, with which she was associated from its inception in 1909.

Midas (in one act).[37] The orchestration is interesting, the music honest, the libretto impressive, and Karsavina charming in the role of the nymph. If *Midas* disappears from the stage, no one will probably notice. It serves merely to show off *Firebird* and *Cockerel* to better advantage. The scenic and musical effects in these two ballets are dazzling; inventiveness permeates every gesture and expression. What ingenuity! How exciting it all is! But not for a moment did I fall under the spell of the music itself. What sort of music is that—just trash. But the production is so intriguing that I'll definitely go to see it again. Stravinsky fails to create the necessary atmosphere of solemnity at the end of *Firebird*; it's crude and doesn't come across sonically. The pagan dances are amusingly staged: while some leap around the stage, others sit on their haunches performing some kind of indecent movements. About *Narcisse, Nightingale, Joseph*—in my next letter. I heard fragments of the last two from backstage.[38] The music for *Joseph* (on top of everything else) seems to have been written hastily: it is ludicrously insignificant. The composer conducts himself. He is a tall, handsome gray-haired gentleman. Massine is a rather quiet young man who has fallen only by chance into this hubbub.[39]

Every morning I work. I am writing my Nyetta anew, but haven't finished the first movement yet. Thanks to Tcherepnin's advice I found an excellent place to work at Breit[kopf] and Härtel's. They have all of your and my collected works in the store. And Kling, the owner, is a good friend of mine.

Thank you for taking care of *Maddalena*. Oh, yes, she is in your hands and it is up to you to give her life. My dear, exhausted creator, congratulations if you've finished your symphony. Its music is still fresh in my memory and I think highly of it. This is not just a compliment. Your symphony is great![40]

---

37. *Midas* was a ballet composed by Maximilian Steinberg, Rimsky-Korsakov's son-in-law. It was first staged by the Ballets Russes on June 2, 1914, with choreography by Fokine.
38. Nicolai Tcherepnin's ballet *Narcisse* was staged orginally by the Ballets Russes, with Fokine's choreography, on April 26, 1911, in Monte Carlo. Stravinsky's opera *The Nightingale*, based on the fairy tale by Hans Christian Andersen, was staged by the Ballets Russes in Paris on May 26, 1914. Richard Strauss's ballet *La Légende de Joseph*, with a libretto by Hugo von Hoffmannsthal, was staged by Fokine for the Ballets Russes in Paris on May 14, 1914.
39. Léonide Massine (1895–1979) was a Russian dancer whose first role with the Ballets Russes was in *La Légende de Joseph*; he would become one of the company's leading male dancers.
40. Prokofiev is referring to Miaskovsky's recently completed Symphony No. 3 in A Minor, op. 15.

Nyamochka, this is all for today, so long and write soon. If you decide to share any of this information with Derzhanovsky, I forbid the publication of anything concerning my negotiations with Diaghilev.

Yours S. Prkfv

I'm very glad your Second Sonata has been published.

[before August 6, 1914]
KISLOVODSK

Dearest Kolyechka:

I sent you a letter by registered mail from London, mailed a regular one from Ostend and called you from Petersburg—and all with the same result, or rather, without any.

Where are you? I am even a little worried about you. Are you in combat or writing your Fourth Symphony? I'm waiting to hear news from you. Send your letters to Kislovodsk at *Poste restante*.[41]

Yours,
Serzh

August 13, 1914
KISLOVODSK

My dear lieutenant:

Just imagine how happy I was to receive a brief letter from you. I was about to start worrying and interrogated everyone: your sister, Borusya, others where you had disappeared. How long will you be stuck in Borovichi? Will they dispatch you with the army to the west? Here in Kislovodsk Belouska,[42] who had been drafted, has been running all over town, beside himself from terror. In the end, to everybody's delight, his mission of defending the motherland will consist in playing viola in the Piatigorsk military orchestra.

I didn't write anything particularly important from Ostend but I did intend to send you another long letter from London. But because I didn't get to it, I decided to talk with you personally. Now I am not even sure when I'll see you again, so let me briefly describe to you what I remember. As a ballet *Joseph* is clumsy and in some places awkward. In terms of music, it is excessively improvisatory with a total lack of any good ideas and plenty of clichés and trite effects

---

41. Miaskovsky had been mobilized for active military duty soon after Germany declared war on Russia on August 1, 1914.

42. Belouska was a nickname for Evsei Yakovlevich Belousov (1881–1945), a cellist and Prokofiev's acquaintance.

(note: this opinion was formed before the declaration of war). *Narcisse* is really nice on stage. Its realism and lyricism are so engrossing that they make you forgive its many sins (with the exception of the vulgar bacchanalia). I have heard *Nightingale* only once, which is not enough to comment on it. In my opinion, there is still too much intentional and unnecessary scraping and scratching that devalues the moments when this scratching is really called for. The second deficiency (in comparison with *Cockerel*, for instance) is its banal humor and lack of excitement. By the way, foreign musicians are much more radical than ours. Many of them accept Stravinsky and know his music very well. Before our parting, Diaghilev remarked that he would expect a ballet from me for next season. On my way through Petersburg I was introduced to Gorodetsky, who seemed to be really inspired by the idea of creating a ballet and promised to write a libretto within the next two weeks. Right now I am not sure whether there will be seasons of Diaghilev's ballets next year, or whether anything will be left of Europe at all. However, regardless of the war, if Gorodevich [Gorodetsky] brings me a really good libretto (the main principles we have already discussed with him together), then I'll create a ballet, and an intricate one at that. Meanwhile I'll continue to spruce up my Nyetta, and rewrite some of it completely: for example, the Intermezzo is 67% new.

I'd be happy to get a letter from you, better yet to get news from you on a regular basis. In any case, I'll stay in Kislovodsk till the beginning of September. I continue to praise your Third Symphony. Besides that, I must also praise Zakharkin. Even though he has been playing one and the same concerto by Rachmaninoff for 8 years now, his style has acquired some finesse and what is still more important—naturalness.[43]

I embrace you, my dear warrior.

Do keep in touch. *Serzh*

September 22, 1914
PETROGRAD, PERVAYA ROTA 4

Nice Kolyechka:

I wrote to you at Borovichi twice—with only silence for a reply. This time I am writing to your new address, which I got from Yurasovich.[44] This draftee got

---

43. This refers to Boris Zakharov, who was learning Rachmaninoff's Second Piano Concerto.

44. Yurasovich is a nickname for Aleksandr Ivanovich Yurasovsky (1890–1922), a composer and conductor.

enlisted as a nurse and is hanging around here in Petrograd waiting to be dispatched to the front. I was really thrilled when he told me about the performance of your Third Symphony coming up in Moscow. If I have any money, I'll go there to hear it. My dear Ziloshka[45] canceled all his concerts, because the Hall of the Nobility is being used as a hospital. I am working on a romance based on Andersen's *Ugly Duckling* and hopelessly looking for Gorodetsky all over Petrograd to start working on the new ballet.

I embrace you and am looking forward to receiving your letter.

Yours Seryozha

October 1, 1914
PETROGRAD

Dear Kolyusya:

Borusya and I are thinking about visiting you in Kapitolovka. We are considering different means of getting there: by bicycle, on horseback, or in a carriage? The last is more likely. Another question: whether to start directly from Petrograd or from Levashovo station, from where (as I can see on the map) it's about seven miles on country roads. So, between what hours are you receiving? Yurasovich told me about your Third Symphony in this way: "And in the RMO[46] Cooper is conducting Miaskovsky's Third Symphony!" Yurasovich disappeared and I have no idea how to get more information about it—Derzhikhvostov [Mr. Bushytail] is down on me and doesn't even send his articles any more.[47] Three days ago Borusya stopped by to purchase a score of your Second Sonata, but he was turned away rudely and told that allegedly they had not received it yet.

I embrace you and cherish the hope of seeing you soon.

Seryozha

December 25, 1914
PETROGRAD

My darling Nyamusya:

Today Andreyev, who has just returned from Galicia, was telling me about meeting with you at the theater in Lvov. I am glad he found you in good spirits.

---

45. Ziloshka is Aleksandr Ziloti. He later gave his concerts in the Mariinsky Theater instead of the Hall of the Nobility (today the Shostakovich Philharmonic Hall).
46. Russian Musical Society
47. Prokofiev refers to Vladimir Derzhanovsky.

I am sending you my season's greetings and hope that you will continue to prosper. I am busy learning my Second Concerto by heart for the concert on January 24,[48] somewhat lazily orchestrating the ballet and moving ahead at a snail's pace. In general, musical life in Petrograd has died down for the moment and I don't know what to tell you about it. Diaghilev, inquiring about my ballet, has asked me to come to Italy. Since he is paying the expenses, I might as well go at the end of January, if the Bucharest-Thessaloníki route remains open. Apparently your comrade is not desired for active duty yet. I embrace you, my friend, and would be happy to receive a little note from you.

Yours, S.P.

January 25, 1915
PETROGRAD

Dearest Nyamusya:

I was awfully happy to receive your letter with the detailed description of your life. I sympathize with all my soul with what you are enduring. Compared to that, it seems even shameful to write about the petty routine of life here. Yesterday I performed my Second Concerto at RMO with great success, although some individuals couldn't restrain themselves and used it as a chance to hiss at me. Malko conducted fairly well, and I conscientiously learnt my part by heart. So whoever was disappointed in music found consolation in the pianist. Auer, Artsybushev, Fitelberg, Ziloti all rather unexpectedly turned out to be of a favorable opinion concerning the concerto. Ziloti still hasn't forgotten your misanthropic attack and tried rigorously to show that his current praise flows naturally out of his former abuse.[49] Dear Glazunov burst out with some rude remarks. Last week at our gathering Zherebtsova sang *Duckling* quite well, which provoked a wide array of opinions.[50] These Evenings of Contemporary Music are becoming noisier and more boisterous. The room was full: a lot of musicians came. Next time we'll listen to your sonata, which so many of us are looking forward to.

---

48. On January 24, 1915, Prokofiev performed his Second Concerto at a concert conducted by Nikolai Malko (1883–1961).
49. In an issue of the journal *Muzyka* (September 18, 1914), under the pseudonym of "Misanthrope," Miaskovsky had written a sharp attack on Ziloti for not paying sufficient attention to new Russian music.
50. On January 17, 1915, at one of the Evenings of Contemporary Music, Anna Zherebtsova-Andreyevna gave the premiere of Prokofiev's *Ugly Duckling*, with the composer at the piano.

I am going to Palermo in a few days to meet with Diaghilev (he is covering the expenses). This will be an exciting trip and is also necessary for the ballet, if only to ensure its production above all. I am traveling with some consul, which should simplify all the formalities at the border. I plan to return home by the end of March.

I embrace you, my dear, take care of yourself and try to finish off those despicable descendants of Schubert as soon as possible.

Yours, Seryozha

Have you received the package with goodies from all of us?

March 1/14, 1915
NAPLES

Dear Kolyechka,

I seriously doubt whether my letters will reach you from here. A week ago I successfully performed my Second Concerto at the Augusteum in Rome. At present I'm in Naples, where Diaghilev and I are trying to rework my ballet. From here I'll go to visit with Stravinsky in Switzerland, at his invitation.[51] Then I hope to go back to Russia. I embrace you, my angel, write to my Petrograd address.

March 21 / April 3, 1915
MILAN

Dear little Kolyechka,

Accept my warmest holiday greetings. For the holidays I am staying in Milan in the company of Stravinsky, Diaghilev, and others. In a day or two I will depart for Petrograd where I hope to get other letters from you. Str[avinsky] and I have become good friends. We get along very well both as individuals and composers. His new *Pribaoutki* with orchestra is just remarkable![52] Both Stravinsky and Diaghilev have become very much interested in you and would like to get to know your works. They both hurl insults at Petrograd with all their might. I embrace you.

S.P.

---

51. The trip to visit Stravinsky did not take place.
52. *Pribaoutki*, four *chansons plaisantes*, for voice and eight instruments, was completed in 1914.

April 10, 1915
PETROGRAD

Dear little Kolyunyechka:

Yesterday I finally got home from Italy safe and sound after a ten-day trip through Brindisi-Thessaloníki-Niš-and Sofia. Today Varlikh and I rehearsed my Second Concerto, which I'll perform on the 13th in a concert together with works by Petrov-Boyarinov, Hartman, and also Stravinsky (*Scherzo fantastique* and "Le Faune").[53] When Varlikh was talking about your Second Symphony and *Silence* his eyes blazed with excitement. I have signed a contract with Diaghilev to create a new ballet (the old ballet has been put aside for the moment) based on themes from Russian life, and also very merry. The piano score is due in August, the complete score in March.[54] The premiere is tentatively scheduled for May 1916 in Paris (if you have defeated the enemy by then). In the summer I'll most likely go to Italy again. By the way, I promised Diaghilev, who is interested in you, to bring him some of your works. Let me know which ones: maybe you could even entrust to me a manuscript, besides the published works? The most progressive trend to which both Stravinsky and Diaghilev now adhere is this: down with the pathetic, down with pathos, down with internationalism. They are making me into a truly Russian composer.

I embrace you, my dearest. I wish I could arrange it so that you weren't so far away.

Yours, Serzh

May 11/24, 1915
TERIOKI

Dearest Nicki, we got to Terioki, took a walk, banged on the piano, thought of you, and regret you're not here with us. Finish off those Germans as soon as possible and come join us.

Sergusya. Borusya.

---

53. On April 13, 1915, Hugo Varlikh (1856–1922) conducted the Court Orchestra in a program that included Prokofiev's Second Piano Concerto (with the composer as soloist); the suite from the ballet *The Scarlet Flower* by Foma Hartman (1885–1956); *Northern Legend* and some songs by Pyotr Petrov-Boyarinov (died 1922); and *Scherzo fantastique* and the song "Le Faune" by Stravinsky.
54. This was the project for the ballet *The Buffoon*, composed during 1915.

MIASKOVSKY to PROKOFIEV

November 3, 1916
REVEL[55]

Majestic Seryozha, your letter about your sad and pensive *Autumnal* had an extremely melancholic effect on me—regrets flared up about the irretrievable past, all those fleeting things which have slipped by, etc. I have heard nothing that interests me—no Sinfoniettas, no *Autumnals*! Everything is boring and inane. [. . .]

My affairs right now are dreadfully boring. Every third night I have to go out to dismal evening work detail; I freeze, I shiver, I don't sleep, and then I waste an entire day recovering my vigor. I think of nothing but the end of all this. On my evenings off I sit and play Ouija and call upon the "spirits" who come up with all sorts of nonsense.

But by hook or by crook I will end up in Peter on the 26th and 27th of November. [. . .] Your name is not listed in *Contemporary Musicians*—someone's grudge? Funny people.

I wish you much success and bliss, my heart!

Your N. Miaskovsky

February 1, 1917
[EN ROUTE]

Dearest Nicki, greetings to you as I travel to Saratov, where my piano recital will take place, for which I've learned everything that I could, beginning from my first opus to the last (but not the "piano puppies").[56] *The Gambler* is already being rehearsed with orchestra.[57] The orchestration is pretty good; everything turned out well, especially the passages. It'll be ready by Easter. I hug you.

Your S.

May 4, 1917
PETROGRAD

My very dearest Nyamurochka, I am more than supernaturally guilty before you for such a long silence. Excuse me magnanimously and accept my most tender,

---

55. Revel, in Estonia, is now known as Tallinn.
56. The concert in Saratov took place on February 2, 1917.
57. The first orchestral rehearsal of *The Gambler* at the Mariinsky took place on January 28, 1917; the premiere was originally scheduled for spring of 1917, but the new administration of the theater, appointed by the Provisional Government after the abdication of the czar, postponed the premiere.

pure, and angelic congratulations. Having finished 20 *Visions fugitives* and having dashed off a Violin Concerto,[58] I have now lost heart and, having bought a telescope, watch the stars. I'm very engrossed with this pastime. *The Gambler* has been postponed until autumn. I still have two piano scores: one the *klavierauszuger*[59] took and the other I'd rather not send you: God forbid it should suddenly get lost. I kiss you on the lips.

May 29, 1917
CHERDIN

My dearest Nicki, I send you greetings from Cherdin but since your geographical knowledge is so elementary, I'll give you some background: it is a tributary of the Kama, 1,000 miles from the mouth. Here the Kama is wild, primeval, and very beautiful with its red mountainous shore covered with dark Siberian pine. I am orchestrating my Violin Concerto and decided to finish the little symphony that you called "boulevard" music.[60] Along the Volga I traveled in the company of Aslanov,[61] he's so in love with you it's disgusting and continues to rejoice in his victory over Cooper in presenting your Third Symphony. Drop me a line in Petrograd if you're not too angry because I write so seldom.

S.

July 24, 1917
KHARKOV

Dear little Nyamochka, I have been very decently exempted from any sort of boring obligations, and have set out for Essentuki.[62] Accept my heartfelt regards from the road and once again give my adoration to the first piece in your second notebook. But for titles like "Fuss and Bother," I do not respect you.[63]

---

58. Prokofiev had recently completed the *Visions fugitives*, a cycle of twenty pieces for solo piano, and his Violin Concerto No. 1 in D Major, op. 19.
59. A person who makes piano scores.
60. Prokofiev is referring to his recently completed Symphony No. 1 in D Major, the "Classical," op. 25, which would become one of his most popular works.
61. Aleksandr Aslanov (1874–1960), a conductor, emigrated from Russia in 1921.
62. Prokofiev was not called to serve in the army because he was the only child of a widowed mother.
63. Prokofiev seems to have in mind a piano piece ("*Sueta*") that Miaskovsky had written but not published separately. The title translates as something like "Fuss and Bother."

May 20, 1918
ARKHARA

Nice Nyamochka,

I am writing to you from Arkhara, remarkable for the the fact that it gave birth to all Arkharians (there's many places fate takes us on the road to America!). Tomorrow we will arrive in Khabarovsk and 30 hours later in Vladivostok. I hug you tenderly and congratulate you on your name day, and wish you success in your orchestrations and in composing the orchestral *morceaux*.

Your S.P.

February 6, 1923[64]
ETTAL

Dear Nikolai Yakovlevich.

I was terribly happy to get your letter, in spite of its slightly artificial, lovingly complimentary tone that reminded me of Tchaikovsky's letters to Nápravník.[65] But your news that you are ready "to immerse yourself for four months" in the orchestration of your Sixth Symphony attests to the fact that you have remained the former Miaskovsky and this instills joy in me. Tomorrow I am going on tour to the most diverse countries[66]—this, of course, is very entertaining, but I very much envy your immersion, for such immersion, when all is said and done, is the most attractive thing on earth. [. . .]

The orchestral score of my Second Concerto perished in the ransacking of my Petersburg apartment. That scoundrel whom you so courteously call Arthur Sergeevich[67] didn't give Asafiev the necessary documents for the timely removal from my apartment of my manuscripts for safekeeping. As a result, the people who moved into the apartment used the concerto to heat the stove. I think next summer I'll proceed with the restoration of the concerto. [. . .]

Well, I kiss you, my dear, and ask you to write. If I do not return from tour, then they will forward your letter to me.

I wish you success with your immersion.

Your loving S. Prokofiev

---

64. Prokofiev and Miaskovsky had lost touch with each other for nearly five years after May 1918, when Prokofiev left Russia, bound for the United States.
65. Eduard Nápravník (1839–1916) was a composer and conductor; he was the chief conductor at the Mariinsky Theater for many years during Tchaikovsky's lifetime.
66. The tour included performances in Barcelona, Paris, Antwerp, Brussels, and London.
67. The Russian composer Arthur Lourié (1892–1966) had emigrated in 1922.

February 12, 1923
GENOA

Dear Kolyechka Miaskovsky, on the way to Spain I send you a hug, wish you success with the orchestration of the Sixth. Regards to the Derzhanovsky family. The other day I wrote to you by registered mail.

I kiss you.

S.P.

January 3, 1924
SÈVRES

Dear Nikolai Yakovlevich.

The other day Borovsky[68] and I, having rehearsed beforehand, played your Fifth Symphony in four-hands piano for Koussevitsky, who followed along with the orchestral score.[69] Koussevitsky responded just as coldly towards the symphony as he did passionately towards your *Caprices*, believing that the symphony is not at all appropriate for performance in Paris. It's no secret that you can't rely on Koussevitsky's taste, but you can't deny his instinct: while in Russia he showed a fine sense for the market, and now, in Paris he is well informed of what is going on in music. He isn't trying to lead music, as Stravinsky wants to do; he isn't trying to bring together and spur on all its leaders, like Diaghilev; but he knows superbly who has gone where and how various circles of listeners and connoisseurs react to what, which is why his attitude towards the Fifth Symphony should not be taken as some kind of random decree by one conductor, but as a reflection of the opinion of a rather important faction.

Of course I argued passionately against his view of the Fifth, but now, just between you and me, I must assail you too, for speaking frankly, I not only am not left in ecstasy by it, but am simply horrified by much if it. Yes! In this symphony I see the clumsy and dead influence of Glazunov! How do you explain the influence of this cadaver? By the isolation of Russia? By the protective halo he has been able to preserve for himself within the boundaries of Petrograd's four walls? For it's well known that Glazunov is not a classic—a classic is a daredevil who discovers new laws that are then accepted by those who follow. Glazunov collected good recipes and then made a nice cookbook out of them. In his technique and orchestrations he is a tasteless collector which is why

68. Aleksandr Borovsky (1889–1968), a Russian pianist, emigrated from Russia in 1920.
69. Miaskovsky's Symphony No. 5 in D Major, op. 18.

those pages where you fall under his influence smell of impotence and decay. [. . .] Glazunov was able to assemble several old recipes and even attract several hearts "through the novelty of mixing two antiques," but his influence is sterile and produces only decay. [. . .]

I am glad to read in your last letter that you feel the earth moving beneath your feet: that means that deep down you are upset and feel something like what I felt glancing at the Fifth Symphony. What to do? Here's what: for now, compose not thinking about music (you always write good music, that's not the problem), but instead concentrate on creating new methods, and a new technique, new orchestration; rack your brains in this direction, sharpen your inventiveness, no matter what it takes, strive for a good, fresh sound; renounce the Petersburg and Moscow schools as you would a morose devil—and you will immediately feel not only the earth beneath your feet but even wings on your back, and mainly—a goal straight ahead. I don't doubt that Aleksandrov, Feinberg, and the others are marvelous lads, but these Medtner-like fragments hang on you like stones and pull you invisibly into a warm, cozy swamp.[70] For those who live in the swamp, the swamp is a paradise; but you, an unspoiled person, let out an involuntary scream upon submersion: "Save me, there is no solid ground underfoot!" And where in a swamp is there solid ground! Only on the bottom.

Should I beg your pardon for this letter? It seems to me that I shouldn't. For it is not only my passionate love for you that guides me, but also my faith in you, and I don't want to think that you could understand me in any other way.

I know you'll tell me that after the Fifth there is a Sixth and a Seventh and that this one, on folk themes, is done in a popular "folk" style. That's true. I don't know either the Sixth or the Seventh, but I know your last sonata and have always been captivated with the ingenuity with which you, for example, avoid the squareness $(4 + 4)$ that appears so frequently in the Fifth Symphony. But even in a "folk" piece one shouldn't resort to Glazunov. [. . .]

Several words about current affairs. [. . .] In *The Fiery Angel* there is little of the divine but tons of the orgasmic. When will I finish orchestrating all of this—only Allah knows. I have finally killed off the Fifth Sonata and am memorizing it. I am also learning a bit of the sixth of the *Caprices* since I'm thinking of playing it at my next piano recital in Paris.

---

70. Anatoly Aleksandrov (1888–1982) was a Soviet composer, pianist, and later professor at the Moscow Conservatory; Samuil Feinberg (1890–1962) was composer and pianist; Nikolai Medtner (1879–1951), a composer and pianist, emigrated in 1921.

I have finally moved permanently from Germany to France, and from now on I ask that you write me in Paris, at American Express. By the way, if they have sent something to Bavaria, then it will not be lost; my mother is still there and she will forward it to me.

I firmly hug and kiss you.

Your loving S. Prokofiev

Koussevitsky continues to be interested in your Seventh Symphony and has asked me to help him get to know it better, as soon as the score arrives.

May 4, 1924
PARIS

Dear Nikolai Yakovlevich,

It will be great if Stokowski plays your Fifth. Stokowski is a talented Austrian,[71] and an Americanized conductor who now occupies a leading position in America. Therefore, if he plays it, immediate attention will be paid to your symphony. I wrote to Ziloti informing him that I have the music—and that I am at his service and asking him to notify me about the date, just as soon as it is announced—so don't turn your back on Europe altogether as you were so hasty to do. Old lady Europe is of course to blame, having twice made promises and then broken them, but here is the explanation: the Paris concert society is young and has so few resources that it couldn't even drag the season to a conclusion. My Violin Concerto was also not performed as promised. [. . .]

My opus 37 is *The Fiery Angel*. I will play the Second Concerto (heavily revised and almost transformed into No. 4) here with Koussevitsky in three days. This thing is so devilishly difficult that I haven't written anything for two months, doing nothing but learning it on the piano. They aren't publishing the Fifth Sonata now, since I want to go ahead first with the "Classical" Symphony. It seems to me that Derzhanovsky exaggerates the success of the sales of my compositions in Moscow: based on information from our Berlin department, there are not that many copies moving there at all. I'll send you the romances to Balmont in a few days. I apologize that I haven't done that yet.[72] [. . .]

Stravinsky is extraordinarily difficult to figure out from the score—one must hear it. Out of the works you named I have heard only *Soldat*: the first time I

---

71. Prokofiev is mistaken about Stokowski's ancestry: he was of Polish-Irish, and not Austrian, heritage.

72. Prokofiev is referring to his Five Poems of Konstantin Balmont for voice and piano, op. 36, composed in 1921.

liked it and it affected me a lot—the second time less so.[73] In any case, you very accurately observed that it is ascetic and at the same time caustic. Tailleferre is nonsense,[74] the *Promenades* of Poulenc are also rather bad, but everyone admires the ballet he wrote for Diaghilev.[75] At the end of the month it will be put on here and I will write to you the about my impressions of it.

I send you a big hug. Get back to the Eighth. Not long ago I saw Zakharov on the way back from America where Hansen[76] had a great success; he is returning there in the fall.

Write.

Your S. Prokofiev

June 1, 1924
Paris

Dear Nikolai Yakovlevich.

Your description of the performance of the Sixth Symphony and your published thematic analysis of it, sent by an anonymous benefactor, arrived almost simultaneously. Many things in your analysis interested me. [. . .]

As for new music here, besides *Pacific 231*[77] I have heard the ballet *Les Biches* by Poulenc, presented by Diaghilev, which greatly disappointed me. It had seemed to me that Poulenc wasn't a bad composer at all but *Biches* is nonsense. I cannot understand why Stravinsky nevertheless praises it and even took offense at me when I accused him of insincerity. Stravinsky's piano concerto is done in the style of Bach and Handel and I don't like it very much.[78] But it's put together solidly, presented boldly, and sounds "hard," mainly because of the brass accompaniment—there are no strings except for the double basses,

---

73. Stravinsky's *L'Histoire du soldat* (*The Soldier's Tale*), to be read, played, and danced, was completed in 1918.

74. Germaine Tailleferre (1892–1983) was a member of the group of French composers known as Les Six.

75. The ten *Promenades* of Francis Poulenc (1899–1963) for piano solo were written in 1924. The ballet Prokofiev has in mind is Poulenc's *Les Biches*, completed in 1923 and staged in 1924 by the Ballets Russes in Paris.

76. Violinist Cecilia Hansen (1897–1989) was the wife of Boris Zakharov, who was a classmate of Prokofiev and Miaskovsky at the St. Petersburg Conservatory.

77. *Pacific 231*, for symphonic orchestra, by Arthur Honegger (1892–1955), was named for an American locomotive and suggested motion from start to full speed to stop. It was composed in 1923 and first performed in Paris by Koussevitsky on May 8, 1924.

78. Stravinsky's Concerto for Piano and Wind Instruments was composed 1923–24 and received its premiere in Paris on May 22, 1924, with Koussevitsky conducting.

and the woodwinds play a smaller role than the brass. In places there appear modern dance-like syncopated rhythms that nicely invigorate the scratched-up Bach. (I should caution you: I do love the old man Sebastian but don't care for imitations of him.) Stravinsky himself played it and not badly at all; he was terribly nervous and put the orchestral score beside him on the bench. But there were no incidents. Of my own things the Second Concerto and *Seven, They Are Seven* have been performed. The Second Concerto was received coolly.[79] Apparently, despite my revisions, I didn't succeed in fully developing the orchestral accompaniment. But *Seven, They Are Seven* had a tumultuous success and indeed it seems this piece has come out well.[80]

Please send me a copy of *Sarcasmes* and inform me how much they cost in dollars or francs: I'll send you the money in my next letter. I received a letter from Ziloti. Stokowski has confirmed his intention of performing your Fifth next season. Wolff will also play it in Paris next season and under better conditions than he could arrange this season.[81] I sent you my romances on texts of Balmont quite a while ago. Right now I am busy correcting proofs of my Third Concerto (the orchestral score). Because of the cramming I had to do on the Second and the performance of *Seven, They Are Seven*, I have delayed this proofreading for two months. I received an invitation from Ossovsky[82] to play next year at the Leningrad Philharmonic Society but have not yet agreed, since there is a possibility I will be going to America. [. . .]

I send you a big hug.

Your S. Prkfv

My address from June 10 until the middle of October: Villa Béthanie, St. Gilles-sur-Vie, Vendée, France.

July 15, 1924
Villa Béthanie, St. Gilles-sur-Vie, Vendée, France

Dear Nikolai Yakovlevich,

I have been very slow in replying to you. [. . .]

Here's another idea I wanted to share with you. Actually, it belongs to

---

79. Prokofiev's revised (reconstructed) version of the Piano Concerto No. 2 was first performed with the composer as soloist in Paris on May 8, 1924, with Koussevitsky conducting.

80. Koussevitsky conducted the premiere of *Seven, They Are Seven* in Paris on May 29, 1924.

81. Albert Wolff (1884–1970) was a French conductor and composer.

82. Aleksandr Ossovsky (1871–1957) was a musicologist and director of the Leningrad Conservatory 1923–25 and 1933–35.

Stravinsky, and I agree with him wholeheartedly. You should do your piano scores yourself. He believes that the preparation of a piano score is also a kind of creative act, or at least a kind of "orchestration for the piano." (Remember that Liszt took considerable liberties in order to attain the best sound for the instrument.) Only the composer himself, working with love and yet possessing complete freedom in manipulating the material, can create a genuine piano score. The piano scores of my violin concerto and of *The Buffoon* are pretty rotten, but in *Oranges* and especially in *The Fiery Angel* I managed to obtain some reasonable results. [. . .]

Many thanks for the entrance application into the Moscow Society of Composers. I am returning it to you with my signature. Please deduct the required entrance fee of ten rubles from the royalties coming from the upcoming performances of my works. I am not in correspondence with Stravinsky and don't know where he is, so I'll have to put off giving him the same entrance application until we meet in Paris.

The question of when I might come to Russia remains very unclear. One of the main reasons is that I have a lot of composing work coming up, and I wouldn't want to tear myself away from it. You know that such a trip would distract me for a long period, if only for emotional reasons.[83] They wrote from Leningrad that they are preparing to stage *The Buffoon* at the Mariinsky.

These are my current composing projects. I'm writing a small ballet for B. Romanov, former ballet master of the Mariinsky Theater; he will stage it in Paris in November. I'm orchestrating it for five instruments and actually consider it to be a quintet, since it consists of six entirely separate and formally distinct movements.[84] Then I'll immediately sit down to write a symphony; I've already sketched out the material, and Koussevitsky will perform it in the spring in America and Paris.[85] Out of greater respect for myself, I have decided to call it my Second Symphony, thereby considering the "Classical" to be my First. Then I want to finish orchestrating *The Fiery Angel*, first of all because it's time to put an end to it, and second because certain voices have been calling for it to be staged. Koussevitsky has undertaken to translate and publish it. So you can see that I have a mass of work to do, and consequently it would be wiser to lock myself up and not go traveling around anywhere!

---

83. Prokofiev would not return to the USSR until early 1927.
84. The ballet *Trapeze* was composed for Boris Romanov's Russian Romantic Ballet. Prokofiev used the same music for his Quintet, op. 39.
85. The Symphony No. 2, op. 40, was completed in 1925.

It's hard for me to describe precisely the essence of the revision of the Second Piano Concerto. The thematic material has remained entirely intact, the contrapuntal fabric has been made slightly more complex, the form has become more graceful, less square, and then I worked to improve both the piano and the orchestral parts. I hope that it will be published by the New Year, when I'll send it to you right away. The slower tempi of the Fifth Sonata are connected with my poor health last summer, when I was planning it out: as a result of the scarlet fever I had five years ago, my heart wasn't working right. But now my health is back to normal, and I have returned in the Quintet to all kinds of allegro tempi.

Stokowski is now in Paris, of course. I asked Eberg[86] to find out from him exactly when he'll be playing your Fifth Symphony in America, so that the materials can be supplied correspondingly. Wolff will play it in Paris. Next season he will be leading a very good series of concerts.

I embrace you. Greetings to Derzhanovsky and Zhilyaev.[87]

> Yours
> S. Prokofiev

> November 9, 1924
> 54, ROUTE DES GARDES, BELLEVUE, SEINE ET OISE, FRANCE

Dear Nikolai Yakovlevich,

I received your letter of October 24, as well as the preceding one, of August 18. I apologize for my long silence and admit that it was caused by the lowest form of professional envy: in your August letter you describe so juicily the completion of your sketches of your musical infant no. 8 that I also wanted to be able to boast in turn of having finished the outline for my Second Symphony. Alas, that event occurred only very recently, after the most wicked kind of effort. Now I'm finishing up the sketches, and in December I hope to get down to the orchestration. So much effort, and yet this little bit of a symphony is only in two movements: the first is an angry allegro (*allegro ben articolato*), the second is a theme with variations. Themes from the first movement are also used in the second, for better cohesion and a feeling of conclusion. It's a shame that your students make it so hard for you to work. My dream is to drag you here to Paris, but for the moment I haven't succeeded in finding a way to do that.

---

86. Ernest Aleksandrovich Eberg was the director of Koussevitsky's Editions Russes and Gutheil publishers in Berlin.
87. Nikolai Sergeevich Zhilyaev (1881–1938) was a composer and music critic.

[. . .] In a week I'm going to Brussels, where I will play my Third Concerto and listen for the first time to the suite from *The Buffoon* (it hasn't yet been played anywhere).[88] I will take your Fifth Symphony along with me. The Brussels conductor Ruhlmann is a sensitive person, and I'm sure that he will like it.

[. . .] Thanks for sharing your extremely interesting impressions of the orchestral performance of my Violin Concerto.[89] In my arrogance I can't help thinking that many of your reproaches can be blamed, however, on insufficient rehearsing by the orchestra and the second-class quality of the conductor. The straining tuba, the bleating trumpet, the fading violas—all these are the symptoms of one disease: a poorly balanced orchestra. This concerto is orchestrated in such a way that if the sonorities of the various sections are not balanced, the result is only God knows what. Koussevitsky achieved this balance—under his baton, the violas played their theme through to the end, and the trumpets sounded as if from a distance, and the tuba emerged like an endearing bumpkin. When I heard the same concerto under a French conductor, I almost fled from the hall. I took the score, looked it all over, and didn't find a single thing that should be changed. Actually, I did make one change, something that you mention in your letter: at the end I added passages for the clarinet and flute, because without some sort of divertissement like that, it sounded painfully similar to the overture from *Lohengrin*! The piano score had already been published by then, so that these passages will have to remain a surprise for those who know the concerto only from the piano score. [. . .]

You must act upon your impulses to start conducting. It's only the first step that is terrifying. At their debuts as conductors, both Rachmaninoff and Stravinsky fell flat on their faces—but that didn't prevent them from becoming excellent interpreters of their own compositions. Your modest task for your first appearance is to try to fall as gracefully as possible, never letting yourself forget even for a moment that this is exactly the way it should be, and that this first attempt will have absolutely no bearing on how it will turn out in the future. Take Stravinsky, who suddenly took it into his head to become a pianist—now that's brave! Tcherepnin has been dreaming his whole life of playing his own concerto, but still hasn't gotten around to it, while Stravinsky just sat down to

---

88. These concerts took place in Brussels on November 15 and 16, under the direction of the French conductor Franz Ruhlmann.

89. Joseph Szigeti (1892–1973) gave a performance of Prokofiev's Violin Concerto No. 1 in Moscow on October 19, 1924. The conductor was Aleksandr Khessin (1869–1955).

work on exercises for a year and a half, and then suddenly went on stage. And now he has more engagements than I do!

In Paris I recently bought your piece "Circles," and although it's in bad taste to praise a composer's old compositions, I must admit that I was just intoxicated by this exquisite thing. *On revient toujours à ses premiers amours.*

I send you a big hug. Please don't let my long silence infect you—it seems I have repented for it with the uncontrolled chattiness of this letter! Note my new address; Bellevue is fifteen minutes from Paris.

Love, S. Prokofiev

March 5, 1925
BELLEVUE

My very dear Nikolai Yakovlevich,

[. . .] The premiere of *Oranges* is taking place in Cologne on March 14, and I am leaving to go there in a few days.[90] After the most desperate sort of effort, I have completed the orchestration of the first movement of my symphony. I now have about 100 pages, notated from top to bottom. After I return from Cologne I'll start to work on orchestrating the variations. I have to hurry: with all the work involved I'll hardly manage to finish by May. The Quintet has not yet been performed, it is supposed to serve as the music for Romanov's ballet, and that will be performed, it seems, no earlier than May. They have the *façon* in Paris of scheduling all the premieres of new music around that one month.

As far as Stravinsky's concerto[91] is concerned, my impressions are mixed. In style and chic construction, Stravinsky has suddenly exhibited a certain stability: the "Bach-ness" of this style could be felt earlier in the Octet, and now, after the concerto, a sonata has followed that is once again in the same style.[92] Stravinsky himself asserts that he is creating a new era with this approach, and that this is the only way one should compose. Personally, I value *Rite* and *Les Noces* more highly.

I send you a big hug, write me in Bellevue.

Love, S. Prokofiev

---

90. *Love for Three Oranges* was staged in Cologne on March 14, 1925.
91. The Concerto for Piano and Wind Instruments.
92. The Sonata for piano was composed in 1924.

August 4, 1925
BOURRON-MARLOTTE, SEINE ET MARNE, FRANCE

Dear Nikolai Yakovlevich,

It's awful how long it's been since I wrote you—simply an unpardonable offense. First I was finishing the symphony, and wanted to wait until I was done to write you; when I completed it, Kuskin[93] took it off immediately to perform it—and I decided to write you after I had the chance to hear it; but after I had heard it, I couldn't even figure out myself what sort of thing it had turned out to be; so, in my state of confusion I kept silent, until my feelings had a chance to settle.[94] And the symphony elicited nothing but bewilderment among everyone else who heard it: I had complicated the piece to such an extent that as I listened, even I couldn't always find the essence—so how could I expect more of anyone else? So—Schluss[95]—it will be a long while before I tackle another complicated work. I'm postponing the publication until next spring, until I have another chance to hear it. Still, somewhere in the depths of my soul there is the hope that a few years from now it will suddenly turn out that the symphony is actually a respectable and even well-made thing. Can it really be that in my declining years, and at the height of my technical powers, I've done a belly flop, and after nine months of feverish work?

After the performance of the symphony, in June and July, I didn't do anything significant—I corrected the proofs of the "Classical" Symphony, as well as the full score, parts and piano score of the Second Concerto. (It came out very flowery, just like the Third—perfect for children—enough then! I'm going to shift to three-part polyphony!) Then I made an arrangement of op. 35, "Songs without Words," for violin and piano—it came out better than it did for solo voice.[96] I redid my arrangement of Schubert waltzes for two pianos on a commission from Romanov, who will give the piece as a ballet with two pianos on the stage, as part of the scenery.[97] As I was doing the rearrangement, I abandonded all restraint and threw in all sorts of cute little counterpoint and ornamentations. On another commission from Romanov, I wrote an additional two numbers for the quintet—for an expansion of the ballet, although these two

93. This is another of his nicknames for Serge Koussevitsky.
94. The premiere of Prokofiev's Second Symphony took place in Paris on June 6, 1925, conducted by Koussevitsky.
95. German for "that's it."
96. The arrangement was called "Five Melodies for Violin and Piano," op. 35-bis.
97. In 1920 in the United States, Prokofiev had written a piano two-hand suite of Schubert waltzes; in 1925 he arranged this suite for two pianos.

numbers will not be included, of course, in the concert version of the Quintet. Romanov will take this ballet and the Schubert one on tour in the fall through Germany, Switzerland, and France, with engagements already lined up for six months. And in a few days I'm going to sit down to work on a new ballet for Diaghilev; it will be simpler than *The Buffoon*, with less plot and more symphonic development.[98] The sets will be done by the Moscow designer Yakoulov. [. . .]

Stokowski came to Paris for a few days, incognito, so that people wouldn't bother him too much. I couldn't ask him about the fate of your Fifth Symphony, since I learned of his arrival only after his departure. This bastard doesn't play my works, either. [. . .] I'm memorizing my Second Concerto, which I have succeeded in forgetting since last year. I've decided to perform it at all the symphonic appearances to which I've been invited: in Sweden, Holland, and America, where, it seems, I'm headed in January and February—let them get used to the piece.

The most interesting item among the new music I heard during the Paris spring *grande saison* turned out to be the ballet *Zéphire et Flore*[99] by Dukelsky, a young Russian composer (age 21), a former student of Glière. Then he went off to America, but a year ago ended up in Paris, where Diaghilev wasted no time in commissioning a ballet from him. This ballet is very well done, with a mass of very beautiful material. At its center is a theme with variations; I'm enclosing the beginning of this theme. Auric has composed a very witty and most merry ballet called *The Sailors* (*Les Matelots*).[100] It enjoyed a bigger success than *Zéphire*, although of course *Zéphire* is more authentic music than these *Sailors*. Honegger let slip a piano concerto, and a most intriguing one at that, although it has absolutely no interest for the pianist.[101] Stravinsky has ended up by writing a horrifying piano sonata, which he performs himself with considerable chic. But musically it's some kind of Bach covered with smallpox.

---

98. The new ballet was *The Steel Gallop*, op. 41. It was first performed by the Ballets Russes in Paris on June 7, 1927.

99. *Zéphire et Flore*, libretto by Boris Kochno and choreography by Léonide Massine, received its premiere in Monte Carlo on April 28, 1925.

100. The ballet *Les Matelots* by Georges Auric (1899–1983), libretto by Boris Kochno and choreography by Léonide Massine, was first performed by the Ballets Russes in Paris on June 17, 1925.

101. Prokofiev is referring to the Concertino for Piano and Orchestra by Arthur Honegger, first performed in Paris on May 23, 1925, by André Vaurabourg and conducted by Koussevitsky.

A rather talented composer has appeared in Italy: Rieti. If he doesn't stray off into Italian vulgarity, then it seems he could turn into a real individual. Amid all the stagnant Germano-French stuff in which we were wallowing this spring, Rieti with his Concerto Grosso shone forth cheerfully and engagingly.[102]

I can't remember if I wrote you about the production of *Oranges* in Cologne. It was not Abendrot who conducted (he was among the opposition), but a young Hungarian named Szenkar.[103] The production was less successful among the people of Cologne (although *Oranges* was performed six times from March to May) than it was among the Berlin critics; as a result, *Oranges* has been accepted by the Staatsoper in Berlin. They have also started talking about doing *Fiery Angel* (which I cannot seem to finish orchestrating) and about *The Buffoon*. Thanks for the invitation to stage *Maddalena* in Moscow, but alas, this undertaking will have to be postponed: after all I must first finish the orchestration of *Angel* before I start picking through my old rags. [. . .]

Well, I send you a big hug. I write you rarely because when I sit down to do it, I can't stop. Regards to Derzhanovsky. All of his letters to which I have yet to reply are lying here in a separate pile. Each time I look at them, and at the number of questions I have to answer, I end up putting my pen back down. [. . .]

Write me in Marlotte, until the end of October. It's a quiet and picturesque little town about two hours from Paris.

Love, S. Prokofiev

[Prokofiev writes out eight measures of Dukelsky's *Zéphire et Flore* at the end of the letter.]

November 9, 1925
STOCKHOLM

Dear Nikolai Yakovlevich,

I played your *Caprices* here.[104] The audience liked them. The critics wrote something about how the absence of atonality in the pieces was attractive. Overall, Stockholm is a sizable village, although your Fourth Sonata is smiling pleasantly in the windows of the music stores. Today I move on to Paris, and hope to discover some news from you waiting for me there. I send you a big hug.

SP

---

102. The Concerto for Five Wind Instruments and Orchestra by Vittorio Rieti (1898–1994) was written in 1924.
103. Eugene Szenkar (1891–1977).
104. Prokofiev played Miaskovsky's *Caprices* in Stockholm on November 5, 1925.

January 8, 1926
ST. PAUL

Dear Nikolai Yakovlevich,

I landed in New York at a very opportune moment: precisely on January 5, Stokowski performed your Fifth Symphony. The Philadelphia Orchestra, which he conducts, is undoubtedly one of the best in the world, and the performance of your symphony was superb. This orchestra gives two performances of each program in Philadelphia (three hours from New York), in addition to coming to New York—so that the performance of your symphony in New York was preceded by two in Philadelphia. Stokowski is very much beloved in New York, the hall was full to bursting and many "name" musicians (Szigeti, Ziloti, Casella,[105] yours truly) listened to your music standing. Stokowski was in full command, and conducted from memory; his single mistake (or mistakelet), as it were, was to draw out the finale of the first movement. But I'm not entirely sure whether he is at fault, or if you let the fading away at the end go on too long.

The symphony enjoyed popular success: not the entire audience, but perhaps half applauded for a very long time. As for the reviews, for the first performance of a new work in New York they were also not bad at all; they write worse things about me. Szigeti, who was at the performance in Philadelphia, told me that it was a success there, too. As for my own impressions, I must continue to scold you for the same old things: for your use of Glazunovian, and in places disgracefully student-like, devices; and for the longeurs of the second movement, which are only aggravated by the fading away at the end. [. . .] But you know the performance of your symphony was for me a real holiday, and I remained in New York especially to hear it—now I'm writing you on my way westward.

In New York I managed to record for Duo-Art your four *Caprices*: numbers 4 and 5, and one and 7. The Duo-Art is a mechanical piano which with the aid of electricity and forced air records all the nuances of a performance—and not too badly at that. In February I will be in New York again and then I'll make corrections to the tapes I've recorded. During this process of editing, it's possible to clean up the pedaling, to indicate the dynamic markings and voicing more precisely, not to mention correcting wrong notes—in a word, everything but mistakes in rhythm. I'm afraid that in the coda of the fifth number I added an extra measure and a half—some extra rolling around in the left hand! [. . .]

---

105. Alfredo Casella (1883–1947) was an Italian composer, pianist, conductor, and critic.

It was nice to hear of the success of the *Scythian Suite*.[106] Can it be that they really banged it out without a conductor? [. . .] I'm interested to know, do you think they'll give permission for the Chaldean idols to be praised?[107] [. . .] One literary correction: *Seven, They Are Seven* is an incantation, and not a cantata.

I send you a big hug and best wishes for the New Year. It's best to write me c/o Guaranty Trust in Paris; they'll track me down from there.

Yours S. Prkfv

February 18, 1926
NEW YORK

Dear Nikolai Yakovlevich,

I wrote you on January 8. Since then I have played your *Caprices* in St. Paul, Denver, Portland, San Francisco, Kansas City and New York; they have been warmly received everywhere—better than in Europe. Besides me, Robert Schmitz, a good French pianist, plays them here.[108] I have edited the recorded tapes for Duo-Art. It's peculiar that the easiest one came out the worst: the first, fourth, fifth, and sixth came out not badly at all, although it's possible you may scold me for the rubatos I took in the sixth.

Here in New York now there is an assemblage of all the most famous conductors: Toscanini, Mengelberg, Klemperer, Furtwängler, Stokowski, and Koussevitsky. One has to give credit to Koussevitsky; he has been competing with them honorably, and always performs to sold-out audiences. I played the Third Concerto with him seven times—in New York, Boston and other cities. I will play it one more time, and then in two weeks' time, I'll start on my way back to France.

Koussevitsky has decided to play your Seventh Symphony in Paris, in one of his four concerts at the Grand Opéra, between May 15 and June 15. Write me immediately to tell me how we can get the musical materials: from Switzerland or from you. [. . .]

What has become of your plans with Monteux? Did he play *The Buffoon*? Have they been rehearsing *Scythian Suite*? Was *Oranges* staged in Leningrad? Who heard them? Which of your new compositions have been performed?

---

106. Persimfans gave the Moscow premiere of *Scythian Suite* on December 14, 1925.
107. Prokofiev is referring to possible official censorship of the religious/pagan content of his *Seven, They Are Seven*.
108. Robert Schmitz (1889–1942).

Write me at the Paris address.

I send you a big hug.

Yours
S. Prkfv

April 21, 1926
NAPLES

Dear Nikolai Yakovlevich,

Just a few words·from Italy, where yesterday I gave my last Italian concert—the last of six—one symphonic concert in Rome and five chamber recitals: in Rome, Siena, Genoa, Florence, and Naples. As you can see from the enclosed programs, I tried in every way possible to be simple and easily digestible, but even this program turned out to be too heavy for Italian stomachs: both my works and yours received an extremely restrained reception.[109] Only the Neapolitans, and, yes, the Florentines let themselves go and shouted for an encore. (That happened in Florence after your "Circles" and in Naples after your op. 25, no. 6.) Actually, I have regarded this tour more as a pretext for a pleasant journey than as a serious musical presentation.

Besides the sun, Raphael, Vesuvius, and the blooming orange trees I have seen Maksim Gorky, Viacheslav Ivanov, and the pope.[110] Tomorrow I head north, to Paris, where I hope to find some news from you waiting for me.

I send you a big hug.

Yours,
S. Prkfv

May 31, 1926
PARIS

Dear Nikolai Yakovlevich,

[. . .] That son of a bitch Koussevitsky will not be performing your Seventh Symphony in Paris. He will play it in the winter in Boston and, besides that,

---

109. The programs consisted of music by Miaskovsky (songs, some of the *Caprices*), Prokofiev (Piano Sonatas Nos. 2 and 3, *Visions fugitives*) and Mussorgsky (excerpts from *Pictures at an Exhibition*).

110. The father of Socialist Realism, the Russian writer Maksim Gorky (1868–1936) was living in Capri; the Symbolist poet and historian Viacheslav Ivanov (1866–1949) left Russia in 1924 and lived in Italy until his death.

perhaps in New York as well.[111] He also served up a piano concerto by the Polish composer Tansman,[112] and a symphonic piece by the American Copland—I nearly died of boredom.[113] Diaghilev has also deceived me over the staging of my new ballet. Instead of mine, he presented ballets by Auric (*Pastorale*), Rieti (*Barabau*), and Lambert (*Romeo and Juliet*).[114] This last one is an Englishman, and thoroughly worthless.[115] The first two are pretty weak, too, although Auric does have a lively C Major theme, slightly circus-like. This will keep his ballet around for a while. Meyerhold has showed up in Paris, and he sat next to me, snorting in disgust. [. . .]

I eagerly await your impressions on the performance of your Eighth Symphony, and send you a big hug.

Yours S. Prkfv

June 28, 1926
SAMOREAU, SEINE ET MARNE, FRANCE

Dear Nikolai Yakovlevich,

[. . .] Damrosch is a poor conductor, old, who doesn't like new music and seeks out new pieces only when he has to, but he is influential (he has been conducting for 40 years already in New York) and leads an excellent orchestra.[116] So to tell the truth, I'm not sure what to advise you. In my opinion, you should give the more substantial symphony to Stokowski, and the easier one to Damrosch: the orchestra will rescue it, and the newspapers are friendly towards Damrosch for old time's sake. I haven't heard a peep out of Ziloti; the old man has lost his mind. I'll wait a little longer and then write him again. [. . .]

But here's my main concern: how about the observances connected with the upcoming centenary of Beethoven's death? When, where, and will you really

---

111. In fact, Koussevitsky did not perform Miaskovsky's Seventh Symphony either in Boston or in New York.

112. The First Piano Concerto by Alexandre Tansman (1897–1986) was first performed by the composer with Serge Koussevitsky in Paris on May 27, 1926.

113. This may have been the *Dance Symphony* (1925) by Aaron Copland.

114. Diaghilev's Ballets Russes gave the premieres of *Pastorale* on May 18, 1926, in Paris (staging by George Balanchine); of *Barabau* on December 11, 1925, in London (choreography by George Balanchine); of *Romeo and Juliet* in Monte Carlo on May 4, 1926 (choreography by Vaclav Nijinsky).

115. Constant Lambert (1905–51) was an English composer, conductor, and critic.

116. Walter Damrosch (1862–1950) had conducted at the Metropolitan Opera House and New York Philharmonic, among others.

come? I'm anxious to know, because of course I would so much like to see you. Write me.

For the meantime, I send you a hug. During the summer I'll be finishing up and orchestrating *The Fiery Angel* for Berlin;[117] cleaning up the Sinfonietta; and composing a piece for small ensemble—an overture for 17 performers, on a commission from New York, for the opening of a new skyscraper.[118] Right now I'm in a country house near Paris. This new address is good until October.

Yours S. Prkfv

September 1, 1926
SAMOREAU

Dear Nikolai Yakovlevich,

I have been immersed all this time in work, which is why I haven't written you. I composed an overture for 17 performers. It was a commission from America, so I had to get it done by the deadline. The orchestra consists of flute, oboe, two clarinets, bassoon, two trumpets, trombone, percussion, celesta, two harps, two pianos, cello, and two string basses. At first it was rather strange to handle such a combination, but then I got used to it and the work started to go faster, especially since the musical material—unlike the Second Symphony—does not undergo extensive development. Besides the overture, I finished and orchestrated during this time one and one-half acts of *The Fiery Angel*—about 200 pages of orchestral score. I managed to cover such a large quantity of pages thanks to a system I have invented of dictating the full score.[119] And you know when someone you are paying is sitting there and waiting for dictation, you don't tend to waste time, whether you like it or not. But you shouldn't think that I hired him for the sake of luxury—actually, it's just the opposite, out of commerical concerns. For if I don't dally with completing *Angel*, they are promising to stage it next season in Berlin.

And so now, from the height of this stack of soiled paper, allow me to swear at you for lapsing (as you wrote in your letter of July) into a state of doing-

---

117. The planned production of *The Fiery Angel* in Berlin did not take place.
118. The Overture in B Major ("American") for chamber orchestra, op. 42. Prokofiev made an arrangement for full symphony orchestra in 1928.
119. Prokofiev's ingenious method of writing out all the indications for orchestration in his piano score later gave rise to unfounded charges that he could not orchestrate. He simply preferred to save time by having someone else write out the orchestration from his very precise notations.

nothing-ness. You're not even trying to compose away from the piano, forgetting the commandments of great Robert and of great Hector![120] I confess that I also work three-quarters of the time at the piano, but in the past I did compose the "Classical" Symphony and *Seven, They Are Seven* without going near a piano.

It seems that my trip to the USSR is becoming more and more tangible: I'm engaged in correspondence (sprinkled with Boleslav's[121] playful letters) with Persimfans and the Leningrad Philharmonic. By the way, what sort of gift did Boleslav give you from me? He raised a terrible hue and cry as soon as I mentioned that he should take something back with him, and here all of a sudden he has brought you a gift! I'm sure that he must have been staging some sort of funny trick, and then took great pleasure in it. [. . .]

Don't follow my example of epistolary silence, and drop me a line as soon as possible. After all, you should come to your own defense, and at least tell me that you have composed half a symphony! I hug you.

Yours, S. Prokfv

December 17, 1926
18, RUE TROYON, PARIS XVII

Dear Nikolai Yakovlevich,

Have the rumors of the triumphant procession of your Sixth Symphony across America already reached you? It was played two times in Philadelphia, and then in New York.[122] Stokowski conducted it in Philadelphia, but he fell ill before the New York concert and was replaced by his assistant, Rodzinski,[123] who had previously conducted the symphony through only at a single rehearsal, when Stokowski wanted to hear it through from the hall. Nonetheless Rodzinski, to judge by the reviews, rose to to the challenge, and even actually made his career on your symphony, since this was his first appearance in New York. I'm enclosing a few of the reviews: they are awfully intelligent, but at the same time generous, which is saying a lot for New York. If I find some more, I will send them along to you. You know, it's high time for you to start learning how either to conduct or to do some sort of performing onstage, so you could have the

---

120. Prokofiev seems to mean Robert Schumann and Hector Berlioz.
121. Boleslav Yavorsky (1877–1942) was a musicologist, pianist, and concert organizer.
122. Miaskovsky's Sixth Symphony was performed in Philadelphia in November 1926, and in New York on November 30, 1926, along with Prokofiev's *Scythian Suite*.
123. Artur Rodzinski (1894–1958).

opportunity (as a new darling of the New York scene) to transform your fame into a checking account. Then you would not have to sell yourself to those Austrians for some endless number of years. [. . .][124]

There's no way I can send you the suite from *Three Oranges*, since they haven't yet begun printing pocket scores, and the large full scores can only be rented out. I must say that I don't value this suite very highly: its specific gravity is incomparably less than my other suites—although it does enjoy success with conductors and audiences. Put aside the piano score of my Fourth Symphony, and I'll get it when I'm in Moscow.

As for my Moscow concert plans, I have decided that it's best to stick with Persimfans and to schedule the rest of my concerts around them: at least these are people who have played my music a lot and plan to play a lot of my music during my stay. [. . .] What were your impressions of your trip to Vienna? I won't even ask about Warsaw: it's a dead city.

I send you a big hug.

Yours, S. Prkfv

April 10, 1927
MONTE CARLO

Dear Nikolai Yakovlevich,

We returned home in fine form, and I'm now in Monte Carlo, rehearsing my new ballet with Diaghilev.[125] I saw Stravinsky: he is writing *Oedipus Rex*, an opera in two scenes.[126] I'm returning to Paris tomorrow: 5, avenue Frémiet, Paris XVI. I send you a big hug, and remember Moscow with pleasure.

Yours, S. Prkfv

Greetings to your dear sisters and to Derzhanovsky.

May 13, 1927
5, AVE. FRÉMIET, PARIS XVI

Dear Nikolai Yakovlevich,

[. . .] After returning from Moscow, I have been in Paris, except for a trip to Monte Carlo for rehearsals of my ballet, and one to Germany, where they

---

124. Prokofiev is referring to Miaskovsky's agreement with Universal Publishers in Vienna.
125. The ballet was *The Steel Gallop*.
126. *Oedipus Rex*, an opera-oratorio with a libretto by Jean Cocteau translated into Latin, was composed in 1926–27. Stravinsky conducted the premiere in Paris on May 30, 1927.

staged a very stupid production of a Dante-style ballet using my *Scythian Suite* (oh, those dear Germans!).[127] In the mornings without fail I'm working on *The Fiery Angel*. But this damned creature has completely consumed me; I had to start working on paper with 36 lines, and to crawl along—with gnashing teeth— at the pace of two measures a day. [. . .] Stravinsky has been delivered of his *Oedipus Rex*, a scenically static opera-oratorio in two scenes, which will be presented in concert by Diaghilev on May 30 in Paris. The librettist is French, the text is Latin, the subject is Greek, the music is Anglo-German (in imitation of Handel), and it will be produced with American money—the height of internationalism! [. . .]

I send you a big hug. Warmest greetings from Lina Ivanovna. Your portraits have been framed and now decorate our living room.

Yours, S. Prkfv

June 18, 1927
Paris

Dear Nikolai Yakovlevich,

I don't know any details about the performance of your Seventh Symphony in New York. When Stokowski played your Sixth, I was better informed, since my *Scythian Suite* was being performed at the same time, and some friends kindly sent me press clippings. I had a very serious conversation with Kusi about your Eighth Symphony. He proclaimed that he will play it in the winter in Boston and in New York, and also in May of 1928 in Paris.[128] Although it's not always characteristic of him to keep his promises, I think that this time his desire is more genuine . . . Koussevitsky has now strengthened his position in America considerably, since his main rival, Stokowski, has fallen ill and will not be conducting this coming season. The rest of the conductors are weaker than Koussevitsky, or if they are good, then they come to America only for a month or two as touring artists who don't feel themselves at home there. [. . .]

My ballet *Steel Gallop* was staged in Paris quite well and not without success—now they have taken it off to London. I heard Stravinsky's *Oedipus* three times; there is much that is interesting about it, but overall it's long and boring.

---

127. This ballet was staged in Berlin on May 7, 1927. The conductor was George Szell.

128. The Eighth Symphony was performed in Boston on November 30 and December 1, 1928, but under the direction of Koussevitsky's assistant, Richard Burgin. Koussevitsky did not perform the symphony in Paris.

The piano score has been published; if you want, I'll send it to you. For the moment, as a follow-up to this lettter, I'm sending you Debussy and the full score of my quintet. I'm still waiting for you to send me the music you promised from the State Publishing House.

I send you a big hug. I wish you success in orchestrating your Ninth Symphony.

Love, S. Prkfv

In a week we'll be moving to the country, at this address: Villa "Les Phares," St. Palais-sur-Mer, Charente Inférieure, France.

You can also write me in Paris at Guaranty.

September 23, 1927

"Les Phares," St. Palais s/Mer, Charente Inférieure, France

Dear Nikolai Yakovlevich,

I have been working quite a lot recently, which is why I haven't written you. I have finished—this time to the end!—*Fiery Angel*, both the full score and the piano score. To the end!—but that's only an illusion: you can't escape corrrecting the proofs, checking the foreign translations, and other such jobs, which always drag along behind what seems to be a completed composition like the train behind a dress. I'm working now on *The Gambler*, which I'm cleaning up from top to bottom, and out of which I think will emerge a very respectable and well-constructed opera. The old version was put together very roughly, so that very good parts ended up right next to really miserable ones. It's terrible to think how long it will take me to finish correcting the proofs of the Second Symphony (full score and parts). [. . .]

I got to know the sonatas of Shostakovich and Mosolov[129] during my trip to the USSR. They seemed interesting to me, especially Shostakovich's. [. . .] I haven't had the time to look over the other compositions: my own music takes so much energy that when I have some free time I would rather get some air than sit down at the piano. [. . .]

Another new composer has appeared on the scene: Nabokov, who is writing an ode on a Lomonosov text, and which Diaghilev plans to stage as a ballet. I don't know this composer, but, judging by the reviews, his music is rather light;

---

129. Aleksandr Vasilievich Mosolov (1900–1973).

the attraction seems to lie in the spiciness of the Nabokov-Diaghilev combination.[130] Borovsky came to see me. He is studying your Second Sonata.

I send you a big hug.

Yours S. Prkfv

January 25, 1928
5, AVENUE FRÉMIET, PARIS XVI

Dear Nikolai Yakovlevich,

I don't even know how to begin, and how to apologize properly for my long silence: I haven't written you now for four whole months, ever since I received your melancholy letter of September 14, which I am now holding in my hands. Alas, it's the same with everyone else; only Asafiev and I have been exchanging letters fairly frequently these days—and they are concerned with *The Gambler*, which may or may not be staged this spring.[131] The revision of this opera has turned out to be in fact a complete recomposition, although the basic material and outline have remained intact. Now I'm hoping to finish this work soon— and, of course, it would be fine if Ekskuzovich could stage it in April. If that were to happen, I would come to the USSR around that time. You already know from Derzhanovsky that I have been refusing to give any kind of concerts, since I have grown completely away from the piano owing to my composing work. Write and tell me what words Derzhanovsky used to curse me for this. The members of Persimfans have simply remained silent since they received my refusal.

[. . .] I have finished *The Fiery Angel*, but we did not manage to meet the deadline for delivering the music, so that it will not be staged in Berlin this season. In my opinion, this is a case of swinishness on the part of Bruno Walter: if he couldn't put it on in the autumn, then he could have done it in the spring. [. . .]

---

130. Nicolas Nabokov (1903–78), a Russian-born composer who lived in Paris, collaborated with Diaghilev and later settled in the United States. Prokofiev is referring to the romantic attraction between the two men. Nabokov's ballet was *Ode*, with a libretto by Kochno and choreography by Massine, first produced on June 6, 1928, in Paris. It was based on a hymn by the eighteenth-century Russian poet Lomonosov praising the Russian Empress Elizabeth.

131. *The Gambler* was not staged in Russia at this time; it was in fact not produced there until April 7, 1974, at the Bolshoi in Moscow.

As for new music, I have seen the manuscript of Dukelsky's new symphony—it's a very cheerful and pleasant thing, with some good ideas and cleverly put together; but I'm not entirely confident that he'll be able to orchestrate it sufficiently well. I have also seen the piano score of Stravinsky's latest. It's a string quintet or sextet, or a concerto grosso, composed for a ballet being staged by Diaghilev—something about Apollo and the Muses.[132] Having played through the piano score just once, I am hesitant to say what I think, since it seems there are many contrapuntal tricks that get lost in the piano score. Of course the thematic material is thin; it's even more simple than *Oedipus*—in this sense the greatest pleasure is to be had in the deciphering. There are reminiscences of Bach, as well as some lighter and more transparent digressions; there are some truly ugly places (too bare), but then there are others that I couldn't understand at all—these are probably the places where the contrapuntal cleverness will emerge more clearly upon examination of the full score. But I repeat: these judgments are very superficial, for I hastily played through this thingamajig in the office of our publishing house, where people were coming and going and making noise.

Don't be angry with me, my dear, and write me about what you are doing, what's happening in Moscow, and—most important—how your Tenth Symphony is coming along.

I send you a big hug, and Lina Ivanovna sends you warmest greetings.

Love, S. Prkfv

March 17, 1928
5, AVENUE FRÉMIET, PARIS XVI

Dear Nikolai Yakovlevich,

So it seems we should congratulate each other with a handshake: you, from the height of two symphonies, and I from the height of *The Gambler* (730 pages of full score plus the piano score). How did your Ninth Symphony go in Leningrad, and did your Tenth go on in Moscow? My trip to Russia is still up in the air: Akopera[133] telegraphed that the production has been agreed upon, but

---

132. The new ballet by Stravinsky was *Apollon musagète*. It was first performed at the Library of Congress on April 27, 1928, with choreography by Adolph Bolm; the first European production was in Paris, with choreography by Balanchine, on June 12, 1928.

133. Akopera was the State Academic Theater of Opera and Ballet, later known as the Kirov.

hasn't sent the contract. If *The Gambler* does not go on this spring, then I'm not sure if we will come or not, although I'd very much like to. In a word, in the course of the next two weeks this will have to be decided one way or the other. [. . .]

You have probably already received Stravinsky's Concertino. Nothing has been heard of Milhaud's Third Quartet in the music stores. As soon as I meet the composer-genius himself, I'll make inquiries in the most respectable way possible. They are starting to print Stravinsky's *Apollon musagète* in the coming days, so that it will be ready for the premiere—so let's say I owe you one. I'm sending you several acts of *Fiery Angel* at the Muzsektor address, in your name, so that the censor won't have any doubts concerning the contents of the package.[134]

I'm very pleased that you are building yourself an apartment. Where? When will it be ready? How many rooms? Will Valentina Yakovlevna live with you?[135] I still have pleasant memories of the performance of your First Symphony in Pavlovsk in 1914, and am therefore happy that the construction of the apartment has forced you to rescue it from the dust.

I send you a big hug. Lina Ivanovna sends her warmest greetings.

Yours S. Prkfv

April 5, 1928
5, AVENUE FRÉMIET, PARIS XVI

Dear Nikolai Yakovlevich,

That you react with unusually painful sensitivity to all the dirty business of rehearsals is something I had noticed back in Leningrad at the rehearsals of your Eighth Symphony; I hope that the cry of despair heard in your last letter will die away after the concert, turning into indulgent grumbling. I experienced similar sensations quite recently during the rehearsals of my Second Symphony in Paris. The highly contrapuntal places came out especially messy. And just like you, I then proclaimed that my next symphony will be clear and transparent. [. . .]

I send you a big hug. Lina Ivanovna sends her most sincere regards.

Yours S. Prkfv

134. Muzsektor was the Musical Divison of the State Publishing Agency.
135. Prokofiev is referring to Miaskovsky's sister, with whom he lived for most of his adult life.

I have decided to put off my trip to the USSR until the autumn, despite the fact that I'd very much like to come, even after the cancellation of *The Gambler*. What about Belyaev's[136] letters regarding a possible production in Moscow—is it serious, or just a bluff to drag the piano score out of me?

May 1, 1928
5, AVENUE FRÉMIET, PARIS XVI

Dear Nikolai Yakovlevich,

I happened to receive your letter about *The Fiery Angel* exactly on the morning of my birthday and it turned out to be the best gift I could possibly imagine. In fact, I've been writing *Fiery Angel* since 1920, but put it aside several times because the subject had started to irritate me; then I took it up again since so much music had been stuffed into it—and so on. In short, I completed it last summer, exerting every last bit of my strength—and in truth, no one has ever shown the interest in it that it deserves. Even the Berlin theater that had been planning to stage it took advantage of my delay in delivering the score to cancel the production.

Your praise was for me the same sort of resurrection of a corpse as was an earlier resurrection of another corpse—the Quintet. During the performance of the Quintet in Moscow, the piece suddenly began to sound right, even after I had been finally convinced that it wasn't worth a damn.

In the first version of *Fiery Angel*, I had ended the opera with Renata's death, but dramatically this seemed boring, particularly in the presence of Faust and Mephistopheles, which recalled the scene of Margarita's death.[137] And since despite all my scheming I had not succeeded in avoiding some static places in the preceding acts, I decided to destroy the final scene (which by the way added nothing new in a musical sense) and to end instead with violent shrieking. If the audience starts nodding off somewhere in the middle of the opera, then at least they will wake up for the final curtain.

In a few days I'm going to Spain for a week.[138] I'll return on the 10th and then I'll send you Act II, along with the ending of Act I. [. . .]

I send you a big hug. Best wishes from Lina Ivanovna.

Love, S. Prkfv

---

136. Viktor Belyaev (1888–1968) was a composer and musical organizer.
137. Prokofiev means the scene of Margarita's death in Gounod's opera *Faust*.
138. Prokofiev performed his Third Piano Concerto in Barcelona on May 8, 1928, with Pablo Casals conducting.

July 9, 1928
5, AVENUE FRÉMIET, PARIS XVI

Dear Nikolai Yakovlevich,

First of all, let me thank you for your very flattering remarks concerning *The Fiery Angel*. I'm awfully glad that you liked it. Asafiev, to whom I sent the piano score, also praises it. A month ago, Koussevitsky performed Act II (in slightly edited form) in Paris, and it had a big success, although the reaction of the audience here was of course rather superficial.[139] Your opinion is more valuable. The Diaghilev clique responded to the opera with hostility, and for some reason Souvchinsky also adopted their point of view. Apparently, they are still of the opinion that one has to write something contemporary, the latest and the very latest—and *Angel* was conceived in 1920. There was also a comic scene: Sabaneyev and Grechaninov came up to me and started to praise Act II to the skies.[140] I was embarrassed and decided that maybe the work is not so good after all.

The failure of *Steel Gallop* in Moscow both upset and angered me. It angered me most of all because Derzhanulkin[141] had slipped this score to Chavitch,[142] a provincial conductor with a limited range who was of course incapable of guaranteeing the work's success—notwithstanding the fact that the Muscovites, desirous of being original at all costs, declared this windmill to be "highly talented." I hope that your analysis of the reasons for its lack of success is correct. At least it seems very insightful to me (they were expecting the familiar and rejected the unfamiliar). In any case, when I come in the autumn, I will have to rehabilitate this thing somehow. The piano score has already been printed and proofed. I hope that you'll receive it in August or September.

And did the publishing house send you (at my request) Stravinsky's *Apollon*? I saw and heard this thing in Diaghilev's production, and in the end found it disappointing. The material is absolutely pitiful and on top of that, stolen from the

---

139. The concert performance of Act II of *The Fiery Angel* took place in Paris on June 14, 1928, with Koussevitsky conducting and Nina Koshetz in the role of Renata.
140. Leonid Sabaneyev (1881–1968) and Aleksandr Grechaninov (1864–1956) were composers who had emigrated from Russia; they represented a very conservative and traditional aesthetic.
141. This is a reference to Vladimir Derzhanovsky.
142. The American conductor Vladimir Chavitch (1888–1947) conducted excerpts from *Steel Gallop* in Moscow on May 27, 1928, in a concert sponsored by the Association for Contemporary Music. Prokofiev and Chavitch had performed together in the United States.

most disgraceful pockets: Gounod, and Delibes, and Wagner, even Minkus. It's all served up with extreme skill and mastery, which would have been more than enough if Stravinsky had not overlooked the most important thing: the most terrible boredom. By the way, in one place, on the last page of the piece, he did after all make a brilliant display, and figured out how to make even a nasty theme sound convincing. I bring this to your attention because when you play through the piano score it's easy to overlook the impression created in the orchestra on this last page. Stravinsky, incidentally, if I'm not mistaken, is very pleased with his work and is already rolling out a new ballet, based on a fairy tale by Andersen.[143]

During May and June I saw quite a few American conductors and became convinced that your name is very highly thought of in that country. Not long ago I had a visit from Krueger[144] from Seattle (a huge city to the north of San Francisco), to whom I showed your Third Symphony. He was very interested in it and it seems will play it next season. At first I was happy about this, but then I started to think that perhaps it's not worth entrusting the American premiere to a provincial city, even if it is a large one. What do you think?

Milhaud's Third Quartet is not available for sale. I asked the composer when it would be printed. He answered that this will be an *oeuvre posthume*. Dukelsky's symphony has turned out to be very interesting and sounds not bad at all in the orchestra. We should figure out how to have it played in Moscow in the winter somehow.

I'm moving to the country in a few days, so write me next time at this address: Château de Vétraz, par Annemasse, Haute Savoie, France.

I send you a big hug. Warmest greetings from Lina Ivanovna.

Yours S. Prkfv

August 3, 1928
Château de Vétraz, par Annemasse (Haute Savoie)
Dear Nikolai Yakovlevich,

Koussevitsky performed Act II of *The Fiery Angel*, cutting (on my advice) the scenes with Glok and the séance. It came out pretty well, and made an impression on the audience, although in Scene 2 the orchestra drowned out the singers, so that I had to alter the dynamic markings. In Moscow did they really

---

143. Prokofiev means Stravinsky's *Le Baiser de la fée* using themes of Tchaikovsky.
144. Karl Krueger (1894–1979), an American, was conductor of the Seattle Symphony 1926–32.

see Wagner's influence on this opera? To hell with that—I didn't have that in mind at all, and have to a large extent parted ways with this composer. By the way, tell your judge of fashion that another judge of fashion, someone who is even considered to be a trendsetter, was not averse once or twice in his *Apollon* to whistle a tune from *The Meistersingers*, so our Moscow friend should not worry about "lagging behind contemporary taste."

[. . .] Since moving to the country I have reorchestrated for large orchestra my overture—the one that flopped so ignominiously in Moscow—and I hope that it will now be more palatable than it was when decked out astringently in the version for 17 instruments. I am now working on several piano pieces,[145] very slowly, since I don't want to dash them off on the spur of the moment, and I'm making a symphonic suite out of *The Fiery Angel*. Just imagine, the material I chose from it has to my complete surprise assumed the form of a four-movement symphony![146] [. . .] I still haven't decided whether or not to call this mishmash a symphony—people would throw stones at me—but it is turning out to be well-proportioned, and I can't conceal the fact that I'm very tempted at the prospect of writing a new symphony "for free"!

I will without fail write to Ansermet about Dukelsky's symphony. Did you finally receive the piano score of *Apollon*? I reminded the publisher about it a second time. I got a letter from Asafiev in Salzburg.[147] He is as happy as a baby, and I am trying my very best to lure him to visit me for a few weeks. Persimfans has demanded that I agree finally to perform with them between October 20 and November 20, so apparently my autumn trip to the USSR is on the way to taking shape.

I firmly squeeze your little paw. Best wishes from Lina Ivanovna.

Yours S. Prkfv

October 2, 1928

CHÂTEAU DE VÉTRAZ, PAR ANNEMASSE (HAUTE SAVOIE), FRANCE

Dear Nikolai Yakovlevich,

[. . .] Don't be angry with me for my long silence; Asafiev came to visit me, and I was so happy to see him—we did a lot of talking, by the way, about you

---

145. These were the *Choses en soi*, two pieces for piano, op. 45.
146. This would become the Symphony No. 3, op. 44.
147. Boris Asafiev had gone to Salzburg with the Opera Studio of the Leningrad Conservatory, of which he was the artistic director. He then went on to France to spend some time with Prokofiev.

and especially about your most recent symphonies, which are of great interest to me. Then we traveled a bit around the mountains, first in the French ones and then in the Swiss, and even crossed through the Passo del San Gottardo, once again remembering you and regretting that you weren't with us. You really must manage next summer to tear yourself away to take some air abroad—and you must let me take care of arranging that. Asafiev was an exceptionally good traveling companion, hungrily taking in the beauties of nature. Lamm[148] was also pleasant, although he did some very silly things, like reporting the mileage incorrectly or taking us down impassable roads. [. . .]

Your insistent instructions to make out of *Fiery Angel* not a suite but my Third Symphony turned out to have real weight: that's what I have decided to do—and am very satisfied with the project. The main advantage of creating a symphony is that while composing it I have reworked the material much more carefully than I would if I had hacked up the opera to make a suite. Asafiev believes that it isn't a symphony concocted from an opera, but an opera and a symphony, both of them using the same material. In short, my Third Symphony is nearly ready; all that remains is to finish orchestrating half of the scherzo.

I am really indignant with you for having composed so little during the first half of the summer. Have you managed to make up for lost time during the second half? [. . .]

In a few days we will make our way to Paris, where we still don't have an apartment, so write us for the moment at Grandes Editions Musicales, 22, rue d'Anjou, Paris VIII.

I send you a big hug. Lina Ivanovna sends her sincere greetings.

Yours S. Prkfv

January 21, 1929
1, RUE OBLIGADO, PARIS XVI, FRANCE

Dear Nikolai Yakovlevich,

If you are so content with my Third Symphony, then allow me to dedicate it to you. After all, if not for your decisive influence it might not exist at all, and some sort of modest little suite from the opera would be crawling around instead. I hope that the finale didn't disappoint you: it seems to me too monolithic and insufficiently symphonic. Did you see the score at Derzhanovsky's?

---

148. Pavel Aleksandrovich Lamm (1882–1951) was a Russian pianist, teacher, and musicologist who helped Prokofiev prepare many of his scores for publication.

That grasshopper didn't even find it necessary to tell me whether he had received it or not, so that even now I don't know if the finale reached you or if it fell through a crack in the mail car.

Actually, in his correspondence with me Derzhanovsky has been rather thoughtless; we were conducting very serious negotiations and then when I was all ready to pack my bags it turned out that there was no firm basis for these negotiations. Meanwhile, I had gotten very excited about going to Moscow. Now I have taken some consolation in the fact that I have nearly completed a new ballet for Diaghilev, which has some very good material.[149] But not long before completing it I was overcome by a condition similar to the one about which you complained in your last letter: the remaining numbers just refused to come together. [. . .] So I gave up composing and orchestrated everything I had already written, but even that didn't help. So now I've put the ballet aside temporarily and have sat down to correct the proofs of the full score of *Steel Gallop*. [. . .]

I send you a big hug. Did you receive Stravinsky's *Le Baiser de la fée* and Dukelsky's sonata? The sonata is inconsistent, although very nice in places. *Le Baiser de la fée* has disappointed many of Stravinsky's admirers, but I find it more appealing than *Apollon*: at least there is some real material, even if it is rented. Lina Ivanovna sends you her warmest greetings. A month ago she composed son op. 2, and is now becoming a person again.[150] Write without fail.

Love, S. Prkfv

March 7, 1929
1, RUE OBLIGADO, PARIS XVI, FRANCE

Dear Nikolai Yakovlevich,

Forgive me for bothering you with this request [. . .] please inquire whether MODPIK[151] could send 150 rubles to my aunt immediately? And if not, then could some of my new royalties at Muzsektor be scraped together? I am enclosing a list for each institution.

Meyerhold has sent me some not very happy news about *The Gambler*: it seems that Akopera cannot obtain the 400-plus dollars needed to present to my publisher in order to receive the orchestra parts. My planned spring trip to the

---

149. The ballet was *Prodigal Son*, op. 46, with a libretto by Boris Kochno. The Ballets Russes gave the premiere, with choreography by George Balanchine, on May 21, 1929.
150. Lina gave birth to their son Oleg on December 14, 1928.
151. MODPIK was the Moscow Society of Playwrights and Opera Composers.

USSR is now up in the air—to my great regret. I'll have to hear *The Gambler* in Brussels, where I'm planning to go for rehearsals in a few days.

Just imagine—your advice to write my Third Symphony has planted an evil seed in me, and now I'm working on my Fourth.[152] I'm including in it some material from my new ballet, some material composed for the ballet but which didn't fit, and some new material composed independently of the ballet. In short, the sonata allegro and introduction are already prepared, also the scherzo (it is a number taken in full from the ballet). I am now working on the andante and the finale, and can already see them in full. This symphony will be less like a mastodon than the Second and Third, but the material is not inferior. It will be a little more than 20 minutes in length.

I send you a big hug and apologize once again for bothering you with this request.

Yours S. Prkfv

April 10, 1929

1, RUE OBLIGADO, PARIS XVI, FRANCE

Dear Nikolai Yakovlevich,

[. . .] You know I am extremely hopeful that this summer you will shake yourself up and come here to visit me, the way that Asafiev did last year. I will make every effort to ensure that you will have comfortable conditions for work. Besides that, I would like to travel around France with you by car; France is especially suitable for such a trip since she is beautiful nearly all over, has good roads, and excellent hotels. I have a project (I don't know if it will succeed) to travel all the way across the Pyrénées from the Atlantic Ocean to the Mediterranean. They say it's very interesting. Lina Ivanovna would also be very happy to see you. Write and tell me if we could realize this project.

Unfortunately, I will definitely not be going to the USSR this spring: in about ten days or two weeks I have to set off for Brussels, where *The Gambler* has been announced for April 29, and around May 10 the Diaghilev troupe will arrive in Paris to complete preparations for the premiere of *Prodigal Son* on May 21 (they will take it to Berlin in the middle of June). [. . .]

Please let me thank you for your efforts on behalf of my aunt, who sent a postcard that she had received the money. Don't forget to send me the name

---

152. Prokofiev used material from his ballet *Prodigal Son* for his Symphony No. 4 in C Major, op. 47.

and address of the legal advisor for MODPIK: I will write him myself, for otherwise they will keep on messing everything up. For example, they sent my last account statement not to me, but to my aunt![153] [. . .]

I send you a hug. Lina Ivanovna wants me to convey her warmest greetings.

Love, S. Prkfv

Write immediately and let me know your reaction to my summer plans.

April 22, 1929

1, RUE OBLIGADO, PARIS XVI, FRANCE

Dear Nikolai Yakovlevich,

[. . .] I'm very sad that you have completely dismissed the idea of a foreign adventure. But don't think that it's so easy to get rid of me. As I see it, you have to overcome nothing more than the following obstacles in order to make this trip a reality: 1) to receive a foreign passport and 2) to be able to spend money on this passport, on the ticket from Moscow to Berlin (which, it seems, can be paid entirely in ten-ruble banknotes) and on the return ticket from the Polish frontier to Moscow. [. . .] Your stay in France will not cost you a single kopeck, since—damn it all—I am so bold, after a 23-year friendship, as to invite you at last to stay with me for a month or two in the country! If this seems to you somehow "awkward," then I fiercely object, and insist that it would be a thousand times more awkward to refuse my invitation. I will obtain a French visa for you. Please think this over, and don't try to find any grounds for refusal. We are planning to move to the country in the first half of July, but that does not mean that you should delay in making arrangements to get a foreign passport, or an application for a French visa.

It's very good to hear that your Ninth Symphony had such a success in Leningrad. I would very much like to play it in a four-hand piano arrangement, along with the Tenth. And how did you find Asafiev? [. . .] The second set of proofs for *Prodigal Son* will be ready upon my return from Brussels, at the beginning of May; then I'll send you the first set right away.

I send you a big hug.

Yours S. Prkfv

---

153. See Prokofiev's letters to Eleonora Damskaya for information on his aunt, Ekaterina Grigorevna Ignatieva; she died in 1929.

May 30, 1929
1, RUE OBLIGADO, PARIS XVI

Dear Nikolai Yakovlevich,

You're exactly right, I'm a terrible pig for not having written you for so long: I have been wandering between my three premieres as if between three pine trees. [. . .]

I have absolutely no intention of accepting your decision to give up on the idea of traveling abroad. In the near future you'll receive an invitation from a certain institution in Paris—with which I have friendly relations—to give a few lectures about music in the USSR. I think that this would remove any obstacles to your trip; a further refusal would be a sign of your own personal caprice. Forgive me for expressing myself so frankly, but it's only because I so much want to see you. I'm sure that if I were now in Moscow, I would be able to persuade you.

The Gambler was staged in Brussels on April 29, and quite respectably at that, with great enthusiasm and excellent success. Just imagine, the audience understood the opera's conclusion very well. The reason had nothing to do with whether the audience could make any sense of Dostoyevsky or not, but that during the course of the opera Aleksei and Polina were seen only episodically— various events were always getting in their way; even in the first scene of the last act, just as something was about to happen, Aleksei would run off to the roulette tables. For that reason, the eyes of the audience are glued to the stage during the final scene: at last they are together. And the scene rushes by rapidly and is full of unexpected events.

Upon my return from Brussels the period of my Third Symphony began. [. . .] We were very anxious because Monteux added two additional rehearsals, especially for the symphony, to the three already scheduled, and besides that, we didn't know if the parts would be ready for the rehearsals. Fortunately they managed to get them ready in time. Monteux was conscientious, but very much *terre-à-terre*, in the manner of Malko.[154] Between rehearsals I kept fooling around with the scherzo (thank God you didn't arrange it for piano yet), and at the performance it had the greatest success—even with Diaghilev and Stravinsky.[155] But you know that still doesn't prevent me from continuing to consider the first movement the most important one.

---

154. Nikolai Andreevich Malko (1883–1961) was a conductor who emigrated from Russia in 1928.

155. Prokofiev's Symphony No. 3 was performed for the first time in Paris on May 17, 1929, with Pierre Monteux conducting.

Running parallel with the symphony was the beginning of rehearsals of *Prodigal Son*. I decided to relive the past and took up the baton myself. The orchestra was substandard and despite all my efforts, I could not cope with either the Robbery or the *pas de cinq*. I am also dissatisfied with the choreography, which doesn't follow the music well and has some annoying tricks that don't fit the subject. But for all that the final number was staged very touchingly, the audience was wiping away tears, and the success was extraordinary. Actually, it seems that nothing I have written for a long time has been so unanimously well-received on all sides as this ballet. [. . .]

I send you a big hug. Warmest greetings from Lina Ivanovna. Both of us are stubbornly hanging onto the hopes of seeing you in the summer, and beg you to cast off your lethargic inertia. Remember Asafiev and how much energy he got from taking in some fresh air. And in your case, I think that the impressions you'll receive from the trip will significantly outweigh the repulsive tedium of dealing with the formalities of setting it up. You should go through them with your eyes tightly closed and ignoring the little stings along the way. I congratulate you on finishing the Lyric Concertino—I like the name very much.

Yours S. Prkfv

June 26, 1929
PARIS

Dear Nikolai Yakovlevich,

I went today to the [Soviet] embassy and chatted at length about the usefulness of your trip to France. I referred only in passing to your engagements here, remarking that I didn't attach too much importance to them since it is possible that in view of your delayed arrival that they might not even take place. I did tell them, however, that your contact with Western musicians and conductors was important in general, since they are expecting from you not only your own music, but also an authoritative evaluation of the musical situation in the USSR. At the embassy they responded warmly to the idea of your arrival and promised to collaborate fully: the diplomatic mail leaving Paris on June 28 will contain a document expressing their desire that you make the trip here, addressed to the head of the Anglo-Romance department of Narkomindel,[156]

---

156. Narkomindel was the People's Commissariat for Education of the Russian Soviet Socialist Republic.

with a copy to Svidersky at Glavnauka.[157] The embassy advisor Arens advises you to go to both these places and inquire what further steps you should take.

Arens also explained to me that in Moscow what they fear most is that a Soviet citizen will fly off abroad in the hope of having money transferred to him from the USSR, and then become stranded—so that the embassy will then have to repatriate him at its own expense. Therefore he advised me to obtain at the Soviet consulate here a form stating that I provide a guarantee for you, which I have done *pro forma* and which I enclose here for you to present along with your request for a passport. I'm very fearful that you, with your annoying lack of faith in my friendship, will jump on me for this and start stamping your feet in indignation—how did I dare to provide a guarantee for you! But I beseech you to shrug off these formalities and to bring your foreign trip to a victorious conclusion.

I have rented for the summer an ancient château (see the postcard) in the center of France, near Lake Bourget. It's a very beautiful and awkward building from the fourteenth century, rebuilt in the seventeenth. Thick walls, towers, tons of space, a clumsy layout, not very comfortable, but with a marvelous view on all sides. There will be two pianos which cannot be heard from one corner of the castle to the other. I will be in a wild rage if you don't come in spite of all this. Soviet citizens are arriving in Paris all the time. You can't see this from Moscow, but we meet them constantly, and they are receiving passports without problems.

We are in Paris until July 5, and from the 7th at the château. If your decision doesn't reach us before the 5th, then before I depart I'll be sure to leave behind all that is necessary for your French visa and for you to receive $100 at the publishing house in Berlin. This means that as soon as I receive word from you, it won't be difficult for me to put everything into action, even though I'll be outside Paris. By the way: when will you send your songs to the publishing house? (The advance, incidentally, doesn't depend on this.)

I send you a big hug. "Awake, o Fafner!"[158]—and let's be on our way.

> Love,
> S. Prkfv

---

157. Glavnauka was the Central Administration of Research, Museum, and Research-Culture Institutions. Aleksei Svidersky (1878–1933) was the head of Art Administration.

158. This is a reference to Fafner, one of the two giant brothers in Wagner's opera *Das Rheingold*.

September 11, 1929

CHÂTEAU DE LA FLÉCHÈRE, CULOZ (AIN), FRANCE

Dear Nikolai Yakovlevich,

I have divided feelings about your failure to come to France. If it was really a case of financial impossibility, then I throw up my hands. However, if that impossibility could have been overcome but was coupled with a lack of desire to conquer your distaste for making the rounds of the necessary offices, then of course I am angry with you. The summer had already been nicely planned—to give you a change of scene through the mountains and lakes, to feed you with various French delicacies, and to treat you to a whole range of wines, beginning with a vintage from 1830. [. . .]

I am still planning to come to the USSR in October, if only for two weeks, and without any concerts.[159] I will also receive my royalties from the Bolshoi in Soviet money. The royalties from the first productions will probably go to cover my expenses during my stay in the USSR, and for my aunt. The succeeding royalties will no doubt start to pile up, so I beg you to count on them to fill the holes in your apartment, since this money will just be lying around unused in any case.

You are wrong to think so coldly of Koussevitsky: your Stokowski is not superior in a cultural-musical sense, works less, and is a big gossip (it's true that his orchestra is exquisite). In any case, I'll wait for news from you concerning which symphony, the Ninth or the Tenth, you want to propose to Koussevitsky. [. . .]

I have just finished redoing my old Sinfonietta: I turned it completely inside out, from top to bottom, and what resulted is a very nice and very well proportioned old-new piece.[160] Now I have sketched out a small orchestral divertissement in four movements, two movements of which had already been sketched out earlier.[161] Stravinsky played his new piano concerto for me, and I liked it better than the first one.[162] In view of the fact that Stravinsky has no doubt already heard plenty of reproaches over the lack of virtuosity in his first concerto, he is now searching for some other label that would save him from the need to pro-

159. Prokofiev arrived in the USSR October 30, 1929, and stayed until November 19.
160. In the summer of 1929, Prokofiev finished another revision of the Sinfonietta in A Major, op. 5, originally composed in 1909 and revised in 1914–15. This third version received the designation op. 48.
161. Prokofiev means the Divertissement for Orchestra, op. 43.
162. Prokofiev is referring to Stravinsky's *Capriccio* for piano and orchestra. Ernest Ansermet conducted its premiere in Paris on December 6, 1929, with Stravinsky as soloist.

duce something virtuoso-like. He had hinted at something like "Divertisse-ment," but when he heard that both you and I are now writing divertissements, he decided to resort to some other title.

I send you a big hug. Greetings from Lina Ivanovna. Write me here.

Yours S. Prkfv

October 19, 1929

GRANDES EDITIONS MUSICALES, 22, RUE D'ANJOU, PARIS VIII

Dear Nikolai Yakovlevich,

Forgive me for the delay in replying, but when we were moving from the country to the city we overturned on the road along with the automobile and had to spend about a week in the hospital. We got off lightly, by the way. [. . .]

My trip to the USSR is starting to look real and there is a good chance that I will be in your embraces by the end of October. [. . .]

I hope that you have received the parcel with *Prodigal Son* and the third movement of my symphony. I send you a big hug. Lina Ivanovna sends her greetings. I'll let you know separately what day I will be arriving.

Yours S. Prkfv

October 23, 1929

6, RUE BASSANO, PARIS XVI

Dear Nikolai Yakovlevich,

I am planning to depart from Paris on October 27, and to arrive in Moscow on the 30th; if I am detained in Berlin, then I'll arrive on the 31st. I'll send you a telegram on the eve of my departure.

Now allow me to trouble you and ask you to reserve a room for me at the Metropol or some other hotel. I am very sorry to bother you, but I don't want to ask Persimfans or the Bolshoi Theater, so as not to make my trip dependent on some particular institution. Perhaps you could ask Derzhanovsky on my behalf, and let him take care of this. No doubt he has lots of connections.

A telegram from him arrived here at the publishing house, inquiring about my health. Apparently the news of my automobile accident has reached Moscow. Actually, the only remaining evidence of this adventure is a knocked-out tooth and black-and-blue bruises all over my body. There is one other prob-lem, too: when I fell, I sprained the muscles in my left hand, so that for the moment I can play anything on the piano except an octave in the left hand.

So, until our pleasant meeting in the near future. You can expect a telegram from me around the 29th. [. . .]

I send you a big hug.

Yours

S. Prkfv

October 29, 1929

WARSAW

I will arrive on Wednesday the 30th at 10:50 A.M. at Belorussia Station.

Prokofiev

December 28, 1929

ON BOARD THE CUNARD R.M.S. *BERENGARIA*

Dear Nikolai Yakovlevich,

[. . .] It's too bad about *Steel Gallop*. Gusman[163] didn't write me about its cancellation—on the contrary, according to him *Steel Gallop* had been presented for evaluation to some committee. [. . .]

I send you a big hug. I have disgraced myself over the strings for Saradzhev[164]—I forgot, but now I have reminders written down everywhere, and I'll bring them in the spring. Warmest greetings from Lina Ivanovna.

Yours S. Prkfv

P.S. Rachmaninoff is also on board this liner. In the evenings, if the sea isn't too rough, we play "Patience" together. How idyllic!

My address until March 26: Mr. Serge Prokofieff, c/o Haensel & Jones, 113 West 57, New York, N.Y.

February 8, 1930

NEW YORK

Dear Nikolai Yakovlevich,

Amid the terrible hustle and bustle of American life I can rarely snatch a moment to write a letter, but we often think of you: Lina Ivanovna is singing your "Circles,"[165] and I am telling people about you, as you can see from the enclosed.

---

163. Boris Evseevich Gusman (1892–1944) was a critic and musical organizer.

164. Konstantin Saradzhev (1877–1954) was a conductor and teacher.

165. Prokofiev's wife Lina sang Miaskovsky's song "Circles" in America on January 23 and February 2, 1930.

We have given seven symphonic and four chamber concerts, and now we are moving across the entire continent to California: five days en route, so we can rest on the train.[166]

I send you a big kiss. Greetings to Valentina Yakovlevna and to Derzhanovsky from both of us.

Yours S. Prkfv

I'm dreaming about writing a string quartet!

February 21, 1930
[EN ROUTE]

Dear Nikolai Yakovlevich,

I'm writing you in the train, en route from California to Chicago. In Los Angeles you have won yourself a passionate admirer among the critics. He published a whole series of articles, which I am enclosing. Rodzinski is supposed to send you another package with reviews of your Sixth Symphony. He performed it not long ago with excellent success. Rodzinski is a protégé of Stokowski and is very interested in you; he's a pleasant person, as long as he doesn't stumble because of his excessively passionate propaganda of contemporary music. I told him about your piece *Diversions*, which is of great interest to him.[167] But where is the music? It would be good if Muzsektor could write him immediately (Dr. Artur Rodzinski, 424 Auditorium, Los Angeles, California, USA), mentioning my name and explaining when and how he can get the score.

I haven't heard a peep from you. Maybe in Chicago I will be met by some fresh mail. I am pleased with the trip: it seems that little by little they have come to believe in me here. I really will be writing a quartet: I have accepted a commission from the Library of Congress (they will get the manuscript), just as Stravishkin did earlier with his *Apollon*.[168]

I send you a big hug.

Yours S. Prkfv

---

166. Prokofiev had already performed in Cleveland, Boston, Brooklyn, New York, Wellesley, Mass., and Philadelphia.

167. Miaskovsky's *Diversions*, op. 32, is three pieces for small orchestra: a Serenade for small orchestra, a Sinfonietta for string orchestra, and a Lyric Concertino for small orchestra.

168. Prokofiev's String Quartet No. 1, op. 50, was written on a commission from the Library of Congress, as was Stravinsky's ballet *Apollon musagète*.

August 26, 1930

VILLA STEVENS, LA NAZE, PAR VALMONDOIS (SEINE-ET-OISE), FRANCE

Dear Nikolai Yakovlevich,

[. . .] I received your letter of August 5, precisely on the day when you announced you would be moving to your new apartment on Sivtsev Vrazhek.[169] So I was thinking about you that entire day, imagining you trailing behind a load of 150 packages of music and catching the ones that fell off. I can deeply sympathize with your torturous search for furniture, but there is an issue much more important for any new apartment than furniture—silence. Will you get that from your neighbors, and is there any "resident with a trombone" in the building, or even worse—with a gramophone? In our new Paris apartment we have not entirely escaped that sort of punishment, and have been nearly driven crazy by—just imagine what—Ravel's *Bolero*, rotating endlessly on the gramophone! (By the way, did you receive the full score that was sent to you c/o Muzsektor?) Our own purchase of furniture is not going smoothly. It's not that there isn't enough furniture in Paris, but rather the opposite—there's too much, so that it's difficult to figure out where they are rolling the prices up, and where they are trying to sell you trash. Of course none of this can compare with your problems, but I wanted to point out that in any city the matter of furnishing requires lots of running around.

It's terrible that you're not composing anything. In such cases you should take consolation in the fact that taking a break freshens up your future material. It seems that I am going to take myself in hand and try to close up shop for six months. Because when I finished the quartet, I was tempted by a commission from the Grand Opéra for a ballet and am now hastily scribbling it down; I have to deliver the piano score in December and the full score at the end of January for a stage production in February or March.[170] And there are still some concerts coming up, and of course I am still dreaming about that trip to the USSR.

I haven't seen Meyerhold for a month now. He went off to take the waters, but I am expecting his appearance any day now, as he announced. Then it will be interesting to find out what news he has. So far, he has told me that the "proletarian composers" had become such an annoyance at the Bolshoi Theater that it has been decided not to allow them in there anymore.

In my last letters, when I was telling you about the absence of new musical

169. Miaskovsky's new apartment was in the Arbat district, Moscow's bohemian quarter.
170. The new ballet was *On the Dnepr*.

events in Paris, I forgot to mention the *Ode* for soprano, chorus, and small orchestra by Igor Markevich, a very young composer who was one of Diaghilev's last discoveries.[171] I can't say that I like the piece very much, since it is constructed of clichés, although they are in the very latest fashion. But the piece has been a hot topic in Paris musical circles. What's most amusing is that the main theme of this *Ode* is extremely reminiscent of the sort of melodies you write. There's a joke about this Igor Markevich making the rounds: Stravinsky's son asked him, "It must be unpleasant for you to also have the name Igor." To which Markevich answered, "It seems to me it would be still more unpleasant also to have the name Stravinsky."

Warmest greetings to you and your sister from both of us, and also to the Derzhanovskys. I still haven't received an answer to my July letter from him. We have been spending most of this summer in Paris—we were detained by various business matters and by torrential rains—and not until mid-August did we make it out to a dacha 30 kilometers from Paris. You should write me here until October 10, at the address given above. But the letters sent to the Paris address will also reach us here regularly.

Yours S. Prkfv

September 25, 1930
Villa Stevens, La Naze, par Valmondois (Seine-et-Oise), France
Dear Nikolai Yakovlevich,

I have composed eight of the twelve numbers for the ballet, but then the work started to go badly, and so its seems after dragging out one more I'll have to start the orchestration and compose the remaining numbers later. Fortunately the Grand Opéra did not impose a subject on me: it will be soft and lightly lyrical. Has your dry period ended now? I know from my own experience how tedious that is, but you shouldn't take it too seriously. Because remember you were moaning and groaning the same way when you started to compose *Diversions*, but see what sort of first-class pieces came out anyway! Of course this sensation is very unpleasant: it also afflicts Stravinsky when he composes each of his works. [. . .]

The piano score of the Divertissement has been published and yesterday I sent it to you at your home address. It will be performed on October 15 by the

---

171. *Ode* by Igor Markevich, for soprano, male choir, and small orchestra, set to verses of Jean Cocteau, was first performed in Paris on June 4, 1930.

Berlin Radio, along with my Overture op. 42 and the Second Piano Concerto, with me as soloist. Whether I will proceed from Berlin to spend two or three weeks in Moscow, or return to Paris to finish the ballet, is a question which I have not yet decided. Of course it would be more prudent to finish calmly composing the piece I am contracted for, and not to postpone it until later (besides, during the first half of the season I am scheduled to play seven concerts in various cities).[172] I am very drawn to the USSR, although to tell the truth no official institutions are making much effort to invite me. If I don't get any further clarification in the near future then in fact I will probably postpone the trip until January, and will attempt meanwhile to get through with the full score.

If you plan to answer promptly, then write me here. If you are delayed in replying, then write to Paris, or around October 14 or 15 to the address of Berlin office of our publisher.

Valentin Haüy lived 150 years ago and was the first inventor of a writing system for the blind, done through the punching of holes in cardboard or thick paper.[173] This system was perfected by Braille and is still in use today. Before her death, my mother saw very poorly and learned how to read by this system. The libraries and various institutions for the blind happen to be located in our neighborhood. This mysterious surname is pronounced as three separate vowels, with the stress on the last (A-u-i). I send you a big hug. I will make inquiries about your nine songs when I am in Paris, but I fear that the publisher is in no hurry to print vocal music, whose sales are the weakest . . .

Yours S. Prkfv

November 9, 1930

5, RUE VALENTIN HAÜY, PARIS XV

Dear Nikolai Yakovlevich,

[. . .] I have composed the ballet, all except one number, and have orchestrated half of it, but apparently it will be more advantageous to produce it not in February but in May, since the Paris season typically dies down after the New Year and then revives again in the spring. So I guess I'll soon sit down to put the finishing touches on the Quartet and to make a piano arrangement of it.

I was at a concert of Richard Strauss, but the composer waved to the audience like a sick fly, and I found his music so unbearable that I couldn't even stay

---

172. The cities were Berlin, Liège, Warsaw, Paris, Ghent, Brussels, and Antwerp.
173. Prokofiev was responding to Miaskovsky's question as to the origin of the name of the street on which he and his family lived in Paris.

to the end. I have seen the printed proofs of Stravinsky's new psalm symphony—it seems to be close in spirit to *Oedipus*, but thank God, without the
diminished seventh chords.[174]

In the next few days I'll be going to Liège and to Warsaw; I'll return around
the 25th and will await some lines from you then. How is your apartment? I
send you a hug. Warmest greetings from my wife to Valentina Yakovlevna and to
you.

Yours S. Prkfv

How is Derzhanulkin?

January 6, 1931
5, RUE VALENTIN HAÜY, PARIS XV

Dear Nikolai Yakovlevich,

Forgive this silent pig, who has entirely forgotten how to stir his little hoof.
By the way, I sent you *Elegy* by Glazunov (whom you so adore) a month ago, but
they told me that the other opus you requested is not yet available. My epistolary irregularity has been caused in part by my concert tours, which piled up in
December. [. . .]

Amid the traveling I have not composed very much, although I did succeed
finally in putting the finishing touches on the Quartet, which will be on its way
to Washington in a few days. The premiere will take place there on April 24, and
it will be published in October. Besides that, I have finished a two-hand piano
arrangement of the "Classical" Symphony; the publisher is promising to bring
it out without delay. The production of the new ballet will take place in the
spring, so I have temporarily put it aside—there's not much left to do anyway.

Koussevitsky performed my Fourth Symphony in Boston in November, and
Monteux did it in Paris on December 18, as part of a concert of my works. In
both places the reception was rather restrained: apparently the public has
grown enamored of being smacked in the face; when a composer goes deeper,
they lose sight of where he is going. Some of the reviews even expressed regret
of this sort: what an example is being set for the young if both Prokofiev and
Stravinsky persist on writing with such pale simplicity! Some passionate
defenders also showed up: Petit,[175] Nabokov, Rieti, and others. Personally, I'd

---

174. Stravinsky composed his *Symphony of Psalms* for children's and mixed voices and
     orchestra in 1930.
175. Raymond Petit (1893–1976) was a French music critic and composer.

like to fix up the finale a little bit, but I believe the rest is so simple and clear that my clients' doubts have amazed me beyond belief.

[. . .] I send you a big hug. My wife sends you her warmest greetings, and we both send greetings to Valentina Yakovlevna.

Love S. Prkfv

May 22, 1931
5, RUE VALENTIN HAÜY, PARIS XV

Dear Nikolai Yakovlevich,

Ordinarily so lively, the spring season in Paris this time around is pale and gray. Today I'm going to the Grand Opéra to hear a new ballet by Roussel, *Bacchus and Ariadne*, but I'm not expecting much, since I've already seen some of it, and that was weak.[176] One place reminded me of nothing so much as the "Flight of the Bumblebee!"[177] Nabokov has a nice new little overture, lively, moderately lyrical, but not very substantial. There's also a cello concerto by a young composer named Krein; at first it's melodic, then dancelike, but in the end it fails to dance us away.[178] [. . .] Dukelsky, who now lives in New York, sent me his latest manuscripts, but his inspiration has somehow just completely dried up. It's a pity, for he had a lot of promise.

As a result, I'm doing more sitting at home and "paying attention to my piano work"; I'm doing a series of concert arrangements of *Prodigal Son* and *The Buffoon*, and also the scherzo from the Sinfonietta and the andante of the Quartet. I don't really want to call these arrangements, so as to avoid the association with the Liszt-Wagner *Tannhäusers*. What I'm doing involves an entirely different method—I'm trying to produce things that will be suitable for concert performance, but that at the same time don't look that way.[179] [. . .]

Stokowski has gone off to the USSR, and he hopes among other Muscovite

176. *Bacchus and Ariadne* by Albert Roussel (1869–1937), with choreography by Serge Lifar, was first produced at the Opéra in Paris on May 22, 1931.

177. "Flight of the Bumblebee" is a famous orchestral interlude from Act III of Rimsky-Korsakov's opera *Tsar Saltan*.

178. The Concerto for Cello and Orchestra, op. 25, by Soviet composer Yulian Grigorevich Krein (1913–?), a student of Paul Dukas, was composed in 1929 and first performed in Paris on May 22, 1931.

179. In 1930–31 Prokofiev wrote Six Pieces for Piano, op. 52. They include arrangements of numbers from Songs without Words, op. 35; the ballet *Prodigal Son*; the Quartet, op. 50; and the Sinfonietta, op. 48.

wonders to view you. Write me if he comes to visit you and in general how his trip went, and what music he decided to play.

I send you a big hug.

Love,

S. Prkfv

July 7, 1931

5, RUE VALENTIN HAÜY, PARIS XV

Dear Nikolai Yakovlevich,

You are probably already in the country. Where is your dacha? How have you settled in? What are you working on? How are you spending your time? Did you manage before your departure to receive the piano score of the "Classical" Symphony and the two little songs lacking both an opus no. and any significance?[180] As usual, we have been detained in the city and have not yet decided where we will go; perhaps to the southwest corner of France, where the Pyrénées meet the Atlantic Ocean, but I'm afraid it will be hot there.

I have finished the sketches for the one-hand concerto, but instead of pleasure I feel annoyance because of numerous spots that still need to be smoothed over.[181] I think I'll put it out of sight for a week and then set to work on finishing it. I have seen Ravel's concerto and agree with you that it is rather dull; of course it is conscientiously composed, but without any spark.[182] [. . .] By the way, my publisher has suddenly come up with the bright idea of sending out copies [of the new one-hand concerto] to famous pianists, and has asked me to come up with a list. Of course I'd like to send about a half-dozen copies to Soviet pianists. During this period when feelings towards me have grown less positive, it wouldn't be out of place to warm up relations with some pieces that could be easily performed. On the list I have placed Feinberg, Oborin, Neuhaus, Sofronitsky, and finally Derzhanovsky, who could serve as a clearing house.[183] [. . .]

180. Prokofiev is referring to two arrangements of Russian folksongs: "On the hill there was a snowball bush" and "White snows."

181. Prokofiev wrote the Piano Concerto No. 4 in B Major, op. 53 (for the left hand), in 1931, on a commission from the Austrian pianist Paul Wittgenstein, who had lost his arm in World War I.

182. The Piano Concerto in D Minor (for the left hand) by Maurice Ravel was composed in 1929–31, also as a commission for Wittgenstein.

183. Samuil Feinberg (1890–1962) was a Soviet composer and pianist; Lev Oborin (1907–74) was a Soviet composer, pianist, and teacher; Henrich Neuhaus (1888–1962) was a

It's too bad that you had so little contact with Stokowski. He told me many interesting and observant things about his trip to the USSR. [. . .] Once when he was at my place, Stokowski looked over your Lyric Concertino, and I thought that when you met in Moscow, you two would come to an agreement about a performance. But he reported that you were silent and inaccessible. In April, Stokowski performed a stage version in New York and Philadelphia of *Steel Gallop*.[184] I hear that the music was brilliantly played, but that the story line and choreography were cut so badly as to be unrecognizable, and therefore unsuccessful. Nonetheless, the hammer and sickle made an appearance, as well as pieces of red fabric and other emblems of Soviet daily life. Stravinsky is scribbling a Violin Concerto; he's completed three of the four movements.[185] Those who have seen it say that this new opus is akin to the *Capriccio*, but more simple, more sonata-like and . . . drier. [. . .] What do you think about this idea of introducing a new orthography, and will it really be carried out? An i with a dot on it—that's in my honor![186]

I send you a big hug. Write to the Paris address.

Yours S. Prkfv

September 11, 1931
CIBOURE [FRANCE]

Dear Nikolai Yakolevich,

I'm not sure who owes whom a letter, but I think I owe you one. I received your last letter of July 21 just before leaving Paris, after which I sent you the proofs of *On the Dnepr* and a postcard from Geneva. I know that you received them, since Asafiev wrote me that he had in turn received the proofs of the ballet. Then I sent you a postcard from the Pyrénées—but from you for the moment there's been nothing but silence. [. . .]

Write and tell me what you got out of my new ballet. Perhaps your letter got lost in the mail? That's not because you sent it to my Paris address: the for-

Soviet pianist and teacher; Vladimir Sofronitsky (1901–61) was a Soviet pianist and teacher.

184. The staged performances by the Philadelphia Orchestra of *Steel Gallop* at the Metropolitan Opera took place on April 21 and 22, 1931.

185. Stravinsky wrote his Violin Concerto in 1931, and it was first performed in Berlin on October 23, 1931.

186. Prokofiev is referring to a proposed reform (never carried out) of Russian orthography, which would have replaced the Russian letter И with a Roman-style i. Prokofiev had always written this letter in the Roman style, which explains his amusement.

warding of my mail from there to our summer residence has been proceeding smoothly, and every day I receive several items. We have been living for a month already near Biarritz, near the border with Spain, and during this time I have accomplished two things: I have learned to swim and I have disposed of the handless concerto. The weather here, by the way, has been pretty lousy; in fact, it seems that all of Western Europe will soon be choking on rain. When will you start composing, and what have you been doing during your summer vacation, if not composing? As the result of various crises, the upcoming concert season looks to be rather limp, although I will still be performing in symphonic concerts in the large cities: London, Brussels, Berlin, Prague, Paris. In Paris, in fact, two programs of my works have been announced.[187] I'm thinking that among new and half-new things I'll include the suites from *The Gambler* and *Steel Gallop*, the Sinfonietta (which has not yet been heard in Paris) and the arrangement of the andante from the Quartet for symphonic quintet. Wittgenstein is busy studying Ravel's Concerto and will hardly have the time this season to memorize mine—maybe he'll do it by spring. But here I am talking only about myself! I'm waiting impatiently for a letter from you, and some information about our musical friends. Is Derzhanovsky going to the Caucasus? How is Asafiev's health—his letters seem lacking in energy, and I can't understand if he is just nervous or if he really does feel bad. I send you a big hug. I will be at the above address until October 7 or 8; after that write to the Paris address.

Yours always

S. Prkfv

September 19, 1931
VILLA CROIX BASQUE, CIBOURE (BASSES PYRÉNÉES)

Dear Nikolai Yakovlevich,

How touching! After a long silence we wrote to each other simultaneously on September 11! So now again the question arises: Whose turn is it to write? So I am hurrying to write you.

First of all, how sad that you were ill all summer, although I think that you must look very nice without a mustache and beard. Couldn't you send me a photograph, even an amateur one? Secondly, your observations on the new bal-

---

187. Actually, there were three symphonic concerts in Paris in the 1931–32 season devoted entirely to Prokofiev's music: one on November 26 conducted by Roger Desormière; one on January 23 conducted by Piero Coppola; and one on March 12 conducted by Franz Ruhlmann.

let are very accurate, despite your temperature of 39 degrees [102° F] when you were looking at it. Yes, it is written in the manner of *Prodigal Son*, but in a somewhat softer and more profound style. The plot of *On the Dnepr* is insignificant: when I was working it out with Lifar, we at first had the idea to build a strong choreographic and musical skeleton, and proceeded from the basis of a softly lyrical mood, punctuated by sudden bursts of energy. That's how we intended to achieve a sense of proportion. That's why separate numbers will have formal titles, such as Men's Dance, Women's Variation, *pas de deux,* and so on. [. . .]

I send you a big hug. I await your music with great interest: I have always liked the Sinfonietta, and the First Symphony is as dear to me as a memory of youth. Get better fast and write.

Yours S. Prkfv

November 9, 1931
5, RUE VALENTIN HAÜY, PARIS XV

Dear Nikolai Yakovlevich,

[. . .] The Grand Opéra has finally started rehearsing my ballet. So as to confirm your tendency to think that anyone who spends a few years outside Russia becomes illiterate in Russian, the ballet will be called *On the Dnepr* (*Na Dnepre*). This title was chosen not, however, because *At the Dnepr* (*U Dnepra*) sounds un-Russian, but because the people at the Opéra found *Sur le Borysthène* more pleasing to the ear than *Au Borysthène*. And although I find *At the Dnepr* (*U Dnepra*) more appealing, I decided to yield to the authority of the Opéra and let them have it their way. [. . .]

Stravinsky's Violin Concerto has been published, and it is cleverly done, but somehow rather dry; I'll send it to you anyway. I welcome your favorable inclination to two-hand piano arrangements. If any foreign editions interest you then let me know and I'll send them to you with pleasure.

I send you a big hug and hope that your health has been completed restored. Warmest greetings from my wife, and also to Valentina Yakovlevna.

Yours S. Prkfv

December 19, 1931
5, RUE VALENTIN HAÜY, PARIS XV

Dear Nikolai Yakovlevich,

Time goes by so quickly that I had hardly noticed that a whole month had flown by since I received your last letter. During the interval I sent you the piano score of the Sinfonietta and Stravinsky's Violin Concerto. The latter was performed in Paris for the first time three days ago. Of course, as is always the case with Stravinsky's things, there was a great deal that was interesting in it. At the same time, I was left with a feeling of emptiness in my soul, and annoyance at the lack of material—or at the difficuty of deciphering the material. The first movement sounds intriguing; but the theme from Tchaikovsky's Fourth Symphony intrudes rather unexpectedly. The second movement goes much faster than you might think from its title—"Aria." I don't especially like the marching theme, but the pizzicato in the strings in the middle of the movement, and the restrained chords in the transition to the reprise, sound very effective. The third movement is the least successful, boring and rather turbid; the ornamented style of the melody is irritating. The finale is lively but unfortunately the entire coda imitates *Rite of Spring*; Stravinsky is very good at coming up with endings, so one might have hoped that he would think of something new. Lourié tried to prove that the thematic material in the fourth movement sounds like Prokofiev, but I didn't think so.

The other new item was the suite from the ballet *Rebus* by Markevich, Diaghilev's latest discovery;[188] Diaghilev was working with Markevich on *Rebus* before he died. I think that it would have turned out to be better-proportioned with more experienced guidance. In his composing, Markevich is following Hindemith's lead. He has definite abilities, but the successful moments still drown in waves of "Beckmesser-ism," which is also so typical of many of Hindemith's works.

[. . .] I have been spending a lot of time lately correcting proofs, but meanwhile I've also nearly finished orchestrating the suite from *The Gambler* and have finished the Sonatina. I've temporarily put the latter aside, since I'm not sure if it has turned out to be worthy of an opus number.[189]

I send you a big hug. Lina Ivanovna sends her warmest greetings.

Yours S. Prkfv

---

188. The Suite from *Rebus* by Igor Markevich, composed in 1931, was first performed in Paris on December 15, 1931, with the composer conducting.
189. The Piano Sonatina No. 1 in E Minor, along with Sonatina No. 2 in G Major, received the opus number 54.

January 11, 1932
PRAGUE

Dear Nikolai Yakovlevich,

Today Malko and I are performing the Third Concerto, and then he will do the *Scythian*. We think of you constantly. When I return to Paris I'll write you in detail, and I'll also send you Ravel's concerto (the two-hand one, not the one-hand one), which has just been published.[190]

I send you a hug.

Yours S. Prkfv

January 25, 1932
5, RUE VALENTIN HAÜY, PARIS XV

Dear Nikolai Yakovlevich,

[. . .] After returning from Prague I performed here with the Third Concerto, and then repeated the andante from the Quartet—rearranged for string orchestra—which had been played in the autumn. Besides that, a local conductor conducted the first Paris performance of the Sinfonietta, whose full score and parts have just been published.[191] A mediocre performance notwithstanding, the Sinfonietta sounded nice and found favor with the audience. I hope that it will now partially displace the "Classical" Symphony, which has been played too much lately. [. . .]

Did you receive the two packages with the music, and how did you like Ravel's concerto? He has announced that when he was composing it, he intended to resurrect the glorious tradition of Mozart and Saint-Saëns, particularly the virtuoso treatment of the solo instrument. But first of all, these two composers were themselves guilty of some miscalculations in that regard, and secondly, Ravel wasn't pulling the wool over anyone's eyes with that announcement, since it was well known that he originally conceived his concerto for his own modest abilities as a soloist, but along the way he decided that he wouldn't play it. After that, he started to make the piano part more difficult. As a result, the writing for the piano is very fragile, but of course the piano and orchestra combine to create such exquisite sonorities that if you didn't look at the score, it would seem that the piano part was really a serious one. At its first perfor-

---

190. Ravel composed his Piano Concerto in G Major in 1929–31; it was first performed in Paris January 14, 1932, with the composer conducting.

191. Piero Coppola conducted the Sinfonietta in a concert in Paris on January 23, 1932.

mance the concerto had a phenomenal success. It was one of the few cases in Paris when the hall was so full that people had to be turned away. By the way, I found it amusing that the theme at the top of the fifth page smacks of Medtner, and that page 20 is pure Rachmaninoff (this impression is further strengthened by the orchestral sonority).

Another new item was Milhaud's opera *Maximilian*, which turned out to be a complete dramatic and musical flop.[192] I cannot remember such unanimous disapproval. I'm not a big fan of Milhaud, but he does come up with interesting discoveries, although they emerge from his head rather than from a strong musical sense. But there was none of that here: just some kind of flat tire.

And finally, I heard Honegger's symphony—although actually it's not new, since Koussevitsky played it in Boston 18 months ago already.[193] In its finale something very nice suddenly appears, similar to his Cello Concerto, but there are boring pages, and the beginning of the finale is frankly taken from Stravinsky's *Pulcinella*. [. . .]

I send you a big hug. Lina Ivanovna sends warmest greetings to you and to Valentina Yakovlevna, as do I.

Yours S. Prkfv

March 18, 1932
5, RUE VALENTIN HAÜY, PARIS XV

Dear Nikolai Yakovlevich,

[. . .] In Paris recently both Rachmaninoff and Medtner gave piano recitals: the former with a big audience and lots of "tra-la-la," the latter modestly. Rachmaninoff played five ballades by Grieg, Liszt, Chopin, and two by Brahms.[194] He played with incredible perfection and brilliance, but dryly; it made you wonder why he had bothered to choose such a romantic program. There was also a new piece by the pianist himself—rather lengthy variations on a theme of Corelli, somewhat trite, fine but not done with much creativity—in short, a textbook exercise.[195] But at the end, after a technical coda *à grand spectacle*, when it seems that everything is all over, suddenly a lyrical extension appears, some-

---

192. The opera *Maximilian* by Darius Milhaud (1892–1974) was composed in 1930 and first staged at the Grand Opéra in Paris on January 4, 1932.
193. The Symphony No. 1 by Arthur Honegger was composed in 1929–30 and first performed in Boston on February 13, 1931, under Koussevitsky.
194. Rachmaninoff gave his recital in Paris on March 10, 1932.
195. Rachmaninoff composed the *Variations on a Theme of Corelli*, op. 42, in 1931, and gave the premiere himself in New York on November 7, 1931.

thing like a second coda—reminiscences of Rachmaninoff's fine old secondary themes. It was as if the recollection suddenly flared up in his dried-up brain that once upon a time he was also a talented melodist.

Medtner's playing left a great deal to be desired.[196] In the technical sense he was irreproachable, but the sound was tedious. Perhaps he did not take into account that the piano had a harsh sound and that the hall was small. Medtner played only his own compositions, two-thirds of them new. It was such dried-up old stuff, so archaic, so thematically and harmonically impoverished, that it seemed that the person sitting in front of me had suddenly gone mad, and having lost his sense of time, was persisting in writing in the style of Karamzin. Even his compositional technique, so celebrated in its time, has degenerated into a rechewing of the same old devices. His fairy tales ("Cinderella" and "Ivan the Fool") came out as nothing more than witticisms uttered by a general.[197] The last of the new pieces was a sonata ("The Stormcloud"), op. 53, no. 2, but I have to admit that I cannot find a thing to say about it. In contrast, the opuses played at the end of the program and for encores, from the prewar period, have not lost their appeal. [. . .]

By the way, a fugue starts in the middle of "The Stormcloud" Sonata, which then turns at midstream into conventional piano technique. I couldn't restrain myself and asked Glazunov, who was sitting next to me, "Aleksandr Konstantinovich, is that an authentic fugue, or just something close?" Glazunov diplomatically muttered something about how he had heard two fugal entrances. The matter was pursued no further. Since he was living outside the city, and I had a car, I offered to take him home after the concert. It was really a colorful event when he crawled into the automobile: he tried to get in front first, then backwards, then head first, and then feet first—it looked like what might have happened if you or I tried to sit down in an upright piano. When at last we were on our way and had reached his house, Glazunov suddenly said, "You know, there really wasn't any fugue at all." So, despite everything else that was going on, he had been reflecting seriously for an entire hour on this question and, in the end, his sense of fairness overcame his sense of diplomacy.

Last Saturday was the premiere of *Four Portraits from "The Gambler."*[198] It

196. Medtner's recital was on March 3, 1932.
197. Medtner's Six Fairy Tales for Piano, op. 51, were composed in 1928 and are "Dedicated to Cinderella and Ivan the Fool."
198. The performance took place in Paris on March 12, 1932, with Franz Ruhlmann conducting.

seems that the piece is a success, and after a few minor adjustments and the redoing of the end of "Polina," it can be published. My method of assembling a portrayal of a particular character from the entire opera and then using this material to construct independent symphonic *morceaux* turned out to be successful. [. . .]

I send you a big hug and hope that with the coming of spring all your ailments will disappear. Tell Derzhanovsky that he was kind enough to force me to write to the Mikhailovsky Theater,[199] but that they have not replied.

Yours S. Prkfv

April 16, 1932
LONDON

Dear Nik Yakovlevich,

On the reverse is the interior of the airplane on which I flew here from Paris. Before leaving I sent you Stravinsky's symphony with chorus.[200] After returning to Paris I'll write you in more detail. I send you a hug.

S. Prkfv

May 12, 1932
5, RUE VALENTIN HAÜY, PARIS XV

Dear Nikolai Yakovlevich,

[. . .] The rumors about my impending arrival in Moscow are based on my correspondence with certain individuals at Narkompros, which is being conducted officially through the embassy in Paris. My work would be something in the nature of looking over the compositions of the graduating class of theoreticians; in order to do this, I would come in the autumn for several weeks and then for the same period in the spring, to look over the new works that had resulted from my first consultation with them.[201] The plan hinges on whether those in charge would agree to my traveling back and forth, but I think that the students would get some benefit from it. Of course, I would never have considered such a project before, since you were cultivating the tender minds of the

---

199. This opera theater in Leningrad was also known as the Maly Opera.

200. Prokofiev is referring to Stravinsky's *Symphony of Psalms*.

201. Upon the invitation of the director of the Moscow Conservatory, Prokofiev was invited to be a professor-consultant in the Composition Department. He worked in this capacity from October 27, 1933, through December 1937, giving consultations to various students.

young composers: you have more experience and more patience in this sphere. But after you wrote me about your departure from the conservatory, this plan began to seem feasible. I am now following all changes on the musical front with interest. [. . .]

I send you a big hug. I am very happy that in the end you feel satisfied with your new symphonies, since you were doing a lot of moaning at the beginning, although I pretended to believe it only out of courtesy. I send you another hug.

Yours S. Prkfv

June 11, 1932
5, RUE VALENTIN HAÜY, PARIS XV

Dear Nikolai Yakovlevich,

I received your letter of May 18, and now I'm awaiting your description of the first performance of your Twelfth Symphony. When a symphonic piece is recorded, it is the publisher who usually signs a contract upon releasing the material to be recorded. Besides that, the composer should be a member of the organization that protects his rights in such cases. There are such organizations in Berlin (Amre) and in Paris (Edifo).

Actually, the income received by yours truly from recordings is insignificant, and would become significant only if they were to be sold in tens of thousands of copies. Among my works, the "Classical" Symphony has been well recorded, and the Suite from *Oranges* has been done pretty well. At the end of June I will go to London to record the Third Concerto.[202] This is a new emotion for me, since I have not yet ever played for the gramophone, and this is a big piece, and with orchestra to boot. Just think—I can't sneeze or mess up!

If my planned teaching engagement in Moscow doesn't work out, I am still saving the time from November 15 to December 5 for the USSR. What do you think, couldn't I play in Moscow and Leningrad my new *Music for Piano and Orchestra*, and who could set that up for me?[203] Or perhaps you could drop a hint about this to someone, and then they could write me? I could also bring with me some other orchestral scores. As for the score of Ravel's concerto, I will try (if the occasion presents itself) to speak with the author himself. Durand

---

202. Prokofiev recorded his Third Piano Concerto with the London Symphony Orchestra, conducted by Piero Coppola.

203. Prokofiev is referring to what eventually he called his Piano Concerto No. 5, op. 55, which was first performed in Berlin on October 31, 1932, with the composer as soloist and Wilhelm Furtwängler conducting.

(the publisher of this piece) would probably demand payment in foreign currency, and a deposit, but if Ravel would like his concerto to be performed in Moscow, the whole matter could progress more smoothly. But I'm not sure if Ravel is in Paris at the moment. [. . .]

Did you receive the corrected proofs of my sonatinas, which were sent to you four days ago? I beg you not to find any mistakes, because it's too late to correct them—the plates have already gone to press. I sent you the proofs first of all because I was impatient to know your opinion, and second because printing often drags out for three weeks here, and I was afraid that by that time you would go off somewhere for the summer, to a piano-less place.

I send you a big hug. Write me about your Twelfth.

Yours S. Prkfv

July 8, 1932
SARK

Dear Nik Yak,

I'm writing you from a fairy-tale kingdom—yes, there are still such places in the wide world. It's a tiny little island in La Manche [the Channel], a protectorate of England, but with its own queen who reigns over 600 subjects and resides in the palace depicted on the other side of this postcard, which is guarded by six cannon. That's how it was in the sixteenth century, and that's how it has remained up until now, owing to some misunderstanding. It's a picturesque islet, the climate is mild, and the numerous tourists soften its medieval character.

I send you a hug. Tomorrow I'm heading back to Paris.

Yours S. Prkfv

July 27, 1932
5, RUE VALENTIN HAÜY, PARIS XV

Dear Nikolai Yakovlevich,

I received both of your certified letters, of June 18 and July 20, and also the postcard. Thanks for your interesting analysis of my sonatinas. [. . .] Why did you come down so hard on me for my style: "lenten in its verticality." But after all that's why they are called sonatinas, because they are one-story compositions! How strange that Saradzhev, who was once a lively fellow, is critical of my new way of composing. And Asafiev also writes: "the lyricization of your recent music is not held in high esteem here." So what's going on? After all, the melodic impulse reaches the soul easiest of all, and the formal design is extremely accessible . . .

So explain to me the reasons for their opposition. [. . .]

You can't imagine what sort of crisis there is now here among all the music publishers. I have become a member of the permanent jury of a new chamber music society in Paris, Triton, which will inaugurate its activity beginning in the autumn; I have also been invited to recommend things for another similar organization, Serenade. [. . .]

That Coates is always straining at the bit—even in old age he will push all the tempi through at breakneck speed. I am disturbed at the way he worked over your Twelfth Symphony. In London recently he recorded the entire *Steel Gallop* for the gramophone, but took such absurdly fast tempi in certain parts that I don't really know what sort of music this record will produce. Actually, I'm going to talk with London today and ask them to put *Steel Gallop* on sale not in complete form, but cutting out the parts that he took too fast. [. . .]

My arrival in the USSR is becoming increasingly evident, but as you might have guessed, it is getting briefer and briefer: I'm playing in Warsaw on November 18 and 19, I'll arrive in Moscow on the 21st, but I'll have to leave around December 5, since I have a symphonic concert in Paris on the 11th, and then America. Concertizing has replaced the original teaching purpose of the trip, although I will try not to take on too much; I'll plan to play once or twice in Moscow and the same in Leningrad.[204] How I'd like it if one of your symphonies was to be performed during my visit! Your news about the change in the attitude of the Proletarian Musicians towards me is very provocative, as well as their hopes for the "beneficial effect" of my upcoming trip. It's hard for me to judge from here, but from the little evidence that I can gather, it seems that of course they have the right to exercise influence, but on the condition that they straighten out their conduct a bit.

I send you a big hug. It seems that we will soon be departing for the south, but you can still write me in Paris, since both regular and certified mail will be forwarded to me regularly.

Yours S. Prkfv

---

204. On November 25 and 26 and December 5, 1932, Nikolai Golovanov conducted symphonic concerts of Prokofiev's music in Moscow. These included the Soviet premieres of *Four Portraits and the Dénouement from "The Gambler"* and the Piano Concerto No. 5 (with Prokofiev as soloist). Vladimir Dranishnikov conducted a concert of Prokofiev's music in Leningrad on December 1. There were also several concerts of his chamber music in both cities.

October 5, 1932
MAISON SADOUL, SAINTE MAXIME (VAR), FRANCE

Dear Nikolai Yakovlevich,

Your analysis of the devices I use in laying out my music is probably correct. When you become infatuated with the search for a new melodic style and for a new simplicity, you can begin to forget how far you have drifted from shore. If this process really does help you to discover a new language, then that is good; if you fall into sterility and mannerisms, then you're finished. So in this regard your letter is a good reminder: you can come up with something new, but you cannot lose the sense of vital momentum. [. . .][205]

We have spent two months on the Mediterranean coast, finding refuge in the south from the rains which have poured upon France in recent summers. It has not been hot, and the swimming excellent; I have gotten somewhat better at swimming, although to tell the truth, not by much. Much of my time has been taken up with correcting the proofs of the full score and parts for the *Portraits* from *The Gambler*. [. . .] No less time has gone to the memorization of my new concerto, which (out of indulgence for your difficult character) I finally have labeled my Fifth Concerto; I crossed out the title *Music for Piano and Orchestra*, although I assure you that it was not Hindemith who came up with the idea of calling music "music"—just take a look at Mozart's *Kleine Nachtmusik*. And so as to annoy you completely with my "lenten vertical style," I have written a sonata for two violins, which has hardly any double stops or chords.[206] When they play it in Moscow at my chamber concert, you'll have to leave the hall.

I'm very happy that Derzhanovsky is undertaking so much frantic activity, and that he is the one I'm corresponding with about the details of my Moscow concerts. Mosfil [Moscow Philharmonic Society] has also sent me an invitation, but I replied that I am already conducting negotiations with the City Committee for Composers. The only problem is that my visit is now beginning to assume a rather lightning-like quality, if you start thinking about all the things I'm supposed to do in the course of a few days. So I'm already starting to dream

205. Prokofiev was responding to Miaskovsky's letter of September 7, 1932, in which he wrote: "If I were to try to sum it up, I would say that the style of your music has become more intellectual. You don't give yourself up to the creative flow so much as you consciously are trying to force it into a specific and, at first glance, more narrow channel."

206. Prokofiev wrote the Sonata in C Major for Two Violins, op. 56, in 1932. It was performed in Moscow on November 27, 1932.

about a second trip in April, when I could take a longer look around and have the chance to do some more tranquil listening. In fact, the time has come to make more frequent visits, and for longer periods.

I send you a hug. I will await your letter in Paris, where I should arrive around the 15th; I also anxiously await your Quartet.

Yours S. Prkfv

October 28, 1932
COPENHAGEN

Dear Nik Yak,

Yesterday I played the Third Concerto here with Malko, but my mind was full of the Fifth—Berlin two days from now. Thanks so much for your Twelfth Symphony, but it arrived right before my departure so I hardly had any time to look it over. I send you a hug. See you very soon.

S.P.

December 21, 1932
ABOARD THE LINER EUROPE

Dear Nik Yak,

I'm writing you in the middle of the ocean, and will drop you a card in New York. We had been rolling a bit en route, but now Neptune has calmed down and the liner is just trembling slightly from the engines, doing their 52 kilometers per hour.

Warmest greetings for the New Year from S. Prkfv.

February 18, 1933
5, RUE VALENTIN HAÜY, PARIS XV

Dear Nikolai Yakovlevich,

Upon my return from America it made me very happy to find your letter. You have turned out to be the only respectable person among the Muscovites—the rest have remained silent. I haven't received any scores in exchange for the rental of my compositions, and I haven't received any chamber pieces by Soviet composers to be performed abroad. It's true that when we were all gathered at Shebalin's[207] place and I gave my little speech about exchanging music, the composers made a brilliant display of restraint, fearing to lose their dignity. But

207. Vissarion Shebalin (1902–63) was a prominent Soviet composer and pedagogue. He was director of the Moscow Conservatory 1942–48.

I'm still convinced that such an exchange would be useful to them, adding foreign weight to the local weight they already have, and besides, it would open the gates to the flow of chamber music literature from abroad. [. . .] By the way, I have established contacts in Boston, New York, and Chicago, and have even brought a whole bunch of American music for small ensemble, which I'll bring with me when I come to Moscow in April.

By the way, as far as April is concerned: they should really write me from Moscow to tell me if they want me to teach at the conservatories (in Moscow and Leningrad), and if they want me for symphonic concerts.[208] Because after all if they have forgotten about my idea of a music exchange, then won't they also forget about me elsewhere? It's too bad that because no music was received in exchange for the use of the scores of my works (the ones I had made in November), I cannot bring in April either my Third Symphony, or the Divertissement, or anything else. [. . .]

In New York I heard Shostakovich's Third Symphony, but it disappointed me to a certain extent: it's fragmentary, and the melodic line is not interesting enough to support the insistent two-voice polyphony. [. . .][209]

Borysthène did not enjoy success in Paris, although a number of musicians (Milhaud, Stravinsky, Rieti, and others) came to its defense. I have made a suite out of it, which I will try to have performed here in the near future so as to rehabilitate this unfairly rejected opus.[210] At the same time, the Sonata for Two Violins is reaping laurels, and after several good performances I can now see how primitively it was played in Moscow and Leningrad.[211] [. . .]

How's your Eleventh Symphony? Is your dissatisfaction with it the result of coquettishness, or did you really see some shortcomings in it? I didn't see any when I heard it in an eight-hand piano arrangement.

I send you a big hug and await your letters.

Yours S. Prkfv

---

208. Prokofiev appeared in four concerts devoted to his music in April 1933, two in Moscow and two in Leningrad.

209. The Symphony No. 3 of Dmitri Shostakovich bears the title "First of May" and is scored for chorus and orchestra, using texts by the Soviet poet Semen Kirsanov (1906–72). It was composed in 1929.

210. *On the Dnepr* had its premiere at the Opéra in Paris on December 16, 1932. Prokofiev turned the score into a suite, op. 51-bis, in 1933.

211. The Paris performance, on December 16, 1932, was given by Samuel Dushkin and Robert Soëtens. The Moscow performance was given by Dmitri Tsyganov and Vasily Shirinsky, and the Leningrad performance by S. Panfilov and Pavel Sergeev.

March 28, 1933
5, RUE VALENTIN HAÜY, PARIS XV

Dear Nikolai Yakovlevich,

I was happy to get your letter of March 8, and glad to learn that you are getting better: the slight peevishness of the letter testifies to the fact that your recovery is proceeding successfully.

As far as your defense of "square" structure in musical compositions goes, I will have to have "a very serious conversation" with you when I arrive. The problem started with Liszt, and the Mighty Handful[212] caught the illness from him, so the current generation is overcoming the mistakes of its fathers and grandfathers. If you don't always appreciate (as you so delicately put it) my asymmetry, then this means that I was not successful in creating the form for these particular compositions. [. . .]

In criticizing Paichadze,[213] you forget that the conditions prevailing in foreign music publishing houses are entirely different from those that prevail in the Soviet market. Paichadze is in his own way correct when he says that it's not enough merely to publish something—people also have to buy it. In other words, something that is published but goes unsold is no better than something that remains unpublished; except for a few copies distributed by the composer to friends, it won't reach an audience. People used to play four-hand piano arrangements, but now they buy gramophone records.

It seems that I'll play on the 11th in Prague, in which case I'll be in Moscow on the 14th for a day or two and then immediately go off to Leningrad, which is where (judging from what Atovmyan[214] says) my concerts will begin. [. . .]

I have found one more article about the performance of your Fourth Symphony in Paris, which I am enclosing. So for now I squeeze your hand hard and rejoice at the prospect of seeing you soon. Be a good fellow and recover completely by then. [. . .]

Yours S. Prkfv

---

212. The Mighty Handful was a group of St. Petersburg composers championed by the critic Vladimir Stasov. Its founders, César Cui and Mily Balakirev, were joined by Borodin, Rimsky-Korsakov, and Mussorgsky.

213. Gavriil Paichadze was director of the Editions Russes de Musique in Paris.

214. Levon Atovmyan (1901–73) was a Soviet composer and concert organizer.

December 23, 1933
5, RUE VALENTIN HAÜY, PARIS XV

Dear Nikolai Yakovlevich,

From the postcard I sent you from Rome you already know how attentively they treated our program there: they rehearsed for 5 days, each day at 12 and at 8, ten rehearsals altogether, each 2 hours and 15 minutes long.[215] You can't find such luxury anywhere anymore. [. . .] The audience responded very well to your Sinfonietta; the critics were a bit surprised that it was so accessible. [. . .]

There's not much good to report about concert life in Paris. There are still seven orchestras, and they continue to consume each other, resulting in impotence and a total lack of rehearsals. The situation is so bad that I don't even want to give any of them my *Symphonic Song*,[216] so that it won't be murdered. I heard Glazunov's saxophone quartet.[217] To my amazement, the harmonic style prevailed over the contrapuntal: the endless four-part chorale became tedious. At the same time, it was entirely obvious that with a stronger contrapuntal structure and with a greater attention to color and certain other devices, a saxophone ensemble has every right to exist and can even stand up quite well in a serious piece of music. The quartet was performed at a concert given at the "Russian" Conservatory here; besides the quartet, the program included my pieces and a few songs by Soviet composers, but they were not performed because the singer was ill. Medtner, an honorary professor of the conservatory, sent an indignant letter that in view of the proximity of the wreckers of culture to Glazunov's noble piece, he was forced to resign his honorary status.

I also went to a chamber concert of new French pieces, but Sauguet's Quintet, and Poulenc's Sextet—both for mixed ensemble—turned out to be completely worthless. Only in a suite by Milhaud did a very pleasant Elegy turn up.

I send you a big hug. I'm working on music for the production at Tairov's theater; I find it impossible to turn it out in a slapdash fashion, just tossing it off, so it's taking an enormous amount of time.[218]

Yours S. Prkfv

215. On December 10, 1933, in Rome, Bernardino Molinari conducted a program of contemporary Russian music that included Miaskovsky's Sinfonietta for String Orchestra, op. 32, no. 2, and Prokofiev's Third Symphony and Fifth Piano Concerto (with Prokofiev as soloist).

216. Prokofiev composed the *Symphonic Song* for large orchestra, op. 57, in 1933.

217. Glazunov wrote his Quartet in B Major for Four Saxophones, op. 109, in 1932. It was first performed in Paris on December 14, 1933.

218. Prokofiev was writing incidental music for a production called *Egyptian Nights* at

January 15, 1934
5, RUE VALENTIN HAÜY, PARIS XV

Dear Nikolai Yakovlevich,

I'm taking advantage of my two-day return to Paris to answer your letter of January 1, which I received in Milan.

Paris makes somewhat different demands on Soviet music than Moscow does. Moscow demands cheerfulness above all; Paris has believed in Soviet cheerfulness for a long time already, but often wonders if this cheerfulness conceals a lack of serious content. You have to forgive the French for this, because their acquaintance with Soviet music began with Mosolov's *Iron Foundry*.[219] So that's why your Thirteenth Symphony would be just the thing to fill in the gap. It would not be a good idea to perform Shostakovich's *Bolt* in Paris, since it is akin to decadent western trends—something that Ansermet already noticed during his stay in Moscow.[220] From Shostakovich, therefore, I would prefer either the Third Symphony or the Piano Concerto. [. . .]

I send you a big hug. Warmest greetings from Lina Ivanovna.

Yours S. Prkfv

March 12, 1934
5, RUE VALENTIN HAÜY, PARIS XV

Dear Nikolai Yakovlevich,

[. . .] I received the letter from Tairov: *Egyptian Nights* has been delayed and is unlikely to be staged even by April. [. . .] I am very glad because that means I will get to the rehearsals; theater orchestras most often play badly and besides that, it's a pretty good piece; now I'll have the time to fix it up. I will arrive in Moscow around April 8th or 9th. [. . .] I have not been able to figure out if Shostakovich can be delivered to Paris for his concert there at the end of April. It would be best to have the composer himself as the soloist, but if that's not

---

Aleksandr Tairov's Chamber Theater in Moscow. The play combined elements of Shaw's *Caesar and Cleopatra*, Pushkin's *Egyptian Nights*, and Shakespeare's *Antony and Cleopatra*. The production had its premiere on December 14, 1934. The famous Soviet actress Alissa Koonen took the role of Cleopatra.

219. *Iron Foundry, Music of Machines*, op. 19, by Aleksandr Mosolov (1900–1973) was composed in 1927 as part of the suite from his ballet *Steel*. It is one of the most famous examples of the glorification of industry and machinery in Soviet music and culture.

220. Shostakovich wrote his ballet *Bolt* in 1930–31; it was later attacked as anti-Soviet.

possible, then you should send the music immediately so that a local pianist will have time to learn it. [. . .]

I'll be leaving Paris during the last days of March, going first to Prague, then to Warsaw. I'll be in Warsaw April 5 or 6 and will stay in the Hotel Europe—in case you have to send me any special messages from Moscow.

I send you a big hug.

Yours S. Prkfv

May 1, 1934
ODESSA

Dear Nik Yak,

Thanks so much for forwarding to me the letter from home: it was long and full of all sorts of stuffing: photos of the children, and so on. It seems that everything at home is fine.[221] Having departed Kharkov and Kiev, I am enjoying the sun and the sea of Odessa and am spending my time beating the manager of the local Philharmonic Society at chess.

I send you a hug.

Yours S. Prkfv

I will be in Leningrad from the 6th to the 13th, and in Moscow, most likely, on the 14th. What you see on the front of the card is not an Oriental chapel but the hall where I'll be playing.

July 20, 1934
5, RUE VALENTIN HAÜY, PARIS XV

Dear Nikolai Yakovlevich,

I went abroad rather unexpectedly, after sending you a bale of scores. Before my departure I got a letter from Asafiev in which he praised your Fifteenth Symphony, which made me very indignant because of your treachery. Didn't you sit across from me on your sofa at the end of June and look at me with an honest expression, as if you weren't composing anything at all? I know that was to pay me back for my reaction to the finale of your Fourteenth Symphony; Valentina Yakovlevna was right when she explained that you wear a beard so you can hide your mean lips and the vengeful lines around them.

---

221. As was often the case during the 1930s when Prokofiev was traveling with increasing frequency to Russia, his family had stayed behind in Paris.

Since my return to Paris I've been living quietly and have not yet decided where to go from here. In any case, your letters will be forwarded to me. [. . .]

Please give my warmest greetings to Valentina Yakovlevna, along with my thanks for forwarding Lina Ivanovna's letter; it reached me en route and was waiting for me in Paris. I send you a hug.

Yours S. Prkfv

I'm playing over the piano score of *Perséphone*; there's much that's interesting in it, but overall it's harsh and difficult.[222]

September 17, 1934
St. Maxime

Dear Nik Yak,

[. . .] I have just finished the suite from *Egyptian Nights* and have no idea how they could have broadcast some of the music on the radio in Moscow.[223] What asses they are if they broadcast some musical fragments from the production, and Tairov isn't so bright either if he gave the music to them without asking me. He could at least have telephoned me. Because surely you know that there is now a phone link with France, which is quite inexpensive from the USSR—7 rubles—but expensive from France—100 francs. When I get back to Paris I will definitely be expecting a telephone call from you: my number is Ségur 88–60. [. . .]

You are too hard on *Perséphone*—it makes a better impression when you hear it. On my way here I stopped in to see Strav[insky]; he is writing a concerto for two pianos and a book about himself. Nouvel is writing a book about Diaghilev in response to the slanderous book written by Nijinsky's wife.[224] Petya[225] is now staying with us, working on developing his tenor, singing *Oedipus* and *Perséphone*; he sends you greetings, and I send you a hug.

Write me in Paris, where I will be arriving sometime between the 25th and the 27th.

Yours S. Prkfv

---

222. Prokofiev is referring to Stravinsky's *Perséphone*, a melodrama in three tableaux, composed in 1933–34.
223. Prokofiev used the music he had written for Tairov's production of *Egyptian Nights* in a suite, op. 61, composed in 1934.
224. Nouvel's book is *Diaghileff, His Artistic and Private Life*, by Arnold Haskell in collaboration with Walter Nouvel (London: Victor Gollancz, 1935). Nijinsky's wife, Romola Nijinsky, had written *Nijinsky* (London: Victor Gollancz, 1933).
225. Pyotr Souvchinsky.

October 8, 1934
5, RUE VALENTIN HAÜY, PARIS XV

Dear Nikolai Yakovlevich,

[. . .] You wrote that the Moscow Philharmonic Society is complaining that I have been giving all my new music to the radio. But after all, both suites—*Kije* and *The Egyptian Nights*—were composed on a commission from the radio.[226] If the Philharmonic wants premieres, then they can have the suite from *On the Dnepr* or the Overture op. 42. Perhaps you could be so kind as to tell them that. But if they want me to bring some additional music, then they have to let me know before the 25th. Besides that, they have to program it so that it would be played during my stay. As far as the orchestral version of *Ugly Duckling* is concerned, there is a plan for Lina Ivanovna to sing it for the Moscow radio.[227] I do not currently have the Second Piano Concerto in my repertoire; as far as my appearance at the Philharmonic in the spring is concerned, that possibility is not yet excluded—we can talk about it when I arrive in November.

We were detained in the south until the beginning of October, so I have not been in touch with Parisian musical life. I leave for Amsterdam the day after tomorrow, and on the 19th I have agreed to conduct the Third Symphony in London, a prospect that strikes terror into me: I'll pull through somehow! Around the 25th I'll make my way first to Kovno, Revel [Tallinn], and so on, so that I can arrive around November 5 in Moscow.

I send you a hug. Write me in Paris.

Yours S. Prkfv

October 24, 1934
5, RUE VALENTIN HAÜY, PARIS XV

Dear Nikolai Yakovlevich,

[. . .] I plan to arrive in Moscow on the 6th by the Red Arrow Express. My itinerary: Revel-Leningrad-Moscow. I am bringing with me the scores you requested, although they are quite expensive—I am trying to get a discount.

On his way from Spain to France, Honegger flipped over along with his

226. On December 21, 1934, in Moscow, the suites *Lt. Kije* and *Egyptian Nights* were performed for the first time, on the radio.
227. Lina Llubera did sing *Ugly Duckling* on the radio in Moscow, in the version for voice and orchestra, but not until November 20, 1937, with Prokofiev conducting.

automobile, which then smashed into a tree. Honneger himself got off pretty easily, but his wife, the pianist Vaurabourg, was seriously injured. [. . .]

I send you a big hug.

Yours S. Prkfv

January 5, 1935
BUDAPEST

Dear Nik Yak,

I couldn't resist sending you this postcard, because of the [Franz Liszt] stamp. You just wait! If you keep on composing, you'll also reach the point where every postal worker will be flogging your face with postmarks. Here in Budapest I'm rehearsing the Third Concerto and *The Buffoon*; it's fun to conduct a real orchestra, which responds to each stroke of the baton like a fine piano does to the push of a finger.

I send you a hug, and wish you Happy New Year.

S. Prkfv

I spoke about your kindness in an interview.

January 24, 1935
5, RUE VALENTIN HAÜY, PARIS XV

Dear Nikolai Yakovlevich,

It took me longer than I planned to get to Paris, since my concert tour expanded a bit. For that reason I didn't get your letter of January 6 till the 21st and am now hurrying to thank you for sending the telegram from the Kiev Radio Theater. I will reply separately to them. [. . .]

Before my departure from Moscow Ostretsov[228] told me that he had been assigned to write a brochure about me. Unfortunately, I couldn't figure out who made the assignment: the Radio Committee or Muzsektor. I am very much opposed to the idea of Ostretsov undertaking this project, since apparently he understands little about my music and does not much like it. It would be much more sensible to assign the writing of the brochure to Asafiev or to Derzhanovsky. [. . .]

I send you a big hug. I really did escape the cold weather, but then in

---

228. Aleksandr Ostretsov (1903–64) was a Soviet music critic.

Yugoslavia the train got stuck in the snow, and after a 13-hour delay I had to rush directly from the station to the concert hall.

Yours

S. Prkfv

February 23, 1935

5, RUE VALENTIN HAÜY, PARIS XV

Dear Nikolai Yakovlevich,

[. . .] Koussevitsky performed your Sinfonietta along with excerpts from *The Buffoon* in Boston on January 25–26. I sent you the program a few days ago. I still haven't received any news as to how the Sinfonietta was received. [. . .]

As for my own work, I have composed hardly anything in recent days. I had to spend a lot of time cleaning up the orchestration of the *Overture on Hebrew Themes*, which dear Derzhanulkin left in a rather lamentable state. [. . .]

Another project was the recording of some gramophone records—a serious matter, since during the four minutes that the disc is recording you can't hit a single wrong note. As a result I had to whip the pieces I was recording into even more irreproachable shape than I would for a concert performance. I have already recorded *Visions fugitives*, the Sonatina-Pastorale, and several other pieces.[229] Tomorrow I'm going to record the Etude op. 52—that will take some sweat.

Rodzinski conducted *Lady Macbeth* in New York, but the reviews were mainly hostile.[230]

I send you a big hug, and plan to be in Moscow around March 12th or 13th.

Yours S. Prkfv

September 11, 1935

POLENOVO

Dear Nik Yak,

[. . .] I have finished the piano score of *Romeo* and have immediately plunged into orchestrating it.[231] For the moment I am maintaining a speed of

---

229. The other pieces included "*Suggestion diabolique,*" *Tales of an Old Grandmother,* and two gavottes.

230. This performance took place at the Metropolitan Opera on February 5, 1935, with Artur Rodzinski conducting.

231. Prokofiev was composing his ballet *Romeo and Juliet,* op. 64, while staying in the country at a sanitorium run by the Bolshoi Theater. The piano score was completed on September 8, 1935.

about 20 pages per day (that means that Lamm can produce about 20 pages in full score from what I'm doing each day), but it is difficult. The main thing is to avoid falling into "Asafievism," the path of least resistance. We were planing to arrive in Moscow on the 15th, but it seems we'll make it only by the 19th—so if any mail arrives for me, then please be so kind as to forward it here.

I send you a big hug.

S.

November 15, 1935
5, RUE VALENTIN HAÜY, PARIS XV

Dear Nikolai Yakovlevich,

I heard from Lina Ivanovna about the success of your Fifteenth Symphony.[232] I'm so sorry that I didn't hear it in its entirety—I liked the little waltz so much! Lina Ivanovna told me on the phone that she had recently been at your place and met Asafiev; then she started to relate the details but the telephone connection suddenly faded out and I couldn't make out what she was saying.

During my time in Paris I have not moved ahead in my own work, since I had to rehearse the Violin Concerto with Soëtens, and also learn with him the Debussy Sonata (for the Africans);[233] run around after visas and all sorts of other matters that have accumulated in Paris, and most of all, correct the sloppy work Derzhanovsky did in order to get *Kije* ready for publication. The children's pieces are ready to go on the market.[234] The Paris performance of the Violin Concerto has been postponed to February, so the premiere will take place in Madrid. [. . .]

I'm going to Spain tomorrow; you'll get some postcards from there with stamps for your collection. [. . .] I send you a hug. Write me at this address: Sociedad Daniel, 14 Los Madrazo, Madrid.

This address will be valid until December 1 and even for a little while longer.

Yours S. Prkfv

---

232. Miaskovsky's Fifteenth Symphony was performed for the first time in Moscow on October 28, 1935.

233. Prokofiev completed his Violin Concerto No. 2 in G Minor, op. 63, in 1935; Robert Soëtens gave the premiere in Madrid on December 1, 1935. He and Soëtens also played some sonatas together on a concert tour through Spain, Portugal, Morocco, Algeria, and Tunisia, including the Debussy Violin Sonata.

234. Prokofiev is referring to "Music for Children," Twelve Easy Pieces for Piano, op. 65.

November 22, 1935
SAN SEBASTIÁN [SPAIN]

Dear Nik Yak,

So far I have "done" three cities: Madrid, Barcelona and San Sebastián. All are very interesting, and the audience hasn't been listening so badly either. The Debussy sonata is coming out fine. [. . .] They played your Sinfonietta in Madrid in October with a small symphony orchestra, and the conductor, Franco, said that it was a success, and that he's planning to play the Lyric Concertino.

I send you a firm embrace.

S.P.

November 27, 1935
LISBON

Dear Nik Yak,

Portugal is a most appealing country, and they aren't even too afraid of new music in Lisbon. Besides that, it's warm and green on the street, and a bright sun is shining!

I send you a hug.

S. Prkfv

December 3, 1935
LE GRAND HÔTEL, FEZ

Fez—the name of the hats (would that be *feski* or *fezki* in Russian?) comes from the name of this city. It's no joke—the French call them *les fez*.

Dear Nik Yak,

Fez is an old Muslim city, 360 kilometers to the south of Gibraltar. But nearby a modern French city has grown up, which is where I am playing. [. . .]

I am also enclosing a program with a thematic analysis of Strav[insky]'s new concerto. There's no doubt that he put the piece together very well, but the themes are emaciated—they are not themes, but themelets.[235]

Africa is extremely fascinating—there's some special air and a special kind of light. The roads are excellent, with many cars and trolley buses, but right alongside them are Arabs in burnooses riding on donkeys, and untouched Arabian cities.

---

235. Prokofiev is referring to Stravinsky's Concerto for Two Solo Pianos, composed 1931–35.

So why, good sir, don't you write me? Lina Iv also has not written me a single letter in three weeks, she sent only two emaciated telegrams.

I send you a big hug. [. . .]

Yours S. Prkfv

The premiere of the Violin Concerto took place in Madrid on December 1. It gave me great pleasure, since it all sounded even better than I thought when I was orchestrating it, wilting from the heat in stuffy Baku. It seems the concerto is a success. The public reception was also excellent—the music somehow immediately reached the audience. Now I still plan to look it over again and to add a few details here and there.

December 16, 1935
ALGIERS

Dear Nik Yak,

My journey is coming to a close—I'm tired of playing the same thing over and over! But just imagine, my Quintet was performed not long ago in Algiers, and, they tell me, not even too badly—so there are some self-sacrificing performers and listeners out there, for whom it's worth the effort. But you know I really feel like getting back to Moscow—the time has come to pull my winter hat out of my trunk.

I squeeze your paw.

Yours S. Prkfrv

December 20, 1935
CARTHAGE

Dear Nik Yak,

I'm sending you a few razors from Carthage. Tunis, where my last concert took place, is not so interesting, but Carthage is very interesting—a few kilometers away is a most impressive spot where Hannibal lost his last battle, which led to the destruction of Carthage by the Romans. As a result, the ruins you see are mainly of Roman origin; all that's left of ancient Carthage are some kitchen utensils and graves.

I send you a hug.

S.P.

July 24, 1936
POLENOVO

Dear Nik Yak,

Thank you for forwarding my letters: I have received two parcels from you and just as many from Val Yak; please convey to her my heartfelt gratitude. I'm especially grateful to you for *P and W* and *QS*, although I didn't intend for *QS* to end up in your hands:[236] I can just imagine how they grumbled about that! In fact, it really is not one of my best opuses, but with the film it will probably come out all right. On the other hand, I hope to resurrect my reputation with *Onegin* (which I am now finishing); it has a lot of real material.[237]

So what are you up to? Is it as hot where you are as it is here in Polenovo—instead of fresh air, the forests have begun to emit a burning smell. Besides working, I'm playing tennis and chess, swimming and reading—Kuprin's stories.[238] Asafiev is here, but we have not had much contact.

I squeeze your little paw.

Yours S.P.

December 24, 1936
14, RUE DU DR. ROUX, PARIS XV

Dear Nik Yak,

I arrived in Brussels the morning of my concert. In the course of the day there were two rehearsals, so that we managed to correct a few things, but it left me nearly dead from fatigue. Then it was on to Bordeaux, Paris, Lausanne, and now I am en route to Prague—so it's not a very peaceful life.[239]

---

236. Prokofiev is referring to *Peter and the Wolf*, A Symphonic Fairy Tale for Children, op. 67, composed in 1936 for the Moscow Children's Musical Theater; and to his score for a film based on Pushkin's story "The Queen of Spades," directed by Mikhail Romm. The film was begun in 1936 but never completed.

237. Prokofiev was writing music for *Eugene Onegin*, op. 71, a dramatic adaptation of Pushkin's verse novel being prepared for production at the Moscow Chamber Theater by Tairov. The production was never staged, however.

238. Aleksandr Ivanovich Kuprin (1870–1938) was a writer of novels and short stories who emigrated to France after the Russian Revolution. He returned to the USSR in 1937 and died there a year later. His work dealt with social ills of his day.

239. Prokofiev conducted a concert of his works on the radio in Brussels on December 2, 1936; on this tour he was performing as conductor and pianist in both symphonic and chamber concerts of his works.

I heard some interesting music in Paris, including Str's Concerto for Two Pianos, with the composer as soloist.[240] It's not easy to grasp: lots of banged-out notes jumping on top of each other, but overall it's very interesting—I have to give it a second hearing. Now Strav has fallen from the heights of *Apollon* and *Perséphone* into the casino, and has completed a ballet on his own subject for an American commission: *Jeu de cartes* in four deals (instead of scenes).[241] I saw only a few pages in passing—it's very well done. Now he has gone off to America to conduct Mozart, Tchaikovsky's Third, and other things(!). I heard in a concert performance Milhaud's *Colomb*,[242] an opera-oratorio composed before *Maximilian*, and much more significant. It has a lot of choral, orchestral and dramatic-scenic inventiveness, and some pleasant melodic material here and there.

The Paris concert of my compositions went well, although there weren't enough rehearsals and as is the custom here, they hadn't completely learned the music.[243] But of course Wolff got the tempi better than Golova[nov],[244] and gave a more subtle performance (as much as could be obtained from 2½ rehearsals). Some Parisians liked the suite from *Romeo*; others heaved sighs of regret over the simplification of my style. In Brussels, to my amazement, they pulled off very well some of my most difficult things: *Seven, They Are Seven* and the *Ov for 17 Instruments*. When I conducted *Scyth* there, I once again came to realize just how monstrously Golova[nov] did it. It's not that I conducted so well; it simply became very clear how badly he conducted.

Right now I'm dashing off some lines about your Sixteenth, at the request of the Soviet embassy—so that it can be sent around to the musical magazines: a brief analysis, as is the custom here before the performance of a new piece. Szenkar's concert will take place here on January 9: your Sixteenth, my Overture op. 72, and Shostak's Concerto performed by a French pianist.[245]

---

240. The premiere of Stravinsky's Concerto for Two Solo Pianos took place in Paris on November 21, 1935; the soloists were Stravinsky and his son Sviatoslav-Soulima.

241. Prokofiev is referring to Stravinsky's ballet *Jeu de cartes* ("The Card Party"), a ballet in three deals, composed in 1936.

242. Milhaud's opera *Christophe Colomb* was composed in 1928.

243. The concert took place on December 19, 1936, in Paris and included a performance of the *Romeo and Juliet* Suite No. 1.

244. Prokofiev is referring to a performance of the *Romeo and Juliet* Suite No. 1 in Moscow on November 24, 1936 (the world premiere), conducted by Nicolai Golovanov. On the same program was the *Scythian Suite*.

245. Prokofiev had helped to organize this performance on January 9, 1937, in Paris; Eugene Szenkar conducted.

So far I have not been blessed with a letter from a single Muscovite. I hope that you will come to your senses—you know I have been selecting beautiful stamps for you. Until January 6 my address is the one given above, and then until February 9: C/o Haensel & Jones, 113 West 57th St., New York, N.Y., USA.

Lina Ivan[ovna] arrived safely and is now resting after her passport troubles. If a package addressed to you arrives with something to be given to my sons, you can call them and someone will come to pick it up. I send you a big hug. Warmest New Year's greetings to Valen Yakov and to you.

Yours S. Prkfv

Rachm[aninoff] really has composed a new symphony.[246] It was performed by Stokowski in New York in the composer's presence, and the public reaction was reserved. Medtner has not printed any new compositions except for a book (a boring one), which I will bring.[247]

January 12, 1937
[EN ROUTE]

Dear Nik Yak,

We got tossed around pretty badly, but now we have left that patch of rough water and are gliding as if upon a lake, as we approach New York, where I will drop this letter into the mail.[248]

Before leaving Paris (I departed on the 6th), I ran over for a few minutes to Szenkar's rehearsal and listened to how they were doing with your symphony. It gains very much upon repeated hearing, and I experienced real pleasure from the excerpts that I heard—which, by the way, sounded excellent. Your use of obviously "Tchaikovskyian" counterpoint in the third movement did lead my soul to grumble a bit; every educated person should refrain from such devices. The orchestra was playing with verve, just as should be the case at the third rehearsal, and even found some misprints in the printed parts. I left instructions to gather all the reviews that will appear after the performance, and I'll give them to you later.

---

246. Rachmaninoff composed his Symphony No. 3 in A Minor, op. 44, in 1935–36, and it was first performed by the Philadelphia Orchestra in Philadelphia on November 6, 1936, conducted by Stokowski.

247. Medtner had written a book, *The Muse and Fashion: A Defense of the Fundamentals of Musical Language*, published in Paris in 1935.

248. On this American tour, Prokofiev performed in Chicago, Boston, and Washington (at the Soviet embassy).

A concert is trying to peck its way out of the shell for Paris in mid-February, and they wanted a first performance of one of your pieces. I racked my brains to think of something and proposed the Lyric Concertino. I think it was the right choice, and the most important thing is that I have the score, which made the performance an immediate and real possibility.

Despite the ship's rolling and pitching, I have still managed to read the proofs of the full score of the Violin Concerto. And have you had a chance to see my Pushkin songs?[249] And perhaps if you have the chance, you could ask [. . .] if they are actually typesetting the things they gathered from me. Otherwise, I wouldn't be surprised to be met upon my return by a pleasant smile and the words: "Oh, yes, S.S., we are just about to set to work on your stuff."

I will be in America until February 10, and this is my address: S. Prokofieff, c/o Haensel & Jones, 113 West 57 St., New York, N.Y., USA.

After February 15 you can reach me in Paris at the Dr. Roux address. I plan to return to Moscow towards the end of February. [. . .]

I send you a big hug.

Yours S. Prkfv

January 29, 1938
Paris

Dear Nicolas-Jacob,

Uf—not a minute to catch my breath. We got to Paris just in time for the last rehearsal; since the preceding ones had been canceled, it lasted twice as long as usual, beginning at 8:30 A.M. and ending at 2 P.M. Somehow we managed to smooth out *Juliet*, the *Russian Overture,* and the First Piano Concerto (with me *au piano*). Then I lay down from 2 to 4, and then the concert took place at 4:30, a Saturday matinee. After the concert we had supper with Stravinsky, who told dirty jokes. It seems he hasn't yet written anything new for the moment. [. . .] After Paris (the next day) we go to Prague, from Prague back through Paris (for a day and a half) to London, where more serious rehearsals have been taking place, and with a first-class orchestra: *R & J, Cl* Symphony, and the Second Violin with Soëtens, who plays better than Fishman and takes more interest in what's going on in the orchestra, although he doesn't have even one-half of Fishman's tone.[250] The next day is a concert in the Soviet embassy, and the day

---

249. Prokofiev is referring to his Three Romances on words by Pushkin for voice and piano, op. 73, composed in 1936.

250. Boris Fishman (1906–65) had performed Prokofiev's Second Violin Concerto in Moscow on November 20, 1937, with the composer conducting.

after that, another at the English VOKS,[251] and the day after that, hurried packing of suitcases and catching the boat. I'm writing this in the train (two hours from the sea), which explains the scribbling.[252] [. . .]

I send you a big hug.

Yours S.˙P.

March 2, 1938
HOLLYWOOD

Dear NYaMushka,

I rejoiced turbulently over the receipt of your sweet little letterette. After all, I've been without news of the musical fields of the Soviet Union for one and a half months now. It took a long time to catch up with me, but I was the one to blame since I have wound up on the shores of the Pacific Ocean. Here we are eleven hours behind what the time is on the shores of the Moscow River—so that when it is 9 P.M. where you are, here it's only 10 A.M. [. . .]

After a series of concerts around America,[253] I have decided to stay a little longer here than I first planned, owing to three reasons: to conduct two concerts in Boston; several concerts of a political nature; and the unexpected interest which Hollywood has shown towards me.[254] Although you're probably chuckling a bit over the last reason for my delay in returning home, you should know that this is a very contemporary field with many diverse possibilities, and one that touches upon thousands of intriguing ideas. So this is the story: we will depart from America on March 30, arrive in Paris on April 4, spend about three days there, and will return to our native land—that is, to our apartment on Zemlyanoi val—around April 9.[255]

---

251. VOKS was the All-Union Society for Cultural Relations with Foreign Countries.
252. This was Prokofiev's last tour abroad; it took him through Europe and the United States.
253. Prokofiev's 1938 American tour included Detroit on February 11 (as conductor of the "Classical" Symphony and soloist in his First Piano Concerto); Denver on February 18 (same program); chamber concerts in New York on February 6 and Denver on February 20; piano recitals in Chicago on February 15 and Denver on February 21 and 23.
254. Prokofiev met with Walt Disney, who was very much interested in having him collaborate on films, and with other Hollywood producers. By this time, of course, he was an experienced film composer. Also, Vernon Duke (Vladimir Dukelsky) had been urging him to work in Hollywood.
255. Prokofiev returned from abroad—for the last time—on April 16, 1938.

Until this all comes to pass, I beseech you to support my starving offspring, and to give my cousin 200 additional rubles towards that end.[256] [. . .]

I have heard little interesting music here, since I have been moving around all the time and playing myself. I slept through Sibelius's Second Symphony and was amused by Felix Mottl's arrangement of Grétry.[257] (That's not Asafiev for you). I heard Toscanini, who played rubbish—but how he played it! He started to learn my *Russian Overture*, but then got scared of something and put it aside (I wasn't in N. York at the time and I don't know the details). I will try to obtain Rach's Third, although they say it's pretty mediocre. [. . .]

I send you a big hug, and greetings to your dear sister. Lina Iv[anovna] is in New York, but I expect her to arrive here any day. It's incredibly warm here, the almond trees are in bloom and the trees are bending under the weight of the oranges.

Yours S. Prkfv

June 29, 1942
HOTEL OF THE HOUSE OF SOVIETS, RM. 143
81 RED ARMY ST.
ALMA-ATA[258]

Dear Nicolas-Jacob,

Probably because I played through *Das Rheingold* in a copy I got from Sheibler, Froh has shown us mercy en route through the desert.[259] In Krasnovodsk it began to rain, and it stopped just before Alma-Ata, so that it wasn't hot in the train, and at night we even needed our coats. Alma-Ata ("father of apples" or "apple father") has turned out to be a pleasant place with straight, wide streets drowning in greenery—several rows of poplars. It would even resemble a country resort if not for the asphalt—in any case, we don't feel like

---

256. Prokofiev's sons Oleg and Sviatoslav had remained in Moscow, where they were attending school.
257. Felix Mottl (1856–1911) made an arrangement for concert performance of three fragments from the opera-ballet *Céphale et Procris, ou l'Amour conjugal*, by André-Ernest-Modeste Grétry (1741–1813), first given at Versailles on December 30, 1773.
258. Prokofiev was in Alma-Ata to work with Sergei Eisenstein on the film *Ivan the Terrible*. The Mosfilm studios were in evacuation there, and it was a center of Soviet wartime film production.
259. Froh, brother of Freia and god of light and the rainbow, was a character in Wagner's opera *Das Rheingold*. Truvor Sheibler (1900–1960) was a composer and conductor.

going to the country from here. The hotel is like the one we stayed in in Nalchik, and the room is also similar.

They have brought me an upright piano made of lemon wood, without any trademark but with a pleasant sound. I have orchestrated all that I can of *War and Peace*, all the scenes except the three big choral ones.[260] [. . .] The idea of bringing Lamm here is not so simple, since there is a shortage of rooms and ration cards, and we could not invite him without those. Furthermore, he sent a letter from which it was impossible to tell if he is coming or not, as if I had managed to do all the groundwork. Out of despair I am trying to train the local half-conductor to decipher my orchestral score, so that I won't be completely stranded if things with Lamm don't get worked out.[261]

How is your overture?[262] Have you finished it? You haven't begun it? You've taken up another project? Of composers we know there are very few here, or none at all, depending on how you count N[ikolai] Kryukov.[263] I have mentioned bringing Shapo[rin] and Nechaev here, and the idea is currently being considered.[264] I send you a big hug. Warmest greetings to both Yakovlevnas—Valentina and Evg[enia].[265] I recall with pleasure how you and I went to fetch the milk. The dog Timur I recall with less pleasure.[266] Write.

Yours S.

October 3, 1942
ALMA-ATA

Dear Nikolya-Zhakob,

At last you've turned up. About two months ago well-informed sources saw the "Tbilisi group" in Tashkent en route somewhere, and even counted 18 people in the group—so I didn't know where you were, and even sent a telegram just in case to Tbilisi, and here it turns out you're right nearby. Because from

260. Prokofiev had begun working on his opera *War and Peace* in 1941.
261. Prokofiev wanted musicologist Pavel Lamm to come to Alma-Ata to help him write out the full orchestral score of *War and Peace*.
262. Prokofiev is referring to Miaskovsky's *Dramatic Overture* for wind orchestra, op. 60.
263. Nikolai Kryukov (1908–61) was a composer who wrote music for films.
264. Yuri Shaporin (1887–1966) was a Soviet composer; among his works is the opera *The Decembrists*. Vasily Nechaev (1895–1956) was a pianist, composer, and teacher.
265. Miaskovsky's sisters.
266. Prokofiev and Miaskovsky, along with many other Soviet cultural figures, lived in evacuation in Tbilisi in the winter and spring of 1941–42. Timur was the dog belonging to the owners of the house where Miaskovsky lived.

here to Frunze as the crow flies is just a couple of steps, but we are separated by a mountain range so that the railroad has to make a big loop. They say Frunze is a kind of smaller Alma-Ata, or, from your point of view, Alma-Ata is a kind of larger version of Frunze.[267]

But judging from the tone of your postcard, you were not exactly received with open arms, and so I went to the administration of the United Film Studio and informed them that a pack of very valuable composers had arrived in Frunze and inquired whether they didn't need someone to come to work. For even greater effect, I declared that I was speaking as a deputy director of the Moscow Composers Union. Unsure if the entire group was in Frunze, I particularly mentioned you and Nechaev, since the latter has been interested in film work, and I also referred to Shapopo [Shaporin]. (Even though he never sent me the photograph, which is a pity—it was great to be with you, but the rest could have been cut out.) The administration replied that there are quite a few films planned, and it would be desirable to bring some composers in, but that everything hinges on availability of living space. This matter will be decided in a few days: either the film studio will receive some apartments—which means the move here might be possible, or the studio won't get any apartments—which means that everyone would have to live on top of each other. For example, Gabriel Popoff [sic][268] came here a month ago without an invitation and, although he received a film to work on, he had to live for about three weeks together with four other people: he, his wife, and three strangers (including one drunk). When he finally got a room, they threw him out a day later. Today he said proudly that he has apparently succeeded in throwing out the one who threw him out.

While the administration is figuring things out, write me, or even better, send me a telegram, and tell me who would come here, and above all, would you come yourself? It's really time that you made up your mind: film work is intriguing, provides a good source of income and doesn't require creative over-exertion, and Alma-Ata is a pleasant city with plenty of money around. Besides films, I am writing a small dramatic cantata[269] and have asked Moscow for a

---

267. Frunze was the capital of the Soviet Central Asian republic of Kirgiz, about 125 miles west of Alma-Ata. A number of composers were evacuated there when Tbilisi was threatened by the advancing German army.

268. Prokofiev is referring to composer Gavriil Popov (1904–72).

269. Prokofiev was composing *Ballad of an Unknown Boy*, op. 93, a cantata for soprano, tenor, chorus, and orchestra to a text by Pavel Antokolsky.

commission for a sonata for flute and piano.[270] Not exactly timely, but pleasant. [...]

I await news from you, send you a big hug, and greetings to your sisters and friends. Mirochka also sends her greetings and is writing to Valentina Yakov-levna.

Yours S. Prkfv

Arrangements for Lamm to come here are looking worse. Part of the work is already waiting for him (one act of the opera and the cantata), but with what sauce will we be able to cook up living space for him?

About a week ago someone called me from Frunze at 8 A.M. But I had returned home at 6 A.M. after a night of recording for the film, the telephone was somewhere in the corridor, I wasn't expecting anything interesting from Frunze, and therefore I didn't go to answer the phone. After I received your postcard I was sorry.

SP

February 27, 1943
ALMA-ATA

Dear Nicolas-Jacob,

So it's been three weeks already that we've been here in the "Father of Apples," trying to adapt once again to its climactic eccentricities.[271] By the way, there are some smiles to be had, from noon until three, when the sunbeams provide some warmth, the streams gurgle, and it smells of springtime—in short, at those moments when you envy us. But the sun soon plunges behind the clouds, the air immediately turns sharp, and nature starts in with all sorts of tricks.

As far as work goes, I have accomplished less so far that I had planned, since the electricity has been turned off, and in the evenings I have had to close up shop, which has made me envy those who have no electrical quotas. I can't remember if I managed to tell you that not long before my departure from Moscow I was persuaded after all to redo the final scene of *War and Peace*, to make it (as it should be) more of an apotheosis. At first I was set against it, but

---

270. This was the Sonata in D Major, op. 94, for flute and piano, composed in 1942–43 on a commission from the Committee on Artistic Affairs of the USSR.

271. Prokofiev had traveled to Moscow in December 1942 in connection with his opera *War and Peace* and returned to Alma-Ata in February 1943.

then I got the idea of writing a chorus singing quickly with a band, using material heard earlier, but in a different arrangement. Then the chorus starts to sing more broadly, the band continues playing its own tune, and the rapid movement shifts from the chorus to the orchestra (without brass). All in all, it seems that the whole venture has come off well, although it has resulted in a lengthening of the final scene by 2 or 3 minutes.

As for the rest, we are living quietly and pleasantly, but (or, if you prefer, *and*) far from music and musicians: the most important musician with whom I have the opportunity to meet is Kryukov (N. N.), and the most vivid new piece of music is *Suvorov*, which I simply cannot force myself to see.[272] So be charitable and write me about what's going on in the musical world.

I send you a big hug, and kiss both of your sister's little hands. Mirochka sends her love to you both.

Yours S. Prkfv

To MIASKOVSKY and HIS SISTER

April 4, 1943
Alma-Ata

Dear Valentina Yakovlevna and her dear relative!

I was very touched by your mutual telegram and thank you for it. I must also thank your dear relative separately because no doubt he was promoting my case behind the scenes—otherwise, why would they have given it to me for such a muddled piece when they didn't give it to me for more simple and clear ones.[273] And what (this is a question for the relative) is Shebalin's Slavic Quartet? Or, more precisely, what relation does it have to the Third Quartet, which I love, and to the Fourth, which I don't? Among the congratulatory telegrams I received was one from Atovmyan, sent on the 21st at 6 A.M., which led me to understand that the night preceding its composition had been spent drinking Ronya [Shebalin] under the table somewhere.[274] Right now I'm selecting all sorts of Kazakh material for a certain rather large piece. There's so much inter-

---

272. The historical opera *Suvorov* by Sergei Vasilenko (1872–1956) was composed in 1941–42 and opened in Alma-Ata on February 23, 1943.

273. On March 19, 1943, Prokofiev was awarded a Stalin Prize second class—his first Stalin Prize—for his Sonata No. 7 for Piano. Miaskovsky was a member of the Stalin Prize jury for music, which is why Prokofiev refers to his influence behind the scenes.

274. Shebalin had won the Stalin Prize first class for his String Quartet No. 5 ("Slavic") in F Major, op. 33.

esting stuff there, a whole untouched sea! I went to a concert given by an orchestra of Kazakh instruments—it sounds quite fascinating and pleasantly off-key as soon as they ascend into the second octave. But for the moment I'm not planning on arranging any of this musical material; it's all in an incipient phase.[275]

And what has become of the arrangements of Zhakob's[276] symphonies? Lamm mentioned in one note, in passing, that several arrangements had been lost, and the composer had to re-create them. What symphonies are these, and how could they have disappeared? And furthermore, what is Zhakob doing that's new, interesting, and pleasant?

I kiss your little hands, dear Valentina Yakovlevna, and your fragrant little beard, dear Nikolai Yakovlevich. [. . .]

Both of yours truly
S. Prkfv

June 12, 1943
ALMA-ATA

Dear Nikolai Yakovlevich,

Your letter of April 24 was most interesting, although it took a lot of effort to decipher all the adjectives concealed by the beauties of your handwriting. We have had no musical events of note here at all, unless you count a few horribly primitive operas by Brusilovsky,[277] which I forced myself to sit through, in my role as a composer intending to write something on Kazakh material.

The main event around which we are now revolving is our upcoming departure for Molotov, in order to complete *Cinderella*, which the Kirovites are promising to begin staging as soon as August, with a view to launching the premiere before the New Year.[278] Since the first two acts have been sketched out

---

275. Prokofiev was gathering material for a "lyric-comic Kazakh opera" called *Khan Buzai*. Although he did a good deal of preparatory work, his failing health and other commitments prevented him from ever completing it.

276. Prokofiev jokingly called Miaskovsky Zhakob (Jacob), from his patronymic Yakovlevich (son of Jacob).

277. Evgeny Brusilovsky (1905–81) was a Soviet composer living in Kazakhstan. His operas included *Aiman-Sholpan* (1938), *The Golden Kernel* (1940), and *Guard, Forward!* (1942).

278. Prokofiev had begun composing *Cinderella* in 1940, but was interrupted by the German invasion in 1941. The Kirov Ballet had been evacuated during the war to Molotov (Perm), and invited Prokofiev go there and finish *Cinderella* for a Kirov production. He went to Perm in June 1943, stayed for four months, and finished the score, but the Kirov staged the ballet nearly three years later, on April 8, 1946.

already (for better or for worse), it seems that I could really finish off the beauty by the theater's deadline. We will leave in the near future via Kuibyshev, where the local administration of the Bolshoi Theater promises to get us onto a river steamer going straight to Molotov. It's unlikely that this part of the journey will be very comfortable, but the Volga is still the Volga, and the Kama the Kama, and as the Americans would say, I "am looking forward with pleasure" to this trip. [. . .]

I would very much like to hear your Eighth Quartet in a genuine performance—even in the piano adaptation it seemed to me vivid, and with many beautiful harmonies: with string players it will sound completely different, of course. It will be interesting to see how you will deal with the sonorities of a violin sonata; I began one a long time ago already, but cannot seem to figure out how to continue—it's hard.[279]

I await another detailed and interesting letter from you, just like your last one, at this address: Molotov, Poste Restante. I send you a big hug, and kiss our adored little sister's little hands.

Yours S. Prkfv

June 10, 1944
IVANOVO

Dear Nicolas-Jacob,

We arrived at the collective farm yesterday and are most pleased with this place.[280] I'm writing you so as to encourage you to leave everything behind and come join us here. The room designated for you is large, quiet, and on the corner of the building. The food is marvelous—fresh, delicious, abundant. The woods here are in no way inferior to the ones we have at Nikolina Gora,[281] and right now, with the young foliage, nothing less than splendid. I just don't understand why the devil you have to hang around in the city!

I send you a big hug.

Greetings to your dear sisters and everyone else from Mirochka.

Yours S. Prkfv

---

279. Prokofiev's Sonata No. 1 for Violin and Piano, op. 80, was completed in 1946.
280. Prokofiev spent the summer at a composers' retreat belonging to the Union of Composers, which had been organized near a collective poultry farm near Ivanovo.
281. Nikolina Gora was a summer colony outside Moscow where Miaskovsky and other prominent musicians lived. In 1947 Prokofiev and Mira would purchase their own dacha there.

August 19, 1945
IVANOVO

Dear Nikolai Yakovlevich,

I'm taking advantage of Vera Yakovlevna's kindness so I can send you a few lines from Ivanovo, where we have spent almost two months already, and have for the most part been enjoying our stay. True, the dear little children scream a lot, but the air is marvelous, the food is delicious, and I feel much better—at least my head aches only on rare days. I'm working an hour or an hour and a half each day, and have sketched out *Ode to the End of the War* and nearly two movements of the Sixth Symphony.[282] Right now I want to sit down to the instrumentation of the *Ode*, and am putting the completion of the symphony aside for now. How is life at Nikolina Gora? I really love that place and remember with pleasure its various nooks and meadows. Give my greetings to the Lamm family. I hope that Pavel Aleksandrovich[283] has managed to resurrect his château. What have you been composing, how do you feel?

Mirochka sends her warmest greetings, and I send you a big hug.

Greetings to your dear sisters from both of us.

Yours S. Prkfv

May 16, 1950
NIKOLINA GORA

Dear Nikolai Yakovlevich,

I embrace you with all my soul. All my thoughts are with you. Come soon to Nikolina Gora.[284]

---

282. *Ode to the End of the War*, op. 105, for eight harps, four pianos, and an orchestra of winds, percussion, and contrabasses, was composed in 1945. Symphony No. 6 in E-flat Minor, op. 111, was completed in 1947.
283. Lamm.
284. Miaskovsky had just undergone a serious operation, after many years of declining health.

To VALENTINA YAKOVLEVNA MENSHIKOVA [née Miaskovskaya]

August 9, 1950
NIKOLINA GORA

Dear Valentina Yakovlevna.

Of course my thoughts are with you every moment right now.[285] To my great regret, I cannot come to Kolyechka's funeral. Please come, my dear, to Nikolina Gora.

Yours Seryozha

I embrace you and Evgenia Yakovlevna with all my soul.

---

285. Miaskovsky died in Moscow on August 8, 1950. Prokofiev's own health was so poor that he was unable to attend the funeral.

INDEX